FACTS AND ARTIFACTS

CURT MUSER received an A.B. degree from Yale University in 1932. After retiring from business in 1966, he studied and researched in pre-Columbian civilizations at Hunter College, Columbia University, and Museo Nacional de Antropología, Mexico City, and he has also done extensive exploration of archaeological sites in Mexico, Guatemala, and Honduras.

Mr. Muser participated in The Metropolitan Museum of Art's centennial exhibition "Before Cortés: Sculpture of Middle America," 1970–71. He found items for inclusion in the exhibition on personal trips to Mexico and Guatemala, and was later twice sent to Mexico by The Metropolitan to complete arrangements with collectors and museums.

He is the contributing editor for "Mesoamerican Architecture" in Cyril Harris's *Historical Architecture Source Book* (1977). He is a member of The Society for American Archaeology and the Chairman of the Board of Trustees of the Museum of the American Indian (Heye Foundation) in New York.

FACTS AND ARTIFACTS OF ANCIENT MIDDLE AMERICA

A Glossary of Terms and Words Used
in the Archaeology and Art History
of pre-Columbian Mexico and Central America

Compiled by

CURT MUSER

E. P. DUTTON | NEW YORK

to Frani

CONTENTS

Color plates follow page   100

LIST OF COLOR PLATES

PREFACE

This volume developed from its author's frustration at the absence of a single comprehensive reference work to facilitate the study of ancient Middle America. It is written from the viewpoint and experience of a student and is therefore dedicated to assisting other new entrants into the field, including the educated traveler.

Up to now there has been no one source available in the field to explain the meaning or the interrelationships of the various terms and names used in the literature. Many words are assumed to be understood, or, as they appear in the texts, are difficult to trace through indexes. Much important information is available only to those able to read the sources in Spanish. Many terms have more than one application, rarely differentiated in the same text. This work attempts to ease the search, and simplify the understanding, of Middle America's past as it has been reconstructed by archaeology and the stylistic analysis of its art.

Proper nouns and terms mentioned in the text are generally cross-referenced to explanatory entries. Maps define the cultural areas and their active centers. Site plans for major centers are included for more detailed analysis and for the convenience of travelers. Finally, chronological tables by cultural areas show the relationships, in time and space, of the cultural phases mentioned in the text.

Faced with the inherent limitations of a small reference work, the author assumes full responsibility for the selection of entries. The spelling of native words while employing the Roman alphabet is at best only an approximation of the native sounds, and therefore shows considerable variation in spelling among authors. We have selected the most common current usage. In the matter of dating, absolute concurrence among scholars does not always obtain. We have used the latest available and most authoritative sources. It must be remembered that although Middle America has a long history, its study is recent. Contemporary archaeological discoveries and new stylistic studies continue to challenge established beliefs. It is this modern detective work that makes the study of New World civilizations so interesting.

In compiling this volume I am particularly indebted to Dr. Muriel Porter Weaver, my mentor in Mesoamerican archaeology, who initially and consistently urged this project. Dr. Michael D. Coe of the Department of Anthropology, Yale University, and Dr. Frederick J. Dockstader, former director of the Museum of the American Indian (Heye Foundation), also gave helpful support along the way. Dr. Ignacio Bernal and Professor Arturo Romano generously encouraged me early in my pursuits while making the facilities of the Museo Nacional de Antropología, Mexico City, available to me. I am most grateful also to those who read my manuscript and added their invaluable criticisms and suggestions. Elizabeth Kennedy Easby reviewed the material on Central America and the highland Maya. Peter David Joralemon of Yale advised on the Olmec and lowland Maya. Allan D. Chapman, Museum Librarian, The Robert Goldwater Library of Primitive Art, The Metropolitan Museum of Art, provided counsel on the Aztecs and compiled the Selected Bibliography.

Permission to publish illustrations is gratefully acknowledged to the American Museum of Natural History, New York (pp. 4, 104, 124, 190); The Art Museum, Princeton University, Princeton, New Jersey (color plate 26); The Trustees of the British Museum, London (color plates 13, 30); Michael D. Coe (pp. 14, 42, 114, 123, 128, 136, 144, 161, 190); Dumbarton Oaks, Washington, D.C. (color plate 14; pp. 41, 68, 180); Field Museum of Natural History, Chicago (p. 92); Peter Joralemon (pp. 68, 180); Alfred A. Knopf, Inc., New York (pp. 49, 62, 72, 83, 123, 125, 127, 191); The Metropolitan Museum of Art, The Michael C. Rockefeller Memorial Collection of Primitive Art, New York (color plates 22, 32); Museum of the American Indian (Heye Foundation), New York (color plates 15, 17–21, 23–25, 27, 28, 31); National Museum of Natural History, Smithsonian Institution, Washington, D.C. (pp. 17, 86, 170, 174); Peabody Museum, Harvard University, Cambridge, Massachusetts (color plate 10); Prentice-Hall, Inc., Englewood Cliffs, New Jersey (pp. 33, 175); and Stanford University Press, Stanford, California (pp. 12, 28, 43, 44, 67, 123, 162, 177).

This volume is enhanced by color illustrations provided by Lee Boltin (color plate 32), Hillel Burger (color plate 10), Carmelo Guadagno (color plate 16), Helga Photo Studio (color plate 12), Justin Kerr (color plates 1–4, 8, 9, 29), Lisa Little (color plate 22), Esther Pasztory (color plate 11), and Muriel Porter Weaver (color plate 5). Original cultural area and site maps for this book were executed by Frank Anthony Dzibela.

MAPS

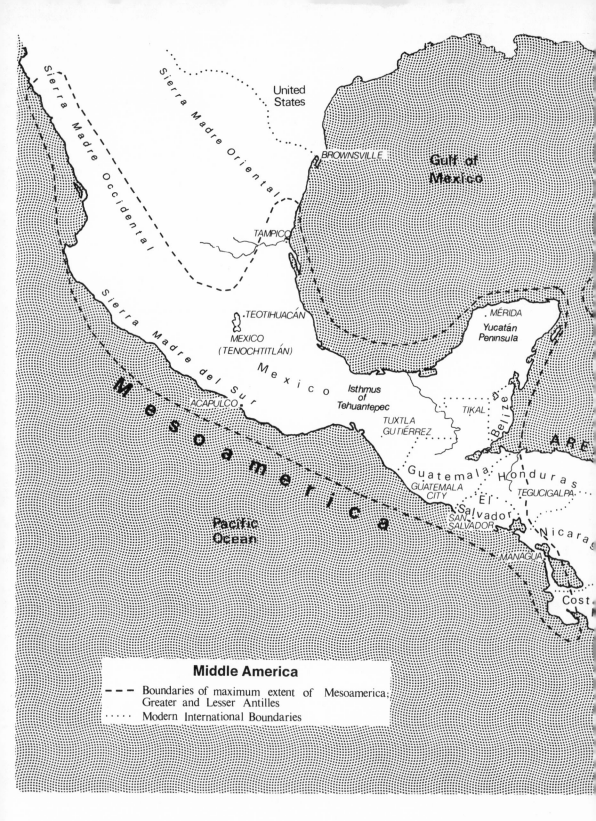

Sierra Madre Occidental

Sierra Madre Oriental

United
States

BROWNSVILLE

Gulf of
Mexico

Sierra Madre del Sur

TAMPICO

·*TEOTIHUACÁN*

*MEXICO
(TENOCHTITLÁN)*

·*MÉRIDA*

Yucatán
Peninsula

M e x i c o

M e s o a m e r i c a

ACAPULCO·

Isthmus
of
Tehuantepec

*TUXTLA
GUTIÉRREZ*

TIKAL

Belize

ARE

Pacific
Ocean

G u a t e m a l a

*GUATEMALA
CITY*

H o n d u r a s

TEGUCIGALPA·

El
Salvador

*SAN
SALVADOR*·

N i c a r a g

·*MANAGUA*

Cost

Middle America

– – – Boundaries of maximum extent of Mesoamerica;
        Greater and Lesser Antilles

· · · · Modern International Boundaries

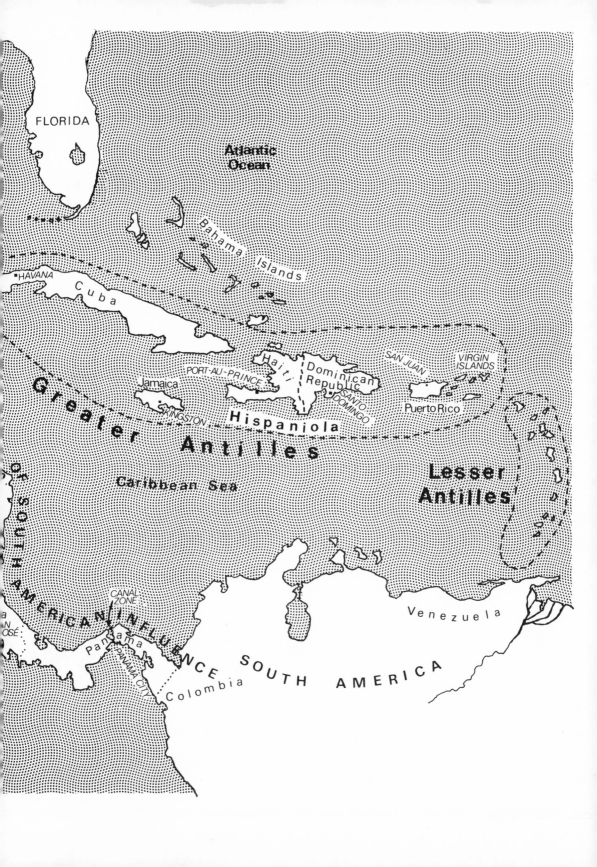

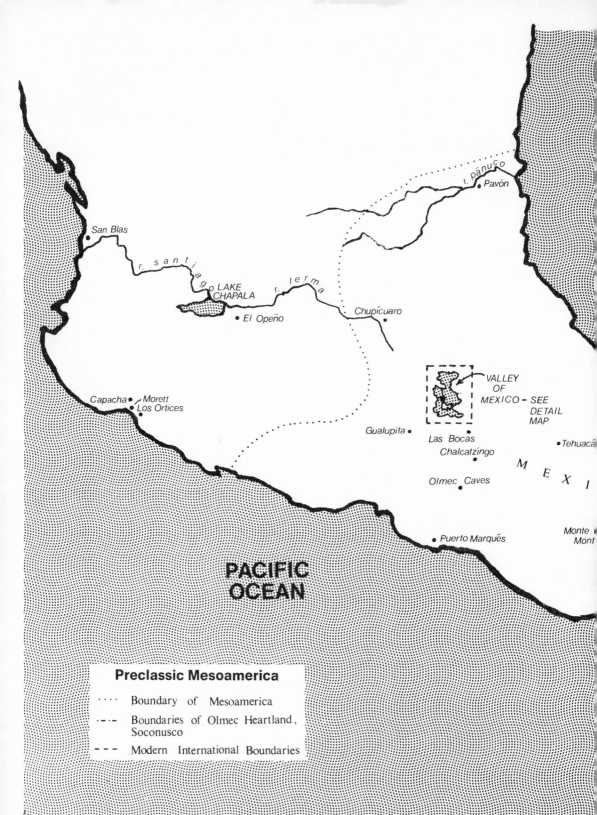

San Blas

r. santiago

LAKE CHAPALA

r. lerma

Chupícuaro

r. pánuco

Pavón

El Opeño

VALLEY OF MEXICO – SEE DETAIL MAP

Capacha
Morett
Los Ortices

Gualupita

Las Bocas

Chalcatzingo

Tehuacá

Olmec Caves

M E X I

Puerto Marqués

Monte
Mont

PACIFIC OCEAN

Preclassic Mesoamerica

· · · · Boundary of Mesoamerica

–·–· Boundaries of Olmec Heartland, Soconusco

– – – Modern International Boundaries

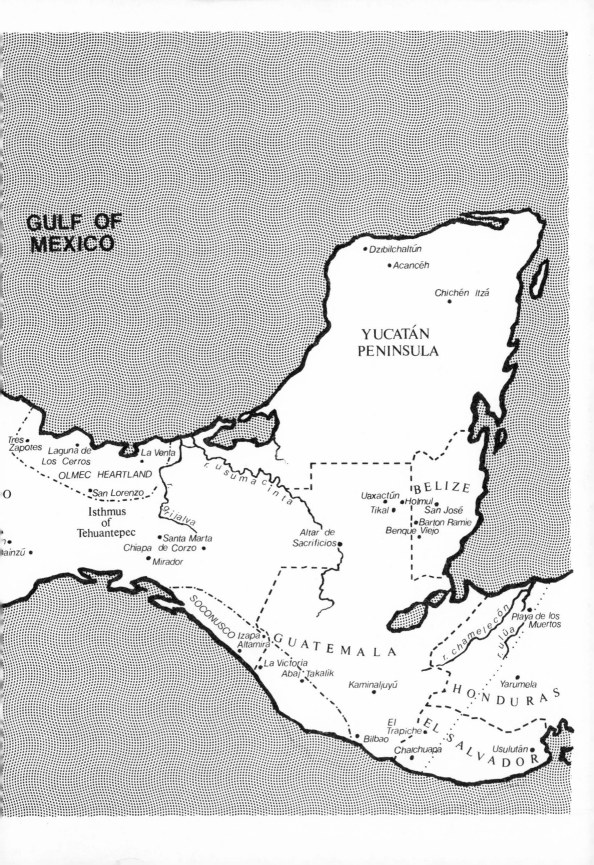

GULF OF
MEXICO

• Dzibilchaltún

• Acancéh

Chichén Itzá •

YUCATÁN
PENINSULA

Tres •
Zapotes
Laguna de
Los Cerros   • La Venta

OLMEC HEARTLAND

r. usumacinta

B E L I Z E

Uaxactún •
Tikal •   Holmul •
            San José •

• San Lorenzo

Isthmus
of
Tehuantepec

Grijalva

• Santa Marta
Chiapa de Corzo •
• Mirador

Altar de
Sacrificios •

• Barton Ramie
Benque Viejo •

O

ainzú •

•ㅇ •

SOCONUSCO Izapa •
Altamira •

G U A T E M A L A

r. chamelecón

r. ulúa

Playa de los
Muertos

• La Victoria
Abaj Takalik •

Kaminaljuyú •

H O N D U R A S

• Yarumela

El
Trapiche •

E L   S A L V A D O R

• Usulután

• Bilbao

Chalchuapa •

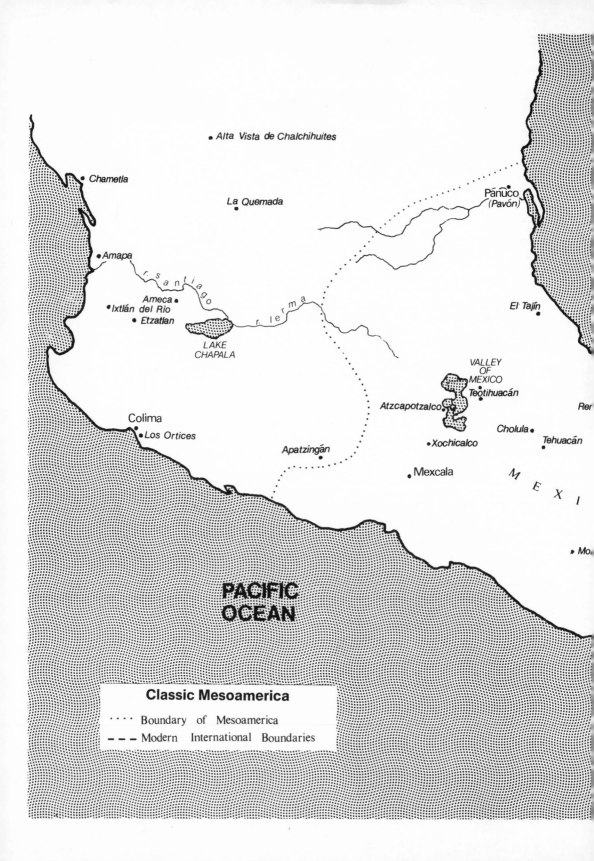

Classic Mesoamerica

- Alta Vista de Chalchihuites
- Chametla
- La Quemada
- Amapa
- Pánuco (Pavón)
- El Tajín

r. santiago

r. lerma

- Ameca
- Ixtlán del Rio
- Etzatlan

LAKE CHAPALA

VALLEY OF MEXICO

- Teotihuacán
- Atzcapotzalco
- Cholula
- Tehuacán

- Colima
- Los Ortices

- Xochicalco

- Apatzingán

- Mexcala

M E X I

Rer

Mo

PACIFIC OCEAN

Classic Mesoamerica

···· Boundary of Mesoamerica

--- Modern International Boundaries

GULF OF
MEXICO

Dzibilchaltún
Acancéh • Izamal
Chichén Itzá • Xcaret
(Polé)
Cobá
• Uxmal
• Kabah
Sayil • Labná
PUUC
STYLE
CHENES
STYLE
Hochob

YUCATÁN
PENINSULA

Jaina

Tulum • Cozumel

RÍO • Xpuhil
BEC • Río Bec
STYLE
Santa
Rita

Cerro de
s Mesas
Potonchán
LAGUNA
DE TÉRMINOS
Comalcalco
r. usumacinta
Calakmul
Altun
Há

Isthmus
of
Tehuantepec
r. grijalva
Palenque
Uaxactún Holmul
Tikal
BELIZE
Piedras Negras
Yaxchilán
Yaxhá
Benque
Viejo
Chiapa de Corzo
Bonampak
Seibal
Lubaantun
Tonalá
Pusilha

• Nebaj

G U A T E M A L A
• Zacualpa
Quiriguá
r. motagua
r. chamelecón
r. ulúa
Kaminaljuyú
Copán
El Baúl
Cotzumalhuapa
H O N D U R A S
Tiquisate

• Tazumal
E L   S A L V A D O R

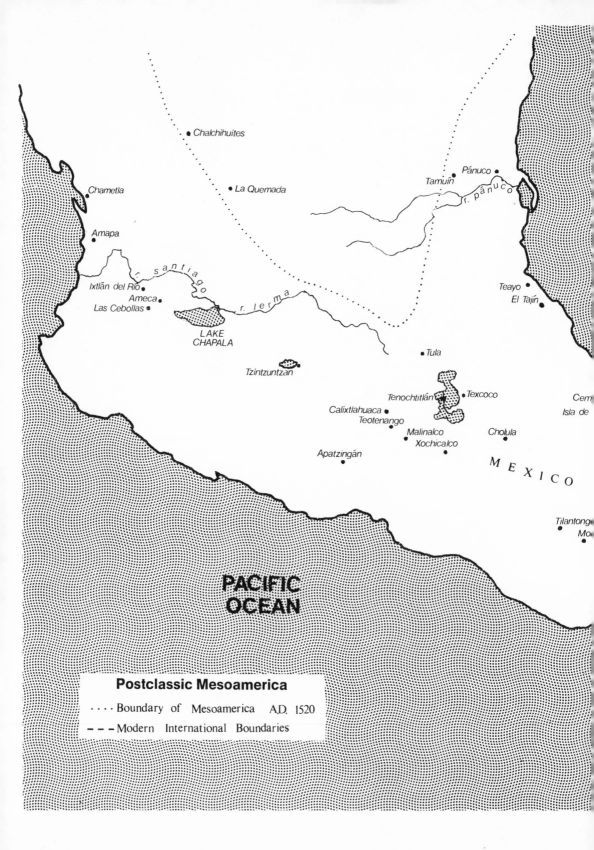

Chalchihuites

La Quemada

Chametla

Amapa

Pánuco
Tamuín
r. pánuco

Ixtlán del Río
Ameca
Las Cebollas

r. santiago
r. lerma

Teayo
El Tajín

LAKE
CHAPALA

Tzintzuntzan

Tula

Tenochtitlán
Texcoco
Calixtlahuaca
Teotenango
Malinalco
Xochicalco
Apatzingán
Cholula

Cem
Isla de

MEXICO

Tilantong
Mo

PACIFIC
OCEAN

Postclassic Mesoamerica

···· Boundary of Mesoamerica A.D. 1520
‒ ‒ ‒ Modern International Boundaries

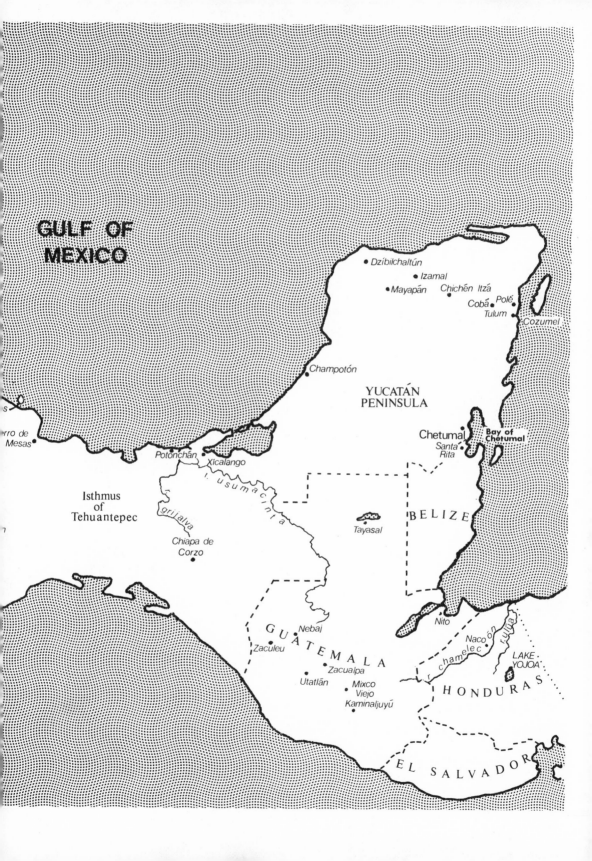

GULF OF
MEXICO

• Dzíbilchaltún
           • Izamal
• Mayapán   Chichén Itzá
                     Cobá • Polé
                     Tulum
                        Cozumel

• Champotón

YUCATÁN
PENINSULA

s

rro de
Mesas•

Potonchán Xicalango

Chetumal   **Bay of
Chetumal**
      Santa
      Rita

l. usumacinta

grijalva

Isthmus
of
Tehuantepec

Chiapa de
Corzo
•

Tayasal
•

B E L I Z E

η

Nito
•

Naco o ó n
   •
G U A T E M A L A   r chamelec   LAKE
   Nebaj   YOJOA
Zaculeu
          Zacualpa
Utatlán   Mixco   H O N D U R A S
          Viejo
      Kaminaljuyú

E L S A L V A D O R

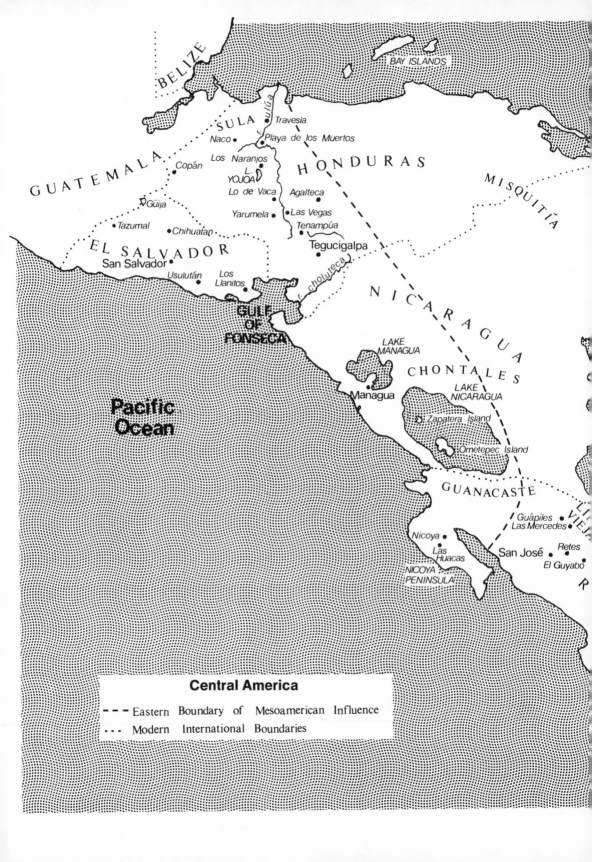

BELIZE

BAY ISLANDS

GUATEMALA

SULA

r. Ulúa

•Travesia

Naco•
•Playa de los Muertos

Los Naranjos•
Copán•
HONDURAS

L.
YOJOA

MISQUITÍA

Lo de Vaca•

Agalteca•

Güija•

Yarumela•
•Las Vegas

Tazumal•
•Chihuatán
Tenampúa•

EL SALVADOR
Tegucigalpa•

San Salvador•

Usulután•   Los
Llanitos•
r. choluteca

GULF
OF
FONSECA

NICARAGUA

LAKE
MANAGUA

CHONTALES

Managua•
LAKE
NICARAGUA

Pacific
Ocean
Zapatera Island•

•Ometepec Island

GUANACASTE

LI..
VIEJ..

•Guápiles
Las Mercedes•

Nicoya•
Las
Huacas•
San José•
•Retes

NICOYA
PENINSULA
•El Guyabo

R..

Central America

– – – Eastern Boundary of Mesoamerican Influence

· · · Modern International Boundaries

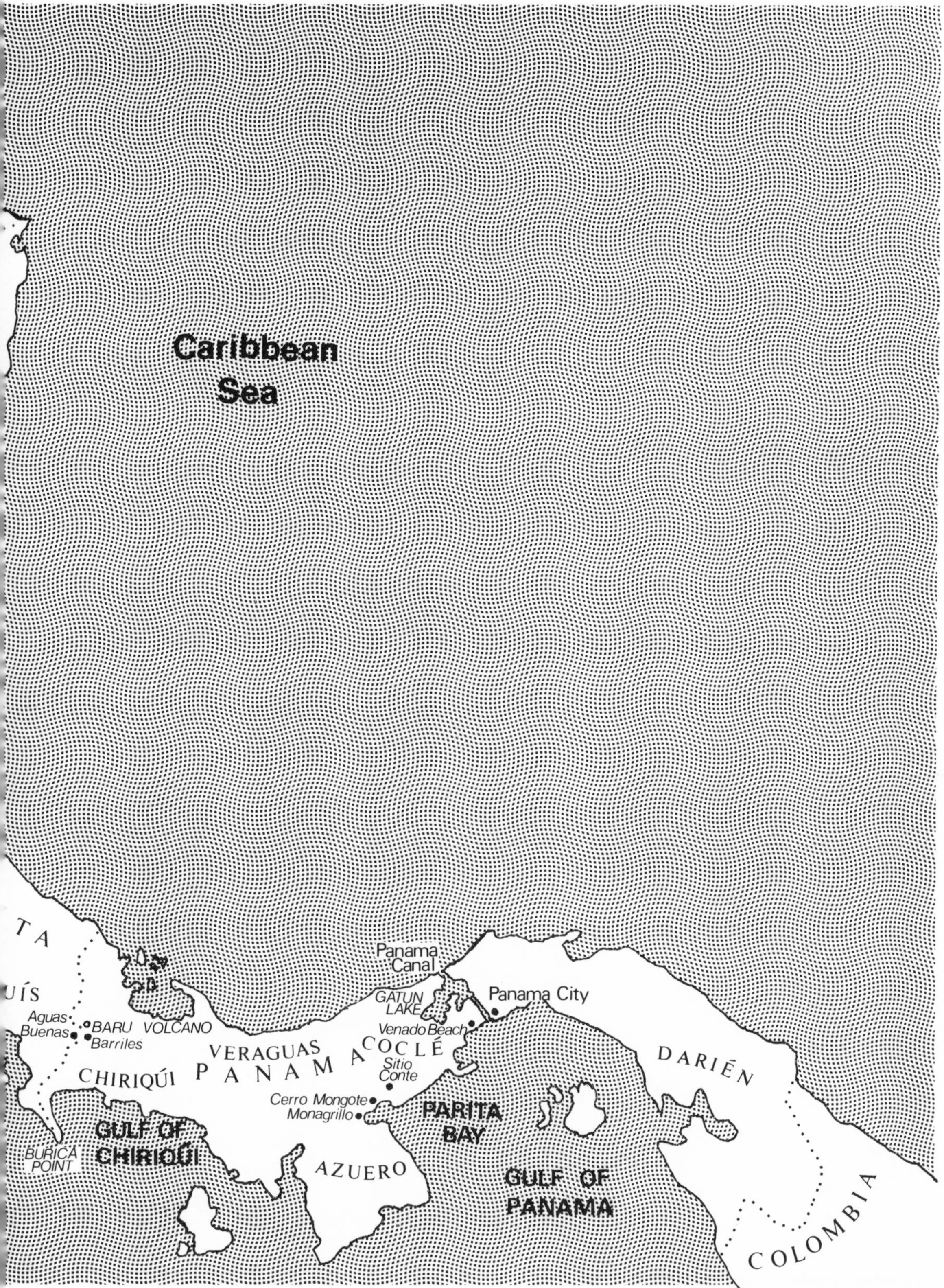

Caribbean
Sea

TA

UÍS

Aguas
Buenas

CHIRIQÚI

BURICA
POINT

GULF OF
CHIRIQÚI

BARU VOLCANO

Barriles

VERAGUAS P A N A M A

Cerro Mongote
Monagrillo

AZUERO

Panama
Canal

GATUN
LAKE

Venado Beach

COCLÉ

Sitio
Conte

PARITA
BAY

GULF OF
PANAMA

Panama City

DARIÉN

COLOMBIA

GUIDE TO PRONUNCIATION

1. *Maya*

Pronunciation of the vowels is similar to Spanish:

a is pronounced as in f*a*ther

e is short as in b*e*t; final *e* is pronounced as in Spanish

i is long *ee*, as in kn*ee*

o is pronounced as in p*o*mp

u is pronounced *oo* as in g*oo*d; hence Uxmal is *Oosh*-mal. *u* preceding other vowels is pronounced *w*.

Consonants are pronounced as in English, except:

c is always hard, like a *k*

x is pronounced *sh; Xul* is pronounced *Shool*

d, f, j, r, and *v* are lacking in Yucatec and most lowland Maya languages; in the highlands, however, *r* is substituted for *l*, hence Cho*l*ti becomes Cho*r*ti.

qu is pronounced as in Spanish, becomes *k* before *e* or *i; Quiriguá* is therefore pronounced *Kee*-ree-gwa

Place names in the Yucatán peninsula are nearly all Maya. In the Guatemalan highlands and adjacent El Salvador they are mainly Nahuatl, retaining names given them by Nahuatl-speaking Indians who participated in the Spanish Conquest under Alvarado. Place names ending in *an, ango, co, pa,* or *te* are usually of Nahuatl derivation.

2. *Nahuatl*

The language of the Aztecs was transcribed in Roman letters by the Spanish conquerors and therefore closely follows the Spanish pronunciation:

a is pronounced as in f*a*ther

e is short as in b*e*t

i is pronounced *ee* as in kn*ee*

o is pronounced as in l*o*rd

c is hard as in *k*, except when followed by *e* or *i*, whereupon it is pronounced *s* as in Spanish, or as in the English word, *s*ong

qu when preceding *e* or *i* sounds like *k*, as in *c*over

z is pronounced *s* as in *S*am

hu is pronounced *w* as in *w*ant

tl is a combination having a separate sound like the *tl* in ra*ttl*er

x is pronounced *sh* as in *sh*oe

The remaining letters are pronounced as in English. Nahuatl words are stressed on the penultimate syllable; variations are indicated by accents in the literature.

a

Abaj Takalik Preclassic site of southwest Guatemalan highlands with monuments in Izapan style. Originally known by the names of two plantations at that location: Santa Margarita and San Isidro Piedra Parada.

Abejas Preclassic phase, 3400–2300 B.C., with evidence of early agriculture, including maize, squash, cotton, chili peppers, beans, etc., Tehuacán Valley, Puebla, Mexico. 2300 B.C. may well be the beginning of pottery in Mesoamerica; falls between the two dates for Pox ware in Guerrero. See also **Purrón.**

Acalán Sometimes called Acalá, it was the region of the Putún Maya, with their capital Itzamkanac, on the Candelaria River, Campeche. Late Classic Putún emigration to the Petén resulted in the same name for the area south of the Pasión River. Under the designation of Lacandón, descendants of the Putún survive along the Usumacinta River.. Acalán was also the Mexican name for Candelaria River.

Acamapichtli Colhua nobleman of Toltec descent chosen first *tlatoani* (king) of the Aztecs, A.D. 1367–87. Fathered nucleus of the *pipiltin,* the Aztec noble class. See **Coxcox.**

Acan God of wine, a term applied to *balché* by the early historians of Yucatán, according to the Motul dictionary.

Acancéh Early Classic Maya site southeast of Mérida, Yucatán. A platform with a *talud-tablero* facade in Teotihuacán style also suggests Mexican influence in its sculptured stucco frieze with anthropomor-phic bats, birds of prey, squirrels, and a serpent recalling the Feathered Serpent deity.

Acantun Four demons with directional colors, prominent in Maya New Year rites and in idol-carving ceremonies. Many references to them in the book, *Ritual of the Bacabs.*

Acaponeta phase See **Aztatlán, Culiacán.**

Ácatl Thirteenth of the 20 Nahuatl day signs, pictured in Mexican codices as bundle of arrows (staffs of cane) held in a bow by leather straps. Ácatl as a Year Bearer, along with Calli, Técpatl, and Tochtli, served to begin the years, there being 13 Ácatl years in each 52-year cycle, oriented to the east. The Maya equivalent day was Ben; the Zapotec equivalent day was Quij. 1 Ácatl is the mythical birth date of Quetzalcóatl, 2 Ácatl of his death. 13 Ácatl represents the sun in the Aztec calendar. The great temple of Tenochtitlán was dedicated on 7 Ácatl. Tezcatlipoca (or Itztlacoliuhqui) was day's patron saint, with an unfavorable augury. See **day names, Aztec.**

acculturation Adoption by one culture of the trait or traits of another, expressed from the standpoint of the recipient. See also **diffusion.**

Ache Fourth of the 20 Zapotecan day names, corresponding to the Aztec Cuetzpalin.

Achi Term applied to cognate Maya language groups Cakchiquel (Guatemalteca), Quiché (Utatlatleca), and Tzutuhil, but most frequently to Cakchiquel.

1

Achiutla Sacred city of Mixtecs, site of the legendary birth of their ancestors from two trees.

Ach Kinchil See **Kinich Ahau.**

Acolhua One of seven Aztec tribal groups believed to have left legendary Chicomoztoc ("seven caves") in A.D. 1168, and then started the long migration to the Valley of Mexico.

Acolhuacán Kingdom of the Acolhua, covering the area east of the Great Lake of the Valley of Mexico; Texcoco was capital. Member of Triple Alliance in the 15th century with Tenochtitlán and Tlacopan. Nezahualcóyotl was its famous poet-king.

acompañantes Zapotec urn figures of Oaxaca tombs, three to seven in number, accompanying a larger deity urn. Representing priests or devotees, they reached greatest importance in Monte Albán III.

Acpaxaco Otomí aquatic goddess, a variant of Chalchiúhtlicue.

Actun Balam Maya site in Belize, south of Caracol, near the Petén border.

adobe In Latin America, a sun-dried clay brick formed in rectangular wooden frames. No fired bricks were used in Mesoamerica until Classic times.

adorno Common Spanish term applied to decorative applications added to the basic entity, as in ceramics.

affix Elements added to edge of the main body of a Maya glyph. On the left, affix is a prefix, on the right, a postfix, above, a superfix, and below, a suffix.

affix: the month Chen, affixed at left

Affixes can generally be moved from left to above and from right to below without altering the meaning of the total glyph. When an element of an affix is introduced into the main body, it is "infixed."

afterlife The Aztec concept of afterlife was determined by the cause of death, leading to four destinations. Tonatiuhichan was the paradise for warriors; Cincalco, the western abode for women who died in childbirth; Tlalocán, the southern paradise for victims of drowning and other causes relating to Tlaloc the rain-god; and Mictlán, the northern underworld for victims of natural causes whose souls after four years were lost forever.

Little is known of the Maya concept of the afterlife. The account in the Popol Vuh, the sacred book of the Quiché Maya, of the progress of hero-twins, Hunahpú and Xbalanqué, through the trials of the underworld represents an elitist approach —the eternal cycle of life and death, ending in deification. It suggests a close relation between ancestor worship and the divine descent of Maya rulers. Accounts of Yucatecan Maya beliefs, recorded after the Spanish Conquest, are obscured by earlier Mexican influences and by the wishful interpretations of Catholic friars.

agave Also called maguey (*Agave americana*), it was important to early Mexicans as a source of paper, thread, needles, pins, soap, pain medicines, fertilizer, thatch for roof and siding, fencing, food, and drink. The juice of the maguey ferments into pulque, distilled into tequila or mescal. The goddess Mayáhuel is identified with the discovery and uses of maguey.

agouti Edible rodent (*Dasyprocta aguti*) of the tropical forest.

Aguacate Name of an archaeological site on Lake Yojoa, Honduras; also the Spanish word for avocado.

Aguacatec One of three Maya languages spoken in the Department of Huehuetenango, Guatemala, the others being Mam and Ixil.

aguada Seasonal waterholes in the lowland limestone surface of the Yucatecan peninsula. Can be natural or of prehistoric construction.

Agua Escondida Eastern Chiapas site in the Lacandón forests.

Aguas Buenas Ceramic phase of Greater Chiriquí in Costa Rica and Panama. Ware was monochrome with appliqué figures, or zoned in red and beige with stylized birds. Contemporary with double-figure stone "slave" sculptures of Barriles. Wares at different sites have been variously dated, stylistically, from c. A.D. 300–800.

Aguascalientes Classic Maya site on the Pasión River, Petén, Guatemala.

Aguateca Classic Maya site in the Pasión River area of the Petén, Guatemala.

Aguilar Upper Preclassic ceramic phase of the Huasteca, c. 600–350 B.C. Sedentary agricultural families settled along the Pánuco River. White Progreso ware was superseded by White Chila, concurrent with the appearance of Red and Gray Aguilar. See also **Huasteca.**

Ah Maya masculine prefix, corresponding to X, or Ix, female prefix.

Ahau 1. Last and most important day of the 20-day Maya month, corresponding to the Aztec day Xóchitl. Ahau was the day of the sun-god Kinich Ahau. Calendrical name for the morning star is 1 Ahau; for the evening star, 7 Ahau. Associated with the number 4. 2. Maya word for lord. Title of the supreme administrator, high priest, and military leader of lowland Maya, the *halach uinic.*

ah canul Mexican mercenaries from Tabasco who sustained the power of the Cocom dynasty of Yucatán during Postclassic Mayapán period.

Ah Chac Mitan Ch'Oc Venus as morning star, linked to 1 Ahau, the day of the planet; translates from Mayan as "he of the great rotten stench."

ah kin Title of Yucatecan Maya priest.

ah kin mai Head of the Maya priestly hierarchy, also called *ahau kan mai,* whose duties included instruction in hieroglyphic writing, genealogies, astronomy, calendar computation, and advice to civil rulers, including matters of war. Next in rank to the *halach uinic,* whose successor he also helped determine as a member of the council.

ah kulel Deputy town chief among the lowland Maya, appointed by the *halach uinic.*

Ah Mucen Cab Honey was so important to Maya economy that this god was created to protect bees. Patron of beekeeping.

Ah Mun Maya corn-god pictured as a young man, often with a maize plant sprouting from his head. Symbolized by the Kan day glyph; associated with the number 8. God E of codices, sometimes called Yum Kaax.

Ah Puch God A of Maya codices, the death-god, corresponding to Mexican Mictlantecuhtli. Pictured with death's-head, bare ribs, spiny vertebral projections. If clothed, is shown bloated, with black spots suggesting decomposition. As chief demon, he presided over the lowest of the nine Maya underworlds. Glyphs include sacrificial flint knife and symbol resembling % sign. His companions were the dog, Moan bird, and owl. Associated with the day Cimi (death), number 10, South, color yellow. Closely allied with god F, god of war and human sacrifice. Principal antagonist of Itzamná. Underworld deities associated with Ah Puch are Yum Cimil, Cizin, and Hun Ahau.

Ahualulco 1. Archaeological site on the Gulf Coast of Tabasco. 2. Ceramic phase, c. A.D. 200–350, named after the site where multiple shaft tombs were discovered near Etzatlán, on Lake Magdalena, Jalisco.

ahuehuete Mexico's national tree, the Moctezuma bald cypress. The tree at Tule, Oaxaca, is believed to be the oldest known, c. 150 ft. (45 m) high, 160 ft. (50 m) in circumference, age estimated at 3,000 years.

Ahuiatéotl Aztec god of voluptuousness, manifestation of Xochipilli.

Ahuiateteo Aztec deities of voluptuousness, the five genies of the South. See also **Macuilxóchitl.**

Ahuíatl See **Macuilxóchitl.**

Ahuítzotl Eighth Aztec ruler, A.D. 1486–1502, successor and younger brother of Tizoc, son of Moctezuma I, father of Cuauhtémoc, the last Aztec king. Aggressive ruler who extended Mexican influence into the Balsas Basin, Guerrero, and east to the Guatemala border, aided by establishment of the *pochteca,* a combination of traders and spies. Reputedly 80,000 victims were sacrificed at his dedication of the Great Temple at Tenochtitlán in 1487.

Ahuizotla-Amantla Former name for Teotihuacán IV cultural phase, now called Metepec, c. A.D. 650–750, of the Valley of Mexico.

Ajalpan Preclassic phase of the Tehuacán Valley sequence, Puebla; comprised Early Ajalpan, c. 1500–1200 B.C., and Late Ajalpan, c. 1200–850 B.C., with its ceramic origins probably in Ocós phase of coastal Guatemala. Few evidences of contact with the Valley of Mexico.

Akab Dzib Late Classic Maya building at Chichén Itzá, in the Puuc style, contemporary with the nearby Nunnery building.

Akbal Third of the 20 Maya day names, identified with darkness and night. Equivalent to the Aztec day Calli, also one of the Year Bearers.

Aké Early Classic northern Yucatán site principally noted for its large colonnade, an architectural feature elsewhere identified with the Postclassic period.

alautun Maya time period of 20 *kinchiltuns,* equal to 23,040,000,000 days. See also **Long Count.**

Algo-es-Algo Middle Preclassic phase of the Cotzumalhuapa area of Pacific coastal Guatemala, c. 750–350 B.C.

Almagre Cultural phase of the Sierra de Tamaulipas, c. 2200–1800 B.C. Early corn domestication is revealed by the presence of cobs of a primitive kind of domesticated maize, which had been discovered earlier at Bat Cave in south-central New Mexico, dated c. 2500 B.C.

almanac, sacred Calendar cycle of 260 days used for ritualistic and divinatory purposes. Called *tzolkin* by Maya; *tonalpohualli* by Mexica. See also **calendar, Mesoamerican.**

almehen Name applied to Maya male nobles, implying known descent in both male and female lines, or *ch'ibal* ("man of lineage"). Represented the hereditary class of magistrates and war captains.

Alta Mira 1. Site in Soconusco region of

Pacific coastal Chiapas, Mexico. Its earliest phase, Barra, c. 1600 B.C., provided pottery suggestive of late Valdivia phase of coastal Ecuador. Middens before 1100 B.C. lack *metates,* artifacts hint at manioc cultivation. 2. Classic Maya site in the southeastern corner of Campeche.

altar 1. Term generally applied to blocky freestanding stone monuments, of which the earliest examples are the Olmec tabletop altars at San Lorenzo and La Venta. Recent work favors interpretation of large La Venta monoliths as royal thrones. Izapan and later Maya altars were generally placed before stelae, usually with related carving. Altar Q at Copán stands alone; commemorates meeting of dignitaries, possibly to correct the calendar. 2. In the Atlantic region of Costa Rica the term is applied to large three-legged *metates,* with "flying panels" underneath the grinding surface, the edges of which are decorated with stylized heads. 3. Ceramic phase: see **Orange, Fine.**

altar, Stela I, Copán

Altar de Sacrificios Classic Maya politicoreligious center near confluence of Chixoy and Pasión rivers in the Petén, Guatemala. Xe pottery there is the earliest known lowland Maya ceramic ware, initiating a sequence from c. 900 B.C. to early Postclassic times. Initial Series dates on stelae and monuments span the years A.D. 455–771.

Alta Verapaz Modern department of highland Guatemala, south of the Petén, with capital of Cobán. Its high, forested Sierra de Chamá was the habitat of the *quetzal* bird, 10,000 of whose feathers were traded from there annually, according to 16th-century chroniclers. Area is a source of the finest Maya carved jade and includes the site of Chamá, renowned for its polychrome pottery.

Alta Vista Important ceremonial center of northwestern Zacatecas, giving name to early phase of Chalchihuites culture, A.D. 300–500. Ceramics show traits of contemporary central Mexico.

altepetl (*altepeme*, pl.) Name for the Aztec city-state, with subdivisions called *calpulli* (*calpultin*, pl.); governed by a hereditary lord, the *tlatoani* (*tlatoque*, pl.).

alter ego Called *nahual* by the Aztecs, it is expressed in a variety of ways: 1. Anciently, the double or auxiliary personality of everyone. 2. Divinity of the day of the *Tonalamatl*, which attended the Aztec for life, was his *nahual*. 3. A living nonhuman being associated with a person at birth and therefore considered his complement. 4. The earthly manifestation of the gods in native mythology: the jaguar was the alter ego of Tezcatlipoca; the dog, of Xólotl; the feathered serpent, of Quetzalcóatl. 5. The animal form into which shamans have the faculty of converting themselves.

Altos Cuchumatanes Mountain range of the western highlands of Guatemala.

Altun Há Large Classic Maya ceremonial center, Belize, whose tombs revealed traces of hieroglyphic books, ceramics, and many jade objects, including a 10-lb. (4.125 kg) head of Kinich Ahau, the sungod. It may be the heaviest known Maya jade carving.

amanteca Member of the privileged Aztec guild of featherworkers, a craft probably of Chichimec origins. Highly prized featherwork is represented by shields, mantles, and the Moctezuma II headdress in the Museum für Völkerkunde, Vienna. Practiced earlier by the Toltecs, the art reached its zenith at the close of the Aztec period.

Amantla Site contemporary with Teotihuacán, which was built over as Atzcapotzalco, capital of the Tepanec state; today part of Mexico City.

Amapa Ceremonial complex of over 100 mounds in central Nayarit, Mexico. Its Early Period, A.D. 250–900, comprises Gavilan, Amapa, and Tuxpan phases; Late Period, A.D. 900–Conquest, is represented by Cerritos, Ixcuintla, Santiago phases. Late Postclassic similarities exist among Amapa polychrome, Mixteca-Puebla, and Aztatlán of Guasave (Sinaloa) ceramics. Metalwork and pottery styles also suggest Central American contact.

Amapala Early Postclassic phase of southern Honduras, c. A.D. 1000–1200.

amapámitl Pennant of white bark paper, a common symbol for sacrifice in the Mexican codices, often shown carried by victims.

amate Spanish word for *amatl*.

amatetehuitl Streamer of white bark paper offered in ritual ceremonies, on which Aztecs rapidly drew symbols of deities in liquid rubber. Sometimes called *tetehuitl*.

Amatitlán Lake and town in central Guatemala highlands. Classic Zarzal site, A.D. 700–1000, found there, with numerous Postclassic lakeside settlements. Noted for *incensarios* recovered from lakeside ceremonies.

amatl Generic Aztec name for wild fig tree (*Ficus cotoni folia*) whose inner bark was utilized to make paper. Corresponds to *huun* of Maya. Also applied to paper itself, and was used in compound words to denote *book*, such as in the *Tonalamatl*, the sacred Book of the Days. See also **bark paper.**

Amatle Classic period of Kaminaljuyú, Guatemalan highlands, c. A.D. 600–750. Coeval with Monte Albán IIIb and lowland Maya Tepeu I. May represent a "provincial-rural" local ceramic development, overlapping with the Teotihuacán-influenced Esperanza phase. Identified with Tiquisate ware and San Juan Plumbate.

Ameca Site on the Ameca River, central Jalisco, Mexico: "Ameca Gray" is a classic-style hollow figurine of Jalisco, either cream or red-slipped, or a combination of both. Typical are the elongated faces with long thin noses, eyes made of round clay pellets under filleted lids, and heads with crossband turbans. Forms are ample and smoothly rounded. Warriors are frequently depicted, armed with clubs, in barrellike armor.

Amerindian Clarifying term applied to natives of the Americas.

Amusgo Mixteca linguistic group at southern Guerrero-Oaxaca border.

Anáhuac Name applied to the Valley of Mexico, which anciently had interconnected lakes with a large coastline, meaning "at the edge of the water" in Nahuatl. The Gulf Coast was referred to as Anáhuac Huixtotin ("coast of salt-gatherers") and the Pacific coast as Anáhuac Xicalanque ("coast of gourd-gatherers"). Today Mexico itself is sometimes called the Republic of Anáhuac.

Anahuacalli ("house of Anáhuac") Museum containing his pre-Columbian collection built by Diego Rivera in Coyoacán, Mexico City.

anáhuatl White pectoral ring, an attribute of Tezcatlipoca and sometimes Huitzilopochtli, occasionally represented by an eye in Mexican codices.

Anales de Cuauhtitlán Also called Codex Chimalpopoca or Historia de los Reinos de Colhuacán, it is valuable for study of Nahua history and literature. Written in Nahuatl at the end of the 16th century.

Anales de los Cakchiqueles History of the Cakchiquel Maya nation of Guatemala. Similar to the Yucatecan *Chilam Balam*, it was transcribed by natives in the 16th century. It recounts migrations, foundings of cities, and struggles with the neighboring Quiché nation. Concludes with mention of the Spanish Conquest under Pedro de Alvarado. Also called *Memorial de Sololá*, after place where it was found, *Memorial de Tecpan-Atitlán*, and *Anales de los Xahil*.

Anales Mexicanos #1 See **codex, early post-Conquest, Mexican; Aubin Codex.**

annealing Metals, such as gold, in the course of being hammered, bent, or otherwise shaped, tend to harden and become brittle. Heating the metal, called annealing, restores its malleability. The process may be repeated many times, until the desired form is achieved.

anthropomorphic In human form.

Antigua (Guatemala) Cakchiquel settlement in the Late Classic period, it was the colonial Spanish capital of Central America from 1543 until its destruction by earthquake in 1773.

Antilles West Indies, an island chain encircling the Caribbean Sea in a giant arch from the northeast tip of Venezuela to the northern tip of Yucatán, Mexico. Greater Antilles include Cuba, Jamaica, Hispaniola (Haiti and Dominican Republic), Puerto Rico, and Virgin Islands. Lesser Antilles, composed of many smaller islands (Leeward and Windward), were natural stepping-stones of migration from South America to Greater Antilles. Geographically part of Middle America, the Antilles' pre-Columbian culture was distinct, with roots in South America. Some contact with the Middle American mainland is suggested but not yet established. Time scale for Caribbean cultures is:

Period I (5000–1000 B.C.) Some islands were inhabited by hunting-gathering peoples with lithic technology.

Period II (1000 B.C.–A.D. 300) Earliest appearance of agriculture and ceramics: Ciboney predominant.

Period III (A.D. 300–1000) Islands settled by Arawak farming group, pushing out Ciboney. Diverse pottery styles include early Taino in Dominican Republic.

Period IV (A.D. 1000–1500) Taino culture of the Island Arawak dominates Greater Antilles. Caribs invade Lesser Antilles from South America.

Apanohuayán See **universe, Aztec.**

Apatzingán Site in the Tepalcatepec basin of Michoacán, with a cultural sequence from the Classic period to the Conquest. Early Classic phases there are Chumbícuaro, Delicias, and Apatzingán.

Ape Nineteenth of the 20 Zapotecan day names, equivalent to the Aztec day Quiáhuitl and the Maya day Cauac.

appliqué Ceramic decorative technique in which embellishment is applied to a completed form by the adding of lumps or strips of clay, such as face effigies or fillets. The clay is usually given further modeling or impressed decoration after application.

Arawak Language and Indian group, widespread in northeastern South America, and the forebears of the Island Arawak. The latter moved north into the Antilles about the time of Christ and by A.D. 1000 had pushed the earlier Ciboney peoples into the peripheral positions they occupied when discovered by Columbus. Agriculturists, the Island Arawak's staple crop remained bitter manioc, similar to the mainland Arawak of Venezuela, the Guianas, and the Amazon valley. They brought a tradition of painted pottery (Saladoid) from Venezuela, later replaced by plainer, no longer painted, ware. The outstanding art of the West Indies was not ceramic, but the carving of ritual objects of stone, shell, bone, and wood, principally by Arawak people, the Taino, during the last 500 years before Columbus. Arawak chiefs were called *caciques,* a name later applied by Spaniards to all native rulers, even in Middle America. See also **Igneri.**

Archaic Archaeological term generally replaced in Mesoamerica by Preclassic. In Central America the term *Formative* replaces Archaic or Preclassic, commonly denoting the early area development stage.

Arenal See **Miraflores-Arenal.**

Arenitas Site in eastern Tabasco.

Arévalo Earliest ceramic phase at Kaminaljuyú, Guatemala, c. 1500–800 B.C. No habitation mounds but outstanding pottery vessels. Clay stamps, small hand-made figurines, and effigy whistles are related to parallel development elsewhere.

Aristide See **Central Panama.**

Armería River originating in southeastern Jalisco that reaches the Pacific near the Colima sites of Armería and Periquillo. The name of a phase of the Colima culture of western Mexico, A.D. 800–1200.

Arroyo Pesquero Olmec site in southern Veracruz, source of life-size jade masks, magnetite mirrors, and hundreds of serpentine and jade celts. The area is also referred to as Las Choapas.

Arrow Sacrifice Sacrificial ceremony, Tlacacaliliztli in Nahuatl, in which the victim was spread-eagled on a frame as the target for arrows; part of the Aztec Ochpanitztli festival honoring the corn-goddess Chicomecóatl. Graffiti found in Temple II, Tikal, suggest its

Arrow Sacrifice
(*Tlacacaliliztli*)

presence also among the Maya.

artifact An object made by man.

Asunción Mita Site in the Department of Jutiapa, Guatemala. Only here and at Papalguapa have corbeled arches been found in the highlands, and only in tombs. It is also most southerly manifestation of the arch, a horizon marker of the Classic period in the Maya lowlands.

Atabeyra Island Arawak goddess of fertility and childbirth.

atadura Molding providing the upper and lower boundaries to the decorative frieze that encircled the upper facade of Classic Maya buildings. It appeared in the lowlands at Río Bec and became a characteristic of the Puuc architectural style.

Atamalcualiztli Major nonannual Aztec ceremony celebrated every eight years in Técpatl years during the 13th or 14th month of 20 days.

atecocolli Nahuatl name for the native trumpet fashioned from a conch shell (*Strombus gigas*), also called *tecciztli.* Maya called it *hub;* Tarascans, *puuaqua;* Zapotec, *paataotocuecheni;* is today popularly called by its Spanish name, *caracol.*

Atemoztli Seventeenth of 18 20-day months of the Nahuatl calendar of 365 days, as celebrated at Tenochtitlán. Tlaloc was the god propitiated. See also **months, Aztec.**

Atetelco Teotihuacán residential building

complex, west of Tetitla. Includes two patios of different periods, the older of which (Patio Blanco) has three porticoes with interior murals of red in two tones, with repetitive patterns of jaguars, priests, and bleeding hearts.

Atitlán Spectacular lake of the Guatemalan highlands, edged by volcanoes, in Department of Sololá. Chukumuk and Chuitinamit are sites on its shore.

Atl Ninth of the 20 Nahuatl day names. Patron deity was Xiuhtecuhtli; its augury was evil. Generally pictured in the Aztec codices as a water-filled vessel. The corresponding Maya day was Muluc; in the Zapotec calendar, Niza or Queza. 1 Atl was the calendrical name of Chalchiúhtlicue, 4 Atl of the fourth sun in Aztec cosmology.

Atlacuilhayán Present-day Tacuba, Mexico City, south of Chapultepec Park.

Atlantean An architectural support in the form of a standing man, identified with the Toltec. Colossal Atlanteans rise on the platform of the pyramid of the Temple of Quetzalcóatl at Tula. Smaller figures supporting stone slabs found at Chichén Itzá's

Atlantean, Chichén Itzá

Temple of the Warriors attest to Toltec influence on Postclassic Yucatán. Earliest Atlantean figures in Mesoamerica, c. 1000 B.C., are carved in high relief on Olmec Monument 2 at Potrero Nuevo in Veracruz.

atlatl Nahuatl word for spear-thrower; a short grooved stick with a hook at one end to hold the spear end and finger loops at other to propel the missile. First appears with lake

atlatl, Codex Colombino

cultures for hunting ducks, antedating the Postclassic bow and arrow in Mesoamerica. Employed in warfare by the Toltec, it became an Aztec symbol of military rank, sometimes elaborately carved and decorated. Called *hulche* by the Maya.

Atlatonan One of four goddesses, impersonated by virgins, symbolically married to the young Aztec warrior who was the honored impersonator of Tezcatlipoca for a year before his sacrifice at the feast of Tóxcatl.

Atlcahualo Second of the 18 months of the Nahuatl calendar of 365 days, as observed in Tenochtitlán. In different regions also called Cuauhuitlehua ("raising of poles," i.e. trees) and Xilomanaliztli ("offering of tender maize ears"). Consecrated to the rain deities, Tlaloc and Chalchiúhtlicue, as well as Quetzalcóatl who as Éhecatl (wind) swept the way for rain. Children were sacrificed to Tlaloc. See also **months, Aztec.**

Atoto See **Cuautepec.**

Atotoztli Daughter of King Coxcoxtli of Colhuacán whose son Acamapichtli became the first Aztec ruler.

Atzan Cultural phase of Zaculeu, Guatemalan highlands, c. 300 B.C.–A.D. 700.

Atzcapotzalco Capital of the Tepanec state, A.D. 1250–1428, until vanquished by the alliance of Tenochtitlán and Texcoco. Today a part of Mexico City. Founded by Otomí and Teotihuacán groups, it was a repository of Teotihuacán cultural traditions (Teotihuacán IV) into the 9th and 10th centuries. See also **Tezozómoc**

Aubin, Codex See **codex, post-Conquest early Mexican, Aubin Codex.**

Aubin Manuscript #20 See **codex, pre-Conquest Mexican, Aubin Manuscript #20.**

auianime Female companions to unmarried Aztec warriors; Xochiquetzal was their patroness; also called *maqui.*

Aurora Early Classic phase of Kaminaljuyú, Guatemalan highlands, c. A.D. 300–400, in period of transition from the inventive Preclassic Miraflores-Arenal to the Mexican-influenced, later Classic Esperanza phase. Stela cult, popular in the Preclassic period, abruptly disappeared—precisely as it embarked on its road to highest development in the southern Maya lowlands.

Autlán Archaeological site of southern Jalisco. Cultural phases include Cofradia, c. A.D. 1000, and Autlán-Mylpa, c. A.D. 1350.

aviform In the form of a bird.

Axayácatl Sixth Aztec ruler, A.D. 1469–81, grandson of Moctezuma I, brother of Tizoc and of Ahuítzotl who succeeded him. Annexed Tlatelolco to Tenochtitlán in 1473. His western expansion was stopped by the Tarascans.

axe A basic tool everywhere, in chipped or grooved stone, the axe took many shapes, and as a sacred symbol, a number of ceremonial forms: 1. Celts, plain, petal- or almond-shaped, were commonest in Middle America. 2. Votive axes (Olmec) incorporate anthropomorphic figure with head carved at the poll and blade left plain. Most are larger than utilitarian celts. 3. Carib axes (Lesser Antilles) are elaborate forms of grooved or eared axes, usually of unusable shape or size. 4. *Hachas* (Veracruz) are only called axes because of the characteristic bladelike edge. Related to the Mesoamerican ritual ball game.

axe gods Costa Rican stylized figure pendants of jade and other stones, probably dating 400 B.C.–A.D. 550. Their thick rounded upper half was carved to represent the top of a figure or bird, the blade below resembled a celt in outline and smooth convex form. They constituted almost a third of Nicoya jade production, less in the Línea Vieja area. Similar pendants have been found at Playa de los Muertos, Honduras, and in Early and Middle Preclassic burials in the highlands of Guatemala, and in Guerrero, Mexico.

axe money T-shaped copper blades resembling axes or food-choppers. Too thin and soft for use as tools, they served as a medium of exchange in 16th-century Mexico. They have been discovered in huge numbers in Oaxaca, other Mexican states, and in distant Ecuador and Peru.

axtaxelli Nahuatl word for tuft of heron feathers, an attribute of Tezcatlipoca, forming part of the Aztec warrior's headdress.

ayacachtli Nahuatl word for a gourd-shaped rattle with beads, seeds, or pebbles inside, today usually called by its Brazilian name, *maraca*. An adaptation, *cacalachtli*, is the rattle of clay pellets in the hollow legs of tripod ceramic vessels or clay incense ladles.

Ayala Phase of the Guardiana branch of the Chalchihuites cultural horizon of Durango, Mexico, c. A.D. 550–700.

Ayampuc Early Postclassic phase of Guatemalan highlands, c. A.D. 900–1200. X Fine Orange ware and Tohil Plumbate characterize its ceramics.

áyotl Nahuatl word for a percussion musical instrument made from a turtle carapace. Prongs on the underside were struck with deer antlers, the sound produced being amplified by the shell. Favorite of the Maya who called it *kayab*.

Ayotla Subphase of Preclassic Ixtapaluca phase of the Valley of Mexico, named after Ayotla excavation near Tlapacoya, c. 1400–1150 B.C.

Azacualpa Archaeological site on the eastern shore of Lake Güija, El Salvador.

Aztatlán Postclassic western Mexican cultural complex characterized by some of the most elaborate prehistoric pottery in the New World. Its diversity was expressed in four- to six-color polychrome vessels, engraving, paint cloisonné, negative painting, and some molded pieces. Widely distributed in Sinaloa and northern Nayarit. Mixtec-Puebla stylistic influence from central Mexico is discernible. Metal artifacts were abundant, primarily of copper, but also of gold and silver.

Aztatlán cultural horizon is identified prominently with three Sinaloa sites: Chametla, Culiacán, and Guasave. At Chametla the earliest phase was Lolandis, c. A.D. 700–900, followed by Acaponeta, 900–1100, and El Taste, 1100–1250. Concurrent phases at Culiacán were Acaponeta and La Divisa. A ceramic phase at Guasave, of the same name, is dated c. A.D. 1200–1400.

Aztec Belonging to the northern Uto-Aztecan language group, legend reports their leaving Chicomoztoc ("seven caves") to begin their migration to the Valley of Mexico. They were composed of seven tribes, generally listed as the Acolhua, Chalca, Mexica, Tepaneca, Tlalhuica, Tlaxcalteca, and Xochimilca. The Aztec empire as encountered at the Conquest grew out of the aggressiveness of the Mexica, who finally prevailed in Valley of Mexico by defeating the Tepaneca of Atzcapotzalco in 1428, aided by Acolhua of Texcoco. In less than 100 years the Aztec realm extended from the Gulf of Mexico to the Pacific Ocean, and as far east as Chiapas. Culturally, the Aztecs built on the preceding Toltec civilization, developing an art form that was direct and heavily formal, combining symbolism with realistic detail, as in the statue of Coatlícue in the Museo Nacional de Antropología, Mexico City. Conquest by Cortés in 1521 abruptly terminated the Aztec empire. See also **Mexican rulers.**

Aztlán Legendary land in northwest Mexico in which Chicomoztoc was located and from which the seven Aztec tribes migrated to the Valley of Mexico.

Azuero Peninsula Portion of Panama south of Parita Bay, comprising the provinces of Herrera, Los Santos, with a strip of Veraguas along its western coast. Known for elaborate goldwork and polychrome ceramics. See also **Central Panama.**

b

baby face Olmec art style expressed in puffy faces with square jaws, mouths with flaring, snarling upper lips and down-turned corners, exposing toothless gums. May represent the mythical union of human and feline from which the Olmec traced their descent. Characteristic of both men and gods as expressed in stone and clay figures. Most distinctive are hollow clay figures with splayed legs and no genitals. Such pieces are found in the Mexican highlands at Tlatilco, Tlapacoya, Las Bocas, and Xochipala, and at San Lorenzo and Tenexpan in the lowlands.

Bacabs Maya deities, sons of Itzamná, who supported the sky at four corners of the earth. The *Chilam Balam* of Chumayel tells of the creation when the 13 lords of the heavens were overcome by the 9 lords of the underworld and the 4 Bacabs were set in place. Each had his own world direction, color, Year Bearer, and name. East: color red, Kan years, called Hobnil; North: color white, Muluc years, called Can Tzional; West: color black, Ix years, called Zac Cimi; South: color yellow, Cauac years, called Hozanek.

They were gods of bees and apiaries, and exercised influence on the luck of the year. Atlantean supports with upraised arms, carved during the Toltec period at Chichén Itzá, were probably Bacabs.

Bacalar Bay and town in southeastern Quintana Roo, Mexico, site of pre-Hispanic Bakhalal.

Bajío 1. Fertile basin in the state of Guanajuato, Mexico, traversed by Lerma River. Known for the Preclassic site of Chupícuaro and the rich silver mines worked into colonial times. 2. Cultural phase of San Lorenzo, southern Veracruz, c. 1350–1250 B.C.

bajos Broad swampy depressions, a source of water during the summer months in the Petén of Guatemala.

Bakhalal Coastal port of Quintana Roo on the Bay of Bacalar; under the dominance of the Putún-Acalán Maya of Tabasco by the tenth century.

Baking Pot Classic Maya ceremonial center on the Belize River, Cayo district, Belize.

baktun Maya time period of 20 *katuns*, 400 *tuns*, or 144,000 days. See also **Long Count.**

Balakbal Classic Maya site, southeastern Campeche, Mexico; near the Petén border.

balam 1. Maya word for jaguar. Applied to invisible guardian spirits who watch over the four sides of Maya *milpas* and four "directional" entrances of villages. 2. See also *Chilam Balam.* 3. According to the Popol Vuh, the names of the first men were Balam-Quitzé, Balam-Acab, Mahucutah, and Iquí-Balam, in the legendary history of the Quiché Maya. 4. Cultural phase of Zacualpa, Guatemalan highlands, c. A.D. 400–700.

Balancán 1. Site in eastern Tabasco, Mexico, with important Classic Maya stelae and ball-game paraphernalia from Classic period Veracruz; Preclassic votive axes suggest earlier Olmec presence. 2. Early Postclassic fine-grained paste pottery, called Z Fine Orange, probably originating in Maya western subregion of eastern Tabasco or southwest Campeche; became the outstanding element in the Cehpech ceramic complex. Varies from other Fine Orange groups in its decorative techniques and vessel forms: an orange, white, or, rarely, a black slip may be used; pottery forms include flaring-sided bowls with ring-stand base and cylindrical vases. Characteristic of the Puuc phase of Yucatán, Z Fine Orange also found its way to Zaculeu and Zacualpa in the western Guatemalan highlands. See **Orange, Fine.**

Balankanche Cave of Balankanche, on the outskirts of Chichén Itzá, contains shrines of Tlaloc, the Maya rain-god. Carbon-dated A.D. 870. The Mexican traits of cave decoration hint at contact during the Early Postclassic period.

balché A mead of fermented honey, with addition of the bark of the balché tree (*Lonchocarpus longistylus*) during processing for its narcotic effect. Favorite Maya intoxicant and purge, with strong religious associations.

ball game, Arawak Possibly introduced from Mesoamerica, its rules are unknown but a solid rubber ball was used. Courts were simple, outlined by erect stone slabs often decorated by petroglyphs of deities, such as at Capa, Puerto Rico. The ball game was limited to Virgin Islands, Puerto Rico, and the Dominican Republic. Collar stones, elbow stones, and *zemis* are generally found at such sites.

ball game, Mesoamerican A definitive aspect of Mesoamerican civilization, it prob-

ball court, **Chichén Itzá**

ably originated in Veracruz, Mexico, home of the rubber tree. Its importance there is archaeologically proven by the presence of all three stone sculptures associated with the game: *yoke, hacha,* and *palma.* Ball courts were called *tlachtli* by the Mexicans; *pok-ta-pok* by the Maya. They had an I-shaped playing area, but it was varied in size and architecture. Courts of the Classic period

generally consisted of raised viewing platforms along the sides, with lower walls sloping inward to the court. Markers were represented by both stone disks emplanted flush in the playing surface and *hachas* tenoned in the parallel facing walls, dividing the length of the court into three sections. In the Postclassic period the facing walls became vertical with a single stone ring embedded high and centrally in each wall; players scored by putting the ball "through the hoop."

Rules of the game are not known, but seem to have varied in time and space. The generally accepted concept of the ritual game at time of the Spanish Conquest called for the ball to be kept aloft, simulating the movement of the sun through the sky. The ball was of solid rubber, weighing about 7 lbs. (3 kg), necessitating protective padding for the players. Hands were not allowed in play, the ball bouncing off hips and shoulders. The *yoke* worn about the waist served this purpose, possibly supplemented by a *palma* resting frontally on the *yoke* to aid the trajectory of the ball. It was a team sport, reputedly played for high stakes, including the players' lives. Relief-sculptured ball-court panels at Classic Tajín and Postclassic Chichén Itzá both portray ball-game ceremonies involving human sacrifice.

Balsas River Second longest river in Mexico, originating in the Mexican states of Tlaxcala and Puebla. Tributaries are Atoyac Poblano, Nexapa, Amacuzac, Zitácuaro, and Tepalcatepec. A part of it in Guerrero is called the Mezcala. The Balsas flows through the fertile Balsas basin of Guerrero before defining the boundary between that state and Michoacán on its way to the Pacific Ocean.

Baluarte phase See **Chametla.**

bark beater Stone block used to pound bark into paper or cloth, usually made to be hafted, with characteristic longitudinal grooved surface.

bark paper Native paper produced by beating the inner bark of the wild fig tree

(*Ficus cotoni folia*), generically called *amatl* in Nahuatl; *huun,* in Maya. All known pre-Conquest Maya codices were written on bark paper, as were the early post-Conquest Mexican manuscripts before the introduction of European paper. Bark paper played a role in Aztec and Maya autosacrificial bloodletting ceremonies, the splattered blood being gathered on strips of paper and offered to the gods.

Barra Earliest ceramic phase of the Soconusco coastal region of Chiapas, before 1600 B.C. Predominance of *tecomates,* absence of ollas or necked jars, decorated by incising, many with crossed lines, and punctation. Resemblance is noted to coeval Colombia and coastal Ecuador. See also **Alta Mira, Valdivia.**

Barra de Navidad Coastal Jalisco site, with an indicated occupation from A.D. 1000–1350.

Barrancon Late Preclassic and Protoclassic mound group near Mapastepec, Chiapas.

Barriles Ceremonial site near Baru volcano, Chiriquí, Panama, at the Costa Rican border. Named for the carved barrel-shaped stones found there. Also noted for "man-on-slave" piggyback stone figures, with human trophy heads in the hands of the top man. Possibly tied to the Chontales region of Nicaragua. Associated with Aguas Buenas phase ceramics.

Barton Creek Cultural phase of Barton Ramie, Belize, c. 500–300 B.C.

Barton Ramie Maya habitation site on the alluvial flats of the Belize River, Belize. Sequence of ceramic phases starts before 1000 B.C. and continues to c. A.D. 1200.

batab Hereditary chief of a Maya village, combining some religious with civil functions like his superior, the *halach uinic.* Shared the responsibility as the captain in war with the elected *nacom.*

bat-god Important Zapotec deity at Monte Albán, related to fertility and maize-god, from Preclassic into Classic times. Also figures prominently in the art and iconography of the Maya, with special relation to the underworld. See **Zotz.** Among the Mexicans the bat-god appears in the codices

Vaticanus 1773, Borgia, and Fejérváry-Mayer. Nahuatl name is Tlacatzinacantli.

batik See **resist painting.**

Bay Islands Caribbean islands off northeastern coast of Honduras.

Bdi'yet Among the Zapotec, one of the Lords of the Night.

beak bird Most prominent Costa Rican jade motif after axe gods. The figure also appears painted on pottery vessels and carved on stone *metates.* Main characteristic is its exaggerated and stylized beak, derived from long-beaked waterfowl, suggesting Antilles influence. All jade beak-bird pendants are drilled horizontally through the neck, so they will hang with the beak projecting when strung on a necklace.

Becan A rare fortified Classic Maya site in eastern Campeche near Xpuhil.

Becker #1, #2, codices See **codex, pre-Conquest Mexican, Becker #1;** and **codex, early post-Conquest Mexican, Becker #2.**

Belize Formerly Crown Colony of British Honduras; also the name of its principal river and Caribbean port. New capital is Belmopan. Country is bounded by Quintana Roo, Campeche, the Petén of Guatemala, and the Caribbean Sea. Maya Mountains in west and south attain over 3,000 ft. (915 m). Archaeological sites include Altun Há, Caracol, Lubaantun, Barton Ramie, San José, and Benque Viejo.

Bellote Small Maya coastal site with burials, near Comalcalco, Tabasco.

Ben Thirteenth day of the 20-day Maya month, corresponding to the Mexican day Ácatl and the Zapotec day Quij. Ben may represent the growing maize plant.

Benque Viejo Maya site on Mopan River, Belize.

Bering Strait Land bridge between Asia and Alaska created by the lowered ocean level during early periods of ice formation. At various times, man (*Homo sapiens*) probably followed the trail of big game into the New World from Asia. Optimum conditions probably prevailed 20,000 years ago.

Beydo Fourth of nine southern Zapotec day names of deities that represented objects or natural forces. Translates as "wind" or "seeds" (not maize).

Bilbao Ceremonial center in the Pacific coastal plain of Guatemala, Algo-es-Algo, its earliest ceramic phase, dates from c. 750 B.C. Bilbao is best known, however, for its important role in the development of the Cotzumalhuapa art style of the region, c. A.D. 650–925.

Binding of the Years See **Tying of Years.**

Bird Jaguar Notable eighth-century Maya ruler depicted on lintel carvings at Yaxchilán.

Bird Jaguar glyph

Biscuit ware A very thin beige ceramic of the Diquís region of Costa Rica, unpainted, highly polished, simple, and elegant. Small appliqué animals on the body or feet of the vessels appear as the only adornment. Has been found with Spanish iron tools, attesting to its late presence.

Boca Costa Pacific piedmont of Guatemala.

Bodley, Codex See **codex, pre-Conquest Mexican, Bodley Codex.**

Bolaños-Juchipila Little-known archaeological area of southern Zacatecas and Jalisco; it formed part of Mesoamerica's northern frontier at the Conquest. Sites include Totoate, Banco de las Casas, Teul, and Las Ventanas. Sometimes referred to as Caxcana, it was contemporary with the Chalchihuites culture of Zacatecas and Durango. Postclassic to the Conquest.

Bold Geometric Red and black-on-orange pottery, with light orange paste and fine temper. Overlapped Ulúa Polychrome in lower Ulúa and Comayagua river valleys, but less broadly traded; found in the Bay Islands and eastern Honduras, c. A.D. 700–900.

bolon Number 9 in Maya.

Bolonchen Large cave in southern Yucatán, anciently used for religious ceremonies. Sometimes called Xtacunbilxunan ("hidden" or "guarded lady"), referring to the

legends in which a girl was hidden there by her lover.

Bolon Dz'acab God K of the Maya codices; sometimes called the "long-nosed god," although his protuberance is probably an extended upper lip. Serpent-footed deity of manikin scepters, god of lineage and descent, his name translates "nine generations." God of Kan years, related to the East. May be Maya equivalent of the Mexican god Tezcatlipoca.

Bolon ti Ku Nine Maya lords of the underworld, worshiped collectively and separately. Names are unknown, but glyphs are identified, included in Long Count inscriptions. Contrasted to Oxlahun ti Ku, the 13 celestial gods. Corresponds to the Aztec Yohualteuctin. See **Lords of the Night.**

Bomba Subphase of Preclassic Tlapacoya, Valley of Mexico, c. 1150–1050 B.C., transitional between the Ixtapaluca and Zacatenco Valley-wide phases.

Bonampak Classic Maya site, c. A.D. 450–800, in jungles of eastern Chiapas, Mexico. Architecture and stelae are of general Usumacinta style. Most noted for its three-room "Temple of the Paintings," all of whose interior surfaces are covered with polychrome murals depicting battles, conferences of dignitaries, dancers, musicians, and sacrifices to the gods. Its composition and detail are rendered with realism and simplicity, making it the closest to European fresco painting of all Mesoamerican art. Realistic, colorful rendition of Maya customs, dress, and warlike activity shed new light. A reinterpretation of the nature of Maya civilization began after its discovery in 1946.

booch Mayan shawl, similar to Mexican *rebozo.*

Book of the Days See *Tonalamatl.*

Borgia Group Term applied collectively to a group of five pre-Hispanic Mexican manuscripts, recorded in native glyphs, named after the principal one, the Codex Borgia. Others are codices Laud, Fejérváry-Mayer, Cospi, and Vaticanus B. Similarity of style is the principal trait governing their relationship. They also share pre-Conquest dating, animal-skin screen-fold format, intricate symbolism and iconography, and complex religious and calendrical content involving elaborations of the 260-day divinatory cycle and associated gods. The history of the codices, all now in Europe, is poorly known, but they seem to originate from the region of the Mixteca-Puebla culture. See **codex, pre-Conquest Mexican.**

Boruca Modern term for a division of the Macro-Chibcha linguistic group of the Pacific southeast of Costa Rica, a region formerly populated by Coto, Tutucaca, Burucaca, and Abubaes.

Boturini, Codex See **codex, early post-Conquest Mexican; Boturini, Codex.**

brachycephalic See **cephalic index.**

breadnut Tree (*Brosimum utile*) whose fruit of high food value probably supplemented the maize diet of the lowland Maya. Today popularly called *ramón.*

bristlecone Bristlecone pine (*Pinus longaeva*), found in the White Mountains of California, is the world's oldest living organism; one such tree is still growing at the age of 4,600 years. Overlapping bristlecone growth-ring sequences reach back into the 7th millennium B.C., and are extended backward as still older wood specimens are found. This accurate dendrochronological scale provided a check on radiocarbon (carbon 14 or C^{14}) dates. Analyses of the same specimens by both methods showed substantial discrepancies and led to the formulation of correction tables for all C^{14} dates within its current limits. Differences increase rapidly in the centuries B.C.; conventional C^{14} dates before 4000 B.C. are more than 800 years too young. See also **radiocarbon (C^{14}) dating.**

British Honduras See **Belize.**

buffware, blackware, brownware, etc. Terms used to describe certain colors of ceramics, achieved directly in the firing of the object.

bule A gray, highly polished globular ceramic vessel with incurving neck, identified with the Middle Preclassic period of Guerrero, Mexico.

Buluc Ch'Abtan An earth deity believed to be god R of the Maya codices.

Burica 1. Narrow Pacific peninsula of southwestern Panama. 2. Ceramic phase of coastal Chiriquí between Punta Burica and the Chiriquí Gulf islands, c. A.D. 500–800; contemporary with the Aguas Buenas phase of Greater Chiriquí.

burnish To polish and give a rich, deeply glowing sheen to ceramic objects by rubbing the surface before firing with a hard object, such as a smooth stone, wood, or bone. Extensively practiced in Mesoamerica.

c

ca Number 2 in Maya.

Caban Seventeenth day of the 20-day Maya month, corresponding to the Aztec day Ollin and the Zapotec Xoo. Word means earth; Caban is the day of the young earth-goddess, the moon, and maize. Associated with the number 1.

cabecitas colosales Term sometimes applied to small Nuiñe-style bodyless spherical heads, in reference to the also bodyless "colossal heads" of the Olmec culture, to which they show similarity. Found near Acatlán, Puebla, they may be ceramic representations of shrunken trophy heads.

Cabo Catoche At northwestern tip of the Yucatán peninsula. Official discovery of Yucatán by Europeans was marked by a battle here in 1517 between the Maya of Ecab province and the Spaniards of the Hernández de Córdoba expedition. The distant view of the Maya settlement so impressed the Spanish that they called it Gran Cairo.

cacao Tropical crop highly prized as food and source of *chocolatl*, a luxury beverage of the priesthood and nobility of Mexico. Itself a major trade item, cacao beans became a medium of exchange throughout Mesoamerica, a custom perhaps introduced by Teotihuacán as simple barter was no longer adequate to sustain the volume and geographic extent of trade in Classic times. Later, Aztec records show that a slave destined for sacrifice, "of good body and capable of sacred dance," was auctioned for 4,000 cacao beans. Cacao beans also became a popular art motif on ceramic vessels, both painted and as an applied adornment.

Cacaxtla Site in southeastern Tlaxcala where important murals were discovered in 1975, including representations of the feathered serpent and man-jaguar. Clay bas-reliefs are of a later period than the murals. It appears to have begun as a ceremonial center, c. A.D. 100–650, followed by the construction of fortifications, A.D. 650–1100.

cacique Arawak tribal chief, a title subsequently applied by the Spanish invaders to Indian leaders generally, including those of the Middle American mainland.

cactli Nahuatl word for a sandal of animal skin or maguey fiber.

Cahyup Late Postclassic Maya site, Department of Baja Veracruz, Guatemala, A.D. 1200–1500.

cajete Archaeological term for a flat Mexican earthenware bowl.

Cakchiquel Maya tribe of the Guatemalan highlands that shared a common Toltec ancestry with the Quiché Maya. The Cakchiquel entered Guatemala c. A.D. 1100 from Tabasco through Chiapas, eventually establishing their capital at Iximché. Their history is told in the *Anales de los Cakchiqueles*.

calabtun Very rare Maya time period of 20 *pictuns*, 160,000 *tuns*, or 57,600,000 days. See **Long Count.**

Calakmul Large Classic Maya site of southern Campeche, Mexico. Erected greatest number of stelae, 103, of which 30 are plain or too weathered to show carving.

Calderitas Postclassic Maya site on Chetumal Bay, Quintana Roo, exhibiting decadent Mayapán influence.

calendar, Mesoamerican The calendar was a definitive achievement of Mesoamerican civilization, unknown in other cultures of the New World, reaching its highest elaboration among the lowland Maya of the Classic period. Study of the movements of celestial bodies produced several time cycles. Among them, the lunar calendar and the Venus cycle were principally employed for astronomical purposes. The two basic time cycles that governed Mesoamerican life were the solar calendar and the ritual calendar. The solar calendar of 365 days, called the Vague Year, was composed of 18 months of 20 days each, with a period of 5 days added at the end. The 360-day period was called *xíhuitl* by Aztecs, *haab* or *tun* by the Maya. The final 5 unlucky days were called *Nemontemi* in Nahuatl, *Uayeb* in Mayan. This calendar answered the needs of an agricultural population and established the monthly feasts to their gods.

The priests used a ritual calendar of 260 days, called *tonalpohualli* by the Aztecs and *tzolkin* by the Maya, primarily for divinatory purposes. The concurrent permutation of the solar and ritual calendars produced the Calendar Round. An exclusively lowland Classic Maya calendrical achievement was the Long Count, which permitted an infinite computation of time from an established mythical starting point, backward or forward.

By means of the Secondary Series the lowland Maya adjusted their 365-day solar calendar slightly more accurately than our Gregorian calendar, introduced almost 1,000 years later, in 1582. Length of modern astronomical year: 365.2422 days; length of former uncorrected Julian year: 365.2500 days; length of current Gregorian year: 365.2425 days; length of Maya solar year: 365.2420 days.

Calendar Round Interval of 52 Vague Years computed by the permutation or intermeshing, in cogwheel fashion, of the 260-day ritual calendar (composed of 20 named days and 13 numbers) with the solar calendar of 365 days (18 months of 20 days, followed by a final 5-day period). The same combination of numbered day with month position could occur only every 52 years, or 18,980 days (equal to both 260 x 73 and 365 x 52). A Maya date might be 1 Kan 1 Pop: 1 Kan being the numbered day in the ritual calendar, and 1 Pop the month position in the solar calendar. This Calendar Round, called a Year Bundle or Xiuhmolpilli in Nahuatl, was of major significance to Mesoamerican peoples. In addition to the Aztecs, Maya, and Zapotec, it governed the Mixtec, Otomí, Huastec, Totonac, Matlatzinca, Tarascans, and others who shared a belief in the ultimate end of the world at the completion of a 52-year cycle.

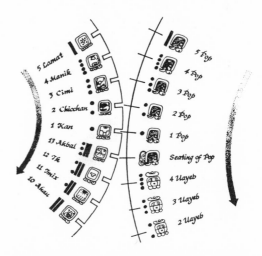

Calendar Round: Diagram shows engagement of *Tonalamatl* wheel of 260 days (*left*) and *haab* wheel of 365 positions (*right*); the combination of the two giving the Calendar Round, or 52-year period.

The appearance of a bright constellation in the midnight sky of the last day of a Calendar Round cycle promised respite for another 52 years, a cause for ritual celebration. The Aztecs observed the New Fire Ceremony, rekindling hearths across the land that had been extinguished in anticipation of the end of the current world. Unlike the earlier lowland Maya of the Classic period with their Long Count, the Aztecs never progressed beyond the concept of a Calendar Round. Since the same date recurred every 52 years, it is often difficult to determine the exact Calendar Round referred to, a limitation that complicates attempts to establish a dependable Aztec chronology based on native records. See also **Yohualtecuhtli, Cerro de la Estrella, Tying of Years.**

Calendar Stone, Aztec Also called the Sun Stone, this circular monolith, over 10 ft. (3.6 m) in diameter, is carved to symbolize graphically the Postclassic Mexican concept of cyclical space and time. The central figure is surrounded by hieroglyphs for the days, months, and suns, or cosmic cycles. Traditional interpretation of the central figure as Tonatiuh, the daytime sun, is challenged by its interpretation as Yohualtecuhtli, associated with cyclical completion, that of the current fifth sun, or world. The Calendar Stone was discovered during repair to the cathedral in Mexico City in 1790. It is now in the Museo Nacional de Antropología, Mexico City. See also **Creation myth, Aztec.**

Calera Last phase of the Postclassic horizon of the Chalchihuites culture of north-central Mexico, c. A.D. 1150–1350.

Calichal Phase of the Chalchihuites cultural horizon of Zacatecas, Mexico, A.D. 500–650.

Calixtlahuaca 1. Center of Matlatzinca culture before its capitulation to the Aztecs under Ahuítzotl in 1476. Prominent round structure is believed to have been dedicated to Quetzalcóatl in his manifestation as Éhecatl, the wind-god. Near the modern city of Toluca, state of Mexico. 2. "Calixtlahuaca ware" is the term applied to the cylindrical, flat-bottomed bowls with incised Olmec motifs first reported in Preclassic levels at this site. Center of manufacture is unknown, but they also appear

in Morelos and at Tlapacoya, Valley of Mexico.

Calli Third of the 20 Nahuatl day signs, pictured in Mexican codices as a house. Calli, as a Year Bearer, along with Ácatl, Técpatl, and Tochtli, served to begin the years, there being 13 Calli years in the 52-year cycle, oriented to the West. The Maya equivalent was Akbal; Zapotec, Guela. Calendrical names identified with Calli are: 1 Calli: one of Cihuateteo, descending; unlucky augury; 2 Calli: Xólotl in Mitla murals; 3 Calli: gods of fire (?); 4 Calli: Mictlantecuhtli; 5 Calli: god of lapidaries, husband of 9 Itzcuintli, their patron goddess (Chantico); 6 Calli: Mictlantecuhtli; 7 Calli: propitious day for merchants' entrance into Mexico; 8 Calli: year of creation of the *macehual;* 10 Calli: year of birth of Ehecatl.

Tepeyolohtli was the patron deity of Calli, with a favorable augury.

calmécac School of higher learning for sons of Aztec nobles, from whom the high chiefs of army, priests, judges, and rulers were chosen. Quetzalcóatl was its patron deity.

calpulli Aztec social and political unit of maximum importance. Constituted the basic family relationship, expressed geographically, and with its own protective deities. Fathers of families in the *calpulli* made up the council led by an elected *teachcauh* who represented them in the higher councils with other *calpulli*, directed land use, imparted justice, presided over festivals and religious ceremonies. Also elected and serving at his side was the *tecuhtli,* leader in war. Other functionaries were the *teopixque,* the priests who presided over the local god cult and directed the *telpochcalli,* the school for commoner youths and warriors. See also **altepetl.**

camahuil (camagüil) Name used in highland Guatemala for primitive stone figure, crudely carved, somewhat similar to the Mixtec *penate,* but without perforations for suspension.

Camaxtli Tlaxcalan god of the hunt and

war, corresponding to Mixcóatl. Revered in Tlaxcala in similar fashion to Huitzilopochtli in Tenochtitlán.

Campanario Site in western Chiapas, near El Ocote.

Campana-San Andrés Classic site in Río Sucio valley of El Salvador; extended into Early Postclassic period. Maya pottery types predominate. Plaza-acropolis architectural arrangement like Copán, but the construction of adobe blocks overlaid with lime plaster imitates Kaminaljuyú.

Campeche Mexican state, bounded by the Gulf of Mexico, Yucatán, Quintana Roo, Belize, Guatemala, and Tabasco. Its capital, of the same name, is an important port and trading center. Campeche contains the Chenes and Río Bec areas, noted for their distinctive architectural styles, as well as the island cemetery of Jaina, famed for its ceramic figurines.

can Number 4 in Maya.

Canan Title applied to various Maya deities, such as Canan Balché, guardian of the forest wildlife, Canan Kax, guardian of the forests, Canan Cacab, guardian of the village, etc.

Cancuén Classic Maya site on the Pasión River, Petén, Guatemala.

Candelaria River flowing west and north through Campeche, emptying into Laguna de Términos; known to Mexicans as the Acalán River. Navigable in the lower and middle regions, it was an important inland route. Itzamkanac, capital of the Acalán Putún Maya, is presumed to have been on its shore. Cuauhtémoc, last of the Aztec rulers, was executed on the Candelaria by Cortés on his way to Honduras in 1524.

candeleros One- or two-holed clay objects perhaps used as censers or to hold blood-splattered paper during native rites. An Early Classic trait of Teotihuacán, examples are found on the Gulf Coast, in Oaxaca, and Guatemala. Named by the Spanish for their resemblance to candle holders.

Canek Postclassic Itzá-Maya ruling family, with its island capital of Tayasal, probably on the site of modern Flores in Lake Petén-Itzá, Petén, Guatemala. Resisted the Spanish Conquest until 1697.

cañitas Oldest type of small solid figurine found in Cuicuilco area of the Valley of Mexico, probably dating from the Tlalpan phase preceding the Olmec intrusion. Extremely simple naked female forms with large falling hairdos. Eyes composed of large holes surrounded by a circle or tiny punctations are typical.

cannibalism Practiced by various tribes in Middle America, notably among the Caribs. Although a recent theory postulates that the Aztecs engaged in it to overcome a dietary protein deficiency, it is more likely that the practice was an extension of human sacrificial rites.

Canutillo Phase of the Río Suchil branch of the Chalchihuites culture, c. A.D. 200–500. It is the earliest known intrusion of Mesoamerica into western Zacatecas.

Capa See **Utuado.**

Capacha Early Preclassic ceramic complex of Colima, Mexico. Openmouthed ollas with cinctured bodies are representative. Stirrup pots carbon-dated 1450 B.C. and other ceramic traits shared with Valdivia and Machalilla phases of coastal Ecuador suggest early South American contact by sea.

caracol 1. Spanish name for native trumpet fashioned from a conch shell (*Strombus gigas*). See *atecocolli.* 2. Classic Maya site in Belize, noted for the rare use of giant date glyphs on circular stone altars. 3. Astronomical observatory at Chichén Itzá, Yucatán; built by Maya in the Classic period, with later Toltec alterations. The building takes its name from the interior spiral staircase. The upper story of the cylindrical tower, 80 ft. (24 m) aboveground, has a small room whose observation openings relate to solstices and equinoxes.

carbon-dating See **radiocarbon (C^{14}) dating.**

cardinal points Fundamental to Mesoamerican religious concepts was the grouping of all beings according to four cardinal points of the compass and central direction, up and down. It explains importance of the numbers 4 and 5 in Mexico, paralleling the Trinity (3) in occidental magic. Among the Aztecs, East (Tlapcopa), North (Mictlampa), West (Cihuatlampa), and South (Huitzlampa) were all assigned colors, trees, birds or animals, divinities, day and year signs, and favorable or unfavorable aspects. Directional assignments varied by cultural area; death ruled from the North for the Aztecs, from the South for the Maya. Unlike the Mexicans, the Maya observed color assignments uniformly: white (*zac*) for North, black (*ek*) for West, yellow (*kan*) for South, and red (*chac*) for East.

Care Language group of central Honduras, probably a Lenca dialect, like Poton.

Carib A warlike people of South American origin who occupied the Lesser Antilles at time of their discovery by Columbus. Less active in agriculture and ceramics than the Island Arawak they replaced some time after A.D. 1000. Man-eaters, they ate their Arawak captives and took their women. The language of the Arawak women prevailed; the descendants of Island Caribs speak an Arawak dialect. Arawak influence on ceramic production further complicates the archaeological reconstruction of the Carib culture. The Carib name is preserved in Caribbean Sea and cannibal, a corruption of *caribal*, the Spanish word for Carib.

Carib axes Stone ceremonial axes of the Lesser Antilles, not proved, however, to have been Carib products. Most have grooves or ears for hafting, but are large, heavy, and not utilitarian. They have a great variety of shapes, often elegant and handsomely finished. Related types have been noticed on the Caribbean coast of Nicaragua.

cartouche Term applied to a closed frame in which Maya day-sign glyphs were contained in Initial Series texts, in codices, and on monuments. Only day-sign glyphs are rendered within a cartouche.

Casas Grandes Outpost of the Southwest culture of the United States, in the state of Chihuahua, Mexico. Prior to c. A.D. 1000, it primarily followed the Southwest culture with its pit houses and kivas. Colonization by the Aztecs after A.D. 1300 introduced the Mesoamerican ball court, platform mounds, and truncated pyramids. Its pottery is notable.

Castillo de Teayo Site in northern Veracruz, founded c. A.D. 815, with a well-preserved Postclassic pyramid in the style of Tula and Calixtlahuaca. Known for its stone sculpture, primarily in the round; stelae and panels show Nahua and Huastec deities.

Catemaco Lake nestled in Tuxtla Mountains of Veracruz. Two small islands of volcanic origin, Agaltepec and Tenaspi, rise from the lake. Fertile area is dotted with ancient mound groups.

Cauac 1. Nineteenth of the 20 Maya day signs, corresponding to the Aztec Quiáhuitl. Associated with the number 3; its augury was unfavorable. See **Year Bearer.** 2. A Preclassic phase of the Maya site of Tikal, Petén, Guatemala, c. 50 B.C.–A.D. 150.

ce Number 1 in Nahuatl. Ce Cipactli (1 alligator) was the first day of the Aztec year at Tenochtitlán, Ce Ácatl (1 reed) is the birthday of Quetzalcóatl, and Ce Técpatl (1 flint) is the calendrical name of Huitzilopochtli.

Ce Ácatl Topiltzin Legendary son of Mixcóatl and Chimalman, born on the calendar day Ce Ácatl in the valley of Morelos. Became the ruler of the Toltecs; founded their capital of Tula. See **Quetzalcóatl.**

Ceh Twelfth month of the *tun*, the Maya year of 360 days.

Cehpech Yucatecan cultural phase, c. A.D. 800–1000, at such Puuc sites as Uxmal, Kabah, Sayil, and Labná. Together with Sotuta phase, c. A.D. 1000–1200, spans "slate-ware interval" of transitional and Early Postclassic ceramic continuity of northern Yucatán.

ceiba (kapok) Sacred tree of the Maya, national tree of Guatemala. See **yaxche.**

celestial band Maya depicted planets and

other celestial bodies by hieroglyphs, frequently arranged in strips or bands. These celestial bands often terminated in heads of the "bicephalic monster" (*Itzamná*) and occasionally in birds' heads. They appear as ornamentation on human figures, particularly as belts, on elongated bodies of monstrous creatures, and as an architectural feature framing doorways. The rendition is identical in codices and on carved monuments.

celestial deities and birds Aztecs conceived of a sky of 13 layers (numbered 1–13), each with its deity and bird for astrological purposes. Among many variations, this is the simplest:

DEITY	BIRD
1. Xiuhtecuhtli (fire-god)	Huitzitzilin (blue hummingbird)
2. Tlaltecuhtli (earth-god)	Quetzalhuitzilin (green hummingbird)
3. Chalchiúhtlicue (water-goddess)	Cocotzin (turtledove)
4. Tonatiuh (sun-god)	Xolin (quail)
5. Cihuateteo (souls of women)	Cacalotl (raven)
6. Mictlantecuhtli (death-god)	Chicuatli (barn owl)
7. Tonacatecuhtli (god of sustenance)	Papalotl (butterfly)
8. Tlaloc (rain-god)	Tlohtli (falcon)
9. Éhecatl-Quetzalcóatl (wind-god)	Chalchiuhtotolin (turkey)
10. Tezcatlipoca (smoking mirror)	Tecolotl (horned owl)
11. Yohualtecuhtli (god of night)	Chiconcuetzalin (macaw)
12. Tlahuizcalpantecuhtli (god of dawn)	Quetzaltototl (quetzal bird)
13. Ometeotl (god of duality)	Toznene (parrot)

celt Ungrooved stone axe, a common ancient woodworking tool and also a ceremonial form. Quantities of celts have been found in Olmec offerings, sometimes placed in patterns; may be a highly polished black stone or greenstone or jade, incised or carved in figural form (votive axes), or made of soft stone and unusable as tools. Celts from the Greater Antilles may also be of jade but generally have a pointed poll. See **axe**.

Cempoala Totonac capital in central Veracruz at the time of the Conquest. Native chief there was first ally of the invading Cortés. Scene of the victory of Cortés over Pánfilo de Narváez, who had been sent to replace him. It was a member of the Narváez expedition who introduced smallpox to Mexico, decimating the native population. The restored site of Cempoala includes the Great Pyramid, the Building of the Chimneys, and a circular terraced structure dedicated to the wind-god.

cenote A natural water hole (*tz'onot* in Maya) in the northern Yucatán peninsula formed by the collapse of the limestone surface crust to expose subterranean water beneath. Cenotes were the principal sources of water in this area of minimal rainfall and no rivers. The most famous is the Sacred Cenote at Chichén Itzá, c. 200 ft. (61 m) in diameter; its water level is 65 ft. (19 m) below ground level, with a water depth of 70 ft. (21 m). Used for ceremonial rites, it is also known as the Well of Sacrifice. Several expeditions have retrieved offerings from its depths, including objects of jade, gold, wood, and stone sculptures. See also **Hunac Ceel**.

Centéotl Mexican god of the maize plant, son of Tlazoltéotl, the earth-goddess. Not to be confused with Xilonen, the "goddess of the tender ear of corn," or Ilamatecuhtli, the "goddess of the old dry ear of corn." All are closely related to Chicomecóatl, goddess of sustenance, and all are depicted with some attribute of the maize plant. Centéotl may descend from Olmec god II. Fourth of the nine Aztec Lords of the Night and, as Centéotl-Xochipilli, seventh Lord of the Day.

centli Nahuatl word for maize.

Central America Land bridge connecting North and South America, containing the modern republics of Guatemala, Honduras, El Salvador, Nicaragua, Costa Rica, and Panama. Before European contact it was an area of cultural thrust, meeting and overlapping, from Mesoamerica to the north and South America below. Mesoamerican civilization permeated all of Guatemala. Its influence extended into El Salvador, the Ulúa-Yojoa and Comayagua basins, and the Gulf of Fonseca in Honduras, and followed the Pacific coast to the Nicoya Peninsula of Costa Rica. South American traditions were evident in Panama and Costa Rica, excluding only the province of Guanacaste, and in the Atlantic watershed of Nicaragua and northeastern Honduras. Large unexplored territories and limited archaeological data inhibit absolute dating of much of the prehistory of southern Central America. The uncontrolled activities of grave robbers, graves being the major source of Central American collections, further complicate attempts at cultural reconstruction. See also **Intermediate Area.**

Central Depression See **Chiapas.**

Central Panama Recent archaeological theory joins the traditionally separate cultures of Coclé, Veraguas, and the Azuero Peninsula into one cultural area, Central Panama (Las Provincias Centrales de Panama). The still limited, controlled excavations within this area provide a tentative chronology and nomenclature:

5000–2000 B.C. Preceramic phase, typified by the midden site of Cerro Mangote, dated to c. 4850 B.C.

2000 B.C.–A.D. 100 Formative phase, with earliest ceramics at Monagrillo, c. 2130 B.C. A later ceramic phase, Sarigua, appears at same site in the first millennium B.C.; develops into scarified/Guacamayo phase c. 225 B.C.–A.D. 100.

A.D. 150–500 Contemporary appearance of bichrome Aristide and trichrome Tonosí ware.

A.D. 500–700 Appearance of true polychrome, Conte Polychrome, a term replacing Early Coclé.

A.D. 700–900 Development into second polychrome phase, Macaracas, replacing former description, Late Coclé.

A.D. 900–Conquest Mendoza ceramic phase.

See **Panama.**

Central Plateau 1. The central Mexican area comprising valleys of Mexico, Tula-Jilotepec, Morelos, Tlaxcala, Puebla, and Toluca. 2. Also name for one of the archaeological regions of southwestern Chiapas, sometimes called the Chiapas Plateau.

centzontli Aztec word for 400, denoting "numberless," often incorporated into names of mythical concepts of Nahuatl culture. Centzonhuitznahuac: the innumerable stars of the southern constellation, symbolically also brothers of Huitzilopochtli; Centzonmimizcoa: the stars of the northern constellation, or the 400 of the cloud serpent: Milky Way; Centzóntotochtin: 400 rabbits, collective name of many pulque gods.

cephalic index A number obtained by dividing the maximum breadth of the cranium by its maximum length and multiplying by 100. Broadly, an index rating of under 80 is called dolichocephalic (long, narrow); above 80 is called brachycephalic (short, wide). Yucatec Maya, with an index averaging 85, are among the most roundheaded people in the world.

ceremonial bar Maya symbol of hierarchical authority. Classic Maya sculpture shows it carried horizontally or diagonally with the arms across the chest. Both ends of the bar commonly terminate in an elaborately stylized serpent's head.

Cerillos Coastal site of Tabasco, Mexico. See **Xicalango.**

Cerritos Ceramic phase of central Nayarit, c. A.D. 1050–1300. See **Amapa.**

Cerro Chacaltepec Late Preclassic phase of Morelos, coeval with the Zacatenco and Ticomán phases of the Valley of Mexico, c. 900 B.C. to beginning of our era.

Cerro Chavin Large fortified site in the Central Plateau of Chiapas dating to the Classic period.

Cerro de la Estrella Prominently situated hill in the Valley of Mexico at the southeast edge of Mexico City, site of the Aztec New Fire Ceremony, called Toxiuhmolpilia in Nahuatl. It celebrated the completion of a 52-year cycle and ushered in the next. See **Calendar Round.**

Cerro de las Mesas Ceremonial site east of

Alvarado Bay, central Veracruz, was strongly influenced by Olmec in Preclassic period. Largest Early Classic cache of jade found in Mesoamerica, numbered over 800 pieces. Early Classic influence from El Tajín was replaced by that of Teotihuacán c. A.D. 650. Stelae 6 and 8, with bar and dots, give Long Count dates of A.D. 468 and 533. Both Maya and Teotihuacán influences mingled in this important center.

Cerro Mangote Shell midden on Parita Bay, Pacific coast of Panama. Near the Monagrillo mounds, but much earlier, 4850 B.C., containing tools and burials, but not pottery.

Cerro Zapote Site near San Salvador that gave its name to Preclassic phase of El Salvador, c. 300 B.C. Perhaps source of the earliest application of the Usulután technique of pottery decoration. Maya polychrome pottery was encountered at the Classic level of excavation.

Chac Maya rain-god, equivalent to the Aztec Tlaloc and Zapotec Cocijo. God B of the codices, patron of day Ik and the number 6. Ancient tradition of the rain-god cult is reflected in lowland Maya inscriptions and codices. Chac is rendered with a long pendulous nose, often ending in an upward curl, a scroll beneath the eye, and is often toothless. He is the most frequently mentioned god in the Maya codices; had four assistants, called Chacs, associated with the cardinal points: Chac Xib Chac: East, color red; Sac Xib Chac: North, color white; Ek Xib Chac: West, color black; Kan Xib Chac: South, color yellow. The name Chac is sometimes also applied to assistant priests in Yucatán.

Chacchob Postclassic walled Maya city of central Yucatán.

Chacmool 1. Life-sized stone figure lying on its back with flexed legs, hands holding a flat receptacle on its stomach, possibly to receive human hearts during sacrificial ceremonies, and with head turned to one side. Although first discovered, and misnamed "red jaguar," which is the meaning of Chacmool in Mayan, at Chichén Itzá, Yucatán, its origin is traced to the Toltec capital of Tula, in the state of Hidalgo. The persistent influence of the Toltecs during the Postclassic period is evidenced by Chacmools in Veracruz at Cempoala, at the Aztec capital of Tenochtitlán, and in the western heartland of the Tarascans in Michoacán. 2. Maya site on Punta Santa Rosa, eastern coast of Quintana Roo.

Chacmultún Most southerly Yucatecan Maya site with buildings in the Puuc style. Noted for its four-story building and remnants of a polychrome mural.

Chaculá Site in the western Guatemalan highlands, with crude Postclassic stone sculpture and pottery.

Chakan Late Preclassic cultural phase of Yucatán, c. A.D. 1–200.

Chakanputún According to chronicles, the homeland of the Putún, closely associated with the history of the Itzá; exact location is uncertain, but has been placed in western Campeche. Possibly one of the three capitals of the Putún, others being Chichén Itzá in Yucatán and Potonchán in the Chontalpa, Tabasco.

Chalca Traditionally one of seven Aztec tribal groups believed to have left the legendary Chicomoztoc ("seven caves") in A.D. 1168, starting their long migration to the Valley of Mexico. Founded Chalco, on bank of the former lake of that name.

Chalcatzingo Important site situated at the pass giving access to Morelos. Inhabited in many epochs and by successive cultures, c. 900 B.C.–A.D. 1200. Most famous for excellently preserved bas-relief sculptures in natural rock, attributed to the Olmecs. Near Cuautla.

chalchíhuatl Symbolic name for human blood supplied by ritual sacrifice: the sustaining nectar demanded by the Aztec gods. Term combines reference to *chalchíhuitl*, most precious jade, and *atl*, water.

Chalchihuites Cultural complex constituting northernmost limit of Mesoamerica. In southern Zacatecas and western Durango, it is characterized by fortified hilltop sites overlooking farming settlements on the plains below. Its cultural development is divided into two branches, Río Suchil in Zacatecas and Guardiana in Durango.

Earliest Zacatecan phase is Canutillo, c. A.D. 200–500, followed by Vesuvio, c. 500–950, in Río Suchil valley. Along the tributary Colorado River, the phases are Alta Vista, A.D. 300–500, Calichal, 500–650, and Retoño, 650–750. Guardiana branch in Durango, chiefly represented by the Schroeder site, developed through four phases: Ayala, c. A.D. 550–700, Las Joyas, 700–950, Río Tunal, 950–1150, and Calera, 1150–1350.

Best-known Chalchihuites site, sometimes separated into its own area culture called Malpaso, is the formidable La Quemada, a fortress site on a hill 600 ft. (150 m) above the plain, and recalling Xochicalco in Morelos.

Chalchihuites shows some early influence of Classic period central Mexico, but the greatest impact from the outside was during the Postclassic, its pottery correlating with both the Aztatlán complex of Sinaloa and distant Tula. Red-on-buff tripods and plain bowls are common. More distinctive is the paint cloisonné decoration applied to tripod vessels. Copper bells, obsidian flaked blades, and a number of stone artifacts are diagnostic of the Chalchihuites Toltec period. Architecture, especially, shows the contribution of Tula in stone pyramids, ball courts, and colonnaded courts. Contact with central Mexico dwindled under the Aztecs, whose thrust was toward the richer southern areas.

chalchíhuitl Nahuatl designation for jade and other rare green stones, including jadeite, green obsidian, fine emerald, green rock crystal, etc., pictured as a round disk with a central hole. Since jade was most highly prized, *chalchíhuitl* by extension referred to anything precious in Nahuatl writing. Following this process, a *chalchíhuitl* sign superimposed on a representation of water became human blood. By itself, jade's green color also caused it to represent water in Maya and Mexican iconography. Highly regarded since Olmec times, jade was carved into pieces of the highest artistic merit throughout Mesoamerica and as far south as Costa Rica.

Chalchiuhcíhuatl An Aztec goddess of the harvest.

Chalchiuhtecólotl With a meaning in Nahuatl of "precious owl," it is a representative form of the god of night, or the black Tezcatlipoca. Found with some frequency in Mexican codices.

Chalchiúhtlicue Feminine counterpart of rain-god Tlaloc in Mexico, invoked as the female life principle. Patron of the fifth day, Cóatl, third of the 13 Lords of the Day, she was also sixth of the nine Lords of the Night. Aztec patron of rivers, floods, and oceans. Gulf of Mexico was called Chalchiuhcueyecatl, "water of the goddess Chalchiúhtlicue." See also **Chicomecóatl, Xilonen.**

Chalchiuhtotolin A form of the Aztec god Tezcatlipoca in the codices, "precious turkey," representative of night and the mysterious. Patron deity of day Técpatl.

Chalchuapa Town and archaeological zone of western El Salvador. Includes sites of Tazumal, Las Victorias, and El Trapiche. Evidence of prosperous occupation goes back to Olmec times.

Chalco Capital of the Chalca people, tributary to the Aztecs, southeast of Mexico City. Formerly on the bank of Lake Chalco, southernmost of connected lakes of Valley of Mexico and important waterway to supply Tenochtitlán. Chalco lies at feet of two snow-capped volcanoes, Popocatépetl and Iztaccíhuatl.

Chalmecatecuhtli God of sacrifice, sometimes identified as 11th of the 13 Lords of the Day in place of Mictlantecuhtli, god of the underworld.

Chamá Maya archaeological site of Alta Verapaz, Guatemala, on the Chixoy River. Its cultural phase was A.D. 200–800. Its Classic polychrome pottery is outstanding and readily identified by black and white chevron bands that border the pictorial field above and below. Many vessels have narrative decoration depicting the gods of their mythology.

Chamax Maya coastal site south of Tulum, Quintana Roo, Mexico.

Chamelecón River of northwest Honduras with outlet in the Caribbean Sea.

Chametla Site on southern coast of Sinaloa, Mexico. Its name is applied to the earliest Classic horizon in western Mexico. Ceramics included relatively elaborate polychrome and some engraved spindle whorls and small figurines. The Chametla horizon is divided into Early Chametla (Tierra del Padre), A.D. 250–500, and Middle Chametla (Baluarte), A.D. 500–700. The Postclassic Aztatlán ceramic horizon followed, in which Chametla played an important role.

chamfer Horizontal molding with intaglio effect, recessed within the walls of a Maya temple or pyramidal platform.

champ-levé Decorative ceramic technique in which the design background is cut away to accent the remaining design in relief. Characteristic of cylindrical vases of Classic Teotihuacán III.

Champotón Gulf port and river of Campeche, Mexico. May be Chakanputún described in the chronicles as the 10th-century home of Putún-Itzás who later settled in and gave their name to Chichén Itzá.

Chamula Town of the Tzotzil Maya south of San Cristóbal de las Casas, Chiapas, but already a center in Classic times.

Chanal Archaeological site near the city of Colima, western Mexico.

Chaneques Mischievous dwarflike poltergeists who dwell in the forest. As rain and thunder deities they recall the Chacs, assistants to the rain-god. Origin may be found in Olmec werejaguars of La Venta.

Chantico Aztec goddess of the hearth, related to Mictlantecuhtli, god of death. Principal deity of Xochimilco and patron of goldworkers, with the calendrical name of 9 Itzcuintli.

Chantino Linguistic group of coastal Oaxaca.

Chantuto Site in coastal Soconusco region of Chiapas.

Chapala 1. Lake between the Mexican states of Jalisco and Michoacán, fed by the Lerma River and emptied by the Río Grande de Santiago, which winds through Jalisco and Nayarit to the Pacific Ocean. 2. Cultural phase of Michoacán highlands with affinities to Tula-Mazapán style in central Mexico, c. A.D. 700.

chapolote Ancient indigenous strain of wild corn. See **maize.**

chapopote Nahuatl word for crude petroleum asphalt, employed in Veracruz to paint ceramic figures.

Chapultepec Its name signifying "grasshopper hill" in Nahuatl, it is the locale reached by the Mexica in their migration to the Valley of Mexico. They were driven out, forced to settle on an island in Lake Texcoco. Chapultepec later became a recreational area for Aztec rulers. In A.D. 1456–57 Moctezuma I had a memorial relief carved into the cliffs, which is barely discernible today. Springs there furnished potable water to Tenochtitlán by aqueduct. Today it is a public park in Mexico City.

Chatino Linguistic group of southwestern Oaxaca.

Chauaca Late Postclassic phase of Yucatán, c. A.D. 1500–Conquest.

Chebel Yax Wife of Itzamná, the Maya creator-god. Drawn in the codices as an old red goddess with a hank of cotton or cloth, overseeing weaving activities.

Chen Ninth month of the *tun,* the Maya year of 360 days. Patron was the moongoddess.

Chenes 1. Region of northeastern state of Campeche, Mexico, whose name is applied to a variant of the Río Bec style of Maya architecture. It is characterized by doorways representing the gaping mouth of a serpent or earth monster. Radiating out from Hochob, the style appears on the west temple entrance of the Pyramid of the Magician at Uxmal and the Nunnery Annex at Chichén Itzá. 2. Maya word for wells.

Chetumal Maya settlement and trading center on Chetumal Bay, east coast of Quintana Roo, Mexico.

chia Lime-leafed sage, used for making a soft drink.

Chiapa de Corzo Site near Tuxtla Gutiérrez in the upper Grijalva basin of Chiapas. Extensive excavations established the chronology for the then little-explored southwestern Chiapas, with these ceramic periods and phases for Chiapa de Corzo:

PERIOD	PHASE	DATES	
I	Cotorra	1400–1000 B.C.	no architecture, unslipped bichrome pottery.
II	Dili	1000–750 B.C.	Las Charcas 3-pronged censers, early La Venta pottery, figurines.
III	Escalera	750–550 B.C.	"waxy slips" on pottery, blackware whistling vessels, building platforms.
IV	Francesa	550–200 B.C.	Monte Albán I and Gulf ceramics, simple ceremonial structures.
V	Guanacaste	200 B.C.–A.D. 1	polished red and black wares, no figurines, Chicanel pottery.
VI	Horcones	A.D. 1–100	cut stone architecture, flat roofs, fine trade pottery from Guatemala, El Salvador, Gulf.
VII	Istmo	A.D. 100–200	transitional.
VIII	Jiquipilas	A.D. 200–350	smudged blackware, first stone-faced pyramid complex.
IX	Laguna	A.D. 350–550	end of construction at site.
X	Maravillas	A.D. 550–900	strong Guatemalan influence, maximum population.
XI	Ruiz	A.D. 900–1250	Tohil Plumbate.
XII	Tuxtla	A.D. 1250–1524	Chiapanec occupation to Conquest.

Reading of the carving on Stela 2 at Chiapa de Corzo, if reliable, gives the oldest Long Count date in Mesoamerica, equivalent to 36 B.C., supporting the theory that the calendar originated outside the Maya area.

Chiapaneca Mangue-speaking people forced out of Cholula area by the Historic Olmecs, settling in Central Depression of Chiapas, where they were known as Chiapaneca. Their capital was built on the site of Chiapa de Corzo c. A.D. 1350. Hostilities between them and the surrounding Maya groups may have caused a branch of the Chiapaneca, the Chorotega-Mangue, to move south to El Salvador and southern Honduras in the area of the Gulf of Fonseca. Their subsequent migrations extended into Nicaragua and Costa Rica. See **Chorotega.**

Chiapas Most southern Mexican state, bordering on Guatemala, and contained by the Pacific Ocean, Oaxaca, Veracruz and Tabasco; capital is Tuxtla Gutiérrez. Northeastern Chiapas, containing Palenque, Toniná, Bonampak, and Yaxchilán, is considered a cultural extension of lowland Maya civilization. South-central Chiapas, contiguous to the highland Maya area, is divided into separate regions: (1) Pacific coastal plain (with Tonalá), (2) Sierra Madre de Chiapas, sparsely populated, (3) Central Depression, or upper Grijalva basin (with Chiapa de Corzo), and (4) Central or Chiapas Plateau (with San Cristóbal-Comitán). See **Chiapa de Corzo.**

Chibcha Language group of northwest Mexico that branched off from Uto-Aztecans c. 4000 B.C., proceeding through Central America to present-day Colombia. See **Macro-Chibcha.**

chicahuaztli A staff, with rattles, pictured in Mexican codices as a symbol of fecundity and an attribute of the deities of earth, maize, and water.

Chicanel Lowland Maya Late Preclassic period, c. 300 B.C.–A.D. 100, showed influence of Izapan style and a strong advance over the preceding Mamom horizon. Pottery showed great variety, mostly legless; but added wide-everted rims, flange protuberances; Usulután and waxy wares were diagnostic. Figurines all but disappeared. Most important was the beginning of architectural innovations, including temple-pyramids, great plazas, terraces, rich tombs, and primitive corbeled vaults with polychrome murals. The famous pyramid E-VII Sub at Uaxactún is of this time.

Chicchan Fifth day of the 20-day Maya month, day of the serpent and its deity who sends the rains. Corresponds to the Mexican day Cóatl, Zee or Zij of the Zapotecs. Associated with the number 9. The name was also applied to the rain-gods of the Chorti Maya of eastern Guatemala and adjacent parts of Honduras and El Salvador.

chicha Native fermented drink made from maize in Mesoamerica. South American influence is noted in Central America where it is made from yuca (manioc), or the fruit of the pejibaye palm.

Chichancanab Saline lake in southeastern Yucatán.

Chicharras Cultural phase at the Olmec site of San Lorenzo, Veracruz, c. 1250–1150 B.C. Marked first appearance of monumental stone carving and Olmec figurines of fine white clay.

Chichén Itzá Large, important religious and political center in northern Yucatán, whose name means "at the rim of the well of the Itzás," referring to the invaders who assumed control in the 10th century. Architecture reflects two periods: Classic Maya of 7th to 10th centuries A.D., and subsequent Postclassic Toltec to 1204 A.D. The Classic influence predominates in southern part of the archaeological zone, including the Akab Dzib, Red House, Deer House, Nunnery, its Annex, and Iglesia. Principally recalling the Puuc style of Uxmal, the Annex facade also reflects the Classic Chenes style. Toltec influence governs the Great Plaza. The Castillo, also called the Temple of Kukulcán, and Temple of the Warriors incorporate Toltec Chacmools, "feathered serpent" motifs, colonnades, and small Atlantean supports. The ball court, with giant scoring rings, narrative frieze panels, and attached Temple of the Jaguars, is the largest in Mesoamerica. Also representing this later period are the Caracol observatory, *tzompantli* ("skull rack"), Platform of the Tigers and

Eagles, Platform of Venus, the Market, and the Ossuary. Chichén Itzá fell to the Cocom, rulers of Mayapán, in the 13th century, after which pilgrims still came, but all construction and influence was at an end.

Chichicastenango Town in the Guatemalan highlands, site of Chuvilá, settled by the ancient Quiché Maya. Parish of Fray Francisco Jiménez, who discovered and translated the Popol Vuh in the 18th century. Small Rossbach museum there contains fine jades and ceramics of the region.

Chichimeca Aztec term loosely applied to hunting and food-gathering nomads of the northern deserts, who at various times invaded the more civilized cultures in the Valley of Mexico. Chichimec invasions parallel those of "barbarians" in Europe in Roman times. Chichimeca applies to all groups migrating south after the fall of Tollán, including the Toltecs themselves. Most important Chichimec group entered the Valley of Mexico in the 12th century, settling at Tenayuca under the leadership of the legendary chief Xólotl. His descendants joined the Acolhua to establish their capital of Texcoco across the Great Lake.

Chichini Preeminent Totonac sun-god.

chicleros Chewing-gum gatherers who tap sapodilla trees in the Yucatecan jungles for their thick sap, chicle. Accidentally coming upon ancient sites, they and their trails were helpful to discoveries by archaeologists.

chicnáhui Number 9 in Nahuatl.

chicome Number 7 in Nahuatl, omen of good luck and fertility. In the esoteric language of seers, calendar names incorporating 7 signify seeds: 7 serpent (Chicomecóatl) is corn; 7 eagle (Chicomecuauhtli) is squash, etc.

Chicomecóatl "Seven Serpent," goddess of vegetation and corn, was also called Chicomolotzin, "seven ears of corn." Codices show her body and face painted red, wearing a paper miter with rosettes. In sculpture she often holds two ears of corn in each hand. Her other names as the fertil-

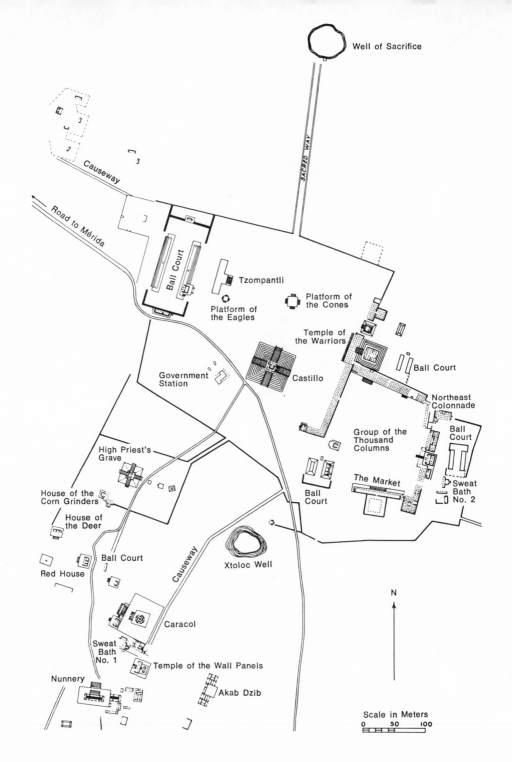

Plate 1. Map of the central section of Chichén Itzá. From S. G. Morley, *The Ancient Maya*, page 283.

ity goddess are Chalchiúhtlicue and Xilonen. 7 Serpent was her feast day in the *Tonalamatl*. See **Centéotl**.

Chicomolotzin See **Chicomecóatl**.

Chicomoztoc "Seven caves," expression of the legendary origin of nomadic tribes that populated the Valley of Mexico; situated in a land called Aztlán, variously placed in Michoacán or Jalisco. La Quemada, Zacatecas, is also mentioned as the site of Chicomoztoc. See also **Aztec**.

chicuacen Number 6 in Nahuatl.

chicueyi Number 8 in Nahuatl.

Chihuahua Mexican state, with capital of same name, bordered on the north by the United States, on the east by Coahuiles, on the south by Durango, and on the west by Sinaloa and Sonora. Casas Grandes is the prominent archaeological site.

chikin Maya word for West. See **world directions, Maya**.

Chikinchel Postclassic cultural phase of Yucatán, A.D. 1450–1550.

Chila Final Postclassic ceramic phase at Apatzingán, Michoacán, c. A.D. 1100.

chilam Chilames, or *chilamoob*, were the upper echelon of the Yucatecan Maya priestly hierarchy, being teachers and prophets.

Chilam Balam Post-Conquest manuscripts written by Yucatecan Maya in European script, relating traditions and myths, calendrical data and medicinal recipes of pre-Hispanic origin. The term is a composite of *chilam* (prophet) and *balam* (jaguar), conveying a sense of the occult but also being the family name of an eminent sage. Of the 18 such books extant, most informative are *Chilam Balam* of Chumayel, Tizimín, Maní, Kaua, Ixil, and the so-called Pérez Codex.

Chilla First of the 20 Zapotecan day names; also called Chilja. Equivalent of the Aztec day Cipactli and the Maya day Imix.

Chilpancingo Capital of state of Guerrero, Mexico. Juxtlahuaca cave with Olmec wall paintings is nearby.

Chimalacatlán Morelos site with traces of four separate cultural horizons from the first to the 16th century A.D., revealing contact with Monte Albán in Oaxaca and Teotihuacán in the Valley of Mexico.

Chimalhuacán Preclassic ceramic phase of Teotihuacán, c. 100 B.C.–A.D. 1, preceding Tzacualli (Teotihuacán I). Named after the site where evidences of pottery, including crude figurines, were found; stylistically related to Ticomán III. Teotihuacán at this time had an estimated population of about 5,000, but architecture is represented only by foundations of huts, fences, and sheds.

chimalli Aztec warrior shield, for war or ceremony, decorated with mosaic or featherwork. The Chimalli Stone of Cuernavaca, celebrating accession of Axayácatl in A.D. 1469, features a carved shield of the god Xipe Totec.

Chimalman Personification of feminine divinity, seen and venerated in various ways: 1. Legendary mother of Ce Ácatl Topiltzin (Quetzalcóatl), wife of Chichimec ruler Mixcóatl who impregnated her with an arrow from his bow. 2. In a contradictory myth, mother of Huitzilopochtli, replacing Coatlícue. 3. Feminine bearer of the cult object during early Aztec migrations. See **Teomama**.

Chimalpa Postclassic phase of the Valley of Mexico (Aztec III), c. A.D. 1325–1500.

Chimalpopoca 1. Third Aztec ruler, A.D. 1415–26, son of Huitzilíhuitl. Grandson of Acamapichtli of Tenochtitlán and Tezozómoc of Atzcapotzalco. Tried to shake off Tepanec yoke; was assassinated at Tezozómoc's orders. 2. Codex Chimalpopoca. See **Anales de Cuauhtitlán**.

China Seventh of the 20 Zapotec day names, meaning deer. Equivalent of the Aztec day Mázatl and the Maya day Manik.

chinampa Artificial islands used by Aztecs for agricultural purposes, today called "floating gardens." Constructed of timber and rush frames, covered with alternating layers of vegetation and mud from the lake bottom. They were firmly anchored in rows, creating canals for canoe traffic. Important food source for land-poor Tenochtitlán. At the Conquest, *chinampas* extended from Tenochtitlán-Tlatelolco south to Xochimilco and east into Lake Chalco, covering an estimated 25,000 acres (10,000 ha), enough to feed up to 200,000 people. A few remain at Xochimilco and Mixquic.

Chinantec Mixtec linguistic minority group of north-central Oaxaca.

Chinantla Archaeological zone of northern Oaxaca. Evidence of earlier Olmec and later Maya influence, finally of Mixtec dominance in the 14th and 15th centuries.

Chinaq Late Classic cultural phase at Zaculeu, northwestern Guatemalan highlands.

Chinautla Hilltop site north of Kaminaljuyú, Guatemala, which gave its name to the Postclassic period there, A.D. 1200–Conquest. Chinautla polychrome and red-on-buff figurines mark the end of the pre-Spanish sequence in the highlands.

chinesco A hollow ceramic figurine style, with vaguely oriental facial cast, of Nayarit, found in shaft tombs dating A.D. 100–250. The *chinesco* style displays a high degree of naturalism, majesty of pose, subtly modeled eyes, and very high polish. A second type has a heart-shaped face, small coffee-bean eyes, and extensive painting in black on the body and face. A third variety is called "Martian" because of its bizarre appearance and striking colors, often with geometric decorations.

Chinikiha Classic Maya site in Usumacinta area of Chiapas, east of Palenque.

Chinkultic Many Late Classic Maya stelae with figures and hieroglyphs and a well-known ball-court marker are associated with this site in the Comitán valley of the Chiapas Plateau, near the Guatemalan border.

Chipal Maya site in the Chixoy River drainage of the Guatemalan highlands, occupied from the Late Classic period to Conquest.

Chipoc Site in the Cobán River drainage, Alta Verapaz, Guatemala. Late Classic Maya phase has ceramics decorated with bending-forward seated personages, exaggerated hand gestures, a thick double scroll, and conch shells. Resist painting was popular c. A.D. 700–1000.

Chircot Name of cemetery site in Cartago valley of Costa Rica Central Highlands, and its ceramic phase dated c. A.D. 1000. Many tombs provided sculpture and pottery consisting of squat jars and three-footed vessels, mostly with appliqué and incised decoration.

Chiriquí 1. Province of southwest Panama, bordering Costa Rica on the west, province of Bocas del Toro along the Continental Divide, Veraguas on the east, the Pacific Gulf of Chiriquí on the south. 2. Greater Chiriquí is an archaeological subarea combining the Chiriquí province of Panama and Diquís region of Costa Rica. 3. "Classic" Chiriquí cultural phase dates from c. A.D. 1200. It is noted for its cast-gold frog-shaped pectorals, stone sculptures including small jaguar *metates,* and fine ceramics.

Chismuyo Ceramic phase of the Choluteca region of southern Honduras, c. A.D. 400.

Chixoy River, also called Salinas, which originates in the Altos Chuchumatanes Mountains of Alta Verapaz, Guatemala. It serves as the border between Chiapas and Guatemala for a short distance, then joins the Pasión River to form the Usumacinta River.

Chocholá Sites near Chocholá, 18½ mi. (30 km) southwest of Mérida, Yucatán, produced spectacular carved vases, the majority cylindrical, some with the paint applied after firing. Light to dark-brown ware, rarely gray or blackish. Late Classic, c. A.D. 600–900.

Chocho-Popoloca Closely related linguistic branches of the Mixtecan division of the Oto-Zapotecan family. Situated in northwest Oaxaca and Puebla. May have been part of the ethnic composition of the Historic Olmecs.

Chocolá Late Preclassic site in the central highlands of Guatemala. Izapa style prevailed, including Stela 1 with seven U-symbols. Its round temple is rare in the highlands.

chocolatera Tripod ceramic vessel with large feet extending outward; possibly used to warm a beverage such as *chocolatl* over an open fire. Characteristic of the Línea Vieja zone of Costa Rica.

chocolatl Nahuatl word for the beverage

made from the cacao bean; prized by the Mexican nobility and priesthood. Source of the English word *chocolate*.

Chol Maya linguistic group centered in the northwest area of Tabasco and northern Chiapas. Palencano Chol is still spoken at Palenque and by the Lacandón of the Chiapas forest. Manche Chol group was established in the southeast Petén, southern Belize, and in the Golfo Dulce region, possibly as a result of trading activities by Palencano Chol–speaking Putún Maya.

Cholollán Early name for Cholula.

Cholula Most important center of the Mexican highlands after the fall of Teotihuacán, near the present-day city of Puebla. The pyramid dedicated to Quetzalcóatl is the largest single structure in the New World, enlarged four times since original Preclassic construction. Now 181 ft. (55 m) high, it covers 40 acres (16 ha), crowned by the colonial church of Los Remedios. Had close connections with the Gulf Coast and Teotihuacán in the Classic period. In the Early Postclassic it was the seat of the Olmeca-Xicalanca (Historic Olmecs), who were finally driven out by Toltec-Chichimecs in A.D. 1292. Mixteca-Puebla polychrome pottery is believed to have centered here in the Postclassic. The site has been extensively excavated, exposing stairs, plazas, and inside the pyramid are miles of tunnels, one with the colorful, lively murals of the *bebedores* ("drinkers").

Cholulteca Designation for Postclassic polychrome pottery at Cholula, divided into Cholulteca I, II, III, with ceramic types known as *laca, mate,* and *"firme."*

Choluteca Both the river and valley, in southern Honduras, furnishing access to the highlands from the Gulf of Fonseca on the Pacific Ocean.

Chontal 1. Nahuatl word meaning foreigner, it was applied to several linguistic groups. One was the Putún Maya of Tabasco; another, completely distinct, was applied to the Chontales of Oaxaca, ostensibly of Nahuatl origin. 2. Local western Mexico art style of Protoclassic times, found above

the Balsas River in Guerrero, Mexico, which was expressed in carved greenstone figures, related to the stone sculpture in nearby Mezcala.

Chontales Department of Chontales at the northern end of Lake Nicaragua gave its name to a late style of monolithic sculpture, c. A.D. 800–1200. Cylindrical or prismatic stone columns, up to 16½ ft. (5 m) in height, were carved in human or animal figures.

Chontalpa Area formed by deltas of the Grijalva, Usumacinta, and Candelaria rivers. Included in the present-day states of Tabasco and Campeche, Mexico. Homeland of the Chontal or Putún Maya, it was referred to as Nonoalco by Mexicans.

Chorotega Linguistic group that left the Soconusco coastal region of Chiapas c. A.D. 800 to settle on Pacific coasts of Nicaragua and Costa Rica. Representing a more advanced northern culture, they were probably responsible for advances during the Middle Polychrome period. The Chorotega were closely followed by the Nicaraos, also from the Soconusco, who drove them out of the isthmus of Rivas and into the Nicoya Peninsula of Costa Rica. See **Chiapaneca.**

Chorti Maya linguistic group inhabiting parts of Guatemala, El Salvador, and southwestern Honduras, specifically around Copán. Probably a dialect of Manche Chol, differing from it in the substitution of *r* for *l*.

Chuen 1. Eleventh day of the 20-day Maya month, associated with arts and crafts. Monkey-faced god C of the codices probably represents Chuen in rebus portraiture, Chuen being the Maya word for monkey. 2. Ceramic period of Tikal, Petén, Guatemala, coinciding with the earliest version of the North Acropolis, c. 200–50 B.C.

Chuh Maya linguistic group of Department of Huehuetenango, Guatemala.

Chuitinamit Fortified Postclassic site on Lake Atitlán, Guatemala, c. A.D. 1000–1200. Built over the former capital of the Tzutuhil Maya nation, Tziquinaha.

Chukumuk Maya ceremonial center on Lake

Atitlán, Guatemala. Its Period I was c. A.D. 200–300, related to Santa Clara, Period II, 300–700, and to Aurora, at Kaminaljuyú.

chultun Bottle-shaped underground cistern used for water storage in northern Yucatán. Among the lowland Maya to the south, the smaller lateral-chambered *chultunes* served for food storage.

Chumayel Place of origin in central Yucatán of the *Chilam Balam* of Chumayel. See *Chilam Balam.*

Chumbícuaro Early Classic phase of the Tierra Caliente region of Michoacán.

Chupícuaro Preclassic village and cemetery in southern Guanajuato, now inundated by the Solis dam of the Lerma River. Contemporary with Teotihuacán I–II, 400 B.C.–A.D. 300. Popular small molded figurines are type H-4, with *pastillaje* decoration and diagonally set, long thin eyes. The elaborate polychrome vessels and hollow figurines invariably had geometric decoration, usually black and cream on red. By Classic times all activity had ceased.

Chutixtiox Postclassic Maya defensive settlement, protected by deep ravines, in Department of Quiché, Guatemala, A.D. 1200–1500.

Cib Sixteenth day of the 20-day Maya month. Cib, meaning wax, is probably the day of the Bacabs, patrons of beekeeping. Corresponds to the Nahuatl day Cozcacuauhtli, and the Zapotec day Loo or Guilloo.

Ciboney Earliest known people to reach the Antilles, possibly by 5000 B.C. Hunters and fishermen, lacking agriculture or ceramics, their archaeological remains are traced in Trinidad, Virgin Islands, Puerto Rico, Hispaniola, and Cuba. Steadily pushed out by the Island Arawaks, they were, at the time of Columbus, restricted to the southwest peninsula of Haiti and western Cuba.

Cihuacóatl 1. "Serpent Woman," a form of the earth-goddess, was related to the West, patron of the Cihuateteo, spirits of women who died in childbirth. Represents the passive principle in Nahuatl dualism. As Tonantzin, she is the mother of mankind; as Coatlícue, she is the venerated mother

of Huitzilopochtli; as Quilaztli, according to legend, she raised Ce Ácatl Topiltzin after his mother Chimalman died in childbirth. She has been transformed into "La Llorana" ("the weeping woman") of a popular Mexican folk tale. See also **Cihuatlampa.** 2. Title of the coruler with the *tlatoani,* or Aztec king; most famous was Tlacaélel.

Cihuapipiltin Souls of deceased Aztec women. See **Cihuateteo.**

Cihuatan Settlement in Department of San Salvador comprising four large squares, pyramidal structures, and a ball court. Also name of Early Postclassic phase of El Salvador.

Cihuateteo Spirits of Aztec women who died in childbirth, residents of Cincalco, the western paradise. Fallen warriors, borne across the morning sky by the sun, were met at midday by the Cihuateteo who then conducted them to the western region of the dead. Protégées of Cihuacóatl, the Cihuateteo descended to earth at times, creating mischief and harm. They are pictured with skulls for heads and feet tipped with claws. Venerated by wizards and witch doctors.

Cihuatlampa Western quadrant of the earth in Aztec cosmology. Its year sign was Calli; day signs were Mázatl, Quiáhuitl, Ozomatli, Calli, and Cuauhtli. Its association was generally unfavorable. Home of the Cihuateteo. See also **Cincalco, cardinal points.**

Cilvituk Maya site of central Campeche.

Cimi 1. Sixth day of 20-day Maya month, corresponding to the Mexican day Miquiztli. The augural animal of Cimi was the owl, portent of death, which is the meaning of Cimi. Its glyph contained a representation of % sign. 2. Cultural phase of Tikal, Guatemala, c. A.D. 150–250.

Cincalco Meaning "house of corn," it was the western paradise for Aztec women who died in childbirth. This was considered equivalent to the death of a warrior in battle—the most honored end to life. See **Cihuatlampa.**

cinnabar Crystals of mercuric sulfide

found in volcanic regions, the source of the vermilion pigment employed in Mesoamerica for the ceremonial painting of jade, corpses, and death-related items.

Cipactli First of the 20 days of the Aztec calendar, corresponding to the Maya day Imix and the Zapotec day Chilla. Lucky symbol of birth, life, and sustenance; Tonacatecuhtli is the patron deity. Cipactli is also the earth monster, the alligator or crocodile, on whose back the world rests in Aztec mythology. When rendered pictorially, a characteristic of Cipactli is the lack of a lower mandible.

Some calendrical names of Cipactli are: 4 Cipactli: god of fire (Xiuhtecuhtli); 6 Cipactli: Ixcuinan (Tlazoltéotl); 9 Cipactli: goddess of death (Mictecacíhuatl).

Cipactonal In Aztec mythology, the first man, conceived as a sorcerer. He and his female counterpart, Oxomoco, invented astrology and the calendar, according to Toltec legend.

circum-Caribbean Term for the cultural area in which the common exposure of peoples to Caribbean sea transport caused them to share certain traits. It included the Indians of Nicaragua, Costa Rica, Panama, Colombia, northern Venezuela, and the West Indies.

cire perdue See **lost wax.**

Citlalicue Feminine counterpart of Citlatona, one of the names for the feminine aspect of the dual god Ometeotl. She is sometimes called Citlalinicue, goddess of the heavens, the Milky Way. Citlalicue in Nahuatl means "she of the skirt of stars." See also **Ometecuhtli.**

Citlatona A name for the masculine aspect of the Aztec god of duality, Ometeotl.

Ciudadela Building complex on the Avenue of the Dead at the center of the original plan of the city of Teotihuacán. It is a gigantic square, approx. 1,300 ft. (400 m) to the side, encompassed by wide platforms on the east, north, and south sides and entered by a wide staircase on the west. The Temple of Quetzalcóatl rises at the east end of a vast patio behind a central large altar. It is a six-tiered *talud-tablero*

construction, elaborately carved in serpent and sea motifs, partially covered by a later superimposition. Completed during the Tlamimilolpa phase of Teotihuacán, c. A.D. 300. Ciudadela suggests itself as a residence for the priesthood serving the ceremonial center.

Cizin Name for a Maya god of the underworld. Derived from *ciz,* flatulence, or "breaking of wind," thereby expressing the putrescence of hell. See also **Ah Puch.**

Classic period Designation in Mesoamerican archaeology coinciding with the Initial Series dating of monuments in the Maya lowlands, c. A.D. 300–900. Initial Series is often used as a substitute term when referring to the Maya; formerly also known by the Egyptianizing phrase of "Old Empire."

It coincides with the flowering of Maya lowland sites such as Tikal, Copán, Uxmal, Palenque, and Yaxchilán. Elsewhere in Mesoamerica, the Classic period is associated with the contemporary development of regional centers such as Teotihuacán in the Valley of Mexico, El Tajín in Veracruz, and Monte Albán in Oaxaca. Classic period is not employed as a cultural timespan designation in Central America below the area that was subject to Mesoamerican influence.

cloisonné See **paint cloisonné.**

Clovis point Stone projectile point made by percussion and pressure-flaking to form a broad groove partway up from the base, on one or both sides. Dating from 12,000 years ago, examples are found from Alaska to Panama. In North America, Clovis and the later Folsom points together relate to the big-game-hunting tradition.

Clovis point

coa Nahuatl word for dibble, or planting stick, used to dig holes into which corn seed is dropped in native *milpa* agriculture.

Coaílhuitl See **Tlacaxipehualiztli.**

Coamiles Nayarit site near Peñitas with

monolithic slabs carved in geometric and curvilinear motifs.

Coapexco Subphase of Preclassic Ixtapaluca phase of the Valley of Mexico, c. 1500–1400 B.C.

coatepantli A serpent wall, sometimes carved in relief, often in the round as at Tenayuca, which guarded the four sides of Aztec temples. The sacred precinct of Tenochtitlán was enclosed by a 1,300 ft. (400 m) square *coatepantli*. The concept is of Toltec origin.

Coatepec A dependency of the Acolhuacán state under Texcoco; earliest ceramics date from c. 2000 B.C.

Coatepeque Lake of southeastern El Salvador.

coati Small raccoonlike arboreal animal of the tropical forest and coastal plains. Regionally also called *pisote*, or *tejón*.

cóatl Nahuatl for snake, symbol of the fifth of the 20 day signs. Chalchiúhtlicue was the patron of the day; its augury was favorable. The corresponding Maya day was Chicchan; Zapotec, Zee or Zij. Associated with the number 9.

Coatlícue Aztec earth-goddess, mother of the moon (Coyolxauhqui), the stars (Centzonhuitznahuac), and Huitzilopochtli. According to myth, when his mother's life was threatened at his birth, Huitzilopochtli decapitated the moon and put the stars to flight. Earth-goddess is also called Tonantzin, Teteoinnan, and Toci. She is concerned with soil and agriculture and presides over the rainy season. A colossal statue of Coatlícue at the Museo Nacional de Antropología, Mexico City, shows her with a skirt of serpents and a necklace of human hands and hearts. It is an outstanding example of Aztec sculpture: melding realism of detail with subjective obsession and with mystic symbolism of the subject as a whole.

Coatzacoalcos River that empties into the Gulf of Mexico at the modern Veracruz city of the same name. One of its tributaries is the Río Chiquito, which gives its name to one of three sites constituting the Olmec zone of San Lorenzo.

Cobá Maya city in Quintana Roo with temple-pyramid, Nohoch-Mul, in late Classic Petén style. Connected by 62-mi. (99 km) causeway (*sacbé*) to Yaxuna. Stone road roller found there was 13 ft. (4 m) long and weighed 5 tons.

coca Narcotic leaf chewed by Andean Indians, its use extended into Central America as far as Nicaragua. The leaf of the cultivated shrub (*Erythroxylon coca*), the source of cocaine, is chewed mixed with lime.

Cocal Postclassic cultural phase of northeastern Honduras and its Bay Islands, c. A.D. 1000–1500.

cochineal Dyestuff derived from the dried scale insect (*Dactylopius coccus*) cultivated on the leaves of the nopal cactus. Reddish-purple dye was important to the Mexican economy, especially in Oaxaca, until the introduction of synthetics. One of the five Mesoamerican "domesticated animals," the others being the dog, the turkey, the duck, and the bee.

Cochuah Cultural phase of Yucatán, c. A.D. 200–600.

Cocijo 1. Zapotec rain-god, equivalent to the Aztec Tlaloc and the Maya Chac. Was pictured with a face combining human, jaguar, and serpent elements, and a characteristic forked tongue representing lightning, the meaning of *cocijo*. 2. In the Zapotec calendar, 65 days, a quarter of the ritual calendar called *piye*, equivalent to the Aztec *tonalpohualli*. The *cocijo* was further divided into five parts of 13 days each, called *cocij* or *tobicocij*.

Cockscomb A name for the Maya Mountains of Belize.

Coclé Central province of Panama, enclosed by other provinces of Veraguas, Colón, Panama, Herrera, and Parita Bay on the Pacific. Sitio Conte is the principal archaeological site. Metalwork from c. A.D. 500 is among the earliest in Central America. Goldwork is related to the Colombian Quimbaya. Use of Colombian emeralds, and alligator motifs resembling Peruvian Paracas textiles, hints at wide contacts. Coclé gold figurines were dredged from the Sacred Cenote at Chichén Itzá, Yucatán; the leg of a gold Coclé figurine was found at Copán, Honduras; a gold claw-shaped pendant dated c. A.D. 500 was unearthed at Altun Há, Belize.

Polychrome ceramics of great elegance showed design motifs of dragon tongue, dragon belt, crab, dancing animals, and humans. Coclé cultural history is divided into Scarified period, 300 B.C.–A.D. 300; Santa Maria, A.D. 300–500; Early Coclé, 500–800; Late Coclé, 800–1300; Herrera, 1300–Conquest. See **Sitio Conte, Central Panama.**

Coco A river, also called the Segovia, that forms part of the international boundary between Nicaragua and Honduras; flows into Caribbean Sea.

cocolli Nahuatl word for maize dough. The word has endured and a *cocol*, now made from wheat flour, can be bought in Mexican bakeries today. Also called *cocotlaxcalli.*

Cocom Dynastic family of Postclassic Yucatán, probably descended from the Toltec invaders. Rulers of Mayapán until sacked by Tutul Xius c. A.D. 1450. At the time of the Spanish Conquest their capital was Sotuta. See also **Hunac Ceel.**

codex Native Mesoamerican manuscript, referred to as codices in the plural, does not fit the European definition of a book with leaves gathered and sewed along one side. Pre-Conquest and early colonial Mesoamerican codices appear in the following formats: 1. *Tira* refers to a manuscript painted or drawn on a long strip composed of sheets of animal skin or paper glued together. It can be folded, or rolled, is read up or down, to right or left. 2. Screen-fold describes a *tira* folded, or pleated, like a screen, with each fold forming a page on both sides. A screen-fold codex makes allowance for the folds between pages, so the paintings do not cross the folds. It is the typical format of surviving pre-Conquest codices, which are usually composed horizontally. Among the Maya, pages were read from left to right; on reaching end of the front, the reader turned to the back

and again read from left to right. In this way the last page of the reverse was the back of the first page of the front. Maya codices were written on bark paper, whereas the surviving pre-Conquest Mexican manuscripts were painted on animal skins. In both cases front and rear surfaces were given a smooth white coating of lime before applying paint. Most pre-Conquest codices were destroyed by zealous friars. 3. A roll is a *tira* that has been rolled rather than folded; a rare form. 4. *Lienzo* denotes a painted cloth made from narrow strips of cotton or maguey fiber sewn together. *Lienzo* can be loosely translated as canvas. No pre-Conquest *lienzos* are known. 5. *Mapa* is a loosely employed term usually applied to a post-Conquest single-panel manuscript of paper. It does not necessarily have any relation to a map in the cartographic sense.

There is no special designation for most single panels or sheets, such as the pre-Conquest Aubin Manuscript #20, executed on a single piece of animal hide.

codex, pre-Conquest Maya Extant pre-Conquest Maya codices deal with the passage of time, rituals, perhaps prophecies for the sequences of *katuns* and *tuns;* divination was based on the 260-day sacred almanac, movements of the planet Venus, etc. None is historical, although it is likely that such records existed, paralleling the dynastic histories now being deciphered on sculptured monuments. Only three, possibly four, have survived destruction or the ravages of time. The lowland Maya region of southeast Mexico and Guatemala is suggested as their provenance. They are:

1. *Dresden Codex.* Finest of the Maya codices in draftsmanship and most interesting in content. Perhaps a copy of an original, it shows Mexican influence and may date from A.D. 1200–50. The Dresden Codex contains divinatory almanacs in almost all sections, multiplication tables for synodical revolutions of Venus; pictures a variety of rituals, gods, eclipse and Venus tables; multiplication tables presumed to have divinatory or calendrical import and

many other references, including disease and agriculture. Also called Codex Dresdensis. Painted on both sides, with four blank pages. A bark paper screen-fold of 39 leaves, each 3½ in. x 8 in. (9 x 20.5 cm), total length, 139 in. (356 cm). Sächsische Landesbibliothek, Dresden, East Germany.

2. *Grolier Codex.* First publicly shown at Grolier Club, New York, in 1971, it was tentatively identified as pre-Conquest, dating to the 13th century. Its authenticity remains the subject of expert debate. The text concerns the Venus tables. Each page fragment shows a standing figure facing a vertical row of day signs on the left, with their numerical coefficients in the dot-and-bar system. The figures show Toltec-Maya traits; the painting stylistically resembles the Laud and Fejérváry-Mayer codices of the Mexican highlands. Bark paper screenfold; 11 pages remain of what may have been 20 pages, their bottoms poorly preserved. Pages measure approx. 7½ in. x 5 in. (18 x 12.5 cm). Museo Nacional de Antropología, Mexico City.

3. *Madrid Codex.* Book of divination based on the sacred almanac, it treats of world directions, colors, and various subjects including hunting, beekeeping, weaving, rainmaking, crops, and diseases. Unlike the Dresden Codex, it contains no astronomy, no multiplication tables, no prophecies, and no reckoning in the Long Count. Probably written in the late 15th century, it was unaccountably and early divided into two parts: the Troano (35 leaves, pp. 22–56, 77, 79–112 of the Madrid Codex) and the Cortesianus (21 leaves, pp. 1–21, 57–76, 78 of the Madrid Codex). In 1880 they were finally identified as parts of one codex, and then referred to as the Tro-Cortesianus. It now totals 56 leaves painted on both sides, pages measure approx. 8¾in. x 4¾ in. (22.6 x 12.2 cm), total length, 268 in. (682 cm). Museo de América, Madrid.

4. *Paris Codex.* Concerned with ritual and the calendar, it is probably later than the Dresden Codex, but also presumed to be a copy of an earlier codex. Front records deities related to 11 successive *katuns* but the hieroglyphic text has not been clarified. Reverse is in poor condition, with vestiges of divinatory almanacs, new year ceremonies, etc. Bark paper screen-fold painted on both sides, the Paris Codex is approx. 58 in. (145 cm) long, its 11 pages measure approx. 5 in. x 7¾ in. (12.5 x 20 cm). Found in a wastebasket in the Bibliothèque Nationale, it was wrapped in a paper bearing the name Pérez in 17th-century script. Hence the references to it as Codex Peresianus, Codex Pérez (not to be confused with the post-Conquest Codex Pérez, one of the books of the *Chilam Balam*). Bibliothèque Nationale, Paris.

codex, pre-Conquest Mexican The term *Mexican* is here applied to all regions of modern Mexico, excluding only the Maya. The Valley of Mexico itself provides no undisputed manuscript of pre-Conquest date, the identified manuscripts having been assigned Puebla-Tlaxcala-Oaxaca provenances. Of the known pre-Conquest codices, five constitute the Borgia Group. Mexican pictorial manuscript writing was pictographic and ideographic, with place and personal names rendered in conventionalized rebus writing. The pre-Conquest survivors are:

1. *Aubin Manuscript #20.* The intricate design of this single sheet, 19⅞ in. x 35½ in. (51 x 91 cm), of animal skin deals with the five sections of the sacred calendar and the five world directions, displaying the five gods of the West and the South, with related symbols at the four corners and in the central position. Also called Le Culte rendu au Soleil, Códice del Culto a Tonatiuh, Fonds Mexicains 20, Códice de Teozoneas. Previously assigned to the Borgia Group, a western Oaxaca provenance is now preferred. Bibliothèque Nationale, Paris.

2. *Becker #1, Codex.* Three loose but consecutive fragments form part of a larger historical manuscript that also contained what is today the Codex Colombino.

Becker #1 is concerned with the life of the Mixtec ruler Eight Deer Tiger Claw, mentioning dates A.D. 1047–68. Also called Manuscrit du Cacique, Codex Saussure, Codex Tzapoteque, Codex Franz Josefino. Western Oaxaca provenance. Skin screen-fold, painted on only one side. 16 leaves (pp. 1–4, 5–14, 15–16). Total length, 156 in. (3.96 m), 7¼ in. (18.7 cm) high. Museum für Völkerkunde, Vienna.

3. *Bodley, Codex.* Important Mixtec historical manuscript referring to the dynastic genealogies of Tilantongo, Teozacoalco, and other unidentified localities of western Oaxaca, from A.D. 692 to the time of writing, c. A.D. 1521. Also called Codex Bodleianus, Códice Bodleiano. Western Oaxaca provenance. Skin screenfold of 23 leaves, 20 painted on both sides, each 10⅛ in. x 11¼ in. (26 x 29 cm). Bodleian Library, Oxford.

4. *Borgia, Codex.* Possibly the most important manuscript for the study of Mexican religion, its gods, rituals, divination, calendar, and iconography. Acknowledged as an outstanding example of Aztec graphic art. Most of its 28 sections are concerned with aspects of the sacred calendar, the *tonalpohualli.* Others are of a complexity that still denies full interpretation. Also called Codex Borgianus, Còdice Borgiano, Manuscrit de Veletri. Preferred provenance is the Mixteca-Puebla-Tlaxcala region. Skin screen-fold of 39 leaves painted on both sides; initial and last pages, formerly fastened to covers, are blank. Total length, approx. 405 in. (c. 1027.34 cm). Pages measure 10½ in. x 10¼ in. (27 x 26.5 cm). Biblioteca Apostolica Vaticana, Rome.

5. *Colombino, Codex.* Life of Eight Deer Tiger Claw (A.D. 1011–63) is presented in characteristic Mixtec style, from A.D. 1028–48. Believed to have been part of the same manuscript with Becker #1. Added Mixtec glosses date from 1541. Also called Codex Dorenberg. Provenance is Tututepec, western Oaxaca. Skin screenfold painted on one side. 24 leaves measuring 7¼ in. x 9¾ in. (18.5 x 25.15 cm) in four fragments, total length, 19 ft., 8 in. (606 cm). Museo Nacional de Antropología, Mexico City.

6. *Cospi, Codex.* Each of the first three sections on the front depicts varying interpretations of the sacred almanac. Fourth section on the back differs in style, and its interpretation remains difficult. It shows gods, perhaps offerings, and sets of bar-and-dot numerals. Has also been called Codex Cospianus, Còdice Cospiano, Còdice di Bologna, Còdice de Bolonia, Libro della China, and is one of the five codices belonging to the Borgia Group. Provenance is probably Mixteca-Puebla area. Initial and last pages are blank, attached to modern covers. Pages measure approx. 7 in. sq. (18 x 18 cm), total length, 11 ft., 10 in. (364 cm). Biblioteca Universitaria, Bologna.

7. *Fejérváry-Mayer, Codex.* Its 17 sections elaborate mostly on aspects of the sacred almanac of 260 days. Some sections on the front of the codex are believed to picture undeciphered ceremonies or offerings; they also show bar-and-dot numerals. Its stylistic affinity to Codex Laud, both among the codices of the Borgia Group, prompts their being called the Fejérváry-Laud subgroup. Fejérváry-Mayer, sometimes abbreviated Codex Mayer, is also known as Codex Pestle. Provenance believed to be Mixteca-Puebla area. Skin screen-fold of 23 leaves, painted on both sides. First and last pages are blank, originally attached to covers. Pages are mostly 68¼ in. sq. (17.5 x 17.5 cm), total length, 13 ft., 1½ in. (4 m). Free Public Museum, Liverpool.

8. *Laud, Codex.* Most of its 11 sections are concerned with interpretations of the *tonalpohualli,* whereas others, including two with bar-and-dot numerals, may relate to ceremonies or offerings. Stylistically similar to Codex Fejérváry-Mayer, it is one of five contained in the Borgia Group. Called Liber Hieroglyphoricum Aegyptorum before its Mexican identity was es-

tablished. Probably of Mixteca-Puebla provenance. Skin screen-fold of 24 leaves, 22 painted on front, 24 on back; first and last pages of front are affixed to leather covers. Pages measure 6⅛ in. x 6½ in. (15.7 x 16.5 cm), total length, 13 ft., 1 in. (3.98 m). Bodleian Library, Oxford.

9. *Nuttall, Codex.* The front of the manuscript is a genealogical and historical narrative delineating the first and second dynasties of Tilantongo, through the marriage of the ruler Eight Deer. Also depicts the genealogy of the rulers of Teozacoalco, through the children of the third ruler of the third dynasty. Pages touching on the Cuilapan genealogy cover 9th to 14th century. Other pages contain genealogies antedating Tilantongo, possibly to establish the divine descent of Mixtec lineages. The back presents a partial history of Eight Deer Tiger Claw from the marriage of his parents in A.D. 1009, to his birth in 1011, to the year 1050. Skin screen-fold of 47 leaves painted on both sides. Pages measure approx. 7½ in. x 10 in. (19 x 25.5 cm). Codex Nuttall is also called Codex Zouche. Its provenance is probably Teozacoalco, western Oaxaca. Codices Nuttall, Becker #1, Bodley, Colombino, and Vienna are sometimes collectively called the Nuttall Group. Cortés is thought to have sent Codex Nuttall, along with Codex Vienna, to Charles V in 1519. British Museum, London.

10. *Vaticanus B, Codex.* It presents a detailed interpretation of the sacred almanac, the *tonalpohualli,* and 28 sections deal with specific aspects of it, such as the 5 x 52 and 20 x 13 days and the deities related to them, as well as other matters such as the world directions. Belongs to the Borgia Group. Also referred to as Codex Vaticanus 3773, Còdice Vaticano Rituale, Còdice Fàbrega. Provenance is probably Mixteca-Puebla area. Skin screen-fold of 49 leaves, of which 48 are painted on both sides; first and last pages, blank, are fastened to original wooden covers. Pages measure 5 in. x 5⅞ in. (13 x 15 cm), total length, 24 ft., 1⅜ in. (7.35 m).

Biblioteca Apostolica Vaticana, Rome.

11. *Vienna, Codex.* The front of the codex comprises 52 pages, calendrical and ceremonial in content, with some reference to 9 wind (Quetzalcóatl), along with lists of place glyphs, dates, and deities or priests. Fire-making ritual appears repeatedly in each of the ten major divisions. Back of the codex is blank, with later Latin inscriptions, excepting 13 pages that concern a genealogy starting two generations before the establishment of the first dynasty at Tilantongo. It ends with the marriage of the third ruler of the dynasty, spanning the period from the 8th century to middle of the 14th. Also called Codex Vindobonensis, Mexicanus I, Codex Hieroglyphicorum Indiae Meridionales, Codex Clementino, Codex Leopoldino, Codex Kreichgauer. Likely provenance is Tilantongo, western Oaxaca. Skin screen-fold of 52 leaves painted on both sides, with original wooden covers. Pages measure 8½ in. x 10⅛ in. (22 x 26 cm). Nationalbibliothek, Vienna.

codex, early post-Conquest Mexican Second in importance only to the surviving pre-Conquest codices were those produced under Spanish patronage by native scribes immediately after the Conquest. The joint motivation of church and state was intellectual, practical, administrative, and explicitly directed toward pre-Conquest rather than colonial matters. A complete census of native pictorial manuscripts appears in vol. 14, *Handbook of the Middle American Indian* (Austin: University of Texas Press, 1975). The following are selected from among hundreds for their authenticity, reliability, and minimum European influence:

1. *Aubin, Codex.* History of the Mexica, starting with their departure from Aztlán in A.D. 1168 and continuing into Spanish colonial times. A year-to-year chronicle, it was composed at different times by different authors, with drawings and a Nahuatl text. The final section lists pre-Conquest rulers and colonial rulers of Tenochtitlán to c. 1608. Written in Mexico City c. 1576–

96 and 1597–1608. Sometimes called Codex of 1576, the date on a copy in Berlin;
also Anales Mexicanos #1. Written on
European paper, 81 leaves measuring 5⅞
in. x 4¼ in. (15 x 11 cm). British Museum, London.

2. *Becker #2, Codex.* Early 16th-cen-
tury historical manuscript, it is divided into
two horizontal sections, with six and nine
native couples, respectively, painted in the
upper and lower registers. Mixtec in style,
they have not been related to genealogies
in any other codices. Skin screen-fold,
painted on only one side. Four leaves. Believed to be of west Oaxacan provenance.
Total length, 45⅝ in. (1.16 m), 10⅜ in.
(26.5 cm) high. Museum für Völkerkunde,
Vienna.

3. *Borbonicus, Codex.* Manuscript concerned with the calendar and religious
ceremonies, possibly written before the
Conquest but not later than 1541. Part I
is a sacred calendar. Presiding deities and
other symbols of the 20 periods appear on
the main panel of each page. Day signs, 9
Lords of the Night, 13 Lords of the Day,
and the 13 birds are drawn in separate
compartments. Noted for its pictorial detail. Part II relates the 9 Lords of the Night
with the Year Bearer days for a 52-year
cycle. Part III is a calendar for the 18
monthly festivals in a New Fire Ceremony
year. Part IV again refers to a monthly
festival and pursues year dates for a 52-
year period. Also called Codex du Corps
Législatif, Codex Législatif, Codex Hamy,
Calendario de Paris. Written at Tenochti-
tlán-Mexico City. Native paper screenfold,
painted on only one side. 36 leaves (pp.
3–38); pages 1–2 and 39–40 are lost. Each
page measures 15¼ in. x 15½ in. (39 x
39.5 cm). Bibliothèque de L'Assemblée
Nationale, Paris.

4. *Boturini, Codex.* Historical chronicle
covering history of the Mexica A.D. 1168–
1355; their departure from Aztlán, arrival
at Chapultepec, to subjugation by Coxcox,
ruler of Colhuacán. Also called Tira de la
Peregrinación, Tira del Museo. Written in
Mexico City in the 16th century. Screen-

fold of bark paper, painted on one side; no
color except for red lines connecting the
dates. 21½ leaves, total length 17 ft.,
10⅛ in. (549 cm), 7¾ in. (19.8 cm)
high. Museo Nacional de Antropología,
Mexico City.

5. *Florentine Codex.* Most comprehensive manuscript dealing with the religion,
calendar, social classes, and natural history
of the pre-Conquest Aztecs. Is believed to
be a copy of the final 12 books of *Historia
de las Cosas de la Nueva España* written
by native scribes under the direction of
Fray Bernardino de Sahagún, and sent to
Europe by him in 1580. Illustrated with
1,846 native drawings, more than half in
Book XI, which concerns natural history.
Written in Tlatelolco, D.F., c. 1575–77, or
1578–80. Also called Còdice Florentino,
parts of it are from the earlier Codices
Matritenses in Madrid. Not a native codex
in format, it is a folio on European paper
in 3 volumes of 345, 372, and 493 leaves.
Biblioteca Medìcea Laurenziana, Florence.
See also **Sahagún, Bernardino de.**

6. *Magliabecchiano, Codex.* Manuscript
composed of native drawings and related
Spanish text, treating the 20-day calendar,
18 monthly festivals, gods, movable ceremonies and customs, and the 52-year cycle.
Also called The Book of Life of the Ancient
Mexicans (Libro de la Vida que los Yndios
antiguamente hacian y Supersticiones y
malos Ritos que tenian y guardavan). Written in the Valley of Mexico probably before 1566. European paper, 92 leaves measuring 6 in. x 8⅜ in. (15.5 x 21.5 cm).
Biblioteca Nazionale Centrale, Florence.

7. *Matritenses, Codices.* Two manuscripts that represent early drafts by Bernardino de Sahagún for his *Historia de las
Cosas de la Nueva España* and therefore
form part of the Florentine Codex. Written
for him by native scribes in Nahuatl and
Spanish at Tlatelolco, D.F. The Codices
Matritenses draw on previous Sahagún
manuscripts known individually' as *Primeros Memoriales* (written at Tepepulco,
Hidalgo, 1559–61), *Manuscrito de Tlatelolco* (written there, 1561–65), and *Memo-*

riales con Escolios (written at Tlatelolco, 1565). Parts of these earlier manuscripts appear in each of the two Madrid codices. One codex resides at the Royal Palace (Códice Matritense del Real Palacio, 303 leaves), the other at the Academy (Códice Matritense de la Academía de la Historia, 342 leaves) in Madrid. Although these codices were completed by 1575, modern knowledge of their existence dates only from 1881. See **Sahagún, Bernardino de.**

8. *Mendoza, Codex.* Manuscript commissioned by the Spanish Viceroy Antonio de Mendoza for Charles V, covering Aztec history, tributes, and ethnography. Part I is a history of Tenochtitlán, A.D. 1325–1521, in terms of its rulers and their conquests. Part II is a pictorial record of tributes rendered by the empire, and Part III graphically portrays Aztec life, including a year-to-year history of an Aztec from birth onward. Also treated are priests, warriors, other professions; life at the court of Moctezuma II, including laws and punishments. This detailed account can only be compared to parts of the later Florentine Codex. Also called Códice Mendocino, it was written in Mexico City c. 1541–42. Written on European paper, 71 numbered leaves, 12¾ in. x 8⅝ in. (32.7 x 22.9 cm), plus added title leaf. Bodleian Library, Oxford.

9. *Ríos, Codex.* Manuscript concerned with religion, calendar, Aztec history, and ethnology. It and the Codex Telleriano-Remensis are thought to be copies of a lost original, the Codex Huitzilopochtli. Together, they are called the Huitzilopochtli Group. Believed to have been copied by a non-Indian artist in Italy, its Italian text is based on commentary by Fray Pedro de los Ríos. The Codex Ríos, in separate sections, relates (*a*) cosmology and mythology, (*b*) the sacred almanac, (*c*) calendar tables for years 1558–1619, (*d*) an illustrated calendar of the 18 monthly festivals, (*e*) customs, including sacrifices, and portraits of Indian types, (*f*) pictorial annals of Aztec migrations and settlement in the Valley of Mexico, A.D. 1195–1549, and (*g*) year

glyphs for 1556–62. The original dates from c. 1566–89, Valley of Mexico. Also called Codex Vaticanus A, Codex Vaticanus 3738, Copia Vaticana. Written on European paper, 101 leaves, measuring 18 in. x 11¼ in. (46 x 29 cm). Biblioteca Apostolica Vaticana, Rome.

10. *Sanchez Solis, Codex.* Traditional historical Mixtec manuscript whose first three pages show a place glyph and two dates followed by a series of human figures. Rest of the codex presents couples that seemingly delineate a 26-generation genealogy. Western Oaxaca provenance, 16th century. Identified place glyphs represent Tequixtepec and Tilantongo, as well as Acatlán, southern Puebla. Also called Codex Egerton 2895, Codex Waecker-Götter, Códice Zapoteco. Skin screen-fold with 16 leaves, of which 16 are painted on front, 13 on back. First and last pages are blank, used as covers. Total length, 14 ft., 4 in. (441 cm); pages measure 8⅜ in. x 10¾ in. (21.5 x 27.7 cm). British Museum, London.

11. *Selden Codex.* There are two unrelated Selden codices in the Bodleian Library, Oxford: (*a*) *Selden I.* Historical Mixtec manuscript describing the dynasties of an unidentified town called Belching Mountain, based on the appearance of its place glyph. It concerns genealogies that also touch on persons from other and known places such as Teozacoalco and Tilantongo. Long thought to be pre-Conquest, it is now dated c. 1556–60, with a western Oaxaca provenance. Also called Códice Selden B, Lienzo de Retapa, MS pictorico de Petapa. Skin screen-fold, only one side retaining legible content. 20 leaves measure 10½ in. x 10½ in. (27.5 x 27.5 cm). (*b*) *Selden II.* The roll opens with a depiction of 9 wind (Quetzalcóatl), the eight celestial layers, and the earth. It continues with a narrative also involving some ritual elements. Manuscript may concern the origin of a yet unidentified dynasty of a town in western Oaxaca. Also called Códice Selden A. 16th century. Native paper roll, painted on one side, mea-

suring 12 ft., 4½ in. x 14⅞ in. (350 x 38 cm).

12. *Telleriano-Remensis, Codex.* Manuscript believed to be derived from a lost original, the Codex Huitzilopochtli, along with the Codex Ríos. It has three main illustrated parts in several native styles and with various Spanish notations, some thought to be the handwriting of Fray Pedro de los Ríos. The first part is a calendar of the 18 months, their related gods, and a symbol for the *Nemontemi;* the second part is a sacred almanac; and the third a pictorial annal for the years 1198–1562. The last two pages, not illustrated, offer historical data in Spanish for the years 1519–57. Leaves are missing from all three main sections but are preserved in the corresponding Codex Ríos. Also called Codex Tellerianus, Codice Le Tellier. Valley of Mexico, c. 1562–63. European paper, 50 leaves, each 12½ in. x 8½ in. (32 x 22 cm). Bibliothèque Nationale, Paris.

Cofradia See **Autlán.**

Coixlahuaca Site of ancient Mixtec capital in state of Oaxaca.

Cojumatlán Late Classic phase of Jalisco, western Mexico, A.D. 600–900.

col Yucatecan Maya word for cornfield, corresponding to Nahuatl *milpa.*

Colhua People who settled in Colhuacán, Valley of Mexico, after the fall of Tula. One of most important groups to maintain a cultural and dynastic link with the Toltecs into later historical times.

Colhuacán (Culhuacán) City-state, in southwest section of present-day Mexico City, founded A.D. 1064 by the Colhua, refugees from Tula. Important until the 15th century when it was subdued by the Tepanecs of Atzcapotzalco. First Mexican sovereign, Acamapichtli, was chosen from its ruling family in order to establish Toltec descent for the Mexica.

Colima Modern Mexican state on the Pacific Ocean, bounded by Jalisco and Michoacán, with capital of the same name. Named for 13,000-ft. (3,960 m) -high Colima volcano. Colima is best known for its hollow ceramic figural sculptures, in the most homogeneous of the western styles, unified by the famous light-orange to deep-red burnished slip with spots of black patina over the surface. Displayed a wide range of zoomorphic representations, including its famous dogs. Ceramics come mostly from shaft tombs, as at Los Ortices and Chanchopa. Other sites include Morett, Playa del Tesoro, Periquilla, Armería. Active from Late Preclassic into Classic period.

collar stone A representation in stone of belts made of wood or other perishable materials used by the Island Arawak ballplayers of the West Indies. Common form suggests the belt was made of a sapling, the longer end of which was bent and strapped to the shorter, leaving the overlapping end projecting. The heavy striking surface was often decorated. The form was oval, never open-ended, in contrast to the usual *yoke* similarly employed in the Mesoamerican ball game.

Colombino, Codex See **codex, pre-Conquest Mexican; Colombino, Codex.**

colors, ceramic Mesoamerican potters used mineral pigments to color their wares, which explains the rather uniform color scheme—mainly blacks, whites, reds, buff, etc.

colors, directional See **world directions.**

colossal heads Term for the bodyless monolithic spherical heads, weighing from 6 to 25 tons, of the Olmec culture, c. 1500–400 B.C. Four were found at La Venta, six at San Lorenzo, two at Tres Zapotes. Superficially alike, the differing details of helmets and facial expressions suggest idealized portraits.

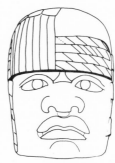

colossal head, San Lorenzo

Comalcalco Westernmost Maya site in Tabasco, offering a rare example of kiln-fired bricks employed in Mesoamerican architecture. A tomb with nine figures sculptured in bas-relief on the walls recalls the art style of Palenque.

comalli Nahuatl word for the ceramic griddle used to bake tortillas, the unleavened corn bread of Mexican natives. Called *comal* today.

Comayagua basin Central plains valley of Honduras, linked to both Gulf and Pacific coasts by Ulúa and Goascoran river systems, respectively.

Comitán Plain Natural corridor leading from upper Grijalva basin of Chiapas (Central Depression) to Guatemala, also called the Central Plateau of Chiapas. Sculpture and stelae of the area indicate a substantial lowland Maya invasion along this route in Late Classic times.

Conchas Preclassic ceramic phase of La Victoria, coastal Guatemala, c. 800–300 B.C.

Conduacan See **Orange, Fine.**

Conte Polychrome See **Central Panama.**

Copador Late Classic ceramic style of western Honduras, especially at Copán, coeval with Ulúa Polychrome of the Honduras-El Salvador area, c. A.D. 700. Pottery decoration is red, purple, and black on light buff, with animals, birds, and human figures, generally seated or lying flat. Upper part of bowls are often decorated with "false glyphs."

copal A resin of several varieties of conifer burned as incense in native ritual ceremonies. Called *copalli* by the Aztecs, *pom* by the Maya. *Copalziquipilli* was the Nahuatl word for a pouch to carry *copal*, a priestly insignia in Mexican art and codices.

Copán Most easterly and a major Classic period Maya ceremonial center in western Honduras. On a bluff overlooking the Copán River, it has several large plazas with stelae and altars, encompassed by temple pyramids and an acropolis, and one of the finest examples of a Classic period ball

Copán emblem glyph

court. Hieroglyphic Stairway is 33 ft. (10 m) broad, rising c. 86 ft. (26 m); its 63 carved steps contain over 2,000 glyphs. Copán is principally noted for its green trachyte stelae whose figures are carved almost in the round, which is unusual among the Maya. They show skill in portraiture, probably representing members of the Caan family, the ruling dynasty also represented at Quiriguá. Copán is considered to have been the intellectual center of the Classic period in the Maya lowlands. Altar Q possibly commemorated a congress of 16 leaders who met to adjust the solar calendar c. A.D. 773.

Copilco Middle Preclassic site, c. 1300–800 B.C., in present-day Villa Obregón, Mexico City. Covered by a thick layer of lava deposited by Xictli volcano. Today in-place exhibits of burials are visible beneath the lava crust.

copilli Conical headdress of Huastec origin and a typical adornment of the god Quetzalcóatl in Mexican codices. Also worn by Aztec priests who assumed the title of Quetzalcóatl.

Coralillo See **Tuxcacuesco.**

corbeled arch Called a "false arch" because it lacks a keystone, it is built up from the walls, each successive stone jutting out over the one below, eventually capped by a flat stone. The weakness of the arch itself required massive walls to support the structures, producing the narrow dark rooms characteristic of most lowland Classic period Maya architecture. Unknown in the highlands of Guatemala, except for its rare occurrences in a few tombs.

cord marking A decorative ceramic technique in which fine cord is wrapped around a paddle and pressed against an unfired clay vessel, leaving the characteristic cord imprint.

Córdoba, Hernández de (d. 1518) Leader of the first Spanish expedition to make contact with the Maya; sailed from Cuba and landed on Yucatán at Cabo Catoche in 1517. First exposure of the natives to European firearms.

cornudo West Mexican hollow ceramic fig-

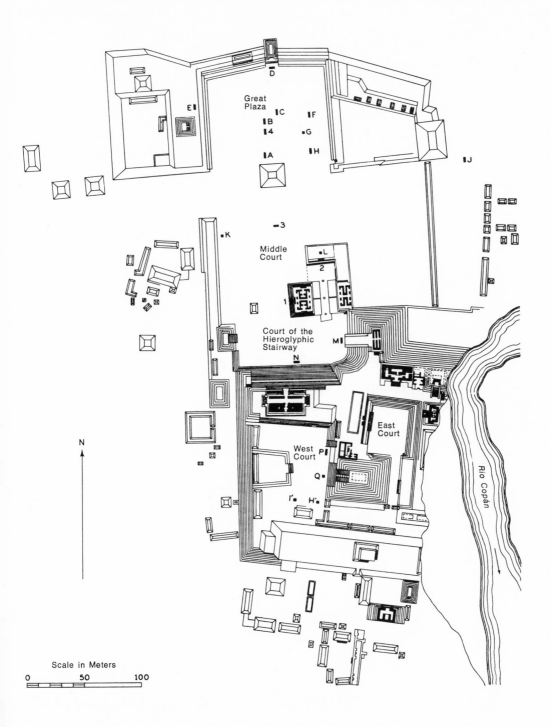

Plate 2. Map of the central section of Copán. From S. G. Morley, *The Ancient Maya,* page 277.

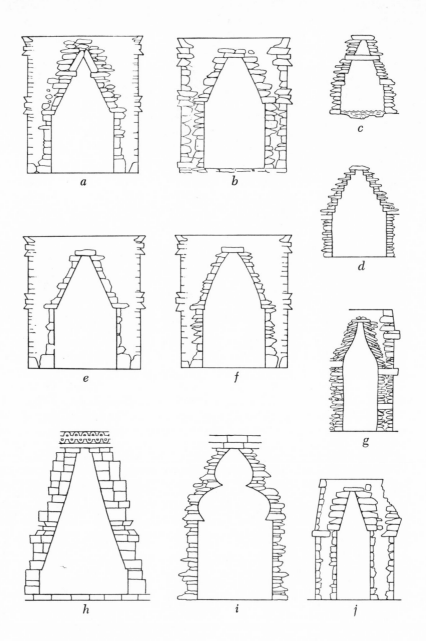

Plate 3. Cross sections of Maya corbeled arches: (*a*) Nunnery Annex, Chichén Itzá; (*b*) section of ordinary arch with flat capstones and undressed sides, characteristic of the Classic period; (*c*) viaduct, Palenque; (*d*) Temple E-X, Uaxactún; (*e*) section of ordinary arch with flat capstones and dressed sides, characteristic of the Postclassic; (*f*) section of ordinary arch with flat capstones, dressed sides, and curved soffit slopes; (*g*) Palace (Structure A-V), Uaxactún; (*h*) arcade through Palace of the Governors, Uxmal; (*i*) trefoil arch, Palace, Palenque; (*j*) second story, Nunnery, Chichén Itzá. From S. G. Morley, *The Ancient Maya*, page 317.

urine with a horn protruding from the forehead. Found in northeast Jalisco shaft-tomb complex; possibly related to shamanism.

Corobán Settlement in eastern El Salvador, active shortly before and during the Spanish occupation.

Corobici Tribe of the Macro-Chibcha language group that inhabited the Nicoya Peninsula and many of the Nicaraguan islands before the invasion by the northern Chorotega-Mangue peoples forced their retreat to the eastern bank of the Tempisque basin, Costa Rica.

correlation of Maya and Gregorian calendars Mesoamerican chronology is based on the Maya lowland sequence and the absolute dating of its Classic period by calendrical correlations. Its relation to Teotihuacán, with its many roots in other regions of Mesoamerica, provides the means for cross-dating. Two theories for correlating Mesoamerican dates are in recent use by archaeologists:

1. *Goodman-Martínez-Thompson correlation* is based on the correspondence of the year 1539 with the 11 *baktun* 16 *katun* ending of the projected Maya Initial Series (Long Count) system of dating. It establishes 3113 B.C. as the starting point of the Maya calendar, employed similarly to our reference to the birth date of Christ in our calendar.

2. *Spinden correlation* is based on the correspondence of 1536 with the date of 12 *baktun* 9 *katun* ending of the projected Long Count. It puts the starting point of the Maya calendar at 3273 B.C.

Period datings of the two systems compare as follows:

queror of Mexico. Sailed from Cuba in February 1519; entered Aztec capital of Tenochtitlán, taking Moctezuma II prisoner, on November 3, 1519. His final subjugation of the Aztecs on August 13, 1521, marked the end of the Mexican empire.

Cortesianus, Codex See **codex, pre-Conquest Maya; Madrid Codex.**

Cospianus, Codex See **codex, pre-Conquest Mexican; Cospi, Codex.**

Costa Chica Pacific coastline extending east from Bay of Acapulco, Guerrero, to Bahía Dulce. Bordered on the north by the Sierra Madre del Sur, the region contains the Early Preclassic site of Puerto Marqués.

Costa Grande Pacific coastline extending northwest from Acapulco. Ceramics there indicate Preclassic and Classic influences from Teotihuacán. Pottery resemblances also suggest contact with Maya area, Nicaragua, and Costa Rica.

Costa Rica Central American republic situated between Nicaragua and Panama, the Caribbean Sea and the Pacific Ocean; San José is the capital. Named by Columbus in 1502, based on an interpretation of the natives' gold ornaments as proof of local wealth. Little or no gold is mined in Costa Rica. The country is divided into four regions: Nicoya in the northwest, Central Highlands (Meseta Central), Atlantic watershed in the northeast, and Diquís to the south bordering on Panama. Culturally, Nicoya is related to Mesoamerica, whereas other regions predominantly exhibit traits introduced from the south. Chronologically it is divided into Early, 300 B.C.–A.D. 500, Middle, A.D. 500–1000, and Late periods, A.D. 1000–Conquest. Costa Rica produced

	LONG COUNT	THOMPSON	SPINDEN	DIFF.
Start of Classic period	8.12.0.0.0	A.D. 278	A.D. 21	257
End, Early Classic period	9.8.0.0.0	A.D. 593	A.D. 333	260
End, Late Classic period	10.3.0.0.0	A.D. 889	A.D. 629	260

Recent investigations, aided by radiocarbon (C^{14}) dating, favor the Goodman-Martínez-Thompson correlation, which is exclusively used in this work.

Cortés, Hernán (1485–1547) Spanish con-

prodigious amounts of stone sculpture, varied ceramics, gold and jade ornaments in ancient times. See also **Línea Vieja, Greater Nicoya, Greater Chiriquí.**

Cotío Representative Maya ceremonial center of Late Classic Amatle phase, west of Kaminaljuyú, with a ball court and adobe-plaster-faced mounds. Reflects the abandonment of Teotihuacán architectural influence.

Cotorra Early Preclassic phase of Chiapa de Corzo, coeval with Chiapa I ceramic period, c. 1400–1000 B.C.

co-tradition A term initially coined by American archaeologists active in Peru, an area co-tradition enlarges upon the concept of a tradition. It refers to the development of several cultures, within a stated area, interrelated over a period of time, exchanging ideas and objects, while retaining a degree of regional and individual identity. See also **Middle Classic horizon.**

Cotzumalhuapa Late Classic phase of Pacific slopes of Guatemala, c. A.D. 650–925, centered in sites of Bilbao, El Baúl, and Santa Lucía Cotzumalhuapa. Mexican influence on sculpture is seen in the emphasis on death, the ceremonial ball game, and the style of hieroglyphic dates. The Cotzumalhuapan style is narrative, emphasizes human sacrifice, and introduces the interlaced vine and flower motif. Ceramics are contemporary with San Juan Plumbate.

Coxcatlán Cave in the state of Puebla, near the Oaxaca border, sheltered samples of earliest corn cultivation in the New World; marked the appearance of sedentary life supported by agriculture. Dates to Early Preclassic period, c. 5000–3400 B.C.

Coxcox A mythical bird of phallic connotation, the deity of war and sacrifice of the early Tepanecs in the Pedregal, Valley of Mexico. Aztecs later identified it with the god Xochipilli, also calling it Coxcoxtli and Quetzalcoxcoxtli. It was further related to worship of the sun in its contest with darkness, the song of the *coxcoxtli* ("wild cock") heralding the dawn of each new day.

Coxcoxtli Mythical king of Colhuacán. One legend has him giving his daughter Atotoztli to the tributary Tenochcas to start a dynasty with Toltec antecedents. Presumably invited to the wedding, he found his daughter had been flayed and her skin was

being worn by a priest officiating at the ceremony honoring Toci, the earth-goddess. A separate legend recounts that the first Aztec king, Acamapichtli, was the son of a union between a Mexican commoner and Atotoztli, Coxcoxtli's daughter. Both accounts underline the consuming need felt by the Aztecs to prove a direct line of descent from the Toltecs and their civilization.

coyolli Vegetable or metal rattles, or bells, whose jingling was caused by dried seeds inside of them. They were worn as dancers' necklaces, bracelets, and anklets. They are shown in sculpture on the cheeks of the Mexican moon-goddess, Coyolxauhqui, providing the basis for her name.

Coyolxauhqui Mexican moon-goddess, daughter of Coatlícue and the ill-fated sister of Huitzilopochtli who decapitated her for conspiring in the death of their mother. Her massive monolithic head, with *coyolli* on her cheeks, is a masterpiece of Aztec sculpture in the Museo Nacional de Antropología, Mexico City.

Coyotlatelco Early Postclassic pottery style widespread in the Valley of Mexico, c. A.D. 900. Preceded Mazapán, also called Xometla. Figurines with thin slablike bodies and long pointed noses were characteristic; ceramic ware was red-on-cream.

Cozcacuauhtli Sixteenth day of the 20-day Nahuatl month, meaning "vulture." Patron deity of the day was Itzpapálotl; its augury was favorable. The Maya equivalent day was Cib; Zapotec, Loo. Being bald, the vulture was a symbol of old age.

Cozumel Island off northeastern coast of Yucatán peninsula. Postclassic center for the worship of the Maya moon-goddess Ix Chel. European discovery was made by Juan de Grijalva, 1518.

Creation myth, Aztec Its concept was one of progression, not evolution, through a series of "suns" or worlds:

First sun was ruled by Tezcatlipoca, struck down by Quetzalcóatl. Giants inhabiting the earth were devoured by jaguars, Tezcatlipoca's *nahual*. Its sign is 4 Océlotl (4 jaguar).

Second sun was ruled by Quetzalcóatl, destroyed by winds. Survivors turned into monkeys. Its sign is 4 Éhecatl (4 wind).

Third sun was ruled by the rain-god Tlaloc, terminated by a rain of fire. Survivors became birds. Its sign is 4 Quiáhuitl (4 rain).

Fourth sun, ruled by Tlaloc's sister Chalchiúhtlicue, was destroyed by floods. Survivors became fish. Its sign is 4 Ácatl (4 water).

Fifth and current sun is ruled by the sun-god Tonatiuh. Its destruction is predicted by earthquake. Its sign is 4 Ollin (4 movement). See also **Calendar Stone, Aztec.**

Creation myth, Maya The Popol Vuh, the sacred book of the Quiché Maya of Guatemala, relates the story of three creations and two destructions by deluge:

In the beginning there was only water and darkness. The gods created earth and populated it with animals. They created man of mud but destroyed him in dissatisfaction with his inability to speak and worship his makers.

The gods then made man of wood. He spoke, looked, and multiplied like man, but lacked a mind. He did not recognize his creators and was destroyed. Survivors of this creation became monkeys.

In their third attempt the gods created man of the dough of yellow and white maize. Came the dawn, the sun rose, and man, the ancestor of the present-day Maya, responded by worshiping his creator-gods. The myth makes no mention of an imminent end to this world.

"crossed-bands" motif A geometric element resembling a Saint Andrew's cross is frequently found in Olmec art and is later prominent also at Izapa. Among the Classic period lowland Maya it became a glyphic element with the meaning of sky or serpent.

Crucero Preclassic phase of the Soconusco, coeval with Chiapas V, c. 300–100 B.C.

Cuadros Preclassic phase of the Soconusco, between the Ocós and Jocotal phases, c. 1000–850 B.C.

Cuanalan-Ticomán See **Ticomán.**

Cuauhcohuatl See **Teomama.**

cuauhicpalli Nahuatl for "eagle seat," it is an Aztec throne decorated with eagle feathers and jaguar skins. See **icpalli.**

Cuauhtémoc ("descending eagle," meaning sunset) Last of the Aztec rulers, reigned 1520–24, nephew of Moctezuma II and Cuitláhuac. Fought Cortés desperately, was captured, and eventually executed while a hostage on the Cortés Honduras expedition of 1524. Venerated today as a national hero in Mexico. See also **Tonatiuh.**

Cuauhtitlán Pre-Conquest settlement of Chichimec origin on the northwestern shore of ancient Lake Texcoco. Its history is told in the Anales de Cuauhtitlán, a part of the Codex Chimalpopoca.

Cuauhtlehuánitl ("ascending eagle," meaning sunrise) See **Tonatiuh.**

Cuauhtli Fifteenth of the 20 Nahuatl day signs. Xipe Totec was the patron deity, with an unfavorable augury. Equivalent to the Maya day Men and the Zapotec day Naa. Word means "eagle" in Nahuatl.

Cuauhuitlehua See **Atlcahualo; months, Aztec.**

cuauhxicalli With a meaning of "eagle vessel" in Nahuatl, it was the stone receptacle for the hearts and blood of Aztec sacrificial victims.

Cuautepec Ceramic subphase of the Zacatenco Preclassic phase of the Valley of Mexico, at El Arbolillo, Zacatenco, and Ticomán, c. 750–650 B.C. It was divided into Early Cuautepec (Late La Pastora) and Late Cuautepec (Atoto at Tlatilco).

Cuaxólotl A variant of Chantico, the goddess of the hearth, with two heads symbolizing the beneficial and harmful aspects of fire.

Cuerauáperi Tarascan creator-goddess, consort of the sun-god, Curicaueri; feminine principle in creation, protectress of birth and sewing.

Cuernavaca Capital of the modern state of Morelos, Mexico. Favorite vacation spot of Aztec kings. Nearby archaeological sites include Xochicalco, Tepoztlán, and Chalcatzingo.

Cuetzpalin Fourth of the 20 Nahuatl day signs; Huehuecóyotl was the day's patron deity, with a favorable augury. Equivalent to the Maya day Kan and the Zapotec day Gueche. Cuetzpalin is the Nahuatl word for lizard. In the codices it is painted with the front half of its body blue and the rear, red, symbolizing night and day. Cuetzpalin represents the creative natural forces, the dying and regeneration of nature. 1 Cuetzpalin is the calendrical name of the god Itztlacoliuhqui, 6 Cuetzpalin of Mictlantecuhtli.

Cuicatec Linguistic group of north-central Oaxaca, Mexico.

Cuicuilco Preclassic site near University City, Mexico, partially covered by lava from the volcano Xictli. A four-stepped circular platform, c. 75 ft. (22 m) high, stone-dressed, may be the earliest pyramid platform of stone, developing out of the earlier earth mounds of Olmec San Lorenzo and La Venta, and initiating the Mesoamerican pyramid. Cuicuilco was the leading city during the Ticomán period of the Valley of Mexico. At Cuicuilco phases I, II, and III, c. 500–200 B.C., were followed by Cuicuilco IV (Tezoyuca) and proto-Teotihuacán Cuicuilco V (Patlachique) to c. A.D. 1.

Cuilapan Oaxacan site, formerly Zapotecan and Mixtec capital, and an important church-convent in colonial times. The famous ceramic sculpture, *Scribe of Cuilapan,* now in the Oaxaca Regional Museum, dates to Monte Albán II, 150–1 B.C.

Cuitláhuac 1. Brother and successor to Moctezuma II, succumbed to illness after a reign of four months in 1520. 2. City in the Valley of Mexico dating from Toltec times, present-day Tláhuac.

cuitlatl 1. With a Nahuatl meaning of excrement, it is rendered in the Mexican codices as a symbol of sin. Teocuitlatl ("excrement of the gods") was the Nahuatl word for gold. 2. Cuitlatl was also the name applied to an algae, cultivated and consumed by the Aztecs, that anciently spawned in the saline lakes of the Valley of Mexico.

Cuitzeo Lake of northwestern Michoacán, Mexico.

Culhuacán See **Colhuacán.**

Culiacán Archaeological site and modern capital of the state of Sinaloa, Mexico. Ceramic phases at Culiacán are Acaponeta, A.D. 900–1100, La Divisa, 1100–1250, Yebalito, 1250–1400, and La Quinta, 1400–Conquest. The last three phases are representative, at the site itself, of the late Postclassic Culiacán horizon of Sinaloa. The Acaponeta phase is related to the Aztatlán horizon of Sinaloa, which precedes and overlaps Culiacán. See **Aztatlán.**

Culuba Archaeological site in northeastern Yucatán, Mexico.

Cumku Eighteenth month of the *tun,* the Maya year of 360 days. Sometimes spelled Cumhu.

Cupul Preclassic phase of Yucatán, c. 1000–800 B.C.

Curicaueri Tarascan fire- and sun-god, of Postclassic western Mexico. Represented masculine principle in creation; Cuerauáperi was his female counterpart.

Curridabat Ceramic complex, c. A.D. 500–850, named after a site in the Costa Rican Central Highlands, characterized by varieties of red and brown incised ceramics and tripod vessels with long rattle feet, decorated with relief figures of animals.

d

Dainzú Site in the Tlacolula section of the Oaxaca valley with over 50 bas-relief stone slabs depicting active ballplayers and priests at the base of the pyramidal structure. Post-Olmec Izapan sculptural influence is suggested. Location also has habitation buildings and a ball court. Late Monte Albán I into II, c. 600–100 B.C. Formerly called Macuilxóchitl, after the nearby modern village.

danzantes Life-sized carvings in bas-relief of human figures on stone slabs at the House of the Danzantes, Monte Albán, Oaxaca. Olmec traits place them in Monte Albán I, 700–350 B.C. Their meaning is uncertain, but their great variety of poses resulted in their being named "the dancers." A more likely interpretation is that of sacrificial victims.

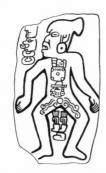

danzante, Monte Albán

Darién Jungle-forested eastern province of Panama, today separated from the Caribbean by the province of San Blas. Enclosed on the west by the province of Panama, on the east by Colombia, on the south by the Pacific. In the 16th century the term was applied to the entire region from today's Canal Zone to Colombia. Little is known about it archaeologically.

dark channeled ware Middle Preclassic period ceramic vessels, black or brown in color, found in Mexico at Tlatilco, Las Bocas, Tlapacoya, Chalcatzingo and at the Olmec site of Río Chiquitos, Veracruz. Decoration is in relief, the wide flat channels are excised from the burnished surface and coated with cinnabar. Two Olmec themes predominate: paw-wing and, more frequently, the jaguar-dragon profile with hand design.

dating, archaeological methods of For some methods employed in Middle America, see **radiocarbon (C^{14}) dating, thermoluminescence, obsidian hydration, fluorine test, dendrochronology, glottochronology.**

dating, Maya method of See **Long Count.**

daub ware A ceramic trait, also called Palma Daub, appearing only in Mamom times at Uaxactún, the southern Maya lowlands. Consists of unpolished and unslipped jars with red vertical or horizontal bands or crude swirls daubed on the body of the vessel.

day names, Aztec The 20 days of the Aztec calendar had pictorial (glyph) representations that, unlike the Maya glyphs, were easy to relate to the names describing them. Each day was combined with its number, had good, bad, or indifferent augury, and a patron deity assigned to it:

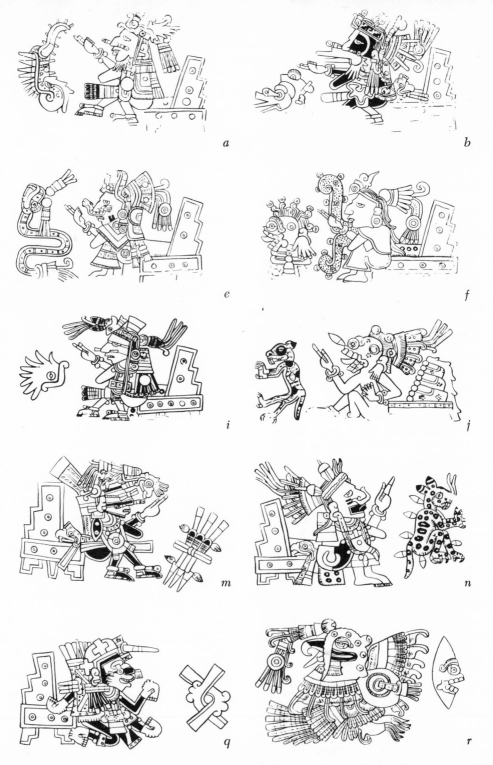

Plate 4. Aztec day names and their patron deities according to the Codex Borgia: (*a*)
Cipactli, Tonacatecuhtli; (*b*) Éhecatl, Quetzalcóatl; (*c*) Calli, Tepeyolohtli; (*d*) Cuetz-
palin, Huehuecóyotl; (*e*) Cóatl, Chalchiúhtlicue; (*f*) Miquiztli, Tecciztécatl; (*g*) Mázatl,
Tlaloc; (*h*) Tochtli, Mayáhuel; (*i*) Atl, Xiuhtecuhtli; (*j*) Itzcuintli, Mictlantecuhtli; (*k*)

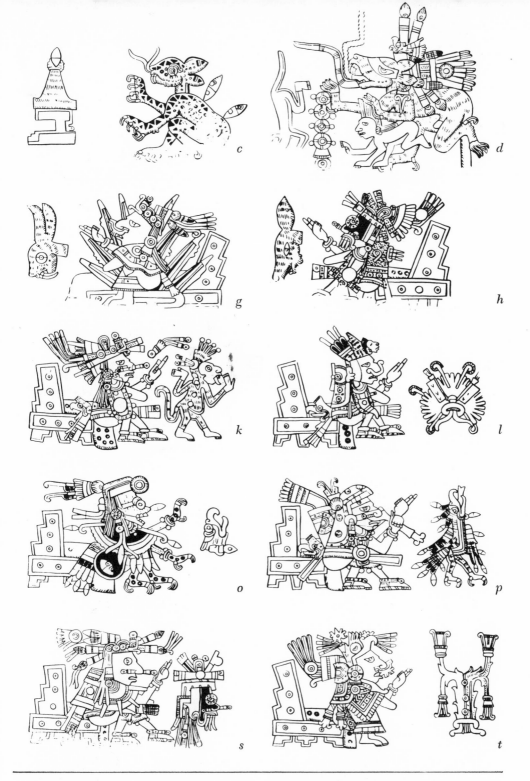

Xochipilli, Ozomatli; (*l*) Patécatl, Malinalli; (*m*) Itztlacoliuhqui, Ácatl; (*n*) Tlazoltéotl, Océlotl; (*o*) Xipe Totec, Cuauhtli; (*p*) Itzpapálotl, Cozcacuauhtli; (*q*) Xólotl, Ollin; (*r*) Chalchiuhtotolin, Técpatl; (*s*) Tonatiuh, Quiáhuitl; (*t*) Xochiquetzal, Xóchitl.

ORDER OF DAYS	GLYPH	MEANING	AUGURY	PATRON
1.	Cipactli	alligator	good	Tonacatecuhtli
2.	Éhecatl	wind	evil	Quetzalcóatl
3.	Calli	house	good	Tepeyolohtli
4.	Cuetzpalin	lizard	good	Huehuecóyotl
5.	Cóatl	serpent	good	Chalchiúhtlicue
6.	Miquiztli	death	evil	Tecciztécatl
7.	Mázatl	deer	good	Tlaloc
8.	Tochtli	rabbit	good	Mayáhuel
9.	Atl	water	evil	Xiuhtecuhtli
10.	Itzcuintli	dog	good	Mictlantecuhtli
11.	Ozomatli	monkey	neutral	Xochipilli
12.	Malinalli	grass	evil	Patécatl
13.	Ácatl	reed	evil	Tezcatlipoca or Itztlacoliuhqui
14.	Océlotl	jaguar	evil	Tlazoltéotl
15.	Cuauhtli	eagle	evil	Xipe Totec
16.	Cozcacuauhtli	vulture	good	Itzpapálotl
17.	Ollin	movement	neutral	Xólotl
18.	Técpatl	flint	good	Tezcatlipoca or Chalchiuhtotolin
19.	Quiáhuitl	rain	evil	Tonatiuh or Chantico
20.	Xóchitl	flower	neutral	Xochiquetzal

day names, Maya The most important element of the Maya calendar was the regular sequence of 20 days, with its attached numbers, 1 to 13. One was meaningless without the other. A specific day was 1 Imix, not merely Imix, followed by 1 Ik, etc. Numbers and days ran concurrently. Since 13 and 20 have no common denominator, the same day name recurred only every 260 days, constituting the *tzolkin*, or ritual year. The combination of the number and day sign determined the luck of the day, but the day name had the dominant influence. Unlike Aztec day names, which plainly related to the glyphic illustrations, some Maya names are unfathomable, some have meanings unrelated to their glyphs. Maya day names follow the same sequence as the Aztec:

ORDER OF DAYS	MAYA NAME (YUCATEC)	GLYPH INTERPRETATION	MEANING OF NAME
1.	Imix	water lily flower	earth monster
2.	Ik	life, breath	life, breath
3.	Akbal	interior of earth	darkness
4.	Kan	maize	ripe maize
5.	Chicchan	celestial snake	celestial snake
6.	Cimi	death-god	death
7.	Manik	hand, scorpion sting(?)	uncertain
8.	Lamat	Venus symbol	uncertain
9.	Muluc	jade, water	collected(?)
10.	Oc	dog	entry (to underworld)
11.	Chuen	uncertain	craftsman
12.	Eb	destructive water	mist, drizzle, rust on plants
13.	Ben	uncertain	uncertain
14.	Ix	jaguar skin, ear	jaguar
15.	Men	old-moon goddess	wise one
16.	Cib	section of shell(?)	wax
17.	Caban	lock of earth-goddess' hair	earth
18.	Etz'nab	knife blade(?)	sharp instrument(?)
19.	Cauac	rain	storm
20.	Ahau	sun-god	lord

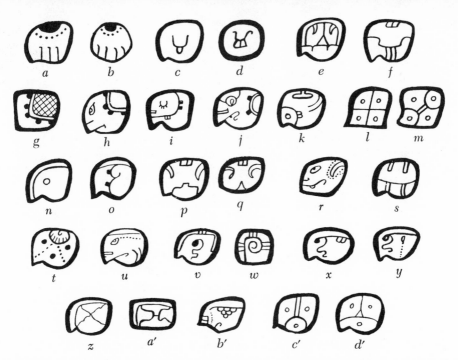

Plate 5a. Maya day signs in the codices: (*a, b*) Imix, (*c, d*) Ik, (*e*) Akbal, (*f*) Kan, (*g, h*) Chicchan, (*i, j*) Cimi, (*k*) Manik, (*l, m*) Lamat, (*n*) Muluc, (*o*) Oc, (*p, q*) Chuen, (*r*) Eb, (*s*) Ben, (*t*) Ix, (*u*) Men, (*v, w*) Cib, (*x, y*) Caban, (*z, a'*) Etz'nab, (*b'*) Cauac, (*c', d'*) Ahau. From S. G. Morley, *An Introduction to the Study of Maya Hieroglyphs*, page 39.

Plate 5b. Maya day signs in the inscriptions: (*a, b*) Imix, (*c*) Ik, (*d, e*) Akbal, (*f*) Kan, (*g*) Chicchan, (*h, i*) Cimi, (*j*) Manik, (*k, l*) Lamat, (*m, n*) Muluc, (*o, p, q*) Oc, (*r*) Chuen, (*s, t, u*) Eb, (*v*) Ben, (*w, x*) Ix, (*y*) Men, (*z*) Cib, (*a', b'*) Caban, (*c'*) Etz'nab, (*d'*) Cauac, (*e', f', g', h', i', j', k'*) Ahau. From S. G. Morley, *An Introduction to the Study of Maya Hieroglyphs*, page 38.

deformation Cranial deformation was common in Mesoamerica; had been practiced by Olmecs in the first millennium before Christ. The head was permanently deformed by binding a small board in an oblique position to the forehead of a newborn child until pressure gave the still plastic cranium the desired form. This practice does not seem to have had any effect on the brain. Other deformations were perforated septa, lower lips, and ears to accommodate adornments. Teeth were filed and drilled for jade inserts. For occasional ritualistic purposes the tongue and other parts of the body were perforated with bone awls or maguey spines to draw blood.

Delicias Early Classic phase of the Tierra Caliente of Michoacán, Mexico.

dendrochronology Science of dating trees, beams, and other timbers by comparing the distinctive sequence of annual growth rings in a specimen with a master sequence established for its region. See also **bristlecone.**

descending god A figure, head down, arms and legs extended, popularly rendered in stucco on building facades on the east coast of the Yucatán peninsula in the Postclassic period. The figure is present at Cobá, Cozumel, and ubiquitous at Tulum where Structure 5 is the Temple of the Descending God. In a region famed for the production of honey, the deity may be Xmulzencab, the Yucatecan bee-gods. More likely it may represent the setting sun, corresponding to Tzontémoc or Cuauhtémoc of the Mexica.

Diablo Earliest cultural phase (nomadic hunters) of the Sierra de Tamaulipas, estimated at 12,000 years ago.

Di Bologna, Codex See **codex, pre-Conquest Mexican; Cospi, Codex.**

diffusion Anthropological term for the spread of a cultural trait from one area or people to another, generally the result of migration, trade, or conquest. See also **acculturation.**

Dili Early Middle Preclassic phase of Chiapa de Corzo, coincident with Chiapa II ceramic period, 1000–750 B.C.

Diquís Southeastern Costa Rica region extending from the Central Valley to the border of Panama, bounded on the north by the Cordillera de Talamanca, on the south by the Pacific Ocean. The Diquís Delta, above the Osa Peninsula, has provided unique spherical granite balls, up to 8 ft. (2½ m) in diameter, of unknown use. Large clay jars, measuring up to 2 ft. (60 cm) at the base and 5 ft. (1½ m) high, presumably for storing *chicha,* have been found. Diquís is also known for its Biscuit ware and small, highly stylized sandstone figures with their arms separated from their trunks by rectangular slits. Cast-gold pendants, enlivened with rows of bangles that often obscure the figure behind them, are stylistically related to Panama.

Diquiyu Archaeological site in the municipality of Tozoatlán in the Mixteca Alta of Oaxaca.

Distance Numbers Many Classic period Maya hieroglyphic texts carry several dates, starting with an Initial Series statement. The Maya evolved a simplified system for arriving at subsequent dates without using the space needed to restate an Initial Series for each date. Expressed in *kins, uinals, tuns, katuns,* etc., and generally placed between the dates they connect, these numbers were added or subtracted to arrive at a date in the Long Count. With exception of the one date fixed by either the Initial Series or the "period ending," all other dates were established by these figures called the Distance Numbers, or Secondary Series.

dolichocephalic See **cephalic index.**

domesticated animals In Mesoamerica there were only five: dog, turkey, duck, bee, and cochineal, a scale insect cultivated on cactus leaves to produce dyestuffs.

Dorenberg, Codex See **codex, pre-Conquest Mexican; Colombino, Codex.**

Dos Pilas Classic Maya site between the Chixoy and Pasión rivers, Guatemala, also called Dos Pozos. An unfinished hieroglyphic stairway is a rare testimony to the sudden interruption of architectural activity at the close of the Classic period.

double-line break Pottery rim decoration consisting of two parallel incised lines, one of which turns up sharply and disappears over the edge. Its broad geographic distribution but limited time span makes it a good Middle Preclassic horizon "marker."

doughnut stones Round perforated stones, probably used as digging-stick weights, found in the Early Classic period of the Guatemalan highlands.

Dresden, Codex See **codex, pre-Conquest Maya; Dresden Codex.**

dualism, religious Manifested itself in Mexican concepts of male and female aspects of a divinity: Tonacatecuhtli and Tonacacíhuatl, Ometecuhtli and Omecíhuatl. In abstract ways they paired day and night, good and bad, life and death. God Tezcatlipoca was black when representing night or war, red to signify day and good. Among the Maya, the sky is male, the earth, female; their intercourse mystically brings life to the world. Light is male, darkness, female, etc.

Dubdo Zapotec god of corn, fifth of the Lords of the Night or underworld. Identified with Aztec Centéotl whose name means corn-god.

duho Ceremonial stool, of either wood or stone, used by the Island Arawak or Taino chiefs. They are low, four-footed, generally with an upward-curving back, often carved in effigy form.

Dulce Guatemalan river furnishing an outlet from Lake Izabal to the Bay of Amatique, Caribbean Sea.

Durán, Diego (1537–88) Spanish-born Dominican friar who lived from childhood in Texcoco and Mexico City. His important work was the *Historia de las Indias de la Nueva España e Islas de Tierra Firma* (History of the Indies of New Spain). Written in Spanish, c. 1579–81, in three parts, illustrated: Part I concerns the history of the Mexica, starting with their migration from Chicomoztoc, through the Spanish Conquest, with special attention given to the dynasties of Tenochtitlán. A portion of this section is based on a lost codex, Cronica X. Part II deals with gods, rites, and native customs. Part III concerns the ancient calendar, including the Calendar Wheel, day signs, and religious festivals of the 18 Aztec months. This work, also called Códice Durán, Durán Atlas, is in the Biblioteca Nacional, Madrid. Popular translations in English are in two separate publications: Part I entitled *The Aztecs* (New York, 1964), Parts II and III, *Book of the Gods and Rites, and the Ancient Calendar* (Norman, Okla., 1971).

Durango Mexican state, with capital of the same name, is enclosed by Chihuahua, Coahuila, Zacatecas, Jalisco, Nayarit, and Sinaloa. Schroeder is the best-known site. See **Chalchihuites.**

Dzahui Mixtec rain- and lightning-god.

Dzibanché The last-known dated Maya inscription, on a jade plaque, is from this site in Quintana Roo, with a date equivalent to A.D. 909.

Dzibilchaltún Extensive archaeological zone in northwestern Yucatán covering more than 18 sq. mi. (c. 46 km²), with some 21,000 temple and habitation sites, occupied from c. 1000 B.C. to the present. Palace Group surrounded the large *cenote,* Xlacah. Temple of the Seven Dolls is rare example of a Maya building with functional windows. Principal axis of the city is defined by a causeway c. 65 ft. (20 m) wide, running east-west for c. 1½ mi. (2½ km).

Dzibilnocac Classic period Maya site of the Chenes region of Campeche with a continuous ceramic history from the Middle Preclassic to the Early Postclassic period. Its main structure of three towers in the Río Bec style, the central one of which supports a simulated temple with false doorways of the serpent-mouth variety, suggests a transition to the Chenes style of architecture.

e

Eagles and Jaguars, orders of Aztec military fraternities pictured in their codices and art. Their mystical origin relates to the sun (eagle) and earth (jaguar), a concept inherited from the Toltecs of Tula. Members were of the highest rank in the most esteemed of Aztec professions—warrior. See also **Malinalco.**

Early Period, Costa Rica Designation of regional cultural sequences of Costa Rica, c. 300 B.C.–A.D. 500. In the Central Highlands, Pavas phase is followed by Curridabat. Línea Vieja was active in the Atlantic watershed, including the newly designated El Bosque phase. In the Diquís area La Concepción phase is followed by Aguas Buenas. In Nicoya Zoned Bichrome is succeeded by the Linear Decorated ceramic phase.

Early Polychrome Ceramic period of Greater Nicoya, c. A.D. 500–800, characterized by the appearance of true polychrome pottery.

earplug After beads, earplugs, or -spools, are probably the most common adornment found in Mesoamerica, dating from the earliest times. The oldest were of baked clay, shell, precious jade, and possibly wood; prominent in Classic Teotihuacán and Monte Albán; the Mexican market at Tlatelolco had them inlaid with mosaics of turquoise and mother-of-pearl. The Mixtecs fashioned them into intricate gold designs; the Guatemalan highlands and western and central Mexico provided fine spools of obsidian. Their most elaborate development was among the Late Classic Maya, as depicted on their monuments and in codices. The most prominent portion of the Classic Maya earplug assembly was the flare, a trumpetlike ring up to 4 in. (10 cm) in diameter, which curved inward to the throat, about 1 in. (2.5 cm) in cross section. A neck and backing plate completed the assembly and held the ornament in the earlobe. Resting against the neck, they caused the flare to face forward.

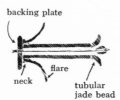

backing plate

flare

neck

tubular jade bead

Classic Maya compound earplug

earth-goddess Three Aztec goddesses, apparently different aspects of the same deity, portray the earth in its dual function of creator and destroyer: Coatlícue (lady of the skirt of serpents), Cihuacóatl (serpent woman), and Tlazoltéotl (goddess of filth).

Eb 1. Twelfth day of the 20-day Maya month, corresponding to the Aztec day Malinalli and the Zapotec day Pija. Eb is the day of the malignant rain deity who sends the mists, dew, and damp weather that produce mildew in crops. 2. Term applied to the earliest pottery finds at Tikal in the Petén of Guatemala, possibly as early as 600 B.C.

Ecab 1. Earliest cultural phase of Yucatán, before 1000 B.C. 2. Maya town visible inland from Cabo Catoche to members of the Córdoba expedition in 1517, which so impressed them that they called it Gran Cairo.

ecacehuaztli Nahuatl word for fan, generally woven of strips of palm leaves; insignia of traveling merchants and their patron deity Yocatecuhtli. For reasons of ceremony or rank, the fan was also made of precious feathers.

Ecatepec Nahuatl for Hill of Éhecatl, state of Mexico; in a cave nearby a polychrome mural painted in the "alfresco" technique was found.

eccentric flint Term applied to flints, sometimes also to obsidian, worked into all sorts of curious shapes. A few are fairly realistic portraits of men, dogs, snakes, and scorpions, but many appear surrealist in concept. They served no useful purpose unless hafted to a ceremonial staff. Usually found in groups in offertory caches beneath stelae and buildings. Manufacture by the Maya seems limited to the areas of the Petén and Belize.

Ecoztli See **Pachtontli.**

Eden Late Preclassic to early Classic ceramic phase of western Honduras, Ulúa-Yojoa region, c. 200 B.C.–A.D. 550.

Edzna Large Classic period Maya site southeast of the city of Campeche. A large plaza, an acropolis, ball courts, and Pyramid of the Four Stories topped by a crested sanctuary are fine examples of Puuc architecture. Stelae date occupation between A.D. 672–810.

Egerton 2895, Codex See **codex, Early post-Conquest Mexican; Sanchez-Solis, Codex.**

ehecailacacózcatl Pectoral in the form of a spiral, obtained by the transverse cutting of a conch shell. An attribute of the god Quetzalcóatl, it is of Huastec origin.

Éhecatl 1. Manifestation of Quetzalcóatl as the wind-god, shown pictorially with bird-beak mask in front of his face. Éhecatl is the Nahuatl word for wind. 2. Second of the 20 Aztec day signs. Corresponds to the Maya day Ik and the Zapotec day Quij Laa. Its patron is Quetzalcóatl; its augury is unfavorable. Calendrical references are: 1 Éhecatl: Iztac Tezcatlipoca, white Tezcatlipoca (Quetzalcóatl); 4 Éhecatl: Xólotl (Quetzalcóatl's twin), also the fourth sun in Aztec cosmology; 6 Éhecatl: the sun; 7 Éhecatl: day of mythical creation of man by Quetzalcóatl; 9 Éhecatl: associated with wind.

Eight Deer Tiger Claw (A.D. 1011–63) Second ruler of the second dynasty of Tilantongo, Oaxaca, he ruled over the Mixteca Alta and to the Pacific province of Tutupec, A.D. 1030–63. Most famous of Mixtec kings, his history is pictured on the reverse of Codex Nuttall, and in Codices Colombino and Becker #1.

Ek Chuah Yucatecan Maya god of merchants and cacao, usually shown traveling with a staff and backpack. Ek means both black and star in Yucatec. He was malevolent as god of war, benevolent as patron of merchants. God M of the codices, in which he appears prominently. Possibly of Putún origin, he was worshiped in the Classic and Postclassic periods. See **Xamen Ek.**

El Arbolillo Middle Preclassic period village site in Guadalupe hills, Valley of Mexico. Gave its name to subphase of the Zacatenco phase, c. 1050–875 B.C.; called Iglesia at Tlatilco.

El Arenal 1. El Arenal phase of the Ahualulco area of Jalisco, lasted to c. A.D. 200, with uncertain beginning. 2. Jalisco pottery type, Arenal Brown, named for its coarse paste; found in shaft tombs in the Magdalena Lake basin. Thick, chunky, powerful bodies characterize the hollow figurines sporting appliqué ear- and nose rings. Bodies are slipped in red with details, such as eyes, in white.

El Baúl Near Santa Lucía Cotzumalhuapa, El Baúl was a prominent site associated with the Cotzumalhuapa Classic phase of coastal Guatemala, strongly influenced from Mexico. The famous Herrera Stela I bears a Long Count date of A.D. 36, which is earlier than any lowland Maya stelae.

El Bosque Ceramic phase of the Early Period in the Atlantic watershed of Costa Rica, c. 300 B.C.–A.D. 500, closely related to the Pavas and Aguas Buenas phases of the highlands. The ceramics are mostly bichrome with red, orange, or dark red pigments applied in zones. Notable are a llama effigy vessel and a fragmentary corncob of South American strain. A radiocarbon date of A.D. 345 ± 165 applies.

elbow stone Served same purpose as a collar stone, but reproduces only the striking surface and decorated section of the belt (*yoke*) used in the Island Arawak ball game of the West Indies. The two tapered arms extending from the tip of the elbow were strapped around the ballplayer's waist with perishable materials.

El Caribe Classic Maya lowland site on the Pasión River, Petén, Guatemala.

El Cayo Classic Maya site on the Chiapas side of the Usumacinta River, between Yaxchilán and Piedras Negras, to which it is artistically linked.

El Guayabo Ceremonial center in the Reventazón River valley of central Costa Rica, active c. A.D. 800–1300; gave its name to a ceramic phase of the Middle Period. Main pyramid, stone pavements, and aqueducts have been excavated. Stone sculptures from there include stone tablets almost 78¾ in. (2 m) high, bordered by figures of birds, monkeys, and jaguars, sometimes accented by patterns in relief guilloche.

El Infiernillo Archaeological phase of the Tierra Caliente of Mexican state of Michoacán, c. A.D. 700. Contemporary with El Romanse of the lower Balsas basin and Chapala of the highlands.

El Jobo Major site on west bank of Melendrez River, east of Ayutla (Ciudad Tecún Umán), at Chiapas border, Guatemala. Large ceremonial structures with stone monuments and plain stelae by the time of the Middle Preclassic period.

El Mirador Maya site of the Guatemalan Petén, near the Campeche border.

El Ocote Ceremonial center in the Central Depression of Chiapas, with massive platform walls of huge squared stone blocks. Chiapa X, c. A.D. 550–950.

El Opeño Preclassic site of northwestern Michoacán, Mexico, with five of the earliest known chambered tombs, possibly dating from 1500 B.C., entered by steps dug into the hard *tepetate;* may be antecedents of the later shaft tombs of the cultures of Jalisco, Colima, and Nayarit. Contained modeled figurines of C and D types found in the Valley of Mexico; vases were decorated in negative painting called *Opeño negativo.*

El Pabellón Maya site on the Usumacinta River, downriver from Altar de Sacrificios, Petén, Guatemala.

El Palmar Late Classic period Maya site in eastern Campeche near Quintana Roo border. Has some of the last dated monuments at the collapse of the Classic period.

El Paraíso 1. Site north of Copán, near the Guatemalan border, in western Honduras. 2. Late Classic to Postclassic site of Guatemalan southern coastal plain.

El Poche Archaeological phase of the lower Balsas basin of Michoacán, c. A.D. 1100.

El Porvenir Classic period Maya site upriver from Altar de Sacrificios on the Pasión River, Petén, Guatemala.

El Puente Archaeological site on upper Chamelecón River, Honduras, between La Florida and Los Higos sites.

El Riego Early Preclassic phase of the Tehuacán Valley, Puebla, c. 6800–5000 B.C. Caves revealed the beginnings of plant domestication to supplement plant gathering and hunting. Ritual burials with offerings and human sacrifice are indicated.

El Romanse Archaeological phase of the lower Balsas basin, Michoacán, c. A.D. 700. See also **El Infiernillo.**

El Salvador Central American republic bounded on the north and east by Honduras, on the west by Guatemala, and on the south by the Pacific Ocean. San Salvador is the capital. Boundaries of the modern state do not represent an archaeological or ethnological region. Western El Salvador was influenced during the Preclassic and Classic periods by the cultures of the Guatemalan highlands, Maya and then Mexican Pipiles. The eastern sector, approximately separated from the west by the lower Lempa River, was dominated by the Lenca group whose presence reached from there north into the Comayagua valley of Honduras.

El Sitio Middle to Late Preclassic period ceremonial site, with plain stelae, some pedestal sculptures, and burials with jade in pottery urns. Appears to have been abandoned before the Classic period. Related to La Victoria and El Jobo, in Guatemala at Chiapas border.

El Tajín Principal ceremonial center of Classic period Veracruz, near modern Tapantla; believed to be the early capital of the Totonacs. Still only partially excavated, the visible site is divided into El Tajín proper and an elevated complex of buildings called Tajín Chico. Its main development dates from A.D. 600 to its subjugation by Toltec-Chichimecs, c. A.D. 1200. Few traces have been found of Preclassic activity.

El Tajín is noted for its architectural emphasis on chiaroscuro, involving niches, friezes of frets, flying cornices, false arches, and flat roofs. The famous Pyramid of the Niches has 365 niches, one for each day of the solar year. Of seven known at the site, the South Ball Court is outstanding, with six carved panels illustrating the ball game and attendant human sacrifice. They portray the typical elaborate scrollwork of El Tajín, employing the "double outline" of two parallel lines that is its hallmark. El Tajín's style borrows recognizably from the Olmec and distant Izapa; during the Classic period contemporary exchanges are noted with Teotihuacán and the Maya. Its ornamented spirals and interlaced outlined ribbons appear on structural carvings as well as on *yokes, hachas,* and *palmas,* ball-game-related items of Veracruz origin, and also on pyrite mosaic mirrors and bas-relief carving. El Tajín influenced the art styles of the Valley of Mexico and cultures as distant as Honduras.

El Taste See **Aztatlán.**

El Tigre Late Postclassic phase of Parita Bay, Panama, c. A.D. 1500.

El Trapiche 1. Preclassic period site in the Chalchuapa zone of El Salvador, near Tazumal, with a 66-ft. (20 m)-high mound in its center. 2. Classic Maya site near Altar de Sacrificios, on the Pasión River, Guatemala. 3. Cultural phase named after the Middle Preclassic site near Cempoala, Veracruz; contemporary with Lower Tres Zapotes.

epcololli Shell ear ornament in the form of a hook, a typical adornment of the god Quetzalcóatl.

epicanthic fold A fold characteristic of eastern Asiatics at the inner corner of the eye, and common among the Yucatecan Maya.

Escalera Middle Preclassic phase of Chiapa de Corzo, coinciding with Chiapa III ceramic period, c. 750–550 B.C.

Escuintla 1. Name of the modern capital and department of the Pacific coast of Guatemala. Found within this area are the Tiquisate culture between the fifth and seventh centuries, and the subsequent Late Classic period Cotzumalhuapa cultural style typified at the site of Bilbao. 2. Late Preclassic site in the Soconusco Pacific coastal region of Chiapas, Mexico.

Eslabones Early Classic phase of the Sierra de Tamaulipas, Mexico, c. A.D. 1–500. House platforms were found around plazas, and some ball courts. Ceramics included modeled and mold-made figurines and vessels of red, black, plain, and brushed finish, often with engraved decoration.

Esperanza Early Classic phase of Guatemalan highlands and El Salvador. Contemporary with lowland Maya Tzakol and Teotihuacán IIIa (Xolalpan) of the Valley of Mexico, c. A.D. 400–600. Following the Aurora phase, Mexican influence made strong inroads. Buildings at Kaminaljuyú were in the Teotihuacán style, tombs contained rich store of jade; lidded slat-legged cylindrical pots and Thin Orange ware were inspired from the north. The Esperanza phase blended the Teotihuacán style were inspired from the north. The Esperanza phase blended the Teotihuacán style such as basal-flanged Tzakol vessels.

Etla Valley northwest of city of Oaxaca, drained by the Atoyac River, and main route of communication to the Valley of Mexico. Important Preclassic period sites include San José Mogote, after which the earliest phase, 1200–900 B.C., was named. Site of Etla itself was Postclassic Zapotec, active after A.D. 1000.

Etzalcualiztli Seventh of the 20-day months of the Nahuatl calendar of 365 days, as celebrated at Tenochtitlán. Feast celebrated the gods of rain Tlaloc and Chalchiúhtlicue.

Etzatlán 1. Town at southern end of Lake Magdalena, Jalisco, near which a large shaft tomb, 52½ ft. (16 m) deep and with three chambers, was discovered on hacienda San Sebastián. Ceramics are believed to date from the time of Christ to c. A.D. 300. The large hollow ceramic figures of the region are chronologically divided into four types: San Sebastián Red, Ojos Variant, Ameca Gray, and El Arenal Brown.

2. Etzatlán phase of the Ahualulco area of Jalisco, c. A.D. 1200–Conquest.

Etz'nab Eighteenth day of the 20-day Maya month. Corresponds to day Técpatl of central Mexico and the day Opa of the Zapotec. Its standard glyph in the Maya codices is a pressure-flaked blade. The day may have been connected with a deity that presided over human sacrifice, possibly god Q. Associated with the number 2.

ex Maya word for breechcloth, same as the Mexican *maxtlatl*.

excising Decorative ceramic technique in which deep grooves, channels, or fields were carved from the surfaces; recessed areas often were left rough and painted with red cinnabar.

f

Fat God Preclassic to Classic period deity of Mesoamerica, especially in Classic Teotihuacán and contemporary central Veracruz. This Falstaffian deity recedes at the end of the Classic; perhaps some of his functions were assumed in the Postclassic period by the Xochipilli-Macuilxóchitl cult of sensuous pleasure.

Feathered Serpent Symbolic name of an important culture-hero and god of Mesoamerica. See **Quetzalcóatl, Kukulcán, Gucumatz.**

Federal District Political subdivision of the Republic of Mexico surrounded by the state of Mexico on the west, north, and east, by Morelos on the south. Contains Tenochtitlán, now Mexico City.

Fejérváry-Mayer, Codex See **codex, pre-Conquest Mexican; Fejérváry-Mayer, Codex.**

figurine A small clay model, usually of a human, and ubiquitous in Mesoamerica. Very popular in Middle Preclassic times, they were mostly solid modeled feminine figures of unknown function, although their use for fertility rites has been suggested. Found at sites such as Tlatilco, they came in many types, which have been classified by letters and sometimes numbers to indicate variations. D-1 is the "pretty lady"; K, the "goggle" type; and the slant-eyed Chupícuaro figurine is H-4. Although rare among the Classic Maya, the realistic and informative genre figurines of the island of Jaina are among the finest expressions of this art form. Small Mesoamerican figurines, especially in Veracruz and at Jaina,

doubled as tiny whistles. See also **Xochipala.**

Filadelfia Archaeological site on the Nicoya Peninsula of Costa Rica.

finca Spanish word for farm, plantation, or ranch in Central America.

Finca Arizona Caches here disgorged tooth-shaped jade pendants of Preclassic and Early Classic horizons; located near Puerto de San José, Pacific coast of Guatemala.

Finca el Paraíso Maya site on southern slope of western Guatemalan highlands where pyrite-encrusted plaques were found dating to the Early Classic period. In the Late Classic it seems to have been the major source of Robles Plumbate pottery.

Fine Orange See **Orange, Fine.**

Fire Ceremony See **New Fire Ceremony.**

fire-god See **Huehuetéotl, Xiuhtecuhtli, Otontecuhtli, gods of the Olmec (I).**

Flacco Cultural phase of the southwest Sierra Madre de Tamaulipas, coeval with Almagre phase of Sierra de Tamaulipas, c. 2200–1800 B.C. Revealed traces of Bat Cave corn; preceramic, peoples were semisedentary macrobands.

flame eyebrows Olmec motif in the form of branched or scroll-like elements representing eyebrows. Characteristic of Olmec gods I and III, sometimes found on god II.

flare Most prominent decorative component of the Maya earplug assembly, usually circular, with face curving inward to a wide trumpetlike throat. Generally of jade in lowland Maya Classic period.

flayed god See **Xipe Totec, Tlazoltéotl.**

"floating gardens" See **chinampa.**

Plate 6. Preclassic clay figurines, chart of interrelationships. From M. Covarrubias, *Indian Art of Mexico and Central America*, page 29.

Floral Park Protoclassic ceramic complex radiating out from Barton Ramie, Belize, as far west as Altar de Sacrificios on the Usumacinta River, c. 100 B.C.–A.D. 300. Intrusive from Honduras and El Salvador. It did not interrupt the cultural process at Tikal and Uaxactún where the Chicanel phase continued to full Classic. True polychrome pottery, combining orange paint and both geometric and conventionalized design. Z-angle bowl with four mammiform supports is distinctive new shape.

Florentine Codex See **codex, early post-Conquest Mexican; Florentine Codex.**

florero Pottery jar with a tall restricted neck and flaring rim, typical of Classic Teotihuacán.

Flores Island capital of the Department of Petén, Guatemala. Generally considered to be the site of Tayasal, last outpost of the Itzá in their resistance to the Spanish Conquest. See also **Canek.**

florescent period A term no longer in favor, it was used to describe the Early Postclassic period in the northern Maya lowlands, c. A.D. 950–1200.

Flowery War War waged by the Aztecs for the purpose of obtaining captives for human sacrifice. Nahuatl word is Xochiyaóyotl; initiated by Tlacaélel during the reign of Moctezuma I.

fluorine test A method of determining the relative age of buried bone. Dating method is based on the measurement of the amount of the fluorine absorbed from ground water that has replaced the original calcium of the bone.

flying panel Descriptive term for a panel of silhouetted figures of men and animals, usually·attached to the underside of the grinding surface and to one leg of the three-legged Costa Rican altars or *metates* carved of volcanic stone.

Fonseca 1. Gulf on the Pacific coast of Honduras, enclosed on the west by El Salvador and on the east by Nicaragua. 2. Middle Period phase of southern Honduras, A.D. 800–1000.

Formative 1. In the pre-Columbian archaeology and art study of Mesoamerica, a term now generally replaced by Preclassic. 2. In lower Central America, a developmental stage characterized by sedentary settlements, agriculture, and craft specialization, along with developed religious concepts verified by funerary offerings and ceremonial structures. The term Preclassic is not employed since it is not followed by a Classic period. A sequence of arbitrary time periods may eventually be adopted that will more closely follow the system used in South America.

"four crossroads" A euphemism, mentioned in the Popol Vuh and books of the *Chilam Balam,* for the entrance to the underworld.

Francesa Middle Preclassic phase of Chiapa de Corzo, Chiapas, coeval with Chiapa IV ceramic period, 550–200 B.C.

g

gadrooning Modeling of pottery with a series of vertical flutings to simulate the appearance of a melon or gourd.

Gavilán Ceramic phase of central Nayarit, c. A.D. 250–500. See also Amapa.

Geche Fourteenth of the 20 Zapotec day names. Its meaning is jaguar, and it is equivalent to the Aztec day Océlotl and the Maya day Ix.

gingerbread A term applied to figurines of solid clay, as opposed to hollow ware, with a flat rendering of the body. Found at Chupícuaro, they were also the most archaic form in Jalisco, although they apparently continued to be made there after new and more advanced techniques were developed.

gladiatorial sacrifice Called *tlahuahuanaliztli* in Nahuatl, it formed part of the celebration of the feast of Tlacaxipehualiztli honoring Xipe Totec during the second of the 18 Aztec months. A valorous victim was bound to the top of a circular gladiatorial stone (*temalacatl*) and made to defend himself against the onslaught of warrior knights. His only weapon was a war club (*macuauhuitl*) on which the dreaded obsidian blades had been replaced by cotton tufts. The custom is believed to be of Oaxacan or Guerreran origin.

gloss An explanatory comment later added onto original native codices, either in Spanish or in a native language; written in European script.

glottochronology A relative dating technique for estimating, by standard comparison of vocabulary samples, the time during which two or more languages or dialects have separately evolved from a common source.

glyph See hieroglyphic writing.

glyph C, Zapotec Of uncertain origin or meaning, this U-shaped element is common to Oaxacan urns. May have its beginnings in the V-cleft observed on some Olmec sculptured heads, or be an abstraction of the mouth of the earth monster. Almost a Zapotec trademark, its generally recognized form is related to Classic Monte Albán IIIb.

glyph, emblem A special symbol identifying a particular Maya center and/or the name of the ruling dynasty, as found on Classic period Maya monuments and stelae.

glyph, false Decorative frieze, generally around the rim of pottery vessels, consisting of elements clearly imitative of Classic period Maya glyphs. The motif appears in El Salvador, Copán (Copador), and on Ulúa-Yojoa polychrome pottery, Honduras.

glyph G The name assigned to the glyph in Maya monumental inscriptions following the Initial Series terminal date and in the seventh position after the introducing glyph. It has nine forms, each one corresponding to one of the Bolon ti Ku, or nine gods of the underworld. It serves to identify the particular god who was the patron of the day determined by the accompanying Initial Series number.

glyph, introducing

The large compound glyph at the head of an Initial Series inscription on Classic Maya stelae, sometimes occupying the space of two or even four glyph blocks. Its constant

introducing glyph, Stela A, Quiriguá

elements are the *tun* sign, the upper affix, and the pair of "comb" symbols, in a few inscriptions replaced by a pair of fish (*xoc*), providing the basis for the word *xoctun* for the introducing glyph. Since the *xoc* and comb signs have the meaning of "count," the total glyph, excepting the variable element, can be translated as "count of the *tuns*." The variable element in the center is the glyph of the deity associated with the 20-day month in which the recorded Initial Series falls.

gods of the Aztec The Mexican pantheon at the Conquest was extensive and complicated by multiple origins and subtle interrelationships. Gods not only had male and female forms, but many different manifestations. The principal deities are listed by spheres of influence to facilitate further study through their individual listings:

1. Major gods: Huitzilopochtli, Quetzalcóatl, Tezcatlipoca.

2. Creative gods: Tloque Nahuaque, Ometecuhtli and Omecíhuatl, Tonacatecuhtli, and Tonacacíhuatl.

3. Fertility gods: Teteoinnan, Tlazoltéotl, Ixcuinan, Toci, Chicomecóatl, Cihuacóatl, Tonantzin, Coatlícue, Centéotl, Xochiquetzal, Xochipilli, Macuilxóchitl, Xipe Totec, Xilonen, Ilamatecuhtli.

4. Gods of rain and storm: Tlaloc, Chalchiúhtlicue, Huixtocíhuatl, Éhecatl, Naapatecuhtli.

5. Fire gods: Xiuhtecuhtli, Huehuetéotl, Chantico.

6. Pulque gods: Mayáhuel, Patécatl, Ometochtli, Tepoztécatl, Tezcatzontécatl, Centzóntotochtin.

7. Gods of the heavens: Tonatiuh, Piltzintécuhtli, Meztli, Tecciztécatl, Mixcóatl, Camaxtli, Itzpapálotl, Tlahuizcalpantecuhtli, Coyolxauhqui, Centzonhuitznahuac, Centzonmimizcoa, Tzitzimime.

8. Gods of the underworld: Mictlantecuhtli, Mictecacíhuatl, Tepeyolohtli, Tlaltecuhtli, Teoyaomiqui, Huahuantli.

9. Other deities: Xólotl, Itztli, Itztlacoliuhqui, Paynal, Yacatecuhtli, Chalchiuhtotolin, Yáotl, Ixtlilton, Cihuateteo, Huehuecóyotl.

gods of the Maya codices Alphabetical designations were given to the gods pictured in Maya codices by P. Schellhas in 1904. These have been most helpful, but a lack of agreement persists about some specific identities.

God A: Death-god, fourth most frequent, shown with death skull and long spine. Of evil influence, he is known as Ah Puch, Yum Cimil, Cizin, and Hun Ahau. Ruled the sixth day, Cimi. His attributes symbolize the number 10; his sign is a % symbol; he is linked with the owl, Moan bird, and dog.

God B: Rain-god, Chac, the "god with the large nose and lolling tongue," is most often depicted. Represented with all four cardinal points, a characteristic shared only with gods C and K, and in one instance, with god F. His day is Ik; he symbolizes the number 6.

God C: Monkey-faced god C probably represents the day Chuen in rebus portraiture. May also be Xamen Ek, the North Star god.

God D: Maya superdeity Itzamná, the Roman-nosed god, second in order of frequency. Often associated with Kin, the sun glyph.

God E: Youthful maize-god, called Ah Mun, third most popular, is the counterpart of the Mexican god Centéotl. Symbolizes the fourth day, Kan, and the number 8.

God F: God of war and human sacrifice, related to god A; resembles Mexican Xipe Totec. Manik is his day.

God G: Sun-god, Kinich Ahau.

God H: Chicchan god. Appears in the Dresden Codex with glyph of day Chicchan ("serpent") on his temple.

Plate 7. Gods of the Aztec: (*a*) Huitzilopochtli: god of the Mexica, Codex Borbonicus, 34, from E. Seler, *Gesammelte Abhandlungen zur Amerikanischen Sprach- und Altertumskunde,* II, page 379, figure 23; (*b*) Tlaloc: rain-god, Codex Magliabecchiano, 89, from Seler, *Gesammelte Abhandlungen,* III, page 342, figure c; (*c*) Quetzalcóatl: god of learning and priesthood, Codex Magliabecchiano, 61, from Seler, *Gesammelte Abhandlungen,* IV, page 111, figure a; (*d*) Tonatiuh: sun-god, Codex Bologna, 12, from Seler, *Gesammelte Abhandlungen,* I, page 345, figure 6; (*e*) Tezcatlipoca: god of providence, Codex Borgia, page 21.

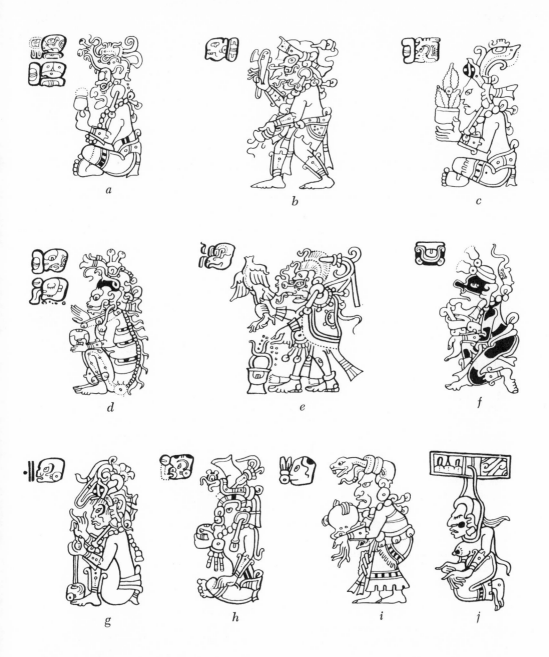

Plate 8. Principal gods of the Maya codices: (*a*) Itzamná, head of the Maya pantheon (god D); (*b*) Chac, the rain-god (god B); (*c*) Ah Mun, the corn-god (god É); (*d*) Ah Puch, the death-god (god A); (*e*) the wind-god, perhaps Kukulcán (god K); (*f*) Ek Chuah, the god of merchants in his aspect of god of war (god M); (*g*) the god of sudden death and of human sacrifice (god F); (*h*) Xamen Ek, the North Star god (god C); (*i*) Ix Chel, the goddess of childbirth and weaving (goddess I); (*j*) Ixtab, the goddess of suicide. From S. G. Morley, *The Ancient Maya*, page 199.

God I: Ix Chel, water-goddess; also of moon, childbirth, procreation, and medicine.

God K: Bolon Dz'acab, the flare-god, related but not identical to god B. Surely represented at Uxmal by masks with flaring protrusions at architectural corners. Perhaps also the serpent-footed deity of manikin scepters. As god of descent, Muluc is his day.

God L: Old black god, perhaps equivalent of the Mexican Mixcóatl. One of the chief lords of underworld, he appears as cigar-smoking god with Moan bird headdress on the doorway of the sanctuary of the Temple of the Cross, Palenque. Akbal is his day.

God M: Ek Chuah, god of traveling merchants, similar to Mexican Yacatecuhtli. Usually shown as an old man with a toothless jaw or a solitary tooth.

God N: God of the end of the year, god of the five *Uayeb* days. Old man identified with Pauahtun and Bacabs, also appears as an Atlantean figure. One of principal rulers of the underworld, patron of the number 5. Frequently identified by a snail shell or turtle carapace, worn on his back, or out of which he is crawling.

God O: Ix Chebel Yax, the old red goddess, spouse of Itzamná.

God Q: Evil god, probably of sacrifice. See **Etz'nab.**

God R: Earth deity, perhaps an anthropomorphic form of the earth monster, shown as a young man. Tentatively identified with Buluc Ch'Abtan.

gods of the Olmec A continuing study of Olmec iconography has tentatively established a pantheon of major Olmec deities. Some of their earlier numerical designations have been eliminated or revised in the face of new evidence:

God I: The Olmec dragon, formerly also referred to as the jaguar monster, is a fantastic creature with cayman, eagle, jaguar, serpent, and human characteristics. Attributes include flame eyebrows, L- or trough-shaped eyes, bulbous nose, cayman jaws and dentition, forked tongue, and jaguar-dragon paw-wing motif. God I is associated with earth, sun, water, and fertility; also linked to royal power and dynastic succession. Olmec dragon seems to be the ancestor of the Maya god Itzamná and possibly the Aztec Xiuhtecuhtli.

God II: The Olmec corn-god is an infant werejaguar; his face has almond-shaped eyes, wide, flat nose, flaring upper lip, and a toothless mouth. Maize symbols sprout from his cleft head, and a complex headband decorates his forehead. God II is associated with corn and other agricultural crops; possibly the antecedent of later Mesoamerican corn-gods such as the Aztec Centéotl.

God III: The Olmec bird monster is a supernatural being with avian and reptilian characteristics. He is usually shown with flare eyebrows, L- or trough-shaped eyes, raptorial beak, prominent cere, and a single, cleft upper fang. Sometimes the feather crest of a harpy eagle decorates the top of his head. The bird monster is shown with paw-wings and his feet are depicted as talons. God III is a deity of the celestial realm with solar associations. He is involved with agricultural fertility; somehow connected with chinless dwarfs.

God IV: The Olmec rain-god is portrayed as an infant werejaguar with almond-shaped eyes, pug nose, flaring upper lip, and a toothless mouth with down-turned corners. A distinctive band decorates his head, crenelated ornaments hang down over his ears. He frequently wears a pectoral with the "crossed-bands" motif. Patron of rain and clouds, he plays important role in fertility ceremonies; antecedent of the Aztec Tlaloc and the Maya Chac.

Olmec god IV

God V: An abandoned designation; its attributes were characteristic of both gods I and IV.

God VI: The Olmec banded-eye god is a mysterious deity usually represented by a disembodied, deeply cleft head. Its eyes are almond-shaped and its mouth toothless with prominent gum ridges. A band or stripe passes through his open eye. God VI may be ancestor to Xipe Totec, the Aztec god of spring and resurrection.

God VII: This divinity is a mythological creature with an avian head crest and wing flap, and a serpentine head and body. Seems to be an aspect of the Olmec dragon, may also be an early version of the Feathered Serpent god of later Mesoamerican peoples.

God VIII: The Olmec fish monster is a supernatural animal with cayman and shark attributes, and not a death-god as previously suggested. Usually has crescent-shaped eye, human nose, cayman's upper jaw and dentition, and a fish's body with fins and a bifid tail. "Crossed-bands" motif sometimes decorates the monster's body. God VIII is associated with standing water and the ocean.

God IX: An abandoned designation.

God X: He is a werejaguar creature with a cleft head, almond-shaped eyes, figure-eight nostril elements, and a toothless mouth with prominent gum ridges. Usually depicted as a disembodied head, his manifestation always occupies a secondary position on complex images.

The Olmec pantheon included several other supernatural animals and spirits, in addition to these major deities.

Golfo Dulce Lake of eastern Guatemala, with outlet to Bay of Amatique, reached by Cortés on his overland expedition from Mexico in 1525. Now called Lake Izabal.

Gran Cairo See **Ecab.**

grater bowl Pottery bowl, usually tripod, with the interior floor roughened by means of incising to provide a

grater bowl (*molcajete*)

surface for grinding seeds, herbs, and chili. Commonly called *molcajete*.

Greater Chiriquí Cultural subarea encompassing the Panamanian province of that name and a large part of adjoining Costa Rica, including the Diquís estuary and Osa Peninsula. Limited exploration has established ceramic phases of La Concepción, 300 B.C.–A.D. 300, Aguas Buenas, A.D. 300–800, including Burica on the Chiriquí Gulf Coast, A.D. 500–800, San Lorenzo on the Gulf Coast, A.D. 800–1200, and "Classic" Chiriquí, A.D. 1200–1500.

Greater Nicoya Cultural subarea comprising Nicoya Peninsula, province of Guanacaste in Costa Rica, and southwest Nicaragua, specifically the isthmus of Rivas and the islands in Lake Nicaragua. Cultural sequence begins with Zoned Bichrome, c. 300 B.C.–A.D. 300, followed by Linear Decorated, A.D. 300–500, and the Early, Middle, and Late Polychrome periods, to Conquest.

Grijalva, Juan de (1489–1527) Captained an expedition sent by Diego de Velásquez, governor of Cuba, in 1518 to seek gold reported by the Córdoba expedition. Grijalva landed on Cozumel, saw Tulum from the sea, skirted the Yucatán peninsula to Campeche, and followed the Gulf Coast as far as the Pánuco River in northern Veracruz. Discovered the Laguna de Términos and the Tabasco River, later renamed the Grijalva River by Cortés in 1519. Died in ambush at Olancho, Honduras, in 1527.

Grolier Codex See **codex, pre-Conquest Maya; Grolier Codex.**

Guacamayo Pottery type that included tall narrow vases of complex profile decorated with incised lines, brush striations, appliqué fillets, and sometimes a band of red paint. Appeared 300 B.C.–A.D. 300 in Azuero Peninsula, Coclé, and Veraguas of Panama. Coeval with scarified pottery. See **Central Panama.**

Guacimo Modern town along the Línea Vieja, eastern Costa Rica. Sites of all periods abound in this locality, especially noted for cemeteries yielding jade, carved stone, and gold. Its basalt statuary, known as "sacrificers," are figures holding an axe in one hand and a severed head in the other.

Guadalupe Middle Preclassic phase of Oaxaca, beginning c. 900 B.C. and eventually blending into the earliest phase of Monte Albán. Close Gulf Coast ties of preceding San José Mogote phase continue, with double-line-break pottery decoration and large hollow figurines as at Las Bocas, Puebla. Solid figurines were type A.

Gualupita Site in Cuernavaca, Morelos, with a long ceramic history. Pottery and figurines of the Middle Preclassic period, contemporaneous with Tlatilco, show Olmec influence; continued with Valley of Mexico contacts into the Postclassic.

Guanacaste 1. Pacific province of Costa Rica, which, combined with the entire Nicoya Peninsula and southwest Nicaragua, composed the Greater Nicoya cultural subarea. Usually considered the southernmost frontier of Mesoamerica. 2. Preclassic phase of Chiapa de Corzo, coeval with ceramic period Chiapa V, 200 B.C.–A.D. 1.

Guanajuato Mexican state bounded by adjoining states of Querétaro, San Luis Potosí, Jalisco, and Michoacán. Contains the Bajío and site of Chupícuaro.

Guápiles Inland terminal of the original Costa Rican railroad, the Línea Vieja, that gave its name to the cultural area of the Atlantic watershed. This area, which included nearby Guacimo, was a sculpture- and jade-producing center, also manufactured objects of gold and *tumbaga* worked in imitation of Panama styles.

Guasave Archaeological site of northern Sinaloa, Mexico. Its name is applied to the most recent and richest phase of the Postclassic Aztatlán complex, A.D. 1200–1400, distinguished by paint cloisonné, turquoise mosaics, iron pyrite beads, onyx and alabaster vases, in addition to intricately decorated polychrome pottery and clay pipes. Motifs reflect the influence of the Mixteca-Puebla culture of central Mexico.

Guatemala Central American republic bounded by Mexico, Belize, the Caribbean Sea, Honduras, El Salvador, and the Pacific Ocean. Its name is derived from the Nahuatl word *quauhtlemallán,* meaning "land of many trees." Guatemala City is its third capital, superseding Antigua, destroyed by earthquake in 1773, and the original colonial capital, nearby Ciudad Vieja, destroyed by volcanic eruption in 1541. The important site of Kaminaljuyú is within the confines of modern Guatemala City.

Gucumatz Quiché Maya name for the Feathered Serpent deity, corresponding to Kukulcán in Yucatecan Maya and Quetzalcóatl in Nahuatl.

Guela Third of the 20 Zapotecan day names; equivalent to the Aztec day Calli and the Maya day Akbal.

Guerra Cultural phase of the Sierra Madre of southwest Tamaulipas, c. 1800–1400 B.C., which developed out of the Flacco phase. Preceramic, population lived in semipermanent villages.

Guerrero 1. Mexican state containing the Sierra Madre del Sur and the Southern Depression. Limited on the north by Michoacán, Mexico, Morelos, and Puebla, on the east by Oaxaca, on the west by Michoacán, and on the south by the Pacific Ocean; includes the Pacific port of Acapulco. The Balsas River and its tributaries supported early settlement and provided the final conquest route for the Aztecs. Known for its fine stone sculptures of jade and other greenstones. Early Olmec influence was followed by Teotihuacán intrusion. Region of Mezcala is particularly noted for its stone carving. 2. Term popularly applied in Costa Rica to male stone figures brandishing a weapon in one raised hand and, frequently, with a trophy head in the other.

Guiengola Large Postclassic site near Tehuantepec, Oaxaca, where the Aztecs suffered defeat by the Zapotec and Mixtec in the 15th century.

Güija Lake on the Guatemala–El Salvador border, with the sites of Azacualpa and Igualtepeque on its shores.

guilloche Decorative motif, an ornamental

braid formed by two or more intertwining bands. Found on ceramic bowls of El Salvador, perhaps related to the Maya mat motif. Carved on some of the Chontales stone sculpture of Nicaragua and on Costa Rican jade figures. Also appears on some Early Polychrome ceramics of Guanacaste, Costa Rica.

h

haab Maya year of 360 days composed of 18 months of 20 days each. It was followed by a period of 5 unlucky days, called *Uayeb,* to arrive at a Vague Year of 365 days. The Mexican equivalent was *xihuitl. Haab* is the same as *tun,* but was occasionally employed in 16th-century Yucatán, and in studies before 1925, to represent the 365-day year.

hacha A wedge-shaped, thin, carved stone, often of intricate design. Frequently tenoned, its use as a marker in the Mesoamerican ritual ball game is suggested. Part of the *yoke-hacha-palma* complex of Classic period Veracruz sculpture. See also **ball game, Mesoamerican; axe, yoke, palma.**

hacha

halach uinic Hereditary top Yucatecan Maya civil ruler, with some priestly functions. Also called *ahau* ("lord"), he ruled aided by a council of leading chiefs, priests, and special councillors called Ah Cuch Cabob. He appointed village chiefs, the *batabs.* In sculpture he is shown holding the double-headed ceremonial bar across his chest, or with the manikin scepter in his hand, symbols of temporal and religious authority.

head variant Maya numerical hieroglyphs occur in two forms in the carved inscriptions: the normal form and the head variant. The former is expressed in bars and dots; the latter is rendered as the head of a deity, man, animal, bird, serpent, or some mythological creature. See **Oxlahun ti Ku; numerical recording, Maya.**

heaven/hell See **universe, Maya; afterlife.**

Hermitage Cultural phase of Barton Ramie, Belize, c. A.D. 100–600.

Herrera 1. Phase of the Parita-Coclé cultural area, c. A.D. 1300–Conquest. 2. South-central province of Panama, bordered by Veraguas, Coclé, the Gulf of Parita, and the province of Los Santos.

hetzmek Ceremony at which Maya children were for the first time carried astride the hip, held by the left hand. The term *hetzmek* is used today to describe this common method of carrying small children. The ceremony was symbolically performed for girls at three months: her destination in life, the hearth, is composed of three stones. For boys it was at four months: the *milpa* he will cultivate has four sides.

hiatus, Classic Maya Between c. A.D. 534–93, the Classic civilization of the Maya lowlands underwent a marked decline in ritual activity, carving, and dedication of Initial Series stelae after 300 years of attachment to the "stela cult." After this hiatus of 60 years, activity resumed for another 300 years. Generally defined in terms of stelae erections, it may have reflected a temporary decline in other aspects of their culture as well. This hiatus probably related to the collapse of imperial authority at Teotihuacán, which had important links to the Classic Maya civilization.

Hidalgo Mexican state north of Mexico City, bordered by states of Mexico, Querétaro, San Luis Potosí, Veracruz, and Tlaxcala. Its capital is Pachuca; its most important archaeological site, Tula.

hieroglyphic writing Writing in Mesoamerica paralleled the typical worldwide stages of development. It began with picture writing, or pictographic glyphs, that clearly depicted the subjects involved. This led to ideographic writing as the next step, in which the glyph became representative, sometimes very abstractly and symbolically, of the idea or thing. Aztec writing seems to have been at the point of arriving at a phonetic system, the third and final stage of writing development, when it was curtailed by the Spanish Conquest. Among the Maya, their hieroglyphs sometimes have phonetic value, but efforts to find a phonetic key to their writing, starting with Bishop Diego de Landa's alphabet in the 16th century, have been unavailing.

Maya hieroglyphic writing employed some 750 symbols, or glyph elements. Partly ideographic, homonyms were used in rebus writing. The limited number of glyphs deciphered are numerical, calendrical, astronomical, along with the identification of certain deities, place names, rulers, and pictured animals and objects. Recently, event glyphs have been separated for the birth, accession, marriage, capture, and death of important personages. A Maya glyph may consist of only one element, or of a main element to which subsidiary elements, affixes, have been attached.

Hieroglyphic inscriptions are carved on stone monuments, on architectural details, on objects of jade, bone, shell, and painted in surviving pre-Conquest codices, on wall murals, and on ceramic vessels of the Classic period. See also **affix, ideogram, pictogram; numerical recording, Aztec, Maya.**

Hispaniola An island of the Greater Antilles comprising modern Haiti and the Dominican Republic. Excavations reveal earliest presence of man in West Indies, perhaps by 5000 B.C. The Taino culture developed there, reaching out to the rest of the Greater Antilles after A.D. 700.

Historia General de las Cosas de la Nueva España See **Sahagún, Bernardino de.**

Historia de las Indias de la Nueva España e Islas de Tierra Firma See **Durán, Diego.**

ho Number 5 in Maya.

Hocaba Cultural phase of Yucatán, c. A.D. 1200–1300.

Hochob Typical, best-studied site with architecture in the Late Classic period Maya Chenes style, in north-central Campeche. Structure 2 is topped by a roof crest formed of two rows of human figures.

hocker Decorative rendering of the human figure, frontal and symmetrical, arms and legs flexed in froglike fashion. Examples are to be found on clay seals of Guerrero, schematic decorations of Tarascan pottery, in ceramic and goldwork motifs of Central America, especially Panama. Aztec and Mixtec codices depict crouching deities in hocker mode.

hocker rendering of Tlaltecuhtli, Codex Borbonicus

Hokaltec A linguistic group of Mexico and Guatemala, represented in Central America by the Subtiaba of northwestern Nicaragua and the Jicaque of north-central Honduras, east of the Ulúa River.

Holactún Maya site of northern Campeche, also called Xcalumkin, source of a coarse black-on-cream Late Classic period pottery.

holcan Mayan soldier.

Holmul Important lowland Maya ceremonial center of the northeastern Petén, Guatemala. Ceramic occupational evidence begins with Protoclassic Holmul I, contemporary with Matzanel at Uaxactún and Floral Park at Barton Ramie. Its unusual polychrome ceramic decoration suggests contact with Late Preclassic Monte Albán, Oaxaca. Remained active through Late Classic Tepeu phase.

homonym Word with the same sound but different meaning, as in rebus writing, was commonly employed in Aztec and Maya writings. Rebus writing was used to overcome the difficulty of expressing an abstract thought. In this way the head of a mythical fish, *Xoc,* was used by the Maya to represent the homonym *xoc,* "count" or "to count." Similarly, the Aztecs used a drawing of teeth (*tlan*) to represent the homonym *tlan,* a "place."

Hondo River with its source in the Petén of Guatemala, which forms the frontier between Belize and Quintana Roo on its course to Chetumal Bay.

Honduras Central American republic, bounded on the north by the Caribbean Sea, on the west by Guatemala, on the southwest by El Salvador and the Pacific Ocean, and on the east by Nicaragua. Tegucigalpa is the capital.

Western Honduras is Mesoamerican throughout its prehistory, whereas eastern Honduras is related to the style and traditions of lower Central America. Western Honduras includes areas drained by rivers that flow south into the Gulf of Fonseca, as well as those drained by the Ulúa River and its tributaries to the north. The far west, with Copán, was culturally a part of the southern Maya lowlands. The Ulúa and Lake Yojoa regions, with Playa de los Muertos, Santa Rita, and Travesia, developed the Ulúa Polychrome that distinguishes western Honduras in the Late Classic. Areas drained by the Aguán, Paulaya, Patuca, and Segovia rivers, flowing to the Caribbean, together with the Bay Islands, define the cultural area of eastern Honduras.

Horcones Late Preclassic phase of Chiapa de Corzo, contemporary with Chiapa VI ceramic period, A.D. 1–100.

horizon A term first applied in the Americas to Peruvian archaeology. It is primarily a spatial continuity presenting cultural traits and assemblages whose nature and mode of occurrence suggest a broad and rapid spread. Cultures linked by a horizon are assumed to be somewhat contemporaneous. A horizon style occupies a great area but a limited amount of time, as opposed to a tradition, which expresses a more limited spread but a longer presence. In Mesoamerica horizons are exemplified by the stylistic influence of the Olmec in Preclassic, Teotihuacán in Classic, and the Toltecs in Postclassic times.

Hormiguero Maya site in the Río Bec area of Campeche.

hotun In Maya time counting, a quarter *katun,* or five years.

Huahuantli See **Teoyaomiqui.**

Huaquero A looter of graves (*huacas*). A word of Peruvian origin, it is now broadly applied throughout Latin America. *Huaqueros* are a major, although illegal, source of pre-Columbian antiquities.

Huasteca Cultural area extending north along the Gulf Coast from the Cazones River in Veracruz to Soto la Marina in Tamaulipas, and including inland southern Tamaulipas, San Luis Potosí, and Hidalgo. Home of the Huastecs, a Maya linguistic group split off from the Mayas of the Yucatán peninsula by the intrusion of other tribes c. 1400 B.C. The stratigraphic sequence on the Pánuco River extends from Early Preclassic to the time of Aztec domination: Pavón: 1100–850 B.C.; Ponce: 850–600 B.C.; Aguilar: 600–350 B.C.; Pánuco I: 350–100 B.C.; Pánuco II: 100 B.C.–A.D. 200; Pánuco III: 200–700; Pánuco IV: 700–1000; Pánuco V: 1000–1250; Pánuco VI: 1250–1521.

The chronicles of the Guatemala Maya refer to Huastec ancestry in the Early Preclassic period (II); Huasteca felt Teotihuacán and Tajín influences in the Classic (III and IV); the Toltecs, the cult of Quetzalcóatl, which may have Huastec roots, and the introduction of clay molds for figurines are manifested in the Early Postclassic (V). Cultural climax was reached at Las Flores and Tamuín during this period; Aztec and Mixtec influences dominated the Late Postclassic (VI), a unique black-on-white pottery style (called Pánuco phase) was its hallmark, especially in effigy vases.

Huatabampo Redware ceramic complex of northern Sinaloa, possibly a mixture of Southwestern and Mesoamerican traits, c. A.D. 900–1200?

huauhtli Mosquito-egg "caviar" harvested from the surface of Lake Texcoco, still occasionally consumed today.

Huave Linguistic group of southeastern Oaxaca.

Huaxtepec Botanical garden created by Moctezuma I near Cuautla, Morelos; now a national park.

hub Maya word for a trumpet made from a conch shell (*Strombus gigas*). See **atecocolli**.

huche Maya word for spear-thrower. See **atlatl**.

Huehuecóyotl The coyote enjoyed a strong cult among the ancients of Mesoamerica. Feather artisans, the *amantecas*, worshiped a god with a coyote as companion (*coyote inahual*). Patron god of the Aztec day Cuetzpalin. His name is often confused with that of the god of fire; he was an enigmatic god of pre-Nahuatl, possibly Otomí, origin.

Huehuetéotl Most ancient of Mesoamerican deities, perhaps originating as Olmec god I. Was the old fire-god, also called Xiuhtecuhtli, with the serpent of fire, *xiuhcóatl*, as his *nahual*. Often shown as a wrinkle-faced, toothless old man bearing a brazier on his head. He occupied first place among the 9 Lords of the Night

Huehuetéotl

(underworld) and the 13 Lords of the Day in Aztec belief.

Huehuetiliztli Period of two Calendar Rounds, or 104 years, in the Aztec count of time. See also **Lubay.**

huéhuetl Aztec three-legged, cylindrical wooden drum, the top covered with a membrane of animal hide, the bottom open. Beaten by hand, it emitted two tones: the higher by striking near the rim of the drum skin, the lower by moving toward the center. The Maya equivalent was *pax;* called *tavenga* among the Tarascans. The Aztec war drum was called *tlalpanhuéhuetl.*

Huehuetlatolli Nahuatl texts of idealized traditions of Aztec life and philosophy, memorized and orally transmitted by the elders on important occasions, prior to the Conquest. An important example of such a text was preserved in writing by Bernardino de Sahagún in Book VI of the Florentine Codex.

Huetamo Postclassic Tarascan site of Michoacán, Mexico.

Huetar Popular generic name, from Huetara, the name of a local chieftain, applied to pre-Columbian artifacts of the Atlantic watershed of Costa Rica.

Huexotla One of the important towns of the Acolhuacán state, originally settled by refugees after the fall of Tula. Near Texcoco, Valley of Mexico, its ruins include a 15-ft. (4½m)-high defensive wall erected A.D. 1409.

Huexotzinco City-state in Puebla, founded by Chichimecs of the same ancestry as the peoples of Tlaxcala; worshiped the same patron god, Mixcóatl-Camaxtli.

Hueymac Last sovereign of Tula. Fled to Chapultepec in A.D. 1168, where he committed suicide according to the Anales de Cuauhtitlán. In the face of conflicting legends, he was most likely a successor to and not a contemporary of Quetzalcóatl.

Hueymiccailhuitl Eleventh of the 18 20-day months, and its feast, as celebrated by the Aztecs at Tenochtitlán. Feast honored the fire-god Xiuhtecuhtli and the patron of merchants, Yacatecuhtli; also called Xocotl-huetzi. The month was represented pictorially by a mummy bundle and/or death symbols. In sacrifice to Xiuhtecuhtli stupefied victims were roasted, and their hearts then torn out. See **months, Aztec.**

Hueypachtli Fourteenth of the 18 20-day months, as celebrated by the Aztecs at Tenochtitlán. Principally dedicated to Tlaloc-Tepictoton, rain deities. Shown pictorially as a *pachtli* plant, an arboreal parasite, as a hill, and as Tlaloc. Alternate names for the period were Tepeilhuitl and Pillahuana. See **months, Aztec.**

Hueytecuilhuitl Ninth of the 18 20-day months, or *veintenas*, celebrated by the Aztecs at Tenochtitlán, dedicated to the maize-goddess Xilonen. Represented pictorially by the "feast day" symbol and/or lords' insignia, the maize deity. Nahuatl word means "great feast of the lords." During the ceremonies the lords feast commoners with food, song, and dance, finally sacrificing impersonators of Xilonen and Cihuacóatl. See **months, Aztec.**

Hueytozoztli Fifth of the 18 20-day months, as celebrated by the Aztecs at Tenochtitlán, honoring the maize deities Centéotl and Chicomecóatl. Represented pictorially by *toctli*, the tender maize plant, with *amatetehuitl*, a paper banner. The fertility ceremony involved a procession of virgins to the temple of the corn-goddess for the blessing of seed and concluded with the sacrifice of the maize-goddess impersonator and children to the rain-god Tlaloc. See **months, Aztec.**

huilacapiztli In the Valley of Mexico, a flute of reed or pottery. In Central America, it refers to the clay ocarinas that reached high development in Nicaragua and Costa Rica. Two animal-shaped flutes from the island of Ometepec in Lake Nicaragua emitted no less than eight pitches each.

huipil Traditional native blouse made of two woven cotton rectangles, often brocaded or embroidered, the typical garb of Maya women even today.

Huistla Postclassic site of the Magdelena Lake basin of Jalisco, c. A.D. 900–1100.

Huitzilíhuitl Mexican ruler, reigned A.D. 1391–1415, son of Acamapichtli. In the face of continuing Tepanec expansion, he subdued the Acolhua to the east, conquering the towns of Texcoco, Acolman, Otumba, and Tulanzingo. Introduced cotton clothing from the tropics; organized lake traffic with fleet of canoes. His name, "hummingbird feather," symbolically relates to the sun, referring to the beauty of the light of day. Married daughter of Tezozómoc, Tepanec ruler of Atzcapotzalco.

huitzilin Nahuatl word for hummingbird.

Huitzilopochtli Exclusively an Aztec god, of war and the sun. Originally a tribal god of the Mexica, he became the patron deity of Tenochtitlán. He is pictured holding his weapon, the fire serpent, *xiuhcóatl* in Nahuatl. His calendrical name was Ce Técpatl ("1 flint"). As one of the four Tezcatlipoca, he is the son of the creator pair Ometecuhtli and Omecíhuatl, according to one myth. In another and popular legend he was also magically born of the earth-goddess Coatlícue. He saved her life by cutting off the head of his sister, the moon-goddess Coyolxauhqui, and dispersing his brothers, the stars, collectively known as Centzonhuitznahuac, because they, together, had plotted his mother's death. In his aspect of the sun he is daily born in the east and descends to the west to illuminate the underworld of the dead. Every morning he renews his struggle with the moon and stars, his victory assuring a new day of life for man. He is conveyed to the sky's center by the souls of fallen warriors. Souls of women who died in childbirth assume his conduct to the west, where his descent is visualized as an eagle falling to earth. He symbolizes the struggle of the Mexicas, "people of the sun," chosen to be warriors. As the god of war he was nurtured by the cult of human sacrifice.

Huitzilopochtli was also the name of the

Aztec tribal god who led them from their homeland, Aztlán. After centuries of migration the eagle, the symbol of Huitzilopochtli, alighted on a cactus on an island in the lake of the moon, Meztliapán, later called Lake Texcoco, thus founding Tenochtitlán.

Huitzilopochtli, Codex See **codex, early Mexican post-Conquest; Ríos, Codex.**

Huitzlampa Fourth quarter of the Aztec universe: the South; the place of the cactus thorns used in human sacrifice; the land of the sun. Assigned color was white; animals, the parrot and rabbit. The fourth sky bearer, in the southern position, was Mictlantecuhtli. Xipe Totec and Macuilxóchitl, deities of regeneration, spring, and flowers, were also associated with the South. Day signs assigned to Huitzlampa were Xóchitl, Malinalli, Cozcacuauhtli, and Tochtli, the last also serving as the year sign. See also **cardinal points.**

huitztli Thorn or spine of the maguey plant, used to draw blood in ceremonial self-sacrifice. Commonly shown in the Aztec codex representations of Quetzalcóatl's headdress, in combination with an *ómitl*, a bone awl used for the same purpose.

Huixtocíhuatl Sister-goddess of the Tlalocs, also related to Tlazoltéotl. Inventor of salt. Represented among four women who gave themselves to the youth impersonating Tezcatlipoca before he was sacrificed in the Aztec festival of Tóxcatl.

hun Number 1 in Maya.

Hunab Ku Supreme, invisible, single creator god of the Yucatec Maya. Possibly an Early Postclassic abstraction of priests; not generally venerated, he was thought of as the father of Itzamná, the most important recognized deity of the Maya pantheon.

Hunac Ceel Head chief of Mayapán who brought the Triple Alliance of Mayapán-Izamal-Chichén Itzá to an end, initiating the hegemony of Mayapán in Yucatán, c. A.D. 1200. He subjugated Chichén Itzá after dramatically diving into the sacred *cenote* and emerging with the prophecy of his own destiny. Also called Cauich.

Hun Ahau Name for a Maya death-god who was associated with Ah Puch.

Hunahpú 1. Twentieth day of the 20-day month of the Quiché Maya of Guatemala. Corresponds to Ahau of the lowland Maya of Yucatán. 2. In the Popol Vuh, the sacred book of the Quiché Maya, Hun Hunahpú and Vucub Hunahpú were sons of the mother-goddess Xmucané. They were defeated by the gods of Xibalba, the underworld, and sacrificed. The head of Hun Hunahpú was hung among the fruits of a calabash tree as a trophy. A daughter of one of the lords of Xibalba, tempted by the forbidden fruit, was impregnated by spittle from the trophy head and became mother of the hero-twins Hunahpú and Xbalanqué. The twins repeated their father's and uncle's visit to the underworld, but after dreadful trials defeated the lords of Xibalba, themselves then becoming heavenly bodies, the sun and moon. 3. Ancient name of a volcano in the Guatemalan highlands; renamed Agua by the Spanish after an eruption-generated flood destroyed their first capital (today called Ciudad Vieja) in 1541.

Hun Chabin Late Classic period mound, with sculptured monuments, near the town of Comitán, Chiapas.

Huntichmul Archaeological site in northeastern Campeche.

huun Maya word for the wild fig tree (*Ficus cotoni folia*) whose inner bark was utilized to produce native paper; also applied to bark paper and books. Corresponds to the Nahuatl term *amatl.* See also **bark paper.**

i

ichcahuipilli Aztec quilted cotton tunic; armor worn by warriors.

Ichpaatun Middle and Late Postclassic site in Quintana Roo, on the Bay of Chetumal, reflecting the decadent Mayapán period.

icpalli Nahuatl word for chair, symbolic of authority, as seen in the codices. Variations include the *cuauhicpalli,* a throne decorated with eagle feathers and, usually, jaguar skin; the *teoicpalli,* depicted in manuscripts, is the seat of the gods in a temple.

ideogram A complex writing method symbolically expressing an idea that was employed by Aztecs and Maya alike. The Aztecs used some arbitrary symbols with no apparent relation to the subject, such as a small pennant to signify 20, a feather to denote 400, etc. Less ambiguously, conquest was rendered by a place-name glyph with a spear thrust into it, or by a temple on fire. Among the Maya, glyphs can take two distinct forms: one is the basic "head form," the other a symbolic, ideographic form that serves to recall the basic glyph. Cimi, death, can be shown directly as a death's-head or by an ideogram resembling our % sign, an attribute of the death-god that is often shown on his body or clothes.

Iglesia See **El Arbolillo.**

Iglesia Vieja Early and Middle Preclassic site in Morelos, Mexico, where excavations produced large quantities of identifiable figurine fragments that were radiocarbon-dated c. 1450–850 B.C.

Igneri Name given by 16th-century Carib Indians to conquered Arawaks of the Lesser Antilles. Sometimes also applied to the Arawaks who preceded the development of the ceremonial Taino culture in the Greater Antilles. Eyeri is a variant of the name, often also used for the distinctive Arawak dialect of the Lesser Antilles.

Igualtepeque Site on the El Salvador shore of Lake Güija, near the Guatemalan border.

iguana house See **Itzamná.**

Ihuatzio Tarascan site opposite Tzintzuntzan on Lake Pátzcuaro, Michoacán. Known for its *yácatas* and stone sculptures of coyotes rearing up on their hind legs.

Ik 1. Second of the 20 Maya day signs, corresponding to the Aztec day Éhecatl. T-shaped sign prominent in its glyph also appears in the name glyph of god B of the codices. Associated with the rain-god and number 6. See **Year Bearer.** 2. Maya wind-god, whose four helpers were collectively called Iques. 3. 110-day period in the Pokom Maya calendar.

Ilamatecuhtli An ancient lunar deity associated with the earth and the maize crop; goddess of the old dry ear of corn. Patron of the feast of Títitl, 18th of the 18 annual Mexican feasts, as observed at Tenochtitlán. Is 13th of the 13 Lords of the Day. See also **Centéotl.**

Ilhuicatl See **universe, Aztec.**

ilhuitl 1. Two reversed scrolls, a characteristic incised Olmec pottery design. 2. Aztec hieroglyph for day or feast.

Ilusiones Late Preclassic and Protoclassic ceramic complex of the Cotzumalhuapa region of Pacific coastal Guatemala, c. 350 B.C.–A.D. 100. Coeval with Miraflores-

Arenal and Santa Clara at Kaminaljuyú, and Chicanel and Matzanel at Uaxactún.

Imix First of the 20 Maya day signs, equivalent to the Aztec day Cipactli. Has associations with earth, water, water lilies, crocodiles, plenty, vegetation, and beginning. Associated with the number 5.

incensario Originating in the Early Preclassic period, the rendition of incense burners

ladle *incensario*

became more elaborate in form. The "old god," seated with a round receptacle on his head, is identified with Teotihuacán. At Monte Albán they became complicated renditions of deities. In the form of ladles, *tlemáhuitl,* they were popular in the Mixteca-Puebla culture, as they had also been among the Maya. Early Chiapa de Corzo *incensarios* had "inner horns" rising about a hole in the center of a low vessel's bottom. See also **urns of Oaxaca.**

incised decoration Pre-Columbian pottery decoration, achieved by using a pointed instrument of wood, bone, stone, or shell to cut lines on a vessel's surface. It was sometimes applied on top of the slip after firing, occasionally before application of the slip.

Indian Church Late Postclassic site of Belize. Buildings display Mexican influence. Incense burners have Mayapán-Tulum affinities. Also called Lamayna.

Infiernillo 1. Cultural phase of the lower Balsas region of Michoacán, c. 700 B.C. 2. Phase of the Sierra Madre of southwest Tamaulipas, 7000–5000 B.C.

infix Detail added to interior of a glyphic element, as in Maya hieroglyphic stone carvings. See **affix.**

Initial Series (I.S.) 1. Maya calendrical count, so called because it was the first series of glyphs after the "introducing glyph" inscribed on stelae. See **Long Count.** 2. A term also formerly applied to the Classic period of lowland Maya civilization, contemporary with the employment of Initial Series dating on monuments, c. A.D. 300–900.

inscriptions A term applied to hieroglyphic

writing when carved in stone or wood, as opposed to its painted rendering in codices.

Intermediate Area A geographic definition of the area and cultures lying between the two New World civilizations of the Central Andes and Mesoamerica. It embraces Central America south and east of Guatemala and northwestern South America, what is now Colombia and Ecuador. Although political development in the area did not go beyond that of chiefdoms, it produced the earliest known pottery of the New World in Ecuador. The outstanding goldworking techniques of Colombia and Panama did not reach Mesoamerica until centuries later.

Irazú Active volcano and tourist attraction in central Costa Rica. Site of Retes on its slope yielded vast stores of stone and wooden ritual objects dating c. A.D. 960.

Isla Conchagüita Island in the Gulf of Fonseca, El Salvador, produced polychrome pottery. Occupied at the time of the Conquest and beyond. Conchagua Vieja is the site with stone house mounds.

Isla de Sacrificios Postclassic site on an island off the modern Gulf Coast port of Veracruz. Period I there, c. A.D. 900–1200, was the twilight of the "smiling figures" tradition in pottery whistles. Periods II and III showed Mixteca-Puebla ceramic influence, an abundance of Fine Orange and Plumbate.

Isla Mujeres Off northeast coast of the Yucatán peninsula; its name, Spanish for "island of women," was inspired by the number of female idols encountered there by early explorers.

Isla Villalba Island in the Gulf of Chiriquí, Panama, where stone pillars ornamented on top by small animal or human figures probably date from the Burica phase, A.D. 300–800. They reflect the northern Preclassic tradition, suggesting cultural intrusion from northern Central America.

Islona de Chantuto Pacific coastal shellmound site in Chiapas dating to preceramic period, 7000–2000 B.C.

Isthmus of Tehuantepec Natural depression in waist of Mesoamerica; only 124 mi. (200 km) wide at that point, is often thought of as the natural frontier between North and Central America. Extends from the Veracruz Gulf Coast plains to the Pacific plains of Oaxaca.

Istmo Late Preclassic phase of Chiapa de Corzo, coinciding with Chiapas VII ceramic period, c. A.D. 100–200.

Itsimte Classic Maya site of central Petén, Guatemala.

Itzá Name applied in Yucatán to the aggressive seafaring branch of the Putún, also called the Chontal Maya, of the Chontalpa area of Tabasco-Campeche. As the "Phoenicians of the New World," they had already established themselves on Cozumel Island when they first invaded Yucatán from the east in A.D. 918, conquering Uucilabnal, renamed Chichén Itzá. Bilingual, closely allied to the Mexicans by trade, they subsequently renewed contact overland with their homeland and were ready to receive the refugees from Tula, presumably under the leadership of Quetzalcóatl (Kukulcán) by A.D. 897. The second invasion, this time from the west, began the Toltec domination of Chichén Itzá. The Itzá during this period established the rival city of Mayapán. By A.D. 1200, under the leadership of Hunac Ceel, Mayapán subdued Chichén Itzá, dominating Yucatán until its own demise c. A.D. 1450. The Itzá persisted, emigrating south where they resisted the Spanish Conquest at their island fortress of Tayasal in Lake Petén-Itzá, Guatemala, until 1697.

Itzamkanac Capital of the Acalán branch of the Putún Maya, on the Candelaria River, Campeche. Believed to be near the modern settlement of El Tigre. Probably visited by Cortés on his Honduras expedition, 1524–25.

Itzamná 1. Supreme Maya deity whose name means "iguana house," was god of creation, the sky, and the earth, abundantly represented in Classic and Postclassic art. Always benign, had celestial and terrestrial manifestations. Father of science and the arts, he is pictured as an old man with a prominent Roman nose and a single tooth.

God D of the codices, patron of the month Zip and the day Muluc. All other gods stem from him and the creator-goddess Chebel Yax. 2. As a Maya concept of the universe, iguana house was primarily a reptilian configuration in which giant iguana (*itzam*) bodies form the walls and roof of a house (*na*), continuing their course to form the floor, too, generally interpreted as the earth's surface.

Itzan Classic Maya site on a tributary of the Pasión River, Petén, Guatemala.

Itzcóatl Aztec king, A.D. 1427–40, uncle of Chimalpopoca whom he succeeded after his assassination by the Tepanecs. Brother-in-law of Ixtlilxóchitl of Texcoco with whom he united to conquer the Tepanecs of Atzcapotzalco, thereby starting the Aztecs on their road to empire.

Itzcuintli 1. Tenth of the 20 Nahuatl day signs, signifying dog; equivalent to the Maya day Oc and the Zapotec day Tella. Mictlantecuhtli was its patron, with a favorable augury. Calendrical names of gods related to this day are: 1 Itzcuintli: name for Xiuhtecuhtli; 5 Itzcuintli: name for Mictlantecuhtli; 9 Itzcuintli: name for Chantico; 13 Itzcuintli: name for Tlahuizcalpantecuhtli. 2. The name is also applied to a breed of dog domesticated and eaten by the Aztecs, often offered in sacrifice. The Mesoamerican belief that dogs guided the dead across the river into the underworld caused them to be buried with the dead. See also **Xólotl, tepescuintli.**

Itzehecayán See **universe, Aztec.**

Itzpapálotl Of Chichimec origin, the earth-goddess, consort of Mixcóatl, their principal god. Nahuatl name means "obsidian butterfly." She was regent of the 16th of the 20 Nahuatl days, Cozcacuauhtli. Is also represented as one of the Tzitzimime, provided with jaguar claws.

Itztapal Nanatzcayán See **universe, Aztec.**

Itztepetl See **universe, Aztec.**

Itztlacoliuhqui Alternate name for Tezcatlipoca as the deity of ice and cold, of sin and misery, the black Tezcatlipoca and the patron of day Ácatl.

Itztli Second of the nine Lords of the Night;

surrogate of Tezcatlipoca in the guise of a sacrificial knife. Nahuatl for "obsidian knife."

Ix 1. Fourteenth day of the 20-day Maya month, corresponding to the Aztec day Océlotl. Day is related to the Jaguar god; in glyphs, circles represent the spots on a jaguar's skin. 2. Maya feminine prefix, sometimes rendered simply as X. Counterpart of Ah, the masculine prefix.

Ixcatec One of the Mixtecan subdivisions of the Oto-Zapotecan language family; a minority group of Oaxaca.

Ix Chebel Yax Goddess O of the Maya codices, the old red goddess, spouse of Itzamná, the creator-god. Patron of painting, brocading, and weaving. Corresponds to Toci or Coatlícue of the Mexica.

Ix Chel Leading Putún Maya deity with important shrine on Cozumel Island. Goddess of the moon, wife of the sun-god Kinich Ahau. Goddess of water with dual aspects: source of life-giving rain and disastrous floods. As the goddess of childbirth, procreation, and medicine, she was the counterpart of the Aztec Tlazoltéotl and Coatlícue. Goddess I of the codices, shown as a female warrior with lance and shield, surrounded by symbols of death and destruction. Caban is her day.

Ixcuinan An aspect of the Aztec goddess Tlazoltéotl, probably introduced to the Valley of Mexico from the Huasteca.

Ixcuintla Archaeological region of Nayarit, western Mexico; source of "Martian" *chinesco* hollow figurines. The name is also applied to a phase of Amapa, Nayarit, c. A.D. 1300.

Ixil 1. Maya town in Yucatán. See also *Chilam Balam*. 2. Mayas of the Mam language group found in departments of Quiché and Huehuetenango, Guatemalan highlands; Nebaj is a major site.

Iximché 1. Fortress capital of the Cakchiquel Maya of the Guatemalan highlands; fell to the Spanish conqueror Pedro de Alvarado in 1524. 2. Native word for the breadnut tree (*Brosimum utile*), *ramón* in Spanish.

Ixkun Classic Maya site, Petén, Guatemala.

Ixlu Late Classic Maya site, central Petén, Guatemala.

Ixtab Maya goddess of suicide, shown in the codices suspended by a rope noose. May be an aspect of the goddess Ix Chel.

Ixtapaluca Early Preclassic site and ceramic phase of the Valley of Mexico, c. 1500–1150 B.C., whose components are known at Ayotla (Tlapacoya) and Tlatilco.

Ixtapantongo Rock paintings, c. 165 ft. (50 m) long and c. 50 ft. (15 m) high, on a palisade at this site in the state of Mexico depict Toltec warriors, gods, and ceremonies.

Ixtlán del Río Southern Nayarit site occupied from the beginning of our era until A.D. 1500. Name of a subcategory of the southern Nayarit figure style. Large hollow figures, models of houses and temples, are found in the tombs. Ixtlán polychrome dates from c. A.D. 250–550. The site contains the Postclassic circular temple of Quetzalcóatl.

ixtle Nahuatl word for maguey.

Ixtlilton Aztec god of health and medical cures; also associated with the dance, the dark brother of Macuilxóchitl and Xochipilli.

Ixtlilxóchitl King of Texcoco, 1409–18. Assassinated by Tezozómoc of Atzcapotzalco; his famous son, Nezahualcóyotl, became an ally of Tenochtitlán and assisted in ending Tepanec rule of the Valley of Mexico.

Ixtutz Late Classic Maya site, southeastern Petén, with several temples and plazas, connecting causeways, and inscribed stelae.

Izabal Guatemala's largest lake. It narrows to form El Golfete, connected with the Caribbean Sea by the Río Dulce where Nito was an important Postclassic trading center.

Izalco Pipil People of Nahuat origin whose culture showed Teotihuacán and El Tajín traits, arrived c. A.D. 300 in western El Salvador, settling the area around Izalco. Other Pipil invasions followed.

Izamal Supported by the nearby salt beds of the northern Yucatán coast, Izamal was a prosperous Maya center from Early Classic times to the fall of Mayapán. Buried under the church of Nuestra Señora de Izamal are the remains of a large pyramid-temple, Kinich-Kakmo, dedicated to the sun-god. It resembles the similar situation of a modern church superimposed on an ancient pyramid at Cholula, Puebla. Chichén Itzá, Mayapán, and Izamal constituted the League of Mayapán until the fall of Chichén Itzá c. A.D. 1200.

Izapa Important Preclassic site of southeastern Chiapas at the Guatemalan border, gave its name to a distinctive art style that peaked c. 150 B.C. Influenced by the Olmec, its new narrative style of relief carving, emphasizing softer curved lines and more violent, elaborate compositions, appeared on stelae and altars. Among the Izapa cult motifs are trophy heads, U-shaped symbols, scroll-eyed dragon masks, descending sky deities, the "long-lipped" god, and the ubiquitous brandished weapon. Glyphs, undeciphered, appear ancestral to Maya writing; they provide the earliest New World written dates, between 35 B.C.–A.D. 36. Influence of the Izapan style is noted at Tres Zapotes, Veracruz; at Kaminaljuyú, Guatemalan highlands, and prefigures the later stone carving in the Maya lowlands.

Izcalli Means "resurrection" in Nahuatl, was the first of the 18 months of the calendar of 365 days, as celebrated at Tenochtitlán. Dedicated to the god Xiuhtecuhtli; every four years his impersonators were sacrificed. Other names for this month and its feasts, referring to separate rituals, were Huauhquiltamalcualiztli ("eating of stuffed tamales"), Izcalli Tlami ("end-Izcalli"), Xochitoca ("plants, flowers"), Xóchilhuitl ("flower feast day"), and Pillahuanaliztli ("drinking of children").

Iz Mictlán Opochcalocán See **universe, Aztec.**

Iztaccíhuatl Snow-peaked extinct volcano, 17,300 ft. (c. 5,300 m) high, of the Sierra Ajusco range that contains the Valley of Mexico to the southeast. With the meaning of "white lady" in Nahuatl, it was worshiped as a manifestation of the mother-goddess who dressed in white.

j

Jacalteca Maya language of the Kanhobol group, spoken in the Department of Huehuetenango, Guatemala.

Jacona Postclassic Tarascan site, Michoacán, Mexico.

jade Brought to Europe in the 16th century, before Chinese jade was known there, by the Spanish conquerors of Mexico. They called it "piedra de ijada," loin stone, root of the word *jade*. Often applied to ancient lapidary work generally, which is predominantly in some kind of greenstone.

Mineralogically, jade may be jadeite, nephrite, or chloromelanite. Nearly all Mesoamerican jade is jadeite, a silicate of sodium and aluminum ($NaAlSi_2 O_6$), often mixed with other minerals. Only known source is in Motagua River valley of Guatemala, but worked jade is found to some extent throughout Middle America and the Greater Antilles, especially in the Valley of Mexico, Oaxaca, the Olmec and Maya regions, and Costa Rica. Principal worked forms were celts, beads, ear ornaments and pendants, figurines in Olmec, Mezcala, and Maya areas, and, rarely, masks among the Maya. Piecing of mosaic work produced larger pieces such as the magnificent life-sized funeral mask of Palenque.

jaguar-dragon paw-wing Olmec decorative pottery motif composed of two separate elements. The jaguar-dragon is a profile head of Olmec god I,

jaguar-dragon paw-wing motif

showing his flame eyebrows, upper jaw only, and bracket gum markings. The paw-wing, representing the thumb and digits, is frequently shown alone on Tlatilco ceramic vessels; when in combination with the jaguar-dragon it is always to the left of the head.

Jaguar god Maya god of the number 7 and the day Akbal.

Jaina Late Classic period ceremonial and cemetery site on an island off the northern Campeche coast of the Yucatán peninsula. Delicately modeled small polychrome figurines, uncommon in the Classic period, provided a wealth of information on Maya dress and ceremonial regalia. Glyphs in stone date the occupation at least as early as A.D. 652.

Jalapa 1. City in Veracruz where the University of Veracruz museum combines outdoor and indoor displays of Veracruz stone sculpture with an outstanding exhibit of ceramics of the region. Cortés passed through in 1519 on his way to Tenochtitlán. 2. Departmental capital east of Guatemala City.

Jalisco Mexican state bordered on the north by Durango, Zacatecas, and Aguascalientes, on the east by San Luis Potosí, Guanajuato, and Michoacán, on the south by Colima and the Pacific Ocean, and on the west by Nayarit. Guadalajara is its capital.

Known for pre-Hispanic shaft tombs rich in ceramic sculpture. Jalisco gave its name to a style of western Mexican pottery, along with Colima and Nayarit; all three formerly and erroneously grouped as Tarascan. Most characteristic ceramics are hollow, highly burnished cream-colored clay figures from the Ameca-Zacoalco zone, with elongated head, sharp nose, eyes of round gray pellets, and hands that are usually extended, palm outward. Often turbaned, many with shoulder scarification, the women's breasts are usually tattooed with geometric designs. For Jalisco pottery types, see **Ameca, El Arenal, San Sebastián Red.** Some prominent sites are in the Lake Magdalena basin: Autlán, Tuxcacuesco, Barra de Navidad. See **Etzatlán.**

Jaral Preclassic phase of western Honduras, c. 500–200 B.C. Identified with the site of Los Naranjos at Lake Yojoa and discovery there of Olmec artifacts.

Jenney Creek Cultural phase of Barton Ramie, Belize, to c. 500 B.C.

Jicaque Non-Maya linguistic stock, astride the Chamelecón and Ulúa river valleys of northern Honduras. Their culture blends Mesoamerican with South American traits.

jícara Modern Spanish word for a bowl made from the gourd of a calabash tree; *xicalli* in Nahuatl.

Jimbal Classic Maya site of the central Petén, Guatemala.

Jiquilpán Classic site of northwest Michoacán, contemporary with Teotihuacán III.

Jiquipilas Early Classic phase of Chiapa de Corzo, coeval with Chiapa VIII ceramic period, c. A.D. 200–350.

Jocotal Early Preclassic Soconusco phase, transitional between Cuadros and Conchas I, c. 850 B.C. The first coastal construction of clay platform houses and pyramidal mounds seems to date from Jocotal.

Jonuta On the Usumacinta River in Tabasco near the Campeche border; it was a stopover for the canoe trade to Yucatán. Fine Orange pottery is believed to have originated in the Tabasco–southwestern Campeche area; type "Z" (Balancan) was made at Jonuta. The fine Classic figurines, many untempered, were as highly prized as those of Jaina, whose mold-made figurines shared the Fine Orange type of paste. The style is linked artistically to Palenque.

Justo Subphase of Preclassic period Tlapacoya, Valley of Mexico, c. 1050 B.C.

Juxtlahuaca Three rock paintings in the Olmec style are found in a cave here, about 3,300 ft. (1,000 m) from the entrance. The largest polychrome mural shows a standing figure facing a smaller, seated, bearded man; the second painting is of a serpent whose eyes contain a Saint Andrew's cross motif, and superimposed flame eyebrows; and the third mural shows an animal, probably a jaguar. It was the first known Olmec mural when discovered in 1966. It was followed by the finding of the Oxtotitlán cave in the vicinity, in 1968. Both cave paintings are dated between 900–700 B.C. East of Chilpancingo, Guerrero.

k

Kabah Maya site near Uxmal whose palace group includes the spectacular Codz-Poop whose c. 150-ft. (45 m)-long facade is made up entirely of identical sculptured Chac masks placed side by side and tier upon tier, for an effect of baroque ostentation. Other structures include Teocalli, Temple of the Meanders, and an archway reputed to mark the beginning of a causeway to Uxmal. Architecture is related to Puuc; pottery to the Cehpech ceramic complex. Site was occupied c. A.D. 650–900.

Kaminaljuyú Important archaeological site within the limits of modern Guatemala City; was the central seat of civic, religious, and political power of the highlands throughout the Preclassic and Classic periods. In the Early Preclassic it was a scattered habitation site, lacking mounds, but already with high-quality monochrome and some bichrome ceramics, finally offering fine kaolin ware.

During the Middle and Late Preclassic periods, Kaminaljuyú was oriented in a roughly north-south direction, in an avenue pattern with huge brightly painted earthen mounds, richly furnished tombs, bottle-shaped storage pits, and plain stelae. In ceramics, the *incensario* cult flourished, hand-modeled figurines in the archaic style were numerous, Usulután ware was popular. Stone sculpture was the finest ever produced in the highlands, including large boulder heads, tenoned silhouette carvings, censers, mushroom stones, and lapidary work including jade.

The Early Classic period introduced temple mounds arranged around plazas, ball courts appear, Teotihuacán influence shows in the *talud-tablero* architectural style, in ceramics with cylindrical tripods with slab legs, Thin Orange, and introduction of the mold process. The stela cult and figurines disappear. The Mexican intrusion is accompanied by their pantheon of gods. Kaminaljuyú seems to have become a colony of Teotihuacán, which may have imposed an elite governing class.

In the Late Classic period the decline of Kaminaljuyú begins, culturally and as the regional focus, ending with abandonment of valley sites in favor of protected hilltop locations throughout the highlands. Ceramics are represented by Tiquisate cream-colored ware, double-chambered, mold-decorated human effigy censers, San Juan Plumbate, Z and Y Fine Orange ware. Clay figurines and effigy whistles disappear. Jade ornaments are fewer, more varied in style.

During the Early Postclassic, the highlands produced X Fine Orange and Tohil Plumbate, which disappeared abruptly c. A.D. 1200. Ceramic development at Kaminaljuyú has suggested a concurrent production of ceremonial luxury ware, perhaps reflecting outside influence on the ruling class, and a more local utility ware for general use. A so-called Kaminaljuyú ceramic sequence is applied generally in the Guatemalan highlands:

Early Preclassic	Arévalo	to 800 B.C.
	Las Charcas A	800–600 B.C.
Middle Preclassic	Las Charcas B	600–500 B.C.
	Providencia	500–400 B.C.
	(Majadas)	(450–350 B.C.)
Late Preclassic	Miraflores-	400 B.C.–
	Arenal	A.D. 100
Protoclassic	Santa Clara	A.D. 100–300
Early Classic	Aurora	A.D. 300–400
	Esperanza	A.D. 400–600
Late Classic	Amatle	A.D. 600–750
	Pamplona	A.D. 750–900
	Ayampuc	A.D. 900–1200
Protohistoric	Chinautla	A.D. 1200–
		Conquest

Kan 1. Fourth of the 20 Maya day signs, symbol of the young maize-god, equivalent to the Aztec day Cuetzpalin. Associated with the number 8, the South, and the color yellow. See **Year Bearer.** 2. Early Classic phase of the central highlands of the Chiapas Plateau. Possibly contemporary with the separation of the Tzeltal and Tzotzil linguistic groups 1,000 to 1,500 years ago.

Kanhobol Maya linguistic group found in the Department of Huehuetenango, Guatemala.

Kankin Fourteenth month of 20 days of the *tun,* the Maya year of 360 days.

katun Contraction of *kal* (20) and *tun,* it is a period of 20 years in the Maya calendar, or 7,200 days. Ends of *katuns* were of supreme importance to the lowland Classic Maya, who erected stelae to mark their completion. See also **Long Count.**

katun glyph

Kaua Town near Chichén Itzá, Yucatán. See also *Chilam Balam.*

Kaxil Uinic Archaeological site in northwest Belize.

Kayab 1. Seventeenth month of 20 days of the *tun,* the Maya year of 360 days. 2. See **áyotl.**

Kedo Zapotec god of justice, one of the Lords of the Night, equated with the Mexican god Mictlantecuhtli.

Kekchi Maya linguistic group affiliated with the Pokom, Guatemalan highlands.

Keuic Yucatecan site south of Sayil and Labná.

kill Term applied to the ceremonial perforation or breaking of ceramic, stone, and gold objects to liberate them from the soul of their previous owner, or to permit the soul of the object to accompany the deceased into the land of the dead. A common funerary practice of Mesoamerica and parts of Central America.

kin 1. Smallest unit of the Maya time count, a day. See **Long Count.** 2. Name for the sun and sun-god among the Maya. Priests were called Ah Kin, "he of the sun."

kin glyph

kinchiltun Maya time count equivalent to 20 *calabtuns,* or 1,152,000,-000 days. See **Long Count.**

Kinich Ahau Yucatecan sun-god, frequently represented in Classic and Postclassic Maya art with a square eye and prominent Roman nose. His head glyph personifies the number 4. Associated with Itzamná as the old sun-god in the sky.

knuckle-duster An object of undetermined use held in the hands of Olmec figures, carved in stone, in jade, and on small engraved celts.

Kohunlich Early Classic Maya site, in southern Quintana Roo, whose pyramid has large stucco god masks flanking its stairway.

kuk Maya name for the *quetzal,* a bird of the Guatemalan and Chiapas mountains treasured for its long green tail feathers which were traded throughout Mesoamerica.

Kukulcán Maya translation of Quetzalcóatl, the feathered serpent, introduced into Yucatán by the Putún Maya in the tenth century. Legendary leader of that name brought Mexican influence into Yucatán and later became the Feathered Serpent deity. The Dresden Codex relates him to the planet Venus, or Quetzalcóatl as the morning star.

1

Laa See **Quij.**

La Amelia Classic Maya site on the Pasión River, Peten, Guatemala.

Labná Great Classic Maya ceremonial center of south-central Yucatán. The architecture is Puuc; the site is famous for its imposing archway leading to a rectangular court surrounded by buildings of the palace type.

labret An ornament inserted in the lower lip, usually cylindrical, with lateral wings for stability.

La Cañada 1. Site southwest of the Tuxtla Mountains of southern Veracruz, possibly occupied by the Olmec. 2. Spanish word meaning "ravine," applied to the valley of Zamora in Michoacán.

Lacandón Tribe and linguistic group of the central Maya area. Currently reduced to a small number residing in the forests of Chiapas along the Usumacinta River. See **Acalán.**

Lacanha Classic Maya site near Bonampak, Chiapas, on the Usumacinta River.

La Ceiba Site at the northern end of Lake Yojoa, Honduras. Identified with nearby Los Naranjos as a source of the Late Classic ceramic known as Ulúa Polychrome. See also **ceiba.**

La Concepción Ceramic phase of the Greater Chiriquí cultural area about the time of Christ, leading into the Aguas Buenas phase. Large monochrome vessels decorated by parallel incising, with areas painted brown on red, known as scarified ware, simulated a zoned treatment.

La Divisa Postclassic ceramic phase of Sinaloa. See **Aztatlán, Culiacán.**

La Florida 1. Late Classic site on upper Chamelecón River, western Honduras. 2. Cultural phase of the Sierra Madre of southwest Tamaulipas, c. 500 B.C. Sedentary population lived in temple-oriented village groups. Ceramics came in a diversity of forms—tripod, effigy, and flanged vessels; figurines, ladles, and whistles.

Laguna 1. Early Classic phase of Chiapa de Corzo, c. A.D. 350–550, contemporary with Chiapa IX ceramic period, Monte Albán IIIa, Tzakol of the lowland Maya, and Esperanza at Kaminaljuyú. 2. Preclassic phase of the Sierra de Tamaulipas, 500 B.C.–A.D. 1, coeval with La Florida of the Sierra Madre of southwestern Tamaulipas.

Laguna de los Cerros Major Preclassic center of the Olmec heartland on a tributary of the San Juan River, south of the Tuxtla Mountains, Veracruz. It may prove to rival San Lorenzo and La Venta in importance, each having produced dozens of large-scale sculptures. Has 95 mounds, largely unexplored. Dates to c. 1000–400 B.C.

Laguna de Términos The Grijalva expedition of 1518 mistook this large lake for a strait separating Yucatán from the mainland, hence its name. The error persisted in some maps until 1603. It is at the mouth of the Candelaria River; was controlled by the seafaring Chontal Maya from their port of Xicalango at the west end of the lake. Located in extreme western Campeche, separated from the Gulf of Mexico by the island of Carmen. The Toltec-Chichimec led by Quetzalcóatl are reputed to have settled there on their trek from Cholula to Yucatán in the 10th century.

Laguneta Ceramic complex, c. A.D. 400–700, at Bilbao, Cotzumalhuapa region of southern Guatemala.

La Honradez Maya site north of Tikal, in the Petén, Guatemala.

lahun Number 10 in Maya.

lahuntun A half-*katun,* or a ten-year period in the Maya time count. See also **Long Count.**

La Juana See **Río Cuautla.**

Lamat Eighth day of the 20-day Maya month, equivalent to the Aztec day Tochtli. Day of the planet Venus; associated with the number 12.

Lamayna See **Indian Church.**

Lambityeco Zapotec site on the Pan American Highway between Oaxaca and Mitla, dating from Monte Albán IIIb–IV, c. A.D. 600–1000.

La Mixteca Mountainous region of western Oaxaca, homeland of the Mixtec people.

La Muñeca Site in the Río Bec region of southeast Campeche where the latest Maya stela corresponds to A.D. 909.

Lana Sixth of the 20 Zapotec day names; corresponds to the Aztec day Miquiztli and the Maya day Cimi.

Landa, Diego de (c. 1524–1579) Born in Cifuentes de la Alcarria, Toledo, Spain, arrived in Yucatán as a Franciscan friar in 1549, became bishop at Mérida in 1572, serving until his death. His *Relación de las Cosas de Yucatán* is still the basic source of information on pre-Hispanic Maya civilization. His contribution to modern understanding of the Maya is often compared to the similar, monumental *Historia General de las Cosas de la Nueva España,* reporting on the Aztec civilization, by Bernardino de Sahagún.

Lao Twentieth of the 20 Zapotec day names; equivalent to the Aztec day Xóchitl and the Maya day Ahau.

Lapa Eighth of the 20 Zapotec day names,

corresponding to the Aztec day Tochtli and the Maya day Lamat.

La Pastora Subphase of the Preclassic Zacatenco phase of the Valley of Mexico, related to the sites of El Arbolillo, Zacatenco, and Ticomán. Early La Pastora (Totolica at Tlatilco) is c. 875–750 B.C.; Late La Pastora extends into Early Cuautepec.

La Perra Cultural phase of Sierra de Tamaulipas, 3000–2200 B.C.

lápida Spanish word applied to carved stone slabs, which often represented genealogical histories. Generally smaller than the earlier stelae, they are characteristic of Late Zapotec culture in Oaxaca, centered about Zaachila after the abandonment of Monte Albán.

La Quemada Largest hilltop fortress of the Chalchihuites culture of Zacatecas; sometimes defined as the center of a separate Malpaso culture. With probable origins in the Early Classic period, its importance relates to the Postclassic, c. A.D. 900–1000, after which it was burned and abandoned. Heavy fortifications and an extensive network of roads recalling Maya causeways suggest its role as a bastion against invasion of Mesoamerica by northern Chichimec tribes.

It has an imposing acropolis, large I-shaped ball courts, and a stone pyramid rising to an apex instead of supporting a temple. Toltec influence is manifested in the Hall of Columns. In spite of its size and preservation, few specimens have been found to establish its cultural history. La Quemada is sometimes referred to as the ruins of Chicomoztoc, the mythical starting point of the nomadic tribes that populated the Valley of Mexico.

La Quinta Late Postclassic ceramic phase of Sinaloa. See **Culiacán.**

La Rama Site in the department of Usulután, El Salvador, where human footprints, estimated to be c. 1500 B.C., were registered in sandstone.

La Salta Cultural phase of Sierra de Tamaulipas, c. A.D. 500–900, developing into

Eslabones. Only four kinds of pottery: polished black, plain, smooth, and brushed utilitarian ware. Settlements were small, many not associated with temples.

Las Bocas Olmec site near Izúcar de Matamoros, Puebla; active in Middle Preclassic period, c. 1200–700 B.C. It is known for hollow, "baby face" ceramic figures, white-rimmed blackware, spouted trays, and black incised pottery known as dark channeled ware, with the Olmec jaguar-paw-wing motif. Contemporary with San Lorenzo in Veracruz and Tlatilco in the Valley of Mexico.

Las Cebollas Extensive cemetery of shaft-chamber tombs near Tequilita, southern Nayarit; source of *chinesco* figurines; c. A.D. 100.

Las Charcas Early to Middle Preclassic phase of Kaminaljuyú, Guatemala. Divided into two periods: A, c. 800–600 B.C., and B, 600–500 B.C. Known for bottle-shaped rubbish pits, similar to those at Tlatilco, and fine white kaolin pottery painted with abstract designs, dragon masks, or realistic renderings of monkeys. Clay temple-pyramids were probably introduced at this time.

Las Choapas See **Arroyo Pesquero.**

Las Flores Site on the Ulúa River in western Honduras, identified with Late Classic Ulúa Polychrome ceramic complex.

Las Higueras Site in southern Veracruz, active sixth to ninth centuries. Three superimposed layers of polychrome murals were successfully removed from one of its structures.

Las Huacas Spanish for "the graves," archaeologists have applied it to two cemetery sites in Central America: 1. Great cemetery site of the Nicoya Peninsula, Costa Rica. It furnished limited pottery but many jadeite ornaments, mace heads, and *metates*. Contemporary with Linear Decorated period, c. A.D. 300, possibly with preceding Zoned Bichrome. 2. Burial site in southern Veraguas, Panama, with Tonosí ceramics, carbon-dated c. A.D. 405.

Las Joyas Early phase of Postclassic horizon

of Chalchihuites culture of north-central Mexico, A.D. 700–950.

Las Limas Site in southern Veracruz where the famous seated greenstone figure holding a werejaguar baby in its arms was discovered. In the purest Olmec style, profusely incised with glyphs, it may date to the 1200–900 B.C. span of the San Lorenzo phase. The object of an international theft, it was recovered in Texas, and returned to the museum at Jalapa.

Las Mercedes Late ceremonial site in the Atlantic watershed of Costa Rica, with stone-faced earth mounds and a plazalike enclosure. Large numbers of stone sculptures, jades, and gold ornaments were found when the railroad (Línea Vieja) was put through the site in the late 1800s. Glass beads of European origin found in tombs there support its occupation to the Conquest.

Las Vegas 1. Site on the Comayagua River, Honduras. 2. Late ceramic complex of Honduras, also found in El Salvador, c. A.D. 1000–1200. Typical ware was called Las Vegas Polychrome, with painted decoration in orange, red, brown, and black on a cream slip. Related to the Middle Polychrome phase of Greater Nicoya.

Las Victorias Site in the Chalchuapa zone of El Salvador, dating to Early and Middle Preclassic periods. Olmecoid figures carved in bas-relief on three sides of a boulder are the most southerly examples of Olmec monumental art. Not to be confused with La Victoria in Chiapas.

Late Period, Costa Rica A term applied to regional cultural sequences of Costa Rica c. A.D. 1000–Conquest. In the Central Highlands, Chircot ceramic phase, in the Cartago valley, it is followed by the Orosí phase at nearby site, both also furnish basalt statuary showing human figures brandishing an axe in one hand and a severed head in the other. Jaguar *metates* are characteristic at this time in the zone of South American influence, from the Atlantic watershed of Costa Rica to Veraguas, Panama. In the Línea Vieja area,

Las Mercedes was an active ceremonial center. In Nicoya, the Late Polychrome ceramic period flourished. The southern Diquís region, a part of Greater Chiriquí, saw the flowering of "Classic Chiriquí."

Late Polychrome A term applied to the ceramic period of Greater Nicoya in Costa Rica and southwestern Nicaragua, c. A.D. 1200–Conquest. Pottery shows more direct Mexican influence than in previous periods.

Laud, Codex See **codex, pre-Conquest Mexican; Laud, Codex.**

La Venta Most famous and the type site of the Olmec culture, situated on an island in the Tonalá River in Tabasco. Its activity spanned c. 1000–400 B.C. Most prominent feature is a 110-ft. (c. 33 m)-high fluted clay and earth pyramid in the shape of a cone. The planned north-south-oriented ceremonial center, a concept initiated at Olmec San Lorenzo, was to be followed by later centers throughout Mesoamerica. La Venta produced colossal sculptured stone heads, stelae, and altars; burial caches revealed finely polished jade and serpentine objects in the Olmec style that influenced all subsequent cultures.

La Victoria Chiapas coastal site on an estuary near the Guatemalan border; dating back to the Ocós phase, c. 1400 B.C., it was an active settlement to c. 300 B.C. Produced a pottery decorated with iridescent paint that was also characteristic of contemporary pots found in coastal Ecuador. Not to be confused with Las Victorias, in El Salvador.

Lempa Principal river of El Salvador; after flowing east for over 62 mi. (100 km), it turns south to form an effective barrier between the western and eastern parts of the country. It was the western area that was culturally influenced by the Maya, and later by Mexican Pipiles in Postclassic times.

Lenca Linguistic group of eastern El Salvador and south-central Honduras. See also **Macro-Chibcha.**

Lerma 1. River of Mexico that flows from valley of Toluca in a northwest direction

to Lake Chapala between the states of Jalisco and Michoacán. As it leaves Lake Chapala to reach the Pacific, it changes its name to Río de Santiago. 2. Cultural phase of the Sierra de Tamaulipas representing a nomadic hunting and gathering society, 8,800 to 10,000 years ago.

Leyden plate Celt-shaped jade plaque 8½ in. x 3 in. (222 mm x 80 mm) found near Puerto Barrios, Guatemala, in 1864. Style of its incising relates to Tikal stela sculpture. It bears one of the earliest undisputed dates, contemporaneous with the carving, in Maya history, 8.14.3.1.12, 1 Eb, 0 Yaxkin, equivalent to A.D. 320. Now in Leyden, Holland.

lienzo See **codex.**

Likin Maya word for East. See **world directions, Maya.**

Linear Decorated Descriptive term applied to ceramic phase of Greater Nicoya, c. A.D. 300–500, first called Early Polychrome A, following Zoned Bichrome. The most important ceramics are of the Guinea incised type, already technically trichrome and leading into later true polychrome. Vessel decoration is mainly incised with bands of geometric motifs, but punctation, modeling, and appliqué motifs are also used. Vessels frequently represent a great variety of animals, mostly birds.

Línea Vieja Archaeological zone of the Atlantic watershed of Costa Rica, named after a railroad line during whose construction in the late 19th century many ancient graves were first discovered. Guápiles and Las Mercedes are the prominent sites. Stone sculptures include human statues and four-legged jaguar *metates*, or altars. Jadeite pendants were found in great quantity. Small bird pendants made of imported gold show close ties with the goldwork of Panama. Presence of Early Classic Maya artifacts also indicates trade with the north, c. A.D. 300–600. The art style of this area is frequently referred to as Huetar.

Lo de Vaca Site near Yarumela in the Comayagua valley of Honduras that gives its name to one of the earliest ceramic complexes, before 200 B.C. Ulúa Bichrome ceramic phase is of this period.

Lolandis Late Classic phase of Sinaloa. See **Aztatlán.**

Loltún Cave in the Puuc region of western Yucatán; a rock carving near its entrance is the only known Preclassic stone sculpture of the Maya lowlands.

Long Count (L.C.) Lowland Classic period Maya calendrical computation, inscribed on their monuments and in their codices. It was computed from a mythical starting point, 13.0.0.0.0, 4 Ahau, 8 Cumku, corresponding to 3113 B.C. according to the Goodman-Martínez-Thompson correlation. It was employed in a similar way to the birthday of Christ in the modern Western calendar, permitting determinations of the past and future. The Maya time count was expressed in numbers of *baktun, katun, tun, uinal,* and *kin.* The Long Count is also called the Initial Series (I.S.) since it initiates the inscriptions carved on monuments of the Classic period.

The Long Count may have originated in the Uaxactún-Tikal area of Guatemala, developing into a full glyphic system. It allowed the Maya to compute endlessly in time, backward and forward, employing Long Count periods: *kinchiltun:* 3,200,000 *tuns* (very rare); *calabtun:* 160,000 *tuns* (very rare); *pictun:* 8,000 *tuns* (rare); *baktun:* 400 *tuns,* or 144,000 days; *katun:* 20 *tuns,* or 7,200 days; *tun:* 18 *uinals,* or 360 days; *uinal:* 20 *kins,* or 20 days.

In some contexts the *tun* is also called *haab; baktun, pictun, calabtun,* and *kinchiltun* are also referred to respectively as a cycle, great cycle, great-great cycle, and great-great-great cycle.

On monuments, Long Count dates are read from top to bottom, in descending time periods. In modern texts, Long Count dates are written horizontally, from left to right, starting with the *baktuns,* followed by *katuns, tuns, uinals,* and *kins.* The earliest contemporaneous Long Count date is on Stela 29 at Tikal, 8.12.14.8.15, corresponding to A.D. 292. The latest known at La Muñeca, Campeche, corresponds to A.D. 909. Together they define the currently known span of the Classic, or Initial Series, period of the lowland Maya civilization.

long-nosed god See **Bolon Dz'acab.**

Loo (Goloo) Eleventh of the 20 Zapotec day names, sometimes called Goloo. It is equivalent to the Aztec day Ozomatli and the Maya day Chuen, representing the monkey-god.

Loo (Guilloo) Sixteenth of the 20 Zapotec days, sometimes called Guilloo. Corresponds to the Aztec day Cozcacuauhtli and the Maya day Cib.

Lords of the Day In the Aztec *Tonalamatl,* or Book of the Days, a series of 13 Lords of the Day, or gods, accompanies day signs and their numbers. The concept may be connected with the 13 heavens. Similarly, a series of 13 *volátiles,* or birds, furnishes related glyphs. Lords and *volátiles* repeat in the following order:

LORD (*god*)	IDENTITY	BIRD
1. Xiuhtecuhtli	fire-god	blue hummingbird
2. Tlaltecuhtli	earth-god	green hummingbird
3. Chalchiúhtlicue	water-goddess	hawk
4. Tonatiuh	sun-god	quail
5. Tlazoltéotl	goddess of love	eagle
6. Teoyaomiqui	god of fallen warriors	screech owl
7. Xochipilli-Centéotl	god of pleasure–corn-god	butterfly
8. Tlaloc	rain-god	eagle
9. Quetzalcóatl	wind-god	turkey
10. Tezcatlipoca	god of sustenance	horned owl
11. Mictlantecuhtli	god of underworld	macaw
12. Tlahuizcalpantecuhtli	god of dawn	quetzal
13. Ilamatecuhtli	sky-goddess	parrot

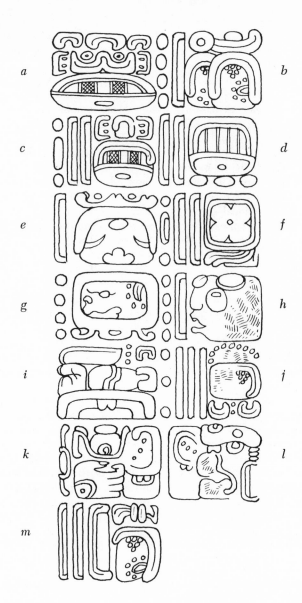

Plate 9. A Classic lowland Maya Long Count date. Stela 24, Naranjo, Guatemala: (*a*) Venus god is patron; (*b*) 9 cycles; (*c*) 12 *katuns;* (*d*) 10 *tuns;* (*e*) 5 *uinals;* (*f*) 12 *kins;* (*g*) 4 Eb; (*h*) ruler of the night; (*i*) start of the lunar count; (*j*) 18 days after the new moon; (*k*) first moon of the group; (*l*) previous moon was 30 days; (*m*) 10 Yax. From Field Museum of Natural History, *The Civilization of the Mayas,* page 57.

As a group the 13 Lords of the Day are called Tonalteuctin in Nahuatl, corresponding to the Maya Oxlahun ti Ku. Of the 13 Lords, 5 preside over the five cosmogonic suns: Tezcatlipoca, Quetzalcóatl, Tlaloc, Chalchiúhtlicue, and Tonatiuh. See **Creation myth, Aztec.**

Lords of the Night Besides the Aztec Lords of the Day and the accompanying *volátiles* (above), there is another series in the *Tonalamatl* called the nine Lords of the Night. They are, with the augury for each, as follows:

LORD (*god*)	IDENTITY	AUGURY
1. Xiuhtecuhtli	fire-god	unfavorable
2. Itztli-Técpatl	god of obsidian– flint	unfavorable
3. Piltzintecuhtli	youthful sun-god	excellent
4. Centéotl	corn-god	excellent
5. Mictlantecuhtli	god of under- world	favorable
6. Chalchiúhtlicue	water-goddess	favorable
7. Tlazoltéotl	goddess of love	unfavorable
8. Tepeyolohtli	heart of the mountain	favorable
9. Tlaloc	rain-god	favorable

The nine Lords of the Night may be associated with the nine layers of the underworld. As a group, the nine Lords of the Night are called Yohualteuctin in Nahuatl, corresponding to the Bolon ti Ku of the Maya.

Los Altos Area of northeastern Jalisco; source of large, hollow male figurines with flat-topped horns projecting from the sides of their heads. Horned figurines were formerly attributed to Zacatecas, decorated with black resist patterns applied over areas of dark ivory and red slip.

Los Angeles Final phase of Sierra de Tamaulipas, A.D. 1300–1750. The culture is less complex and sophisticated than in preceding phases; caves are again used for habitation.

Los Higos Classic Maya site on upper Chamelecón River, western Honduras.

Los Llanitos Classic site of eastern El Salvador in the valley of the Río Grande de San Miguel; has most southerly known I-shaped ball court.

Los Naranjos Site at north end of Lake Yojoa, Honduras. Active from Jaral phase, c. 500–200 B.C., through Classic to c. A.D. 950. Identified with Ulúa Polychrome and Fine Orange ware.

Los Ortices S te in central Colima, western Mexico. The Los Ortices phase was Protoclassic, c. 100 B.C.–A.D. 250, and known for its shaft tombs.

Los Tuxtlas Mountain range paralleling the coast of southern Veracruz. Source of stone for the monumental Olmec sculptures.

lost wax A worldwide method of casting metal, especially suitable for intricate forms. Frequently referred to with the French phrase, *cire perdue*. An exact model of the desired piece was shaped in wax, sometimes over a core; the outer mold of clay was then applied and heated, causing the wax to melt and become "lost" through holes provided in the mold. The metal was then poured in to replace it. After cooling, the mold was broken, revealing the metal form. Found in the Mochica culture of Peru, the process was diffused to Colombia and Central America, ultimately reaching Mexico where the art was highly developed by the Mixtec of Oaxaca.

Lubaantun Late Classic Maya site of southern Belize. Noted for its mold-made whistle figurines, which were rare in the Maya Classic period except on the island of Jaina and the nearby coast of Campeche.

Lubay In Classic Maya calendrical computation, a period of two Calendar Rounds, or 104 years, corresponds to the Aztec Huehuetiliztli. At its end, 65 synodical revolutions of Venus (584 days each), 104 Vague Years (365 days each), and 146 rounds of the *tzolkin* (260 days) will have elapsed and "come to rest." Lubay comes from the Maya word *lub,* "resting place at end of day"; depicted by full-figure glyphs on Stela D at Copán.

Lum Late Postclassic phase of the Central Plateau of Chiapas, represented at Chamula.

Luna ware Postclassic pottery of Nicaragua and northwest Costa Rica produced into the 16th century, distinguished by its fine-line geometric painting and preslip incising. The background is white, and the motifs are associated with the feathered serpent, black or brown silhouetted figures, dots, stepped frets, and pompons, recalling Cholula and Tlaxcala, home of the Nicarao. Luna is the family name of a hacienda owner at Moyogalpa, Nicaragua, where this ceramic type was discovered.

lunar calendar Among Maya, a time measurement consisting of 29 and a fraction days between two successive new moons. See also **calendar, Mesoamerican.**

Lunar Series See **Supplementary Series.**

m

Mac Thirteenth month of the *tun*, the Maya year of 360 days.

Macaracas See **Central Panama**.

macehual Commoner in Aztec society.

Machaquilá Classic Maya site on river of same name, tributary of the Pasión River, Petén, Guatemala.

Macro-Chibcha Central American language group at the time of the Conquest, extending into Colombia. It was represented by three subsidiary languages spoken in the Pacific zone of northern Central America: Corobici of northwestern Costa Rica, Ulva of southern Honduras and central Nicaragua, and Lenca of eastern El Salvador, central and northwestern Honduras. Macro-Chibcha in Central America possibly represented a back-migration from Colombia. See also **Chibcha**.

Macro-Maya A major language group of Mexico and Guatemala that split into several branches: the Huastec of northern Veracruz, Totonac of central Veracruz, Zoque of the isthmus region, and the Maya of eastern Chiapas, parts of Tabasco, the Yucatán peninsula, Guatemala, and western parts of Honduras and El Salvador.

macuauhuitl The wooden war club of the Mexica, edged on opposing sides with obsidian blades.

macuauhuitl

macuilli Number 5 in Nahuatl.

Macuilxóchitl 1. Aztec god of pleasure, the ball game, and *patolli*. Identified with, and possibly calendrical name (5 flower) of, Xochipilli, but more representative of excesses. Also called Ahuíatl or Ahuiatéotl, one of the five genies of the South, the Ahuiateteo. 2. Modern village in valley of Oaxaca. See **Dainzú**.

Madrid Codex See **codex, pre-Conquest Maya; Madrid Codex**.

Magdalena 1. Lake in Jalisco near Nayarit border. See also **Etzatlán, San Sebastián**. 2. Middle Classic phase of San Augustín Acasaguastlán, Guatemala.

Magliabecchiano, Codex See **codex, early post-Conquest Mexican; Magliabecchiano, Codex**.

maguey See **agave**.

mahtlactli Number 10 in Nahuatl.

mai Gourd, container of powdered tobacco, worn and shown in the codices as the badge of priesthood; perhaps of Yucatecan origin, it was used in much of Mesoamerica.

maize Mainstay of the Mesoamerican diet, earliest traces of which were found in a cave in the Tehuacán Valley, Puebla, carbon-dated 5200–3400 B.C. Earliest corncobs seem prototypes of *chapalote* and *na!-tel* strains previously discovered in Bat Cave, New Mexico, and in the dry caves of southwestern Tamaulipas, Mexico. Evidence of domestication appears by 3000 B.C. By 2300 B.C., hybridization is seen by cross-fertilization with wild grasses, probably *teosinte* or *Tripsacum*.

Centli is Nahuatl for ear of corn; *tlaolli*, for grain, depicted by the Mexicans in four

95

varieties: yellow, blue, red, and white. Aztecs revered Centéotl, the masculine corngod, and his feminine counterparts, Xilonen and Chicomecóatl. Maize is god E of Maya codices, patron of the number 8. Maya recognized only a male corn deity, Ah Mun.

Majadas See **Providencia (Majadas).**

malacate Spindle whorl, usually of clay; a perforated round disk used as a weight in spinning thread.

Malalaca Postclassic phase of Choluteca region of southern Honduras, A.D. 1200–1500.

Malinalco Late Aztec ceremonial site on a high mountain slope southeast of Toluca. This monolithic shrine, dedicated to the warrior fraternities of Eagles and Jaguars, was carved out of the living rock. Source of the famous, intricately carved wooden drum, *tlalpanhuéhuetl,* now in the Toluca museum.

Malinalli Symbol of the 12th day of the Nahuatl calendar. Patron deity was Patécatl; its augury was unfavorable. Equivalent of the Maya day Eb and the Zapotec day Pija. Malinalli calendrical names include: 1 Malinalli: Tlazoltéotl, earth-/love-goddess; 8 Malinalli: Coatlícue, earth-goddess.

Malinche, La 1. Extinct volcano between Puebla and Tlaxcala, anciently called Matlalcueye after the second wife of the rain-god Tlaloc. 2. Native woman of Tabasco, mistress and interpreter for Hernán Cortés during his conquest of Mexico. Originally named Malintzin, she was baptized Marina by the Spanish.

Malpaso Postclassic cultural development of Zacatecas, directly on the northern frontier of Mesoamerica, contemporary with Chalchihuites. It may have been related to or a part of the Tarascan political domain. La Quemada is said to be of the Malpaso culture.

Mam 1. Maya linguistic group which at the Conquest occupied the area of the Guatemalan departments of Huehuetenango, San Marcos, and the Mexican district of Soconusco, Chiapas. 2. Old Mayan deity who

carries the symbol of the year, generally pictured with a shell; an evil deity who lives beneath mountains causing earthquakes. Perhaps the same as god N of the codices and similar to the Mexican god Tepeyolohtli.

mamalhuaztli Nahuatl word for pieces of wood rubbed together to produce fire.

mammiform Description of a type of ceramic vessel support, or foot, shaped like a breast or nipple.

mammiform supports

Mamom Preclassic lowland Maya ceramic horizon, observed at Uaxactún and Tikal in the Petén of Guatemala, c. 1000–300 B.C. It probably represented a simple village culture whose remains are principally monochrome pottery and figurines.

Managua 1. Capital of modern Nicaragua. 2. Lake in Nicaragua containing the island of Momotombito. 3. Managua ceramic ware is probably of the Late Period, found in southwest Nicaragua and northwest Costa Rica. Characterized by tripod bowls with solid legs, slightly flaring sides, and flat bottoms, incised on the inside, recalling the grater bowls of the Mexicans and Maya.

Manche Chol Maya linguistic group who occupied the southeast corner of the Petén, southern Belize, and the Golfo Dulce region west of the mouth of the Motagua River. See **Chol.**

Mangue A subdivision of the Chorotegan language group; a tongue spoken in Pacific Nicaragua and Costa Rica, between Managua and Subtiaba.

Maní Postclassic capital of the Xiu family in central Yucatán, after the abandonment of Uxmal. See also *Chilam Balam.*

Manik Seventh of the 20 Maya day names; corresponds to the Aztec day Mázatl and the Zapotec day China. Associated with the number 11.

manikin scepter Classic Maya scepter, symbol of the *halach uinic's* authority. The top is an anthropomorphic figure, with the long upturned lip of god K, Bolon Dz'acab. Its lower extremity is curved, ending in a serpent's head. Common in monumental carvings, especially Yaxchilán lintels.

manioc A tuber also called yuca and cassava. It was domesticated in tropical South America and may have been cultivated in the Central American tropics as a staple food before maize. In the 16th century the "sweet" variety was grown. In Panama the "bitter," which requires leaching to remove the prussic acid before grating and roasting, was also consumed.

mano Cylindrical stone muller for grinding corn on the Mesoamerican *metate*.

manuscripts, Mesoamerican See **codex.**

Manuscrit du Cacique See **codex, pre-Conquest Mexican; Becker #1, Codex.**

Manuscrito de Tlatelolco See **Codex, early post-Conquest Mexican; Matritenses, Codices.**

mapa See **codex.**

maqui See **auianime.**

Maravillas Classic phase of Chiapa de Corzo, coeval with Chiapa X ceramic period, c. A.D. 550–900.

Mariato Site on Azuero Peninsula, carbon-dated A.D. 190–550. Ceramics are Tonosí. See **Central Panama.**

Maribio Mexican peoples who settled Pacific Nicaragua in the Early Postclassic period. Affected by the unrest at Cholula, they left western Mexico, where they were known as the Tlapaneca-Yope; brought the cult of Xipe Totec to Central America.

Marismas Nacionales Estuary-lagoon complex of the Pacific coastal plain of southern Sinaloa and northern Nayarit, Mexico, with prehistoric shell-mound sites.

"Martian" figurine See **chinesco.**

masa Spanish word for a dough of lime-treated corn from which tortillas are made. Nahuatl word is *nixtamal.*

Matanchén Nonceramic complex of coastal Nayarit, dating c. 2000 B.C., followed by San Blas ceramic complex c. 500 B.C.

Matillas See **Orange, Fine.**

Matlalcueitl "Lady of the green skirts," second wife of the rain-god Tlaloc after Tezcatlipoca absconded with his first, the god-dess Xochiquetzal. Also called Matlalcueye. See also **Malinche, La.**

Matlatzinca Indigenous group, linguistically related to the Otomí, but probably of Toltec cultural background, which resided in the valley of Tollocán. Calixtlahuaca, near present-day Toluca, was their capital when conquered by the Aztecs in A.D. 1476.

Matritenses, Codices See **codex, early post-Conquest Mexican; Matritenses, Codices.**

Matzanel Protoclassic period at Uaxactún, Petén, Guatemala, c. A.D. 100–200. Coeval with Holmul I phase in Belize.

Maxcanú Late Classic Yucatecan site, southwest of Mérida. Produced light to dark brown (sometimes gray) carved pottery ware, mostly cylindrical in shape, c. A.D. 600–900.

Maxtla Son of Tezozómoc, Tepanec ruler of Atzcapotzalco. Succeeded in A.D. 1426 by arranging his brother's assassination.

maxtlatl Mexican article of clothing, similar to a breechcloth; called *ex* among the Maya.

Maya A branch of the Macro-Maya language group that migrated from North America to the highlands of Guatemala probably by 2500 B.C. Within the next 1,000 years some emigrated to the Gulf Coast, settling the Huasteca and remaining apart from the evolution of the great Maya civilization. Others continued to the north to populate the Petén-Yucatán peninsula, retaining contact with the highland Maya. The emerging Maya civilization, with periodic influences from Mexico, eventually encompassed all of Guatemala, eastern Chiapas, parts of Tabasco, the Yucatán peninsula, westernmost Honduras, and western El Salvador. The Maya are the largest homogeneous group of Indians north of Peru; their language still defines the limits of the high Maya civilization that vanished 1,000 years ago. The Classic period, c. A.D. 300–900, of the southern lowland Maya made large contributions to Mesoamerican civilization. Their astronomical studies and invention of the concept of zero produced intricate mathematics, a highly accurate calendar, and the ability to determine time to infinity. Hieroglyphic writing, as seen on their monuments and represented in the later codices, was highly developed. Stelae reached their height in number and quality, with detailed carving and Initial Series dating. In architecture they built on the Teotihuacán tradition, added roof combs, and invented the corbeled vault that expanded the structural possibilities. Their polychrome ceramic vessels are among the finest in the world. See **Pipil; Long Count; calendar, Mesoamerican; Calendar Round; hieroglyphic writing; numerical recording, Maya.**

Maya areas The geographic scope of the Maya civilization is archaeologically divided into three contiguous areas:

1. *Southern area* comprises the Guatemalan highlands, parts of Chiapas, Pacific coastal Guatemala, and El Salvador west of the Lempa River. Important sites include Izapa, Zacualpa, Zaculeu, Kaminaljuyú, El Baúl, Tiquisate, Amatitlán, Mixco Viejo, Utatlán, Toniná, and Iximché.

2. *Central area* comprises the Petén of Guatemala, the Usumacinta drainage into Tabasco, southern Campeche, Belize, the Motagua River valley of Guatemala, and westernmost Honduras. It is also called the Southern Lowlands. Major sites include Comalcalco, Palenque, Yaxchilán, Bonampak, Piedras Negras, Altar de Sacrificios, Seibal, Uaxactún, Tikal, Naranjo, Yaxhá, Copán, Quiriguá, Lubaantun, Holmul, and Altun Há.

3. *Northern area* comprises the rest of the Yucatán peninsula, including northern Campeche, and the states of Yucatán and Quintana Roo. It is also called the Northern Lowlands. Important sites include Acancéh, Dzibilchaltún, Chichén Itzá, Mayapán, Uxmal, Kabah, Sayil, Labná, Cobá, Tulum, Jaina, Santa Rosa Xtampak, Xpuhil, Hochob, and Río Bec. See also **Mesoamerica.**

Maya social classes Lowland Maya society at the time of the Spanish Conquest was composed of three classes:

1. *Nobles, almehen* in Maya, were the administrators, priests, controllers of commerce. At the top was the *halach uinic*

("true man"), also called *ahau* ("lord"), supreme administrator, high priest, and military leader. He appointed the *bacabs* ("town chiefs") and the *ah kulel* ("deputies").

2. *Commoners, yalba-uinic* or *pizil cach* in Maya, were farmers, fishermen, small merchants, and the source of labor for public works; they formed the main body of the population.

3. *Slaves, ppentacob* in Maya, were a class formed of convicted criminals, debtors, and plebeian captives.

Mayáhuel Aztec goddess of maguey and its derivative, pulque; her 400 breasts fed the unnumbered (400) gods of drunkenness, the Centzóntotochtin. Widely worshiped, they derived local names from the tribes whose patrons they were. Most important was Ometochtli, general god of pulque. Mayáhuel's consort was Patécatl, the god who "cured" pulque and changed it into a drink with magical and intoxicating power. Mayáhuel is the deity of the eighth day, Tochtli, and Ce Tochtli (1 rabbit) is her sign.

Mayapán Postclassic period Maya state, seat of the Cocom family of Itzá lineage. Was joined in a Triple Alliance with Chichén Itzá, the leading city, and Izamal from the 10th to 13th century. After A.D. 1200, led by Hunac Ceel, Mayapán subjugated Chichén Itzá, initiating the period of its dominance in Yucatán, until its fall c. 1450 in a revolt of the Maya nobles against the Cocom dynasty, abetted by the rival Xiu, another family of Mexican antecedents.

The wall enclosing the city's 2,000 dwellings suggests a military preoccupation. Cultural decadence is seen in its architecture, such as the temple-pyramid of Kukulcán, a poorly constructed imitation of the Castillo at Chichén Itzá. Slateware pottery so typical of Yucatán for 1,000 years disappeared, replaced by inferior products such as idolatrous ceremonial censers in anthropomorphic form made of coarse buff paste, unslipped but painted after firing, in garish multicolored designs.

mayeque Bondsmen or slaves in Aztec society, permanently attached to the lands of the hereditary lord.

Mayer, Codex See **codex, pre-Conquest Mexican; Fejérváry-Mayer, Codex.**

Mayoid Maya influence expressed in the art styles of other peoples, such as Ulúa Mayoid pottery of Late Classic period in western Honduras.

Mazahua Branch of the Otomían subdivision of the Oto-Zapotecan language group. The Otomí-Mazahua were dominant in the north of the Valley of Mexico and the northern plains of the Toluca valley.

Mazapán Ceramic phase of the Valley of Mexico, c. A.D. 1000, marking the Toltec horizon that developed out of earlier Coyotlatelco. The style is distinguished by pottery decorated in parallel wavy red lines on buff.

Mazatec Branch of the Mixtecan subdivision of the Oto-Zapotecan language group, found at the northern tip of Oaxaca, including the Tehuacán Valley.

Mázatl Seventh of the 20 Nahuatl day signs, with Tlaloc as its patron deity, and a favorable augury. Equivalent to the Maya day Manik and the Zapotec day China. For the Aztecs, the deer (*mázatl*) symbolized drought and fire. Associated calendrical names are: 1 Mázatl: name of the creator-gods; 4 Mázatl: name of Itztlacoliuhqui; 5 Mázatl: a form of Xólotl.

Mbaz Zapotec earth-god or -goddess; one of the Lords of the Night. Corresponds to the Mexican Tepeyolohtli or Tlazoltéotl.

Mdi One of the Zapotec Lords of the Night; equivalent to the Mexican Tlaloc.

Mejor es Algo Early Classic ceramic complex at Bilbao, Cotzumalhuapa region of southern Guatemala, c. A.D. 100–400.

Men Fifteenth of the 20 Maya day signs; corresponds to the Mexican day Cuauhtli and the Zapotec day Naa. Men was the day of the patroness of weaving, the aged moon-goddess.

Mendoza 1. See **codex, early post-Conquest Mexican; Codex Mendoza.** 2. Final polychrome ceramic phase of Central Panama, c. A.D. 900–Conquest, also called El Hatillo.

The naturalism of Conte and Macaracas animal designs is replaced by extreme geometric treatment. See **Central Panama.**

Mérida Capital of the modern Mexican state of Yucatán. Founded in 1542 by Francisco de Montejo, the Younger, on the site of the Maya town of Tihoo.

Mesa de Guaje Cultural phase of Sierra Madre of southwest Tamaulipas, 1400–500 B.C. Evidence of hybridized maize, along with the cultivation of beans, squash, and cotton; it introduced black, red, and plain flat-bottomed ceramic bowls.

mescal Drink distilled from the fermented juice of the mescal agave plant; popular in Oaxaca. Similar to tequila.

Mesoamerica Area of Mexico and Central America in which the common presence of certain pre-Hispanic culture traits permits the classification of the separate cultures within the area as one civilization. The concept was first proposed, geographically and culturally, by Paul Kirchhoff in 1943.

Geographically, Mesoamerica can be marked on the north along the Sinaloa, Lerma, and Pánuco rivers, separating the nomadic tribes of the northern desert from the agricultural population of Mesoamerica. It includes central and southern Mexico, the Yucatán peninsula, Guatemala, El Salvador, parts of Honduras and Nicaragua, and northern Costa Rica. The southern boundary runs from the Caribbean mouth of the Motagua River, Guatemala, in a southwestern line through Central America, passing Lake Nicaragua, to the Gulf of Nicoya, Costa Rica. This is, conversely considered, the limit of a primarily South American cultural influence in Central America.

Characteristic Mesoamerican cultural traits include writing, solar and ritual calendars intermeshed to produce a 52-year cycle, terraced pyramids, stuccoed floors, ceremonial ball game and courts, human and autosacrifice; a complicated pantheon of gods, and a cosmic concept expressed in the four cardinal directions and center, each with assigned colors and deities. The dependence on maize as the staple food was not exclusive in the New World, but basic to Mesoamerican life and symbolism. The chronology of its cultural sequences is shown below with occasionally used alternate names for the periods:

Preclassic period	2300 B.C.–A.D. 300	Archaic, Formative, Developmental
Classic period	A.D. 300–900	Regional, florescent, theocratic, Old Empire, Initial Series in southern lowlands
Postclassic period	A.D. 900–1521	New Empire, florescent, Mexican, militaristic, in northern lowlands

See also **nuclear area.**

mesocephalic Physical anthropological term meaning "medium headed," where the maximum width of the cranium is between 75 percent and 80 percent of the length. See **cephalic index.**

metallurgy The absence of iron in Middle America precluded use of this metal in tools. Metalwork was principally in gold and copper, and almost exclusively for ornament. Probably introduced from Colombia, goldsmithing appeared in Coclé, Panama, by the fifth century A.D. There was no goldwork in Mesoamerica during the Classic period. It reached Oaxaca c. A.D. 900, where the fine Mixtec craftsmanship showed Central American influence. The Toltecs at Chichén Itzá produced objects of gold and copper in quantity. The Tarascans of Michoacán worked copper and some gold. Pre-Columbian goldworking techniques included hammered stretching and shaping with the knowledge of annealing and repoussé, casting in open and closed molds (lost-wax process), alloying of copper and gold (*tumbaga*), incising, and inlaying with other metals and precious stones.

metaphorgram Among the Maya, a glyph that corresponds to a figure of speech or a recognized symbol, such as the burden glyph (*cuch*) with the meaning of fate or destiny.

metate Flat-surfaced stone mortar, generally rectangular, with legs, was employed with a stone muller (*mano*) for

metate, Costa Rica

grinding grain. *Manos* and *metates* are associated with Tehuacán as early as 4000 B.C., with Veracruz by 1200 B.C. Subsequently in general use throughout Mesoamerica, their presence serves archaeologically to indicate dependence on maize as opposed to manioc. Central Panama and Costa Rica elaborated *metates* in the form of jaguars and birds, with three legs and a "flying panel," oval, circular, or rectangular tops, often bordered by little heads. See also **altar.**

Metepec Cultural phase of the Valley of Mexico, also called Teotihuacán IV, c. A.D. 650–750. It was a period of decadence following the collapse of Teotihuacán itself, with some of its population resettled in nearby regions. The period was formerly called Ahuizotla-Amantla.

mexayácatl Mask made from the thigh skin of a sacrificed victim, worn by a ritual performer representing Centéotl (male maize deity) during the Ochpanitztli ceremony.

Mexica One of seven Aztec tribal groups traditionally believed to have left the legendary Chicomoztoc ("seven caves"), and the last to reach the Valley of Mexico, settling at Chapultepec. Predatory and antagonistic, they were subdued, scattered, and finally forced to live on an island in Lake Texcoco; according to myth the site was indicated to them by an eagle perched on a nopal cactus (*tenochtli*) with a snake in its beak; thus Tenochtitlán, today's Mexico City, was founded. Tributary to the Tepanecs of Atzcapotzalco, they fought in their wars of conquest until 1428 when they combined with Texcoco to crush the Tepanec empire, laying the foundation for the Aztec expansion that persisted until the Spanish Conquest. As citizens of

1. Temple I facing Great Plaza. c. A.D. 700. North Acropolis to the left. Tikal, Guatemala. Photograph: Justin Kerr.

2. View of the Great Plaza from the North Platform. Current construction dates from A.D. 500–1000. Building of the *"danzantes"* is in the center distance. Monte Albán, Oaxaca, Mexico. Photograph: Justin Kerr.

3. Atlantean columns on the platform of the pyramid of Quetzalcóatl. c. A.D. 1000. Tula, Hidalgo,
Mexico. Photograph: Justin Kerr.

4. Platform of the Temple of the
Warriors. Between 11th and 13th
centuries. A Chacmool is centered
in front of two "serpent" columns.
Chichén Itzá, Yucatán. Photograph:
Justin Kerr.

5. Classic Maya ball court. A.D. 775. Three circular markers appear in the playing surface; three others, in the form of stylized macaw heads, are spaced at the top of each sloping wall. Copán, Honduras. Photograph: Muriel Porter Weaver.

6. Colossal head. c. 800–400 B.C. Found at Olmec site of La Venta. Installed at Parque Museo de La Venta, Villa Hermosa, Tabasco, Mexico. Photograph: Curt Muser.

7. Detail of Mixtec stone mosaic work. A.D. 1150–1500. Interior walls of Hall of Columns. Mitla, Oaxaca, Mexico. Photograph: Curt Muser.

8. Detail of Puuc-style decorative frieze. A.D. 800–1000. On a Late Classic Maya building on the west side of the Nunnery Quadrangle. Uxmal, Yucatán. Photograph: Justin Kerr.

9. Detail of stucco panel. c. A.D. 700–770. In Palace, House A, pier C, at Classic Maya center of Palenque. Chiapas, Mexico. Photograph: Justin Kerr.

10. Late Classic Maya wall painting. c. A.D. 800. Room 2, Building of the Murals. Portrays the treatment of prisoners. Bonampak, Chiapas, Mexico. Peabody Museum, Harvard University, Cambridge, Massachusetts. Photograph by Hillel Burger of a watercolor by Antonio Tejeda.

11. Early Classic interior wall murals. A.D. 400–700. In the residential compounds at Teotihuacán: (*a*) detail of Tepantitla mural showing insects and figures with speech scrolls in a representation of Tlalocán; (*b*) detail of mural in the Hall of the Red Quetzals, Tetitla. Mexico. Photograph: Esther Pasztory.

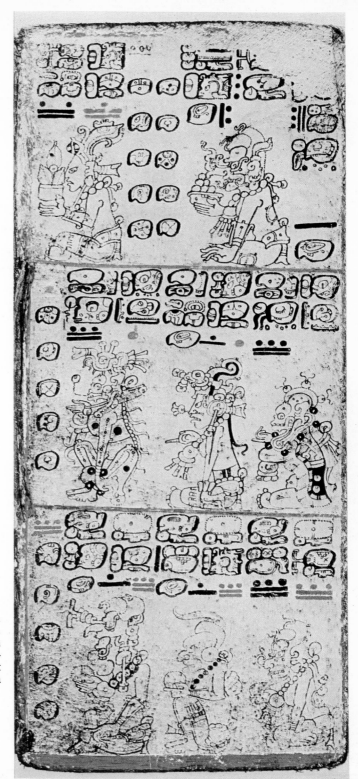

12. Page 12 of the Dresden Codex showing various gods. Probably dates to the 13th century. Sächsische Landesbibliothek, Dresden, East Germany. Photograph: Helga Photo Studio, New York.

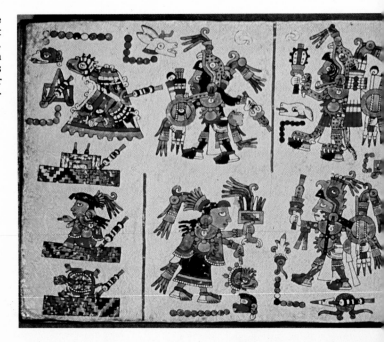

13. Page from the reverse side of the pre-Conquest Nuttall Codex. 15th century. The page depicts an event in the life of the most famous Mixtec ruler, Eight Deer Tiger Claw. The British Museum, London.

14. Roll-out of design on Late Classic Maya cylindrical pot. c. A.D. 800. 8 in. (20.3 cm) high. Six figures and glyphs. Believed to be from Altamira at Campeche-Petén border. Yucatán peninsula. Dumbarton Oaks, Washington, D.C.

15. Early Classic Teotihuacán-style blackware lidded pot. A.D. 200–500. 13½ in. (35 cm) high. Kaminaljuyú, Guatemala. Museum of the American Indian (Heye Foundation), New York.

16. Late Classic vessel. A.D. 600–1000. 5⅛ in. (13 cm) high. Three waterfowl are shown around the circumference. Probably from Tenampúa, Ulúa valley, Honduras. Private collection. Photograph: Carmelo Guadagno.

17 (*left*). Late Classic jaguar effigy vessel. A.D. 800–1200. 14 in. (36 cm) high. The legs contain pebbles, making it a combined vase and rattle. Nicoya, Costa Rica. Museum of the American Indian (Heye Foundation). 18 (*right*). Late Postclassic Mixteca-Puebla-style vase. A.D. 1350–1520. 10 in. (25 cm) high. Cholula, Puebla, Mexico. Museum of the American Indian (Heye Foundation).

19 (*left*). Postclassic Maya Plumbate animal effigy vessel. A.D. 1000–1200. 7½ in. (19 cm) high. Campeche, Mexico. Museum of the American Indian (Heye Foundation). 20 (*right*). Postclassic Maya carved clay bowl. A.D. 1500(?) 7½ in. (19 cm) high. The carving is in a pattern of monkeys, serpents, and deities. San Augustín Acasaguastlán, Guatemala. Museum of the American Indian (Heye Foundation).

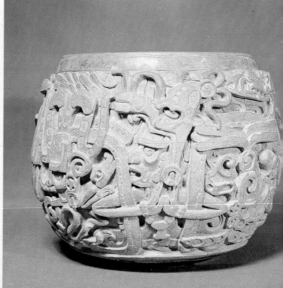

21. Dish painted with design of the crocodile god. A.D. 1000–1500. Diam. 10½ in. (26.5 cm). Veraguas, Panama. Museum of the American Indian (Heye Foundation).

22. Hollow Middle Preclassic baby figure. 800–300 B.C. 13 in. (33 cm). The figure's cap recalls the "helmet" on Olmec colossal heads. Las Bocas, Puebla, Mexico. The Metropolitan Museum of Art, New York. Photograph: Lisa Little.

23. Mother and child hollow ceramic effigy. A.D. 300–900. 18 in. (45 cm). Jalisco, Mexico. Museum of the American Indian (Heye Foundation).

24. Classic Veracruz pottery figures (whistles). A.D. 300–600. 6 in. x 6 in. (15 cm x 15 cm). The figures are on a swing; their bodies are painted to simulate clothing; the string is modern. Museum of the American Indian (Heye Foundation).

25. Late Classic Maya clay whistle. A.D. 550–900. 5½ in. (14 cm). The whistle probably was also used as an ear ornament. Island of Jaina, Campeche, Mexico. Museum of the American Indian (Heye Foundation).

26. Seated shaman and youth. Before 1500 B.C. Shaman: 5½ in. (13.5 cm); youth: 4½ in. (11 cm). Xochipala, Guerrero, Mexico. The Art Museum, Princeton University, Princeton, New Jersey.

27. Black stone carving of a kneeling Olmec figure. 1000–500 B.C. 9¾ in. (25 cm). The hollow in the top of its head suggests its use as an *incensario*. Found in Alta Verapaz, Guatemala. Museum of the American Indian (Heye Foundation).

28. Stone axe gods. A.D. 750–1250. Figure at left: 3⅜ in. (9.5 cm). Nicoya, Costa Rica. Museum of the American Indian (Heye Foundation).

29. Late Classic Maya death mask of jade mosaic. c. A.D. 683. 9½ in. (24 cm). Found in the sarcophagus of the ruler Lord Shield-Pacal in the crypt of the Temple of the Inscriptions. The eyes are inlaid shell and obsidian. Palenque, Chiapas, Mexico. Museo Nacional de Antropología, Mexico City. Photograph: Justin Kerr.

30. Aztec pendant ornament. c. A.D. 1500. 17 in. (43 cm) long. Turquoise mosaic covers the front of the body; the back is hollowed-out wood. The heads are entirely covered with a mosaic of turquoise and red and white shell. The eyes were probably set with shell and polished disks of iron pyrites. The British Museum.

31. Cast-gold pendant depicting a musician. A.D. 1000–1500. 3¼ in. (8.25 cm). Chiriquí, Costa Rica. Museum of the American Indian (Heye Foundation).

32. Jadeite beak bird. A.D. 1–1500. 3⅝ in. (9.1 cm). In place of wings, the arms are doubled over its chest; a human head is at its feet. Línea Vieja area, Costa Rica. The Metropolitan Museum of Art. Photograph: Lee Boltin.

Tenochtitlán they were called the Tenochca. Emphasizing their claim to Toltec
ancestry, they called themselves Colhua-
Mexica. See also **Coxcoxtli.**

Mexican absorption Term used for a period
in Yucatán, A.D. 1204–1539, between the
fall of the Itzás at Chichén Itzá and the
Spanish Conquest.

Mexicano 1. Small linguistic group on the
southern coast of Oaxaca. 2. Modern synonym for Nahuatl or other Nahua dialects
spoken by natives.

Mexican period Term sometimes applied to
the period of Toltec influence in Yucatán
between c. A.D. 987 and the fall of Chichén
Itzá, A.D. 1204.

Mexican Plateau See **Central Plateau.**

Mexican rulers The Mexica were born to
calendrical names, but their rulers chose
official names drawn from myths and religion, perhaps to guard against the harmful
magic use of their number and day name.

it on the south. Its capital is Tolula. Important sites include Teotenango, Malinalco, and Calixtlahuaca.

Mezcala 1. Alternate name for the Balsas
River in Guerrero. 2. "Mezcala zone" refers to the area in Guerrero, south of the
Balsas River, famous for distinctive small
stone sculptures characterized by simplicity of design and detail; rendered with
straight cuts and planes, forms tend to be
geometric. Types include human effigies,
masks, miniature temples, and animal effigies. Active c. 500 B.C.–A.D. 400. See
Guerrero.

meztli 1. Nahuatl word for the moon; sometimes also the god Tezcatlipoca in one of
his nocturnal aspects. 2. The basic Aztec
legend of the moon's creation refers to an
assembly of gods at Teotihuacán at which
both the sun and moon were born of the
self-sacrificial cremation of two gods:
Nanahuatzin, poor and syphilitic, jumped

Acamapichtli	"handful of reeds"	1367–87
Huitzilíhuitl	"hummingbird feather"	1391–1415
Chimalpopoca	"smoking shield"	1415–26
Itzcóatl	"obsidian snake"	1427–40
Moctezuma (I) Ilhuicamina	"angry lord who shoots into the sky"	1440–68
Axayácatl	"water face"	1469–81
Tizoc	"leg of chalk"	1481–86
Ahuítzotl	"water monster"	1486–1502
Moctezuma (II) Xocoyotzin	"angry lord, youngest son"	1502–20
Cuitláhuac	"lord of Cuitláhuac, keeper of the kingdom"	1520
Cuauhtémoc	"descending eagle"	1520–24

Mexico 1. Literally, "place of the Mexica,"
or metaphorically, "place of the moon."
Earliest use of the name, stemming from
the Mexica tribal founders, is by chroniclers mentioning the neighboring cities of
Mexico-Tenochtitlán and Mexico-Tlate-
lolco, today in downtown Mexico City.
Starting in the 18th century, Mexico referred to the area formerly called New
Spain, today the Republic of Mexico. 2.
Modern state in the western part of the
Mexican Plateau, limited by the contiguous states of Hidalgo, Puebla, Tlaxcala,
Morelos, Guerrero, Michoacán, and Queré-
taro. The Federal District is contained by

into the fire first, becoming the sun; Tecciztécatl, rich but cowardly, reluctantly followed and reappeared as the moon, which
was then as bright as the sun. One of the
assembled gods then threw a rabbit into
the moon's face, obscuring its brightness.
This explains the frequent presence of a
rabbit in the Mexican codex representations of the moon. 3. *Meztlipohualli* is the
Aztec count of the lunar months.

Meztliapán "Moon lake," an esoteric name
for Lake Texcoco.

Miccailhuitontli Tenth of the 18 months of
the Nahuatl year of 365 days, as celebrated
at Tenochtitlán. It honored deities in gen-

eral, but especially Huitzilopochtli and Tezcatlipoca. Alternate name was Tlaxochimaco. See **months, Aztec.**

Miccaotli 1. "Road of the Dead," the north-south-oriented axis-thoroughfare of Teotihuacán. So called by the 16th-century Spanish who mistook the bordering earthen mounds, since excavated to reveal the city, for ancient graves. 2. Alternate designation for the Teotihuacán II cultural phase, on the threshold of the Classic florescence at Teotihuacán, c. A.D. 150–250. Paint cloisonné and Thin Orange pottery were introduced. Sculptural activity was related to architecture, including the rain-god and serpent relief panels of the Temple of Quetzalcóatl. This period marks the expansion of the city to 22½ sq. mi. (58 km²), with an estimated population of 45,000.

Michoacán Mexican state bounded on the north by Lake Chapala and the Lerma River, on the south by Balsas River, touches the states of Guerrero and Mexico to the east, Pacific Ocean and the states of Jalisco and Colima to the west, Jalisco, Guanajuato, and Querétaro to the north. Some prominent sites are Tzintzuntzan, El Opeño, and Apatzingán. The Tarascans, centered about Lake Pátzcuaro, were a powerful cultural group in the Postclassic period.

Mictecacíhuatl Consort of Mictlantecuhtli, the Aztec god of the underworld.

Mictlampa North in the Nahuatl concept of the universe and its four directions. Region of the dead of natural causes. Its year sign was Técpatl ("flint"); its day signs included Océlotl, Miquiztli, Técpatl, Itzcuintli, and Éhecatl. Its association was bad and barren.

Mictlán Specifically the northern underworld, destination of Aztecs who died a natural death. After undergoing nine magical trials, souls found repose or disappeared forever after four years. Xibalba is the Maya equivalent.

Mictlantecuhtli Aztec lord of the underworld and of Itzcuintli, tenth of the 20 Nahuatl day names; appears as fifth of the nine Lords of the Night, and variously as the sixth or eleventh of the 13 Lords of the Day. One of the most popular Nahuatl gods, his feminine counterpart was Mictecacíhuatl. In the codices his body is shown covered with human bones, a human skull is his mask, human bones are his earplugs. His hair is black, curled, and studded with starlike eyes since he dwells in the dark regions. Animals associated with him are the bat, spider, and owl.

midden A refuse heap marking a former habitation area.

Middle America Variously defined, for purposes of this volume it is the area comprised of Mesoamerica, the rest of Central America including Panama, and the islands of the West Indies.

Middle Classic horizon A recent term applied to the Teotihuacán cultural horizon in Mesoamerica. Its first phase, Teotihuacán, c. A.D. 400–550, was dominated by that metropolis and its culture. It represents a rapid extension of economic power to foreign centers as distant as Kaminaljuyú, Tikal, Uaxactún, and Copán.

The second phase, Teotihuacanoid, c. A.D. 550–700, shows absorption and reintegration of Mexican forms consolidated into new styles; some floresced after Teotihuacán's collapse, c. A.D. 650, in regions such as Cotzumalhuapa, Yucatán, Usumacinta, and at Xochicalco. This unifying intrusion of the Teotihuacán style in art and architecture upon the separate regional cultures has been referred to as the Middle American co-tradition.

Middle Period, Costa Rica Term applied to regional cultural sequences of Costa Rica, A.D. 500–1000. Curridabat ceramics persist in the Central Highlands. Stone sculpture reaches high development generally, introducing the *sukia* and standing figures with trophy heads. Elaborate wood carving at Retes dates to A.D. 960. Guayabo in the Reventazón River valley achieved maximum expression as a ceremonial center. In Nicoya, Linear Decorated gave way to the Early and Middle Polychrome periods. In the Diquís (Greater Chiriquí) region, Aguas Buenas persisted with Burica and San Lorenzo phases in the Pacific coastal area. Goldworking was probably introduced during the Middle Period from Panama.

Middle Polychrome Term for the ceramic period of Greater Nicoya, in Costa Rica and southwestern Nicaragua, c. A.D. 800–1200.

milpa Nahuatl word for the native cornfields of Mesoamerica and the swidden type of agriculture employed. This method, called "slash-and-burn," required the felling of trees, burning of stumps, and clearing of underbrush for planting. Corn seeds were dropped into holes dug into the ground by *coas*, or planting sticks. Because the natives lacked the plow, soil conditions and weeds usually limited the productivity of a *milpa* to two to three years, after which it was allowed to revert to forest and new *milpas* had to be cleared. *Milpa* cultivation still obtains today.

Miquiztli Sixth of the 20 Nahuatl day signs with a meaning of "death." Its patron deity was Tecciztécatl, its augury unfavorable. Corresponds to the Maya day Cimi and the Zapotec day Lana. Pictured in the codices by a skeleton or a skull with round hollow eyes under a heavy brow and with a hole in its side, a reminder of the skull rack, *tzompantli*. Miquiztli appears in several calendrical names of deities: 1 Miquiztli: Tezcatlipoca, god of sustenance; 5 Miquiztli: Tonatiuh or Xochipilli; 13 Miquiztli: god of death.

Mirador Early Preclassic site of western Chiapas.

Miraflores Archaeological site in Tabasco. Palenque emblem glyphs found there suggest its relationship to that Classic period Maya center.

Miraflores-Arenal Late Preclassic period at Kaminaljuyú, Guatemalan highlands, c. 400 B.C.–A.D. 100; achieved peak of Preclassic development, including the finest stone carvings ever produced in the highlands. They included large human and jaguar heads, silhouetted stone carvings, stelae, mushroom stones, and jades. In ceramic ware, hollow-foot supports were introduced, also censers with three top loop handles, and solid handmade figurines. In architecture there was a zeal for building religious and civic buildings and huge brightly painted pyramids, differentiating it from earlier phases.

mirror The use of mirrors in ancient Middle America extends from Panama to northern Mexico. Highly polished concave mirrors of magnetite, ilmenite, and hematite were found in Olmec offerings at La Venta. Their function remains obscure: they could have served to ignite kindling; perforations at the edges suggest they were worn as pendants; La Venta Monument 23 surely has a concave mirror on its chest.

By the Early Classic period plaques of stone and wood were faced with beautifully fitted and ground polygonal pieces of refractory pyrite crystals. They were prominent at Kaminaljuyú, where circular slate mirror backs were intricately carved with designs in El Tajín (Veracruz) style. Mirrors were also found in the earliest graves at Sitio Conte, Panama. The Aztec god Tezcatlipoca ("the mirror that smokes") is identified in the codices by a smoking mirror in place of a foot torn off by the earth monster. Frequently another mirror adorns his temple.

mise-en-couleur French term commonly employed to describe a treatment of alloyed gold, *tumbaga*, by which the copper content of the surface is removed by acid, leaving a thin coating of pure gold. Also called "pickling."

Misquito The largest tribe of the Caribbean lowlands of Nicaragua and eastern Honduras; the region is called Misquitía.

Mitla Center in the eastern Oaxaca valley of the waning Zapotec civilization after the Mixtec Postclassic expansion c. A.D. 1000. Striking architecture is a blend of Zapotec and Mixtec styles. Mitla's freestanding palace structures are famed for the detailed geometric stone mosaic work that decorates their facades, principally in variations of the "stepped-fret" motif. Cruciform tombs are built in the Zapotec style—large, intricately carved stone blocks laid without the use of mortar.

Mitnal Lowland Maya name for the underworld, possibly a derivative of the Nahuatl Mictlán, and corresponding to Xibalba of the Quiché Maya of Guatemala. Ah Puch ruled as the lord of death.

Mixcóatl Leader of the Toltec-Chichimec tribe that settled in Colhuacán. Chimalman bore him a son, Ce Ácatl Topiltzin, later known as Quetzalcóatl. He was murdered, later deified, becoming the god of the hunt. His name in Nahuatl means "cloud serpent," probably a reference to the Milky Way. A leading god of the Chichimec, he was revered in the Tlaxcala-Puebla region as Camaxtli.

Mixco Viejo Pokoman Maya fortress-city, Department of Chimaltenango, Guatemala. Established in the Late Classic period, it fell to the Spaniards in 1525. Comprises 12 groups of palaces and temples around paved courts with altar platforms.

Mixe Linguistic group of northeast Oaxaca.

Mixquic See **chinampa.**

Mixtec A branch of the Oto-Zapotecan language group from the mountains of the Mixteca Alta that settled in the valley of Oaxaca. By c. A.D. 1000 the Mixtec confederation of city-states initiated a highly developed civilization, strongly influencing the later Aztecs. Mixtec dynastic history is documented to A.D. 692, including the account of the famous ruler Eight Deer Tiger Claw. Famous for polychrome ceramics; their outstanding goldwork shows Central American contact. Seven of remaining pre-Conquest codices are Mixtec. The Mixtec availed themselves of ancient Zapotec tombs at Monte Albán, burying their leaders with rich treasure: Tomb 7 is the most famous, its contents now on display in the Oaxaca Regional Museum. Mitla attests to their artistic innovation in architectural decoration, murals, and beautifully carved interiors of cruciform tombs.

Mixteca The region inhabited by the Mixtec peoples. It is divided into the Mixteca Baja in western and northeastern Oaxaca, Mixteca Alta to the east and south, and the Mixteca de la Costa in the Pacific coastal lowlands.

Mixteca-Puebla An art style that, starting in the early Postclassic period after the fall of Tula, gradually dominated central Mexico. It is essentially a synthesis of the styles of Teotihuacán, Xochicalco, and Veracruz; Cholula in Puebla became the creative center. Since its motifs and techniques and those of the Mixteca were nearly identical, the style is called Mixteca-Puebla. Polychrome pottery and codices, such as the Borgia, typify it. Original pottery shapes were effigy jars, tripod censers with walls perforated in geometric frieze decorations, pitchers, and vases. They culminated in polychrome tripod vessels painted with scenes and motifs almost identical to the codices; the finest are Mixtec in subject matter. Widely traded from the Atlantic to the Pacific, and from Sinaloa to Nicaragua. Contemporary with the Aztecs.

Mixtequilla Region in the modern state of Veracruz, between the Papaloapán and Cotaxtla rivers, whose best-known sites are Cerro de las Mesas and Nopiloa.

Moan bird Mythical bird of ill omen depicted in Maya art, possibly based on the Yucatecan screech owl. It is related to Ah Puch, the "black god" of death, as his symbol and attendant.

Moan bird

Moctezuma I Fifth ruler of Tenochtitlán, A.D. 1440–68, Moctezuma Ilhuicamina ("angry lord who shoots into the sky"), was the cousin of his predecessor, Itzcóatl. Under him the Mexica began their great expansion, extending their domain to the Gulf of Mexico. Influenced by his ally, Nezahualcóyotl of Texcoco, he created zoological and botanical gardens. "Flowery Wars" to obtain sacrificial victims were initiated in his reign.

Moctezuma II Moctezuma Xocoyotzin ("angry lord, youngest son") was the ninth Aztec ruler, A.D. 1502–20. He was the son of Axayácatl, the sixth Aztec king, and the grandson of Moctezuma I. He died in Tenochtitlán while a prisoner of Cortés.

Mol Eighth month of the *tun,* the Maya year of 360 days.

molcajete See **grater bowl.**

Momotombito Island in Lake Managua, Nicaragua. Gray basalt columnar figures found there date c. A.D. 800–1500. The volcano Momotombo rises on the nearby mainland shore.

momoztli Postclassic Mexican offertory shrine, usually found at crossroads or centers of plazas.

Monagrillo Shell midden site on Parita Bay, Pacific coast of Panama, near the earlier mounds of Cerro Mangote. Earliest known ceramic complex on the isthmus, 2130 B.C., its pottery origins are to be found in the earliest ceramics of Colombia or Ecuador.

Mongolian spot Small irregularly shaped spot at the base of the spine of a baby at birth; purple to bluish in color, it gradually fades to slate, and finally disappears before the tenth birthday. Characteristic of the peoples of eastern Asia, it is common among American Indians.

Monte Albán Major Zapotec ceremonial center on a flattened mountaintop, c. 2,000 ft. (600 m) above the modern city of Oaxaca. The identity of its earliest inhabitants is not established. Monte Albán cultural phases define the development of Oaxacan civilization.

Monte Albán I, 700–350 B.C., shows the connections of this area with the Olmec sites of La Venta in Tabasco, Tlatilco in the Valley of Mexico, and sites in Morelos. In ceramics, the ceremonial grayware that was to characterize Monte Albán was already evident but utility ware was yellow or brown. By the middle of the seventh century the site itself was inhabited; oldest extant building, named for the bas-relief sculptures of the *danzantes,* is of this pe-

riod, as are the earliest known examples of writing, and the Mesoamerican Calendar Round.

Monte Albán II, 350 B.C.–A.D. 100, was more closely related to the lowland cultures of Chiapas and the Maya. Anthropomorphic ceramic figures, tetrapod vessels, and vases with animal figures appeared. The Great Plaza was leveled, Mound J (observatory) was built, along with the famous subterranean tombs.

Transitional Monte Albán II–IIIa, A.D. 100–300, marked the appearance of the unique funerary urns whose representations of deities recall Teotihuacán II figurines. See **urns of Oaxaca.**

Monte Albán IIIa, A.D. 300–600, presents the first proof of occupation by Zapotec intruders from the Mixteca Alta. Although drawing heavily on Teotihuacán during the Early Classic period, they imposed their own regional stamp, as in the architectural development of the "scapulary tablet" out of the *talud-tablero* building facades of Teotihuacán. The I-shaped ball court and quadrangular plazas surrounded by buildings arose around the Great Plaza. In ceramics, Teotihuacán-inspired jars with spouts, tripod vessels, polished grayware with engraved or incised decoration appeared, along with Thin Orange pottery.

Monte Albán IIIb, A.D. 600–900, marked the zenith of building activity, introduction of monolithic columns, and completion of the Great Plaza as seen today. It was a period of consolidation and isolation from the rest of Mesoamerica, thereby perhaps laying the foundation for the marked aesthetic and technical decadence of Monte Albán IV. Toward the end of IIIb, Monte Albán relinquished its dominance over the region.

Monte Albán IV, A.D. 900–1150, gave rise to the Mixtec culture, commingling with the Zapotec c. A.D. 1000. Monte Albán was not abandoned, but became a necropolis. Mixtec treasures found in Tomb 7, among others, demonstrate their reuse beginning at this time.

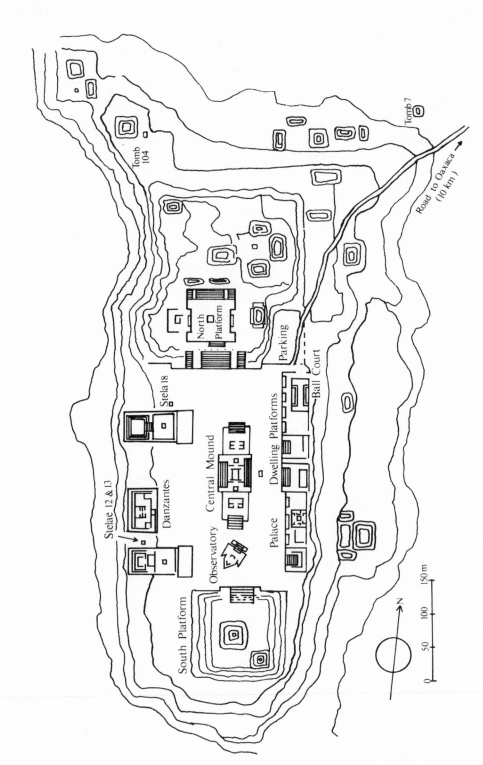

Plate 10. Central Monte Albán.

Monte Albán V, A.D. 1150–Conquest, essentially refers to the Mixtec presence in the valley of Oaxaca. Sites such as Mitla and Yagul were civic rather than ceremonial centers, such as Monte Albán had been. See **Oaxaca.**

Monte Alto Preclassic site, c. 500 B.C.–A.D. 100, near Democracia, southern Guatemala. Colossal bodyless boulder heads recall those of the Olmec only in size. Rendered with closed eyes, they may be portraits of dead rulers.

Monte Negro Hill near Tilantongo in the Mixteca Alta, Oaxaca. The name is also applied to an important settlement of Middle Preclassic times in the valley of Oaxaca, contemporary with Monte Albán I; abandoned c. 300 B.C.

Montezuma See **Moctezuma II.**

months, Aztec The Aztec solar year of 365 days was composed of 18 months of 20 days (*xíhuitl*), followed by a period of five unlucky days (*Nemontemi*). Each of the 20-day months had its *veintena* ceremonies dedicated to various deities (described in detail under the headings of individual months): 1. Izcalli: "resurrection"; 2. Atlcahualo: "they leave the water"; 3. Tlacaxipehualiztli: "flaying of men"; 4. Tozoztontli: "short watch"; 5. Hueytozoztli: "great watch"; 6. Tóxcatl: "dry thing"; 7. Etzalcualiztli: "meal of maize and beans"; 8. Tecuilhuitontli: "small feast of the lords"; 9. Hueytecuilhuitl: "great feast of the lords"; 10. Miccailhuitontli: "small feast of the dead"; 11. Hueymiccailhuitl: "great feast of the dead"; 12. Ochpanitztli: "road sweeping"; 13. Pachtontli: "a bit of hay"; 14. Hueypachtli: "much hay"; 15. Quecholli: "precious feather"; 16. Panquetzaliztli: "raising of banners"; 17. Atemoztli: "the water falls"; 18. Títitl: "shrunk, or wrinkled."

The order of the months of 20 days, or *veintenas*, was universally observed in the Mexican Plateau, but it is uncertain which was the generally observed first month. Izcalli, which spanned January 24–February 12 of our modern calendar in 1521, appears to have begun the year in Tenoch-titlán. See also **religious ceremonies, Aztec.**

months, Maya The Maya solar year of 365 days was composed of 18 months of 20 days (*tun* or *haab*), followed by five unlucky days (*Uayeb*). The names of the months, sequentially, were: 1. Pop, 2. Uo, 3. Zip, 4. Zotz, 5. Tzec, 6. Xul, 7. Yaxkin, 8. Mol, 9. Chen, 10. Yax, 11. Zac, 12. Ceh, 13. Mac, 14. Kankin, 15. Muan, 16. Pax, 17. Kayab, 18. Cumku (followed by *Uayeb*).

The day of the month in the 365-day Maya calendar was stated by a number preceding the name of the month. Since Maya chronology was based on elapsed time, the first day of the first month is 0 Pop, the last day of the same 20-day month thereby becoming 19 Pop. The first day of the following month is then 0 Uo, followed by 1 Uo, 2 Uo, etc., proceeding to 19 Uo. The Maya system of numbering the position of the days in the months is identical with the modern method of counting astronomical time; both are based on elapsed time and therefore only possible with the knowledge of zero.

moon See **meztli; u; lunar calendar.**

Moon Count See **Supplementary Series.**

moon-god, goddess See **meztli, Tecciztécatl, Coyolxauhqui, Ix Chel, Xaratanga.**

Mopan Maya linguistic group and river of southern Belize.

Morelos State of modern Mexico bordered by the Federal District, and the states of Mexico, Guerrero, and Puebla. Capital is Cuernavaca. Archaeological sites include Xochicalco, Chalcatzingo, Tepoztlán.

Morett Pacific coastal site in Colima, with possible occupancy from 500 B.C. Early ceramics, with zoning in red and white, show similarity to Conchas phase of Guatemala and early material from Ecuador.

mortuary complex An assembly of features found in the death rituals of a people: the tombs, burial practices, and associated offerings.

mosaic This technique was employed in Mesoamerica in the Classic and Postclassic periods. Mirrors of fitted pieces of pyrite attached to wood or stone were found at

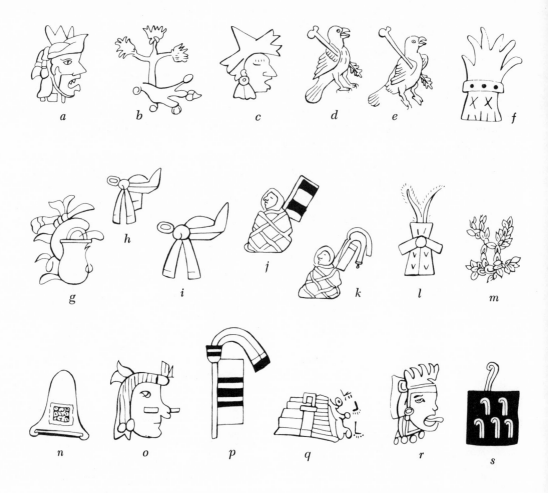

Plate 11. Eighteen Aztec month signs and *Nemontemi:* (*a*) Izcalli, (*b*) Atlcahualo, (*c*) Tlacaxipehualiztli, (*d*) Tozoztontli, (*e*) Hueytozoztli, (*f*) Tóxcatl, (*g*) Etzalcualiztli, (*h*) Tecuilhuitontli, (*i*) Hueytecuilhuitl, (*j*) Miccailhuitontli, (*k*) Hueymiccailhuitl, (*l*) Ochpanitztli, (*m*) Pachtontli, (*n*) Hueypachtli, (*o*) Quecholli, (*p*) Panquetzaliztli, (*q*) Atemoztli, (*r*) Títitl, (*s*) *Nemontemi* (last 5 days).

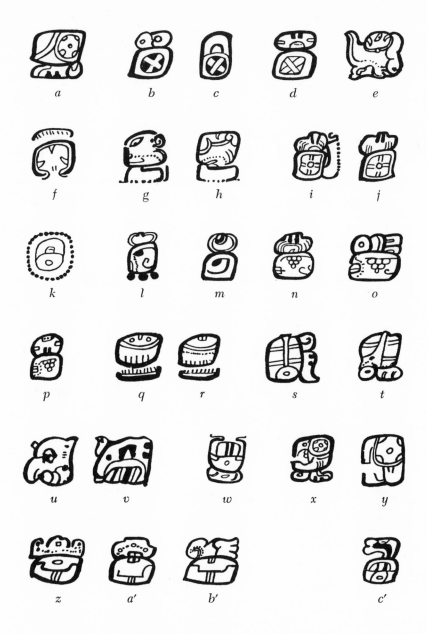

Plate 12. Maya month signs in the codices: (*a*) Pop, (*b, c*) Uo, (*d*) Zip, (*e*) Zotz, (*f*) Tzec, (*g, h*) Xul, (*i, j*) Yaxkin, (*k*) Mol, (*l, m*) Chen, (*n*) Yax, (*o*) Zac, (*p*) Ceh, (*q, r*) Mac, (*s, t*) Kankin, (*u, v*) Muan, (*w*) Pax, (*x, y*) Kayab, (*z, a', b'*) Cumku, (*c'*) *Uayeb*. From S. G. Morley, *An Introduction to the Study of Maya Hieroglyphs*, page 50.

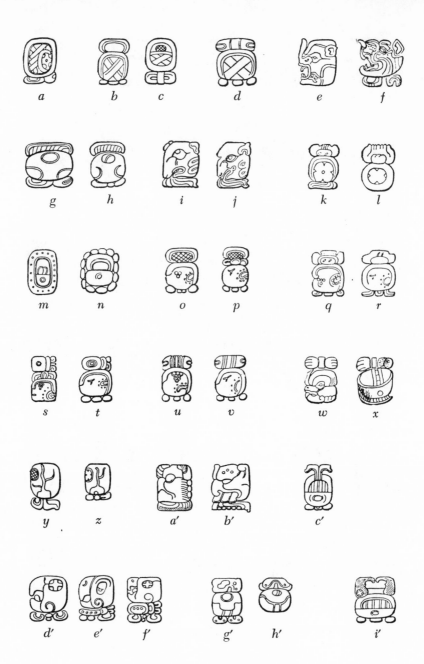

Plate 13. Maya month signs in the inscriptions: (*a*) Pop, (*b, c*) Uo, (*d*) Zip, (*e, f*) Zotz, (*g, h*) Tzec, (*i, j*) Xul, (*k, l*) Yaxkin, (*m, n*) Mol, (*o, p*) Chen, (*q, r*) Yax, (*s, t*) Zac, (*u, v*) Ceh, (*w, x*) Mac, (*y, z*) Kankin, (*a', b'*) Muan, (*c'*) Pax, (*d', e', f'*) Kayab, (*g', h'*) Cumku, (*i'*) *Uayeb*. From S. G. Morley, *An Introduction to the Study of Maya Hieroglyphs*, page 49.

Plate 14. Middle American musical instruments. *Percussion:* (*a*) horizontal drum (*teponaztli*); (*b*) vertical drum (*huéhuetl*); (*c*) turtle carapace struck with antlers (*áyotl*). *Wind instruments:* (*d*) conch shell trumpet (*atecocolli*); (*e*) clay flute (*tlapitzalli*); (*f*) pottery whistle, Veracruz; (*g*) ceramic ocarina (*huilacapiztli*), Costa Rica. *Rattles:* (*h*) spherical clay rattle (*ayacachtli*). *Rasps:* (*i*) bone rasp (*omichicahuaztli*). Drawings by Frank Anthony Dzibela.

Piedras Negras and Kaminaljuyú. Jade mosaic masks were uncovered in the Temple of the Inscriptions at Palenque. Turquoise mosaic disks and masks were produced by the Aztecs. In architecture, intricate stone mosaic work distinguishes Puuc facades such as those at Uxmal in Yucatán, and the Mixtec palace walls at Mitla in Oaxaca.

Mosquito See **Misquito.**

Motagua The Motagua River rises in the Department of El Quiché, Guatemala, and flows into the Gulf of Honduras on the Caribbean coast. San Augustín Acasaguastlán and Quiriguá are sites along its course. Originally called Nimaya, or Great River.

Motozintlec Maya language group of Chiapas, Mexico.

Motul 1. Maya city of northern Yucatán, seat of the Pech family at the Conquest. 2. Yucatecan ceramic phase, contemporary with Tepeu I–II in the southern lowlands, c. A.D. 600–800. 3. Motul dictionary, composed c. 1590, is the finest Maya-Spanish dictionary, attributed to Fray Antonio de Ciudad Real. Today in the John Carter Brown Library, Providence, R. I.

Mountain Cow An assembly of small Classic period Maya sites in the southern Cayo district of Belize. Mayas called it Hatzcap Ceel.

Mount Hope Cultural phase of Barton Ramie, Belize, 300 B.C.–A.D. 100.

movable ceremonies See **religious ceremonies, Aztec.**

Mse One of the Zapotec Lords of the Night; equivalent to the Aztec goddess Tlazoltéotl.

Muan Fifteenth month of the *tun*, the Maya year of 360 days.

Mul-Chic Small Maya site of western Yucatán, with painted murals depicting warriors and priests; active A.D. 600–800.

Muluc Ninth of the 20 Maya days, corresponds to the Aztec day Atl. Its glyph is the head of a fish, possibly *xoc*. The day's augury was favorable. See **Year Bearer.**

mushroom stone Small mushroom-shaped stone sculpture, up to a foot high, sometimes with annular, tripod, or effigy base. Found throughout the Guatemalan highlands and on the Pacific slope, more rarely in the lowlands, and in Chiapas and El Salvador. Appeared in the Preclassic period but manufacture ceased at the end of the Classic.

musical instruments Ancient Middle American music was produced by percussion instruments (*huéhuetl, teponaztli, áyotl*), trumpets (*atecocolli*), flutes (*huilacapiztli, tlapitzalli*), rasps (*omichicahuaztli*), rattles (*ayacachtli*), whistles, or ocarinas (*huilacapiztli*). The use of stringed instruments in pre-Columbian times has not been established.

n

na Common Maya hut.

Naa Fifteenth of the 20 Zapotec day names, equivalent to the Aztec day Cuauhtli and the Maya day Men.

Naachtun Lowland Classic period Maya site in the northern Petén of Guatemala, near the Campeche border.

Naapatecuhtli One of the Tlalocs, with the meaning "four times lord."

Nacaste Cultural phase at San Lorenzo, southern Veracruz, marking the end of Olmec civilization there, c. 900–700 B.C. Mutilation of monuments and appearance of non-Olmec wares suggest outside interference.

Naco Commercial center for the Ulúa valley at the time of the Conquest, situated on an affluent of the Chamelecón river. Naco is also the name of the only ceramic complex in Honduras assigned to the late Mexican-influenced Postclassic period. Red- or black-on-white is diagnostic of Naco ware, also found at Agalteca, Honduras.

nacom Maya war chief, elected for a period of three years, sharing some responsibilities with the hereditary ruler of the town, the *batab*.

nacon A class of Maya priests charged with the duty of tearing out the heart of a sacrificial victim, subservient to the regular priest, the *ah kin*.

Nacxit 1. Abbreviated name given in their histories by the Quiché and Cakchiquel Maya to the "king of the east," or Quetzalcóatl, as related in the Popol Vuh. 2. A name for Venus, it has been interpreted to mean "four steps," the steps Venus takes in space. Mentioned in the *Chilam Balam* of Tizimín.

Nahua An important subdivision of the Uto-Aztecan linguistic strain that probably had its roots in western Mexico; also the peoples who spoke it. Two major dialects of it are Nahuat and Nahuatl.

nahual Nahuatl word for alter ego.

Nahuat A dialect of Nahua spoken on the Gulf Coast of Mexico and as far south as Nicaragua in isolated areas.

Nahuatl Dialect of Nahua centered in the Valley of Mexico, still spoken today, that became the lingua franca of Mesoamerica. Sometimes also called Aztec and Mexicano.

nahui Number 4 in Nahuatl.

Nakum Lowland Classic period Maya site in the central Petén, Guatemala.

nal-tel Strain of wild corn discovered in dry caves of Tamaulipas and the Tehuacán Valley, Puebla. See **maize.**

nanahualtin Nahuatl word for sorcerers who possessed the faculty of adopting the shape of animals, primarily that of the jaguar, dedicating themselves to nocturnal mischief.

Nanahuatzin The syphilitic god, an aspect of Xólotl, god of twins and the deformed. Appeared as the accomplice of Tecciztécatl in the myth of the creation of the fifth sun. An antecedent of Huitzilopochtli and probably identified with him. See also **meztli.**

Naranjo 1. Classic Maya site in the central Petén, Guatemala. 2. River in Costa Rica, formerly called Río de los Manques.

Naranjo emblem glyph

Nayarit Mexican state on the Pacific Ocean, bounded by Sinaloa, Durango, and Jalisco; Tepic is the capital. Along with Colima and Jalisco, one of three prominent western Mexico art styles. Rich polychrome, facial painting, multiple-ring nose and earplugs, arms like ropes of clay distinguish Nayarit ceramic figure types. Great variety includes grotesque figures with "elephantine" legs, the gay rendering of village scenes, and the sophisticated *chinesco* figures. Among Nayarit sites are Ixtlán del Río, Las Cebollas, Etzatlán, Amapa, Peñitas, and Coamiles.

Ndan Zapotec god of the ocean, principal god of the hierarchy, and one of the nine Lords of the Night. Sometimes a goddess, or bisexual.

Ndo'yet Zapotec god of death and one of the nine day names representing objects or natural forces.

Ndozin A Zapotec god of justice and death, and one of the nine Lords of the Night. The messenger of Ndan.

Nebaj Maya site in the Department of Quiché, northern Guatemalan highlands. A well-documented ceramic sequence, from the Early Classic period to the Postclassic, has been derived from tombs and caches.

negative painting See resist painting.

Nemontemi The last 5 days, of unfavorable augury, at end of the Aztec Vague Year, following the 18 months of 20 days. Corresponds to *Uayeb* of the Maya.

Nentli Meaning "worthless," it is an alternate word for *Nemontemi.*

New Empire A term formerly applied to the Toltec-influenced Postclassic period of the northern lowland Maya. See also Mesoamerica.

New Fire Ceremony See Toxiuhmolpilia, Cerro de la Estrella, Calendar Round.

Nezahualcóyotl (A.D. 1402–72) King of Texcoco, son of Ixtlilxóchitl I, who was slain by Tezozómoc, the Tepanec king of Atzcapotzalco. He later aided the Aztecs in destroying Atzcapotzalco. Nezahualcóyotl was an inspired poet, he codified the ancient laws of Texcoco, and founded probably the first library in the Americas. As an engineer he helped plan the city of Tenochtitlán, the building of its aqueduct, and the great dike across Lake Texcoco to hold back the brackish waters from the fertile *chinampas* in the sweet waters of Lake Chalco. As a religious theorist his concept of the Tloque Nahuaque, abstract, invisible god, was far ahead of his time and the nearest approach to monotheism in Mesoamerica. He was contemporary and counselor to both Itzcóatl and Moctezuma I of Tenochtitlán. His name means "fasting coyote."

Nezahualpilli (A.D. 1460–1515) 1. King of Texcoco, succeeding his father, Nezahualcóyotl. Similarly gifted, his reign saw economic, social, and cultural progress; his capital was recognized as the intellectual center of the Valley of Mexico. 2. A name of the god Tezcatlipoca as the patron of princes.

Nicaragua Largest Central American republic, extending from Honduras to Costa Rica, and from the Caribbean Sea to the Pacific Ocean. Managua is the capital. It contains two large lakes, Managua and Nicaragua, the latter with the archaeologically important islands of Ometepec and Zapatera. Most of the population is on the Pacific side and bears witness to the Mexican migrations of the Chorotega-Mangue, the Maribio, and Nicarao in Classic and Postclassic times. The Atlantic slope includes a portion of the Misquitía that extends into eastern Honduras and is the homeland of the large Misquito tribe. Preceramic deposits on the Misquitía coast may date in the third millennium B.C.

Nicarao A Nahuat-Pipil group that left the coastal Soconusco region of Chiapas c. A.D.

800, settling in Nicaragua and driving out the Chorotega peoples who had preceded them.

Nicoya Peninsula on the Pacific coast of Costa Rica. Originally populated by peoples of southern origin who were forced out in Late Classic times by Mexican invaders, the northern Chorotega and Nahuat-speaking Nicarao. The Nicoya cultural area is composed of the province of Guanacaste and the entire peninsula, and known for its fine polychrome pottery, closely related to the Late Classic Maya style. The Papagayo group of Middle Polychrome ceramics is also called Nicoya. Large cemeteries furnished fine jade objects along with pottery. Nicoya is the only part of Costa Rica with large stone sculptures in quantity, including three-legged rimless *metates* and statues.

Pacific Nicaragua, together with the Nicoya Peninsula, is referred to as the Greater Nicoya archaeological subarea.

Nito An important trading center at the Caribbean mouth of the Río Dulce, Guatemala. Reached overland by Cortés. Commercial contact with the distant Gulf of Mexico was attested by the existence of a quarter occupied by Acalán merchants from their capital of Itzamkanac on the Candelaria River of Campeche.

Niza Ninth of the 20 Zapotec day names. Equivalent to the Aztec day Atl and the Maya day Muluc. Sometimes called Queza.

Noche Triste Spanish for "sad night," it is applied to the night of June 30, 1520, when Cortés and his men attempted to escape from Tenochtitlán by one of the causeways; he was attacked by the Aztecs with a loss of 600 men and 80 horses.

Nocuchich Late Classic period Maya site of northern Campeche-Chenes area, but with Río Bec cultural influence. An uncommon lone-standing tower resembles a narrow, attenuated roof comb.

Nogales Phase of the Sierra de Tamaulipas, 5000–3000 B.C.

Nohmul Classic Maya site of northern Belize; caches contained figurines, rare for the Classic period.

Nohol Maya word for South. See **world directions, Maya.**

Nonoalca A Nahuat-Pipil group that settled in the southern Veracruz-Tabasco area after the fall of Teotihuacán. According to the Popol Vuh some continued on to Guatemala and became the forebears of the Quiché Maya. Others joined the Toltec-Chichimec to form the Toltec state at Tula c. A.D. 900. Excellent artisans, they excelled in jade carving and in metalworking. After the fall of Tula, a Nonoalca group moved south to become a major element in the population of Chalco. See also **Pipil.**

Nonoalco Intermediate zone on the Gulf Coast drainage of the Usumacinta and Grijalva rivers between peoples of the north and Maya to the south, who spoke a different language, hence its name, which means "land of the dumb" in Nahuatl. Identified with Tlapallán, the legendary region to which Quetzalcóatl repaired after leaving Tula. Also called Chontalpa, as the homeland of the Chontal, or Putún, Maya.

Nopiloa Site in the Mixtequilla region of southern Veracruz. Gave its name to the "smiling figure" ceramic complex, often confused with similar figurines from Remojadas to the north. Smaller Mayoid figurines, generally whistles or rattles, show similarity to those from Jaina, Campeche, and Jonuta, Tabasco. Ceramic production spanned c. A.D. 500–900.

Northern Lowlands See **Maya areas.**

nuclear area An area that generates vigorous cultural change and also exerts its influence on other cultures. It thereby establishes itself as the focus (nucleus) of cultural development. Mesoamerica and the Central Andes of South America are therefore defined as the two nuclear civilizations of the New World. The term *nuclear America* groups Mesoamerica, the Intermediate Area (where South American and Mexican cultural influences meet), and the Central Andes into one cultural-historical unit. Smaller nuclear areas may exist within the larger concept. Within Mesoamerica, the Valley of Mexico was one of several nuclear subareas.

Ñuiñe Late Middle Classic period regional art style found in the upper Balsas River basin of the Mixteca Baja, southern Puebla. Perhaps the precursor of the later Mixteca-Puebla style, it was influenced by Teotihuacán and Monte Albán. Thin Orange pottery production, c. A.D. 200–500, was centered at Ixcaquixtla in the Ñuiñe region. It is also the source of the *cabecitas colosales*, small bodiless spherical stone heads. Coeval with Xochicalco and Cotzumalhuapa, between the fall of Teotihuacán and the rise of Tula.

numbers The basic numbers and ten in Nahuatl and Maya are:

NUMBER	NAHUATL	MAYA
1.	ce	hun
2.	ome	ca
3.	yeyi	ox
4.	nahui	can
5.	macuilli	ho
6.	chicuacen	uac
7.	chicome	uuc
8.	chicueyi	uaxac
9.	chicnahui	bolon
10.	mahtlactli	lahun

As in English, these numbers are compounded to form 13 to 19, inclusive. Maya 14 is *can lahun,* compounded of *lahun* and *can;* among the Aztecs it is *mahtlactli ihuan nahui.* There was a definite deity-number relationship among the Maya. The deities of the moon, sun, jaguar, maize, death, and earth were respectively associated with the numbers 1, 4, 7, 8, 10, and 11. See also **numerical recording, Aztec; Maya.**

numerical recording, Aztec The Aztecs employed the vigesimal system of counting, as did other Mesoamerican peoples. Numbers 1 to 19 were represented by corresponding numbers of dots or circles. Unlike the Maya, bars were rarely used to denote 5, even though they had earlier been used at Teotihuacán and Xochicalco. They did not record Long Count dates and therefore did not avail themselves of either position numerals or the zero. To indicate quantities larger than 19, the Aztecs employed a system of symbols, such as a flag for 20, a feather for 400, etc. These symbols are prominent in the remaining tribute codices, shown with pictured goods, and thereby provide a simple accounting of tributes paid.

numerical recording, Maya The Maya employed only three symbols: a dot for 1, a bar for 5, and a stylized clam shell for 0:

| 0 | 1 | 3 | 5 | 19 |

To represent large numbers, the Maya used a vigesimal system of position numerals based on multiples of 20, which is similar to our decimal system employing the unit 10. Whereas we write numbers from right to left in increasing multiples of 10, the Maya proceeded from bottom to top. Their first position included the numbers 1 to 19. In the second position each unit had the value of 20, in the third position the value of 400, etc., thus permitting the total to be added vertically. To show 20 by a single dot, it was placed in the second position, above a zero in the first position. The comparison below shows how to arrive at 1,920, compared to the decimal system:

MODERN DECIMAL		MAYA VIGESIMAL		
100s:	1,000	400s:	••••	(1,600)
10s:	900	20s:	≡̇	(320)
1s:	20	1s:	⬭	(0)
	1,920			1,920

Calendrical computations followed the same system, with the sole exception that the third position (*tun*) had a value of 360 (18 months of 20 days) instead of 400.

Head variants (head glyphs) were also used to represent numbers on carved monuments. Number 10 was a death's-head; for numbers 11 to 19, the glyph combined an attribute of death (e.g. a lower jawbone) with that of the lower number. Such compounded head variants differed widely, confounding modern decipherment. In a few texts, such as the Initial Series on Stela D at Copán, full-figure glyphs are used, vastly aiding in the identification of the animal or being represented by the head form.

Nuttall, Codex See **codex, pre-Conquest Mexican; Nuttall, Codex.**

O

Oaxaca Mexican state, with capital of same name, bounded by the Pacific Ocean, Guerrero, Puebla, Veracruz, and Chiapas. Zapotec and Mixtec are the dominant tribes to this day. Sites include Monte Negro, Monte Albán, Mitla, Yagul, Lambityeco, Dainzú, and Zaachila.

Obiyel Guaobiran Island Arawak dog deity; keeper of the souls of the recently departed.

obsidian Volcanic glass that can be flaked by percussion or pressure to make fine prismatic blades for cutting tools or projectile points. Usually black, it is also found in shades of green, white, or red. Abundant in volcanic highlands, it was an important trade item in all areas.

obsidian hydration A method of archaeological dating of obsidian that has been worked by man. Since water is absorbed at a constant rate after obsidian has been flaked, the resulting hydration layer on the newly exposed surface can be measured and converted into the elapsed time.

Oc Tenth of the 20 Yucatecan Maya day names, corresponding to the Aztec day Itzcuintli; the Maya equivalent of Xólotl was its patron.

Ocampo Cultural phase of southwest Sierra Madre de Tamaulipas, contemporary with Nogales phase of Sierra de Tamaulipas, c. 4000–3000 B.C.

Océlotl 1. Océlotl is the Nahuatl word for jaguar (*Felis onca*). It must not be confused with the smaller ocelot (*Felis pardalis*) that the Aztecs separately and derivatively called *tlacoocélotl*. 2. Fourteenth of the 20 Nahuatl day signs. Tlazoltéotl was its deity; its augury was unfavorable. Equivalent to the Maya day Ix and the Zapotec day Gueche. Mythologically, *océlotl* is the beast that devours the sun, thus signifying the earth; also symbolic of night. Revered as a symbol of the "Jaguar knights," an Aztec warrior fraternity. Jaguar calendrical references are: 1 Océlotl: Xipe Totec, god of regeneration and jewelers; 4 Océlotl: sign of the first world in Aztec cosmology; 5 Océlotl: patron god of the *amantecas*, featherworkers; 8 Océlotl: birthday of Tepeyolohtli; 9 Océlotl: Tlaloc, rain-god; 13 Océlotl: a form of the goddess Coatlícue.

Ochpanitztli Harvest festival, the 12th of the 18 20-day months of the Aztec calendar, as celebrated at Tenochtitlán, honoring Teteoinnan, mother of the gods—the old earth-goddess, also called Toci. In another aspect she was the corn-goddess Chicomecóatl. See **months, Aztec.**

Ocós Early Preclassic site on the Guatemalan coast near La Victoria at the Chiapas border. Rocker stamping, cord marking, shell stamping, and an iridescent paint seemingly related to the Chorrera phase of Ecuador are diagnostic of the Ocós ceramic phase, at least 1500 B.C., and no later than 1350 B.C. Its influence penetrated as far as Veracruz at San Lorenzo.

octli Among the Nahuatl, any fermented drink, but generally applied to the fermented juice of the maguey, today called pulque. Among the ancients the use of intoxicants was restricted to men over 70, women in labor, religious ceremonies, and warriors preparing for battle, when it was called *teotli*, the divine drink.

Ojochí Earliest occupation of San Lorenzo site, southern Veracruz. This phase is related to the Barra and Ocós phases of the Soconusco, c. 1500–1350 B.C., with comparable ceramic forms and figurines.

Old Empire Outdated designation for the lowland Maya Classic period, encompassing the Tzakol and Tepeu phases; distinguished from New Empire, former name for the period of Toltec influence in Postclassic northern Yucatán. See also **Mesoamerica.**

old fire-god See **Huehuetéotl.**

olla Spanish word for a pottery jar with a flaring neck.

olla

ollama is the Nahuatl word for ball game; *ollamani* for a player in the Mesoamerican ball game.

olli Nahuatl word for the rubber latex of the *Castilla elastica* tree.

Ollin Seventeenth of the 20 Nahuatl day signs, with the meaning of "movement." Xólotl was the patron deity, with an indifferent augury. Corresponds to the Maya day Caban and the Zapotec day Xoo. It appears in the calendrical names: 1 Ollin: the god Xólotl; 4 Ollin: sign of the fifth and current world, destined to destruction by earthquake.

Olmec A Middle Preclassic period people of unknown antecedents, whose heartland was southern Veracruz and western Tabasco. Olmec is Nahuatl for "rubber people." Active c. 1500–400 B.C., they are sometimes also called the Metropolitan Olmecs to distinguish them from the later, nonrelated, Historic Olmecs.

Beginning c. 1200 B.C. they exerted the first culturally unifying influence on Mesoamerica from their sites of San Lorenzo and La Venta. This phenomenon, often re-

ferred to as the Olmec horizon, spread to central Veracruz, and south into the Valley of Mexico, Morelos, Guerrero, Oaxaca, and as far as the Chiapas coast, based on ceramic evidence related stylistically to San Lorenzo. Monuments carved in the Olmec style occur as far east as El Salvador. The means by which this was accomplished, whether by trade, conquest, colonization, or a combination of them, has not been determined. The presence in Olmec art of many elements that have known meanings in later traditions leaves no doubt that the Olmec introduced many of the deities, myths, rituals, and calendrical concepts that appear in the cultures of the Maya, Zapotecs, Mixtecs, and Aztecs. There is reason to believe, although evidence is scant, that they had a writing system.

Mesoamerican site planning and architecture find their roots in the Olmec north-south site orientation, pyramids, *talud* or sloping wall, use of platforms to raise buildings and temples, and the ceremonial courts or plazas.

In large sculpture, colossal heads, altars, and stelae typify the culture. Smaller sculptures in the round, of jade and serpentine, in the form of celts, figurines, and pendants were masterfully executed, highly polished, and not to be excelled by their followers. The Olmec art style is unique in its iconographic symbolism, avoidance of geometric abstraction for curvilinear naturalism, with a characteristic monumentality, no matter how small the object. The Olmec hallmark is the werejaguar, which combines elements of man and feline. Inclined to obesity and sexless, it had a snarling mouth, toothless gums, or long curving fangs. Although the Olmecs were primarily carvers of stone, their influence is seen in the "baby face" ceramic figurines, clearly of werejaguar derivation, at Olmec colonies such as Tlatilco in the Valley of Mexico. Their style is also evident in the cave paintings of Oxtotitlán and Juxtlahuaca in Guerrero. The wide influence of the Olmec art style supports the reference to the Olmec as the Mesoamerican "mother culture."

Olmec, Colonial A term sometimes applied to sites where Olmec culture appears as an adjunct to, but not part of, the local culture. The Olmecs appear to have colonized some sites that remained principally inhabited by local peoples, such as Tlatilco in the Valley of Mexico, Chalcatzingo in Morelos, others in Veracruz and Guerrero.

Olmec gods See **gods of the Olmec.**

Olmec, Historic Also called the Olmec-Xicalanca or Tepeu Oliman of the chronicles, they ruled Cholula from c. A.D. 800 until driven out by the Toltec-Chichimecs in 1292. They appear to have been of a triethnic composition, including Mixtec, Nahua, and Chocho-Popoloca, with no relation to the Preclassic Olmec of the Gulf Coast. Their tyrannical ways caused the exodus, sometime after A.D. 800, of the Pipiles to the Gulf Coast and to Central America.

Olmec, Metropolitan The term defines the Middle Preclassic Olmecs of the Olmec "heartland" of southern Veracruz and western Tabasco. It avoids confusion with the Postclassic Historic Olmec, an unrelated group settled about Cholula. See **Tenocelome.**

Olmecoid A term applied to Olmecs who lived with alien groups, influencing the predominant local culture; also the resultant art style.

ololiuhqui Morning glory (*Rivea corymbosa* [L.] *Hallier filius*), a botanical hallucinogen known to the ancients of Mesoamerica.

Omácatl Calendrical name (2 Ácatl) of the Aztec god Tezcatlipoca in his role of god of banquets.

ome Number 2 in Nahuatl.

Omecíhuatl The opposite and feminine version of Ometecuhtli. Also called Tonacacíhuatl, Citlalicue.

Ometecuhtli Masculine aspect of the Aztec dual creative principle, Ometeotl, from which all other gods descended; also called Tonacatecuhtli, Citlatona. He and his opposite, Omecíhuatl, lived in the 13th, the highest, celestial layer called Omeyocán

("the place of two"). Patrons of the first day of the *Tonalamatl*, Cipactli; representative of the earth.

Their four sons related to world directions and colors: 1. Red Tezcatlipoca, with Xipe and Camaxtli as variants, is identified with the East. 2. Black Tezcatlipoca is identified with the North. 3. White Tezcatlipoca, also called Quetzalcóatl, is identified with the West. 4. Blue Tezcatlipoca, also called Huitzilopochtli, is identified with the South.

Ometeotl Bisexual primordial expression of the divinity: two gods in one, Ometeotl means "twice god" in Nahuatl. An Aztec priestly concept too abstract to have developed an active cult.

Ometepec 1. Archaeological site of Guerrero, contemporary with Monte Albán III. 2. Island in Lake Nicaragua, Nicaragua.

Ometochtli Generic calendrical name (2 rabbit, or *tochtli*) of the Centzóntotochtin (400, or innumerable, rabbits), collective name for the many gods of pulque. Patécatl and the goddess Mayáhuel were the most prominent.

Omeyocán The supreme 13th celestial layer of the Aztec stratification of the universe; source of the principle of duality—active and passive, masculine and feminine, light and darkness—underlying Mexican thought. Home of the divine pair, Ometecuhtli and Omecíhuatl.

omichicahuaztli Nahuatl word for a musical instrument (rasp) consisting of a dried, striated deer bone or human femur that is scraped by a smaller bone to produce doleful sounds for the accompaniment of funeral dirges. Frequently laid above a resonator such as a conch shell or skull.

ómitl Nahuatl word for a bone awl used to draw blood in ceremonial self-sacrifice. Commonly depicted in the headdress of Quetzalcóatl in the codices in combination with a *huitztli*, a spine of the maguey plant that was similarly employed.

Opa Eighteenth of the 20 Zapotec day names, corresponding to the Aztec day Técpatl and the Maya day Etz'nab.

Opiyel Guaobiran See **Obiyel Guaobiran.**

Opochtli One of the Tlalocs, identified with the South; god of those who lived on the water, inventor of the fishing net, dart thrower, three-pronged harpoon, boatman's pole, and the bird snare.

Orange, Fine Pottery of fine-grained paste, free of temper, of western Maya lowlands origin; probably Laguna de Términos, lower Usumacinta and Grijalva rivers region. Alphabetically listed, the six groups of Fine Orange span 950 years.

Altar: Called Y. Part of the Maya Tepeu III ceramic complex, A.D. 800–900. Designs blend Classic Maya and Nahuatl features, characteristic of the Putún culture.

Balancán: Called Z. Part of the Cehpech ceramic complex of Yucatán, A.D. 800–1000. Identified with the Puuc phase, it also reached into the Guatemalan highlands at Zaculeu and Zacualpa. Called Ximba at Altar de Sacrificios in the Petén, A.D. 900–1000.

Conduacan: Part of the Chikinchel ceramic complex of Yucatán, A.D. 1450–1550.

Dzibilchaltún: Part of the Motul ceramic complex of Yucatán, A.D. 600–800.

Matillas: Part of the Mayapán ceramic complex of Yucatán, A.D. 1250–1450.

Silho: Called X. Part of the Sotuto ceramic complex of Yucatán, A.D. 1000–1200. Important as an Early Postclassic horizon marker in the area south of central Veracruz, northern Yucatán, and Guatemala. Corresponds to the era of Toltec influence.

Orange, Thin A fine paste thin-walled pottery with a distinctive mica schist temper, diagnostic of the Teotihuacán II period, widely traded throughout Mesoamerica in Classic times. The source of the clay is believed to be the Ixcaquixtla zone of Puebla. Pinkish-orange in color, it could be as thin as an eggshell, often decorated with incised and dotted patterns.

Orosí Cemetery site in Central Valley of Costa Rica that gives its name to a Late Period Costa Rican Highlands phase, c. A.D. 1400.

Osa Peninsula Shelters the Gulf of Dulce on Pacific coast of Costa Rica just below the Diquís Delta.

Otomangue One of the main linguistic groups of Mexico, represented in Central America by the Chorotega-Mangue tongues of the Pacific coast of Honduras, Nicaragua, and Costa Rica.

Otomí An ancient language group principally settled in the region north and west of the Valley of Mexico. Referred to in one legend as the Otontlaca, of Chichimec origin. They moved into the Valley of Mexico after the Chichimec invasion under Xólotl. Their leader married a daughter of Xólotl and established the kingdom of Xaltocán, subsequently incorporated into the Tepanec empire under Tezozómoc. Conquered by the Aztecs and later by the Spaniards, the remnants of the Otomí peoples remain in the mountains north of the Valley of Mexico.

Otontecuhtli Patron god of the Otomí, a form of fire-god. Similarly worshiped by the Tepaneca and Mazahua. Also called Xócotl.

Otontlaca See **Otomí.**

ox Number 3 in Maya.

Oxkintok Maya site of western Yucatán where the earliest known inscribed date for the Yucatán region correlates to A.D. 475.

Oxlahun ti Ku Collective name of the 13 Maya gods of the upper world whose separate names are unknown. Possibly the 13 head-variant numerals of the Maya arithmetic system represent the heads of these gods. The concept is analogous to the Aztec Tonalteuctin, a collective reference to the 13 Lords of the Day.

Oxomoco In Aztec mythology, the first woman. See **Cipactonal.**

Oxpemul Maya site in the Río Bec region of Campeche.

Oxtotícpac Proto-Coyotlatelco phase of the Teotihuacán valley, named after a terraced hill site near the city. Surviving Teotihuacán tradition is blended with some new ceramic styles, contributed perhaps by Xochicalco or Cholula, c. A.D. 750–900.

Oxtotitlán Site of a cave in Guerrero containing Middle Preclassic rock paintings attributed to the Olmecs.

Ozomatli Eleventh of the 20 Nahuatl day signs, signifying "monkey." Corresponds to the Maya day Chuen and the Zapotec day Loo or Guilloo. Xochipilli was the patron deity; its augury was indifferent. Calendrical names related to this day are: 1 Ozomatli: one of the Cihuapipiltin; 2 Ozomatli: feast day of merchants; 6 Ozomatli: Tecciztécatl, the moon-god; 8 Ozomatli: moon-god; 9 Ozomatli: Itzpapálotl; 12 Ozomatli: Huehuecóyotl, god of music and dance.

The Aztecs considered the monkey as an animal of pleasure and, by extension, also identified it with concupiscence.

Óztotl Nahuatl for "cave of the mountain," it signifies the West, the way to the Aztec underworld; also the mythical place of tribal origin, as in the reference to Chicomoztoc ("seven caves").

p

Pacal Lord Shield-Pacal was the first major king of Palenque, ruled A.D. 615–83, leaving an indelible mark on its architecture and sculpture. Built and was buried in the sarcophagus of the Temple of the Inscriptions.

Pachtontli Thirteenth of the 18 months of the calendar of 365 days, as celebrated at Tenochtitlán. Propitiated the gods in general but particularly Huitzilopochtli, Tezcatlipoca, and Yacatecuhtli. Its pictorial representation was *pachtli,* an arboreal parasitic plant. Alternate names were Teotleco and Ecoztli. See **months, Aztec.**

padlock stone Variety of Veracruz open-work stone sculpture of unknown use, many resembling padlocks. May correspond to the forms carried by the ballplayers portrayed on the bench of the Great Ball Court at Chichén Itzá.

padlock stone

paint cloisonné A technique of gourd and pottery polychrome decoration in which the surface color is cut out, scraped away, and the hollow is filled with another color; then it is smoothed off to the level of the original layer. Typical of western Mexico, Teotihuacán, and the Mixteca Puebla.

palace An archaeological term applied in Mesoamerica to public buildings of unknown use, as dis-  tinct from temples. Erected on raised platforms, palaces generally consist of two ranges of windowless chambers, one behind the other. Entered by doorways in the front wall, access to rear rooms is by a door in the back wall of the outer chamber. Maya palaces varied in size from three-room buildings to the 325-ft. (98 m)-long Palace of the Governors at Uxmal.

plan of Palace of the Governors, Uxmal

Palangana 1. Olmec cultural phase at San Lorenzo, southern Veracruz, 700–400 B.C. Its new pottery style suggests contacts with La Venta, Tres Zapotes, and Mamom of the Maya lowlands. It marked the end of Olmec civilization there. 2. Large basin-shaped ball court, an innovation during the Amatle phase at Kaminaljuyú, Guatemala; a similar type may have existed at San Lorenzo. It was an enclosure with surrounding walls of even height and no end zones.

Palencano Chol See **Chol.**

Palenque Classic Maya center of the Usumacinta River drainage, magnificently placed in the foothills of the Chiapas Mountains overlooking the Tabasco plain to the Gulf of  Mexico; active c. A.D. 600–900. It is architecturally distinguished by its temples of the Sun, Cross, Foliated Cross, and Inscriptions, the last with a famous tomb. It was erected as a memorial to himself by Lord Shield-Pacal (A.D. 615–83); his re-

Palenque emblem glyph

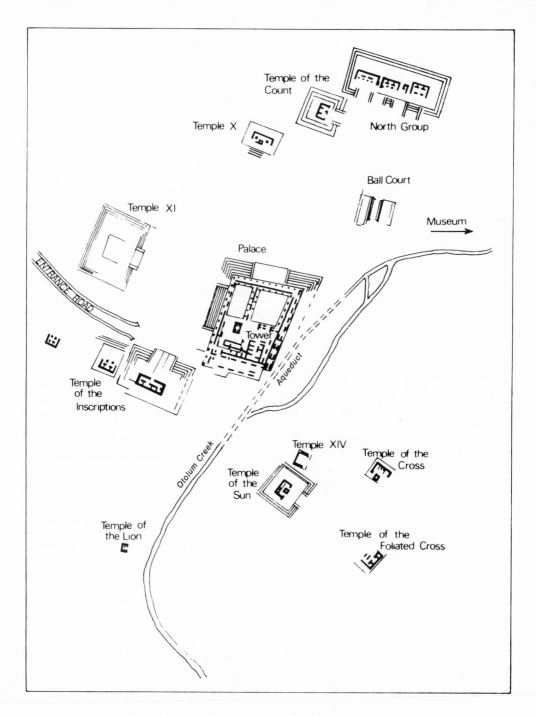

Plate 15. Palenque.

mains reside within a richly carved sarcophagus. An unusual feature of Palenque
is the multiple-court palace with a square
tower.

Lacking stelae, its renowned sculpture is
expressed in molded-stucco relief decoration of the buildings, the elaborately carved
sanctuary tablets, as well as portrait heads
carved in the round. Ceramics, jade, and
mosaic work further express the highest
sensitivity of Classic Maya art. Its ceramics, which showed little direct affiliation
with that of the Petén lowland Maya, are
divided into these complexes: 1. Picota:
possibly Protoclassic to Early Classic; 2.
Motiepa: Middle to Late Early Classic;
3. Otolum: contemporary with Tepeu I,
c. A.D. 600–700; 4. Murcielagos: Early and
Middle Tepeu II, A.D. 700–770; 5. Balunta:
Late Tepeu II, Early Tepeu III, A.D. 770–
850.

Paleo-Indian Designation of the early nomadic hunters who entered the New
World in late Pleistocene times across the
Bering Strait from eastern Asia. Their only
utensils were crude scrapers, knives, and
chopping tools; they belonged to the pre-
projectile horizon.

palma One of three
sculptural   forms,
along with *yokes* and
hachas,   identified
with   the   Meso-
american ball game.
Found only in Vera-
cruz, it may repre-
sent in stone a plas-
tron worn by the
players. Pictured in
the South Ball Court
reliefs at Tajín, rest-
ing frontally on the
yoke of a ballplayer.
See also **ball game,**
Mesoamerican.

palma

Palmar 1. Site in the Diquís region of Costa
Rica. Human figures predominate in its
sculpture, varying from columnar forms of
igneous rock to slotted slab figures of sandstone. 2. Ceramic ware of Pacific Nicaragua

and northwest Costa Rica of the Zoned
Bichrome period, c. 300 B.C.–A.D. 300.

Palmillas Cultural phase of the Sierra Madre
of southwest Tamaulipas, A.D. 1–500, coeval with Eslabones of the Sierra Madre de
Tamaulipas.

Palo Blanco Phase of the Tehuacán Valley,
Puebla, sequence. Early Palo Blanco, 150
B.C.–A.D. 250, had Thin Orange and the
same traits as Horcones, Istmo and Jiquipilas of Chiapas. Late Palo Blanco, A.D. 250–
700, was closely affiliated with the Tlamimilolpa phase of the Valley of Mexico.

Pame Early peoples of the eastern Sierra
Madre Oriental adjoining the Huasteca;
led a seminomadic life with rudimentary
agriculture. The Chichimec group led by
Xólotl may have been Pame.

Pamplona Late Classic cultural phase of the
Guatemalan highlands, c. A.D. 750–900.
The Postclassic period was anticipated po-
litically by the abandonment of valley sites
for the security of hilltops. Ceramics seem
inferior to the preceding Esperanza-Amatle
phases; painted ware becomes rare. Tiquisate ware, mold-decorated human effigy
censers, Z and Y Fine Orange ceramics,
and mushroom stones are characteristic;
pottery figurines and clay effigy whistles
reappear.

Panama Southernmost Central American
Republic, bounded on the east by Colombia, of which it originally was a part, on
the west by Costa Rica, and extending between the Caribbean Sea and the Pacific
Ocean. Its capital is Panama City; it is
bisected by the Panama Canal Zone.

Traditionally, it has been archaeologically separated into four cultural areas: 1.
Darién to the east, with little-explored
jungles; 2. Chiriquí to the west; 3. Veraguas and the Azuero Peninsula to the
south; and 4. Coclé, west of, but combined
with, the Venado Beach site within the
Canal Zone. Recent archaeological investigation tends to support the theory that
the cultural areas of Coclé, Veraguas, and
Azuero constituted one single culture, at
least by A.D. 500. See **Central Panama.**

To facilitate the reader's cross-referencing to published works, the chronology table in this volume retains the traditional ceramic phase chronology and terminology.

Pancuecuetlayán See **universe, Aztec.**

Panquetzaliztli Sixteenth of the 18 20-day Nahuatl months, as celebrated at Tenochtitlán. Principal feast honored Huitzilopochtli. See also **months, Aztec.**

Pantaleón Site in the Cotzumalhuapa zone of southern Guatemala.

Pánuco 1. Late Postclassic phase of the Huasteca, also called Pánuco VI, A.D. 1200– Conquest. See also **Huasteca.** 2. One of Mexico's largest rivers, Tampico, upstream, is an important Gulf port. Due to the artificial drainage completed in 1900, the Valley of Mexico is one of its sources today. According to Aztec tradition, the first inhabitants arrived in the Huasteca from the east, possibly explaining the name Pánuco, also called Pantlán, or Panutla, "place of the crossing." See **Huasteca.**

Papagayo Cemetery site on the Bay of Culebra, Costa Rica, which gave its name to a Middle Polychrome, A.D. 800–1200, group of pottery, also called Nicoya, characterized by orange, red, and blackish-brown painting on a cream-colored slip. Shapes included tripod plates and bowls with zoomorphic supports, and pear-shaped bowls with a pedestal base, often in animal form.

Papaloapán River and basin of south-central Veracruz, Mexico.

paper See **bark paper.**

paradise See **afterlife.**

páramos Wet grasslands or forests at high elevation.

Paris Codex See **codex, pre-Conquest Maya; Paris Codex.**

Parita Bay Bay facing the Gulf of Panama, province of Coclé, Panama. The area has the earliest Central American pottery-making sites, associated with refuse mounds. Among them, Monagrillo provides a C[14] date of 2130 B.C.

Pasión The Pasión River is an important tributary of the Usumacinta River, in the Petén forests of Guatemala. Along this trade route to the Guatemalan highlands are many Classic period Maya sites, including Altar de Sacrificios, Seibal, and Cancuén.

Paso Caballo Paso Caballo waxy ware is a hallmark of the Late Preclassic Chicanel period in the Maya lowlands. It has a thin, soft, uniform slip, burnished and fashioned to achieve a "waxy" feel.

pastillaje Spanish term used to describe the application of small rolled bits of clay to ceramic figurines before firing, and then refined by a wooden modeling stick to simulate clothing, jewelry, headdresses, and other decorations. A common technique in Preclassic Veracruz, the Valley of Mexico, and western Mexico.

Patécatl Aztec god of wine (pulque), husband of Mayáhuel, goddess of maguey. Regent of Malinalli, the 12th day of the Nahuatl calendar, he was identified with medicine, herbs, and narcotic plants.

Patlachique See **Cuicuilco.**

patojo A shoe-shaped ceramic vessel found at various times in cultures ranging from the southern United States to Peru. Its presence is peculiarly irregular,

patojo

disappearing from a site only to return at a later date. In Oaxaca *patojos* are found in Monte Albán I and V; in the Guatemalan highlands in Las Charcas A phase only to reappear in the Postclassic; in central Mexico they disappear after Chupícuaro, but reappear in the Postclassic Tarascan florescence. See also **Zapatera.**

patolli Game of chance played by the Mexica, it is similar to pachisi of southern Asia. Archaeological evidence of the game is found as early as Teotihuacán. With astronomical and religious significance, the game was dedicated to the gods Macuilxóchitl and Ometochtli.

Patuca River of eastern Honduras; the Guayape and Jalan are tributaries.

Pátzcuaro 1. Lake in the state of Michoacán, Mexico. It is bordered by the ancient sites of Tzintzuntzan, Ihuatzio, and Pátzcuaro. 2. Pátzcuaro was the capital of the Tarascans before the founding of Tzintzuntzan. 3. Colonial capital of Michoacán, later removed to Morelia.

Pauahtun In Maya mythology, the winds and the four cardinal points from which they blew, known then as the red, white, black, and yellow Pauahtun. Identified with rain, they may be Chacs or *bacabs*. Probably equivalent to god N of the codices.

Pavas Cultural phase of the Costa Rican highlands, encompassing the region's oldest known materials, falls within the Early Period, c. 300 B.C.–A.D. 500, followed by the Curridabat phase. Named for a site with numerous bottle-shaped tombs. The ceramics are zonally decorated with both plastic and painted motifs: incision, scarification, brushing, appliqué, roller-dentation, reed-impression, and rocker stamping. They have much in common with El Bosque, Zoned Bichrome, and Aguas Buenas phases of adjacent areas.

Pavón Site in the Pánuco valley, and name of the earliest ceramic phase of the Huasteca, c. 1100 B.C.–850 B.C. Dominant types are Progreso Metallic and White Progreso; common forms are ollas and plates with flaring sides and flat bottoms. Small modeled figurines recall Middle Preclassic period of the Valley of Mexico. See also **Huasteca.**

paw-wing See **jaguar-dragon paw-wing.**

Pax 1. Sixteenth of the 18 months of the *tun,* the Maya year of 360 days. 2. Upright drum of the Classic period Maya. Fashioned of a hollowed tree trunk, with the top covered with animal skin, it was played by hand like the Aztec *huéhuetl.* The Maya also had a ritual timbal of clay called *kayum.*

Paya A division of the Macro-Chibcha linguistic group, in eastern Honduras.

Paynal In Aztec mythology, the messenger of Huitzilopochtli.

pectoral Ornament worn on the breast.

Pedregal Area in the San Ángel suburb of Mexico City covered by a rough, deep layer of basalt, resulting from the eruption of the volcano Xictli probably between 300–200 B.C. Ancient sites covered by the lava flow include Cuicuilco and Copilco.

pejibaye Palm (*Guilielma utilis*) and its rather mealy vegetablelike fruit cultivated as a basic food, exclusively in Panama and Costa Rica.

penate Small, angular figure pendant, possibly serving as an amulet, carved from jade, greenish or white stone, is characteristic of the Mixtec (Monte Albán V) period of Oaxaca. *Penates* were generally perforated with two holes for suspension. The features were summarily rendered by straight incised lines or drilled circles. Somewhat similar figures, called *camahuiles,* were produced in the Guatemalan highlands, but without perforations.

penate

Peñitas Northern Nayarit site on the San Pedro River, with an archaeological sequence beginning in the fourth century A.D. and ending in the late 13th century. Its phases are Tamarindo, c. A.D. 200, with vertically ribbed red vessels similar to Colima; Chala, c. A.D. 300–600, related to the Tierra del Padre phase at Chametla, Sinaloa; and Mitlan, A.D. 1050–1300, with similarities to the Early Postclassic period of central Mexico.

peo Zapotec word for month, also moon.

Peor es Nada 1. Postclassic ceramic complex at Bilbao, region of Cotzumalhuapa, southern Guatemala, c. A.D. 925–Conquest. 2. Late Classic site at the southern end of the Sula Plain, Honduras; a source of carved marble vases.

Peresianus, Codex See **codex, pre-Conquest Maya; Paris Codex.**

Pérez, Codex See *Chilam Balam;* **codex, pre-Conquest Maya; Paris Codex.**

period ending In the Mayas' consciousness of the march of time, each end of a period, *tun, katun,* or *baktun,* was celebrated. Ends of *katuns* (20 years) were of major importance and around them evolved most calculations recorded in the Classic period. Maya periods are not counted until completed and are named for the day on which they end, which is always Ahau.

Periquillo Name of a site and Late Classic phase of Colima, western Mexico, A.D. 1200–Conquest.

petatl Called *petate* in modern Mexican, it is a woven mat of straw or palm leaves. Among the ancients, it became a symbol of authority, like the Maya *pop*, which translated as "throne."

Petén The northernmost department of Guatemala, a forested jungle wedging into the Yucatán peninsula. It is bordered by the Mexican states of Chiapas and Tabasco on the west, Campeche and Quintana Roo on the north, and Belize on the eastern boundary. Capital is the island city of Flores. Area saw full development of the Maya southern lowland civilization in sites such as Uaxactún, Tikal, Piedras Negras, Altar de Sacrificios, Yaxhá, Holmul, etc.

Petén-Itzá Largest of several lakes in the Petén, containing the island of Flores, believed to have been the site of Tayasal, the last stronghold of the Itzás against the Spaniards. Anciently called Chaltuna.

petroglyph An engraving on natural rock displaying various designs or figures; examples are widely distributed in Mesoamerica, and as far north as the western United States.

peyote A small cactus (*Lophophora williamsii*) rich in peyotine and mescaline that produces visual and auditory hallucinations. Used anciently and today in native ceremonies. The term *mescal buttons* is erroneously applied to the dried tops of the peyote. It has no relation to mescal, a drink derived from the distillation of the fermented juice of the century plant. Peyote grows in northern Mexico, from Sonora and Tamaulipas to Zacatecas and Querétaro.

phytomorphic In plant form. Applied to artifacts in fruit or/vegetable shape.

pichancha Monte Albán II pottery form, used to strain cooked corn, or maize.

pictogram Earliest form in the development of a writing system. Sometimes called "picture writing," it is a literal presentation of the subject. Among the Aztecs, the glyph for *calli* ("house") is a recognizable rendition of a house. See also **hieroglyphic writing.**

pictun Maya time period of 20 *baktuns,* 8,000 *tuns,* or 2,880,000 days. See also **Long Count.**

Piedras Negras Classic Maya site, with a large acropolis, situated on an important trade route along the Usumacinta River, in western Petén, Guatemala. Famed

Piedras Negras emblem glyph

for stelae showing figures seated in niches, sculpted panels of figures, and columns of glyphs, and the fine detail of their rendition. The study of these figures first established that the carvings represented a historic presentation relating to dynastic occurrences, involving identifiable persons, and furnished the basis for the recognition of the interrelationships of rulers of the separate Maya centers. The artistic style of Piedras Negras is eclectic, linking it with distant Copán and northeastern Petén.

piggyback See **Barriles.**

Pija Twelfth of the 20 Zapotec day names, equivalent to the Aztec day Malinalli and the Maya day Eb.

pilli (*pipiltin,* pl.) Nahuatl for prince or noble child; it describes the Aztec aristocracy, the lineage of the *tlatoani.*

Piltzintecuhtli Youthful manifestation of the sun-god Tonatiuh, referred to as the "young god," third of the nine Lords of the Night, or underworld. Also a manifestation of Xochipilli.

Pipil A term loosely applied to the speech and culture of various Nahuat-speaking groups whose influence penetrated southern Mesoamerica and Central America from the Mexican highlands. Reference is made to several periods of intrusion, from the early Classic period to Late Postclassic, and the accompanying introduction of northern deity cults and art styles. Pipil is a Conquest-period term and was then used to describe the latter-day descendants of the ninth-century Mexican invaders found in El Salvador and Nicaragua. See also **Nicarao.**

pisote See **coati.**

Pitao Cozobi Benevolent Zapotec god related to maize, sometimes represented in the guise of a bat.

piye Ritual 260-day calendar of the Zapotecs, same as the Aztec *tonalpohualli* and Maya *tzolkin*. It was divided into four periods of 65 days called *cocijos*, but also, confusingly, *piye* or *pije*.

pizarra Yucateca Spanish term for "Yucatecan slate," it applied to pottery made with a soapy, lustrous gray appearance during the Puuc period of Yucatán, c. A.D. 600–1000.

Playa de los Muertos Type site of the Middle Preclassic period culture of Honduras, along the Ulúa River on the Sula Plain, c. 900–600 B.C. Contemporary with Mamom of the Maya lowlands, its pottery has analogies with the Preclassic of the Valley of Mexico. Most widely distributed elements are hand-modeled, highly polished solid figurines. Early period provided jade pendants and jadeite axe gods. Unpainted or monochrome pottery predominated.

Playa del Tesoro Archaeological site on Manzanillo Bay, Colima, dating to the Classic period.

Plumbate The importance of Plumbate ware lies in the wide trade, from Mexico to El Salvador, engendered by its qualities, creating a "Plumbate horizon" that coincided with Toltec dominance in Mesoamerica.

Plumbate is characterized by slips of high iron content fired at unusually high temperatures, c. 1,742°F. (c. 950°C.), resulting in a lustrous, glazelike finish, the only Mesoamerican semivitrified ware. It is extremely hard, its characteristic pale and olive-gray surface relieved by softer oxidized areas of orange and reddish brown; it can also be all brown or gray. San Juan is its earliest form, diagnostic of the Late

Classic Santa Lucía phase of Cotzumalhuapa, Guatemala, mostly in cylindrical vessels without effigies. San Juan was followed by Robles, a transitional ware with molded decorations. Plumbate reached the height of its development and broad trade acceptance as Tohil Plumbate in the Early Postclassic period. It is the distinctive, elaborately decorated ware, famous for its effigy vessels, whose distribution coincided with the Toltec dominance, even though it was not of their creation. Plumbate manufacture apparently ceased at the beginning of the Protohistoric period, c. A.D. 1200.

pochteca Aztec merchant class, probably hereditary, specializing in luxury goods for its ruler. Under Mexican military protection, they traveled widely, serving the state as emissaries and spies. The Maya probably had a similar class of merchants, shown on painted Maya pottery vessels holding a fan, their badge of office. Yacatecuhtli was the Aztec patron deity, corresponding to Ek Chuah of the Maya.

Pokomam 1. A branch of the Macro-Maya linguistic group, often simply called Pokom, which settled in the area about Lake Amatitlán, Guatemala, with its capital at Mixco Viejo. The Pokomam also occupied El Salvador west of the Lempa River, representing the easternmost extension of the Maya realm. 2. Late Classic phase of Zacualpa, Guatemala, A.D. 700–1000.

Pokomchi Maya linguistic group of Alta and Baja Verapaz, Guatemalan highlands.

pok-ta-pok Maya word for the Mesoamerican ritual ball game, comparable to the Aztec *tlachtli*. See **ball game, Mesoamerican.**

Polé Legendary mainland port of Quintana Roo opposite Cozumel Island, by which the Itzá (Putún or Chontal Maya) first invaded Yucatán, A.D. 918. Probably corresponds to modern Xcaret.

poll That part of a celt which is opposite to the blade.

pom Maya word for *copal* incense. See **copal.**

Pomona Early Classic period Maya site in

the Stann Creek area of Belize. The "Pomona flare" is the largest such earplug component ever discovered; it measures 7 in. (18 cm) in diameter, with eight glyph blocks incised in pairs in its jade surface.

Ponce Preclassic ceramic phase of the Huasteca, c. 850–600 B.C. Metallic Progreso and White Progreso of the Pavón phase persist. Black Ponce ware appears. See also **Huasteca.**

Pop 1. First month of the 18 months of the *tun,* the Maya year of 360 days. On New Year's day, the first day of Pop, houses were swept clean and all utensils of daily use were renewed. 2. The mat (*pop* in Maya) was the symbol of authority, justice, and noble birth; also interpreted as "throne." Quiché Maya chronicles refer to rulers as *ahau-ahpop,* "lord of the mat," and his assistant, destined to succeed him, as *ahpop camhá.*

Popocatépetl Snow-capped volcano southeast of Mexico City; second highest mountain in Mexico, after Orizaba, rising to 17,887 ft. (5,452 m) above sea level. Means "smoking mountain" in Nahuatl.

Popoloca See **Chocho-Popoloca.**

Popol Vuh Sacred book of the Quiché Maya of highland Guatemala, discovered at the beginning of the 18th century by Fray Francisco Jiménez while he was parish priest at Chichicastenango. He both copied the original Quiché text of the manuscript, now lost, and translated it into Spanish. It contains the cosmogonical concepts and ancient traditions of the Quiché, the history of their origin, and the chronology of their kings down to 1550. Written by natives between the years 1554–58, it is now in the Newberry Library, Chicago. See also **Hunahpú.**

posole An unfermented beverage of ground maize and water.

Postclassic period Broad archaeological designation applied in Mesoamerica to the time span between c. A.D. 900 and the Conquest. Its early and late phases are related to the rise of two dominant polities in Mexico. Its inception is linked to the rise of the Toltecs, out of Tula, whose in-

fluence was felt in Mesoamerica up to c. A.D. 1200. The second phase of the Postclassic saw the hegemony of the Aztecs of Tenochtitlán during the 15th and early 16th centuries. Other representative states of the period were Mixtecan Mitla in Oaxaca, Tarascan Tzintzuntzan in Michoacán, and Totonacan Cempoala in southern Veracruz.

The Postclassic in the Maya area witnessed a shift of the center of civilization from the southern lowlands to northern Yucatán. Chichén Itzá became the ruling city after the Toltec (Itzá) invasion in the 10th century, retaining its position until c. A.D. 1200. It was superseded by Mayapán, which in turn was sacked c. A.D. 1450. Thereafter, until the Conquest, the lowland Maya area presented a group of warring city-states.

The Postclassic was a period of widespread trade, extending into Central America from the north. Mesoamerican influence there is noted in feathered-serpent motifs on ceramics, the appearance of deity names, and the calendar. Diagnostic ceramic wares of the Mesoamerican Early Postclassic were X Fine Orange, Tohil Plumbate, and effigy vessels of Nicoya Polychrome. The Mixteca-Puebla style horizon was unmistakable in the second phase.

Postclassic Maya is sometimes called the "Mexican Period," or "Toltec Maya," but the earlier term, "New Empire," has been abandoned. The term Postclassic is not applicable in Central America below the area subject to Mesoamerican cultural influence.

postfix See **affix.**

pot irrigation Irrigation of cultivated land where the water table is high; wells are sunk at intervals in the fields, and water is drawn out by buckets or scoops and distributed among the plants.

Poton A dialect of Lenca spoken in western San Miguel, El Salvador, beyond the Lempa River.

Potonchán Site at mouth of the Grijalva River, probably the chief port of the seafaring Putún, controlling the water trade route from the Grijalva and Usumacinta rivers to Yucatán.

Potosino Language of Maya origin spoken in San Luis Potosí and Tamaulipas.

Potrero Nuevo Preclassic Olmec site near San Lorenzo, Veracruz. Altars from here contain the earliest Mesoamerican examples of Atlanteans supporting altars or ceilings. See **San Lorenzo Tenochtitlán.**

potsherd Fragment of a pottery vessel or figure; also a sherd or shard.

Pox ware Name describing Early Preclassic period Mexican pottery, from the pitted secondary surface of the sherds. Found principally at Puerto Marqués, Guerrero, it may be the earliest identified Mexican ceramic, carbon-dated to 2440 B.C. *Tecomates* are the dominant form. Similar to the earliest pottery of the Tehuacán Valley (Puebla), the Purrón phase.

ppentacob Slaves among the lowland Maya; became so by birth, punishment for stealing, being captured in war, being an orphan, or acquisition by purchase or trade.

Precious Twin Esoteric Nahuatl name of the god Quetzalcóatl as the brother of his twin, Xólotl. *Quetzal* feathers were the symbol of something "precious" and *cóatl* ("serpent") in rebus writing also means "twin brother."

Preclassic period A general archaeological designation in Mesoamerica for the time span starting with establishment of sedentary cultures c. 2000 B.C. and ending with the rise of urban centers c. A.D. 250, sometimes called Formative. In lower Central America Preclassic is not in use because of the absence of a Classic period; there Formative still describes the early area development stage.

The Preclassic period comprises three phases, with Protoclassic sometimes placed at the end for cultural areas of more rapid development:

1. *Early Preclassic* introduced first religious centers and pottery, starting with the Purrón phase of the Tehuacán Valley of Puebla and coastal Guerrero, c. 2300–

1500 B.C., and extending to c. 900 B.C. Early Preclassic is related to the Ixtapaluca phase of the Valley of Mexico, Pavón of the Huasteca, San Lorenzo of southern Veracruz, Olmec caves of Guerrero, Chiapa I, Ocós of the Soconusco, and Arévalo-Las Charcas of the Maya highlands.

2. *Middle Preclassic* produced fine pottery, ceremonial objects, well-stocked burials, and the spread of mound building 900–400 B.C. It encompasses the Zacatenco phase of the Valley of Mexico, Monte Albán I of Oaxaca, Olmec San Lorenzo and La Venta, Chiapa II–IV, Conchas I–II of the Soconusco, late Las Charcas and Providencia of the Maya highlands, and Mamom of the lowlands.

3. *Late Preclassic* shows increasing ceremonial architecture and complexity of material goods up to c. A.D. 250. Protoclassic, when applicable, is generally placed c. 100 B.C.–A.D. 250. Late Preclassic is represented by Chupícuaro and El Opeño in western Mexico, Ticomán-Cuicuilco in the Valley of Mexico, Monte Albán I–II in Oaxaca, lower Tres Zapotes on the Gulf Coast, Chiapa III–IV, Izapa, Miraflores-Arenal of the Guatemalan highlands, and Chicanel of the Maya lowlands.

prefix See **affix.**

pretty lady Small modeled terra-cotta figurines found in Middle Preclassic burials, prominently at Tlatilco, Valley of Mexico. The term applies specifically to type D-1.

primary burial Direct inhumation of the fully articulated corpse. See **secondary burial.**

Primeros Memoriales See **codex, early post-Conquest Mexican; Matritenses, Codices.**

Protoclassic period A transitional phase of the Mesoamerican Late Preclassic period, used in some areas where more rapid local development caused Classic period features to blend with the end of the Preclassic, c. 100 B.C.–A.D. 250. It is identified with the shaft-tomb complex of western Mexico, Monte Albán II–IIIa, Teotihuacán I–II of the Valley of Mexico, Lower Remojadas and Middle Tres Zapotes of Veracruz, Izapa, Chiapa V–VII, Santa Clara of the Guatemalan highlands, and Matzanel of the lowlands.

provenance Location where an object is known to have been found in modern times. Sometimes called provenience.

Providencia (**Majadas**) Preclassic phase at Kaminaljuyú, Guatemalan highlands, c. 500–400 B.C. Produced stone pedestal sculptures, "bench" figures, mushroom stones, and carved stelae. Marked the re-appearance of solid hand-modeled fig-urines. New ceramic styles included ves-sels with solid conical feet; the Usulután decorative technique became popular. Coeval with early Chicanel in the lowlands.

Puebla Mexican state, with capital of same name, bounded by the adjoining states of Hidalgo, Tlaxcala, Veracruz, Oaxaca, Guerrero, Morelos, and Mexico. Most prominent site is Cholula. Its Tehuacán Valley provided the longest record of hu-man occupation in the New World, before 7000 B.C.–Conquest.

Puerto Marqués Midden site on the Pacific coast of Guerrero, south of Acapulco. See **Pox ware.**

pulque A fermented drink of low alcoholic content made from the sap of the maguey plant, and mythically, an invention of the goddess Mayáhuel. Its distillate is gener-ally sold today as tequila; mescal is typical of Oaxaca.

punctate decoration A pottery decoration achieved by punching a sharp tool into the wet clay. If punctation is elongated, it is known as dash punctation; using an awl produces a cuneiform dent called awl punctation.

Pupuluca Non-Maya group of uncertain lin-guistic affiliation at the southern Guate-mala–El Salvador border.

Purrón Early Preclassic phase of the Tehua-cán Valley sequence of Puebla, 2300–1500 B.C. Earliest evidence of tempered pottery manufacture in Mesoamerica dates from early Purrón, correlating with the Pox ware of Puerto Marqués in Guerrero.

Pusilha Classic Maya site of southern Belize, near the Petén border.

Pustunich Postclassic site of southwestern Campeche.

Putún Chontal Maya of the southern Cam-peche and Tabasco delta regions of the Usumacinta and Grijalva rivers. Outstand-ing seamen and merchants, they virtually controlled, between A.D. 850–950, north-ern Tabasco, southern Campeche; Cozu-mel, Bakhalal, and Chetumal on the east coast of Yucatán, where they were called the Itzás.

Other Putún groups followed the Usuma-cinta and Pasión rivers inland, perhaps gaining temporary control of Yaxchilán A.D. 730–750, establishing a trading post at Altar de Sacrificios c. A.D. 800, con-quering Seibal c. A.D. 850, and pushing on as far as Ucanal near the border of Belize. After the abandonment of ceremonial cen-ters, remnants settled south of the Pasión River, calling the region Acalán. Under the loose designation of Lacandón they main-tained independence until 1695; a few de-scendants remain to this day. See **Itzá.**

Puuc Hilly region (*puuc* is Maya for "land of low hills") of western Yucatán that also gave its name to a Classic period Maya architectural style incorporating many as-pects of Río Bec and Chenes, to c. A.D. 900. It innovated freestanding palace struc-tures about large courts, with the lower sections of vertical facades faced in plain limestone veneer. The upper building facade was an exuberant frieze of mass-produced carved segments joined in a mosaic of latticework, stepped-fret, re-peated sky-serpents, and mask motifs. Wide moldings encircling the buildings contained the decorative band. Columnar doorways alternated with rectangular openings; half-columns were repeated in long rows. Puuc architecture developed monumental arch-ways and, occasionally, storied and cham-bered pyramids. Uxmal is the largest and best-known Puuc site, others include Ka-bah, Labná, and Sayil. The Puuc style may have influenced the architectural mosaic ornamentation observed at Postclassic Mitla in Oaxaca.

pyramid In Mesoamerica, a mound or raised platform constructed to support a temple. Usually terraced, a stairway on one or more sides led to the leveled top. Contrary to earlier beliefs, some of them were erected to contain the tomb of a ruler, as in the Temple of the Inscriptions at Palenque, Chiapas.

q

Q-complex A term formulated for a group of early southern Mesoamerican ceramic traits: swollen mammiform pottery supports, bridge spouts, spool-shaped pot stands, and lavish use of polychrome stucco. These elements were found in the Protoclassic luxury tombs of Monte Albán II; Chiapa VI (Horcones), Holmul I, and Matzanel phases of the Maya lowlands.

quadripartite badge Maya glyphic emblem incorporating a leaflike element, a shell representation, and most importantly, the "crossed-bands" motif of Olmec origin. This combination is known as the

quadripartite badge, Temple of the Cross, Palenque

"triadic" symbol, but with the flattened U added, it becomes the quadripartite badge of kingly authority. A variant of it appears on the tomb in the Temple of the Cross at Palenque, Chiapas, and is found associated with carvings of rulers, on their headdresses; also on two-headed monsters and altars at Classic period Maya sites as far away from each other as Copán, Quiriguá, and Yaxchilán.

Quankyak Early Postclassic phase of the western Guatemalan highlands.

quauhpilli (*quauhpipiltin*, pl.) Axtec commoner who achieved the status and some of the prerogatives of nobility through distinction in warfare.

Quecholli Fifteenth of the 18 20-day months of the Nahuatl calendar of 365 days, as observed at Tenochtitlán. Major deities propitiated were Mixcóatl-Camaxtli and their female consorts. Alternate names for the month were Tlacoquecholli ("half-Quecholli") and Tlamiquecholli ("end-Quecholli").

quechquémitl A triangular overblouse worn since ancient times in Mexico.

Quelepa Site on the Pan American Highway west of San Miguel, El Salvador; coeval with Tazumal, c. A.D. 400–1200; most easterly example of a ceremonial site with direction-oriented mounds.

Querétaro Mexican state, with capital of the same name, bounded by the adjacent states of Mexico, Michoacán, Guanajuato, San Luis Potosí, and Hidalgo.

quetzal (*Pharomachrus mocinno*) Bird of the humid, mountain cloud forests of Guatemala and Chiapas whose long, brilliant green tail feathers were highly prized. Prominent in the headdresses of Mesoamerican rulers, it was an important trade item. Its rarity and green color, as with jade, made it a symbol of preciousness. National bird of Guatemala.

Quetzalcóatl One of the most widely venerated creator gods of Postclassic Mesoamerica, he was, historically, also a priest-ruler of Tula. The Maya called him Kukulcán in the lowlands; he was Gucumatz to the Quiché Maya of the Guatemalan highlands. The "feathered serpent," the meaning of his name in Nahuatl, was known at Teotihuacán and possibly finds its origin in Olmec god VII. In Nahuatl mythology he was the bearded god of learning and priesthood, father and creator, source of the arts, agriculture, and science, brother of Xipe Totec, Tezcatlipoca, and Huitzilopochtli, and patron of the day Éhecatl. His many aspects include the wind-god (Éhecatl), morning star (Tlahuizcalpantecuhtli), and evening star (Xólotl, his twin). See **Precious Twin.** He is the 9th of the 13 Lords of the Day. In the Creation myth he ruled the second "sun," or world. See **Creation myth, Aztec.**

He is depicted in the codices with a variety of attributes, not all of them always shown. His conical hat (*copilli*) is divided vertically into a dark and light part, the former is sometimes a jaguar skin. It is bordered by a band from which emanate the instruments of autosacrifice (*ómitl, huitztli*), with a flower symbolizing blood. At the nape of his neck is a fan of black crow feathers from which red macaw feathers project. As Éhecatl he wears a red bird-beak mask, below which his beard protrudes. His body is black, his profile face vertically divided into a yellow front and black behind, separated by a dark band descending through the eye. His ear ornament is a jade disk with a pendant "twisted shell" ornament (*epcololli*). His definitive breastplate is the transverse cut of a strombus (conch) shell (*ehecailacacózcatl*). He frequently carries a spear-thrower (*xiuhátlatl*), symbol of the fire-god. He was the legendary historic figure Ce Ácatl ("one reed": his birthday) Topiltzin Quetzalcóatl, son of the Chichimec ruler Mixcóatl. An enlightened ruler, he was forced out of Tula before A.D. 1000, proceeding to Cholula, and then on to Yucatán where, as leader of the second Itzá invasion of Chichén Itzá, he was called Kukulcán. He had prophesied his return to the Valley of Mexico in a year Ce Ácatl (which 1519 was), thereby predisposing the Aztecs to capitulate when Cortés appeared by sea from the east in 1519.

Quetzalcóatl was also assumed as a title by Aztec priests.

Quetzalpapalotl A mythological animal that gave its name to the Palace of Quetzalpapalotl (also referred to by its Spanish name, Palacio de Quetzalmariposa) at Teotihuacán where its representation is carved in bas-relief on supporting pillars. The name can be translated as "precious butterfly."

Quiáhuitl Nineteenth of the 20 Nahuatl day signs, equivalent to the Maya day Cauac and the Zapotec day Ape. Among calendrical names, 9 Quiáhuitl is Tlaloc, 4 Quiáhuitl is the designation of the third "sun," or world, in the Aztec Creation myth.

Quiché Dominant Maya tribe of the Guatemalan highlands. They entered along the Usumacinta River and through Chiapas from the Tabasco Gulf Coast area in the Early Postclassic period, c. A.D. 1000–1200. The history of the peregrination of their ancestors, a Nonoalca-Pipil-Toltec-Chichimec group, is described in the Popol Vuh. Their highland capital was Utatlán, north of Lake Atitlán. The worship of Tohil united the three Quiché groups: Quiché, Tamub, and Ilocab.

Quij 1. or Ij, Laa, 13th of the 20 Zapotec day names, corresponding to the Aztec day Ácatl and the Maya day Ben. 2. or Laa, second of the 20 Zapotec day names, equivalent to the Aztec day Éhecatl and the Maya day Ik.

Quilaztli Aztec goddess of pregnancy, childbirth, and the sweat bath, a manifestation of Cihuacóatl.

Quinametzin Giants created during the first "sun," or world, of Aztec mythology; they were devoured by jaguars, Tezcatlipoca's *nahual.* The ancients credited them with building Teotihuacán, based on an erroneous identification of prehistoric mammoth bones found in the valley.

Quintana Roo Mexican state on the northeastern shore of the Yucatán peninsula, bounded by the Caribbean Sea, the Mexican state of Yucatán, Guatemala, and Belize. Chetumal is the capital. Major sites include Tulum and Cobá.

quiquiztli Large conch shell used as a trumpet, also called *tecciztli;* used in war and by Aztec priests.

Quiriguá Maya center in the lower Motagua River valley of Guatemala. In the eighth century A.D. a ruler from nearby Copán was imposed on Qui-

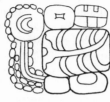

Quiriguá emblem glyph

riguá, establishing a dynasty during which most of the monumental sculpture commemorating the history of the Caan family over some 75 years was erected. The site is famed for its unusual and enormous, intricately carved zoomorphs and the loftiness of its sandstone stelae. Stela E, rising 35 ft. (10.5 m) and weighing 65 tons, was erected A.D. 771 and is the largest block of stone ever carved by the Maya.

Quiroga Postclassic Tarascan site of Michoacán.

r

Rabinal Maya town, tribe, and language of the Postclassic period in the central highlands of Guatemala. *Rabinal Achi,* translated as "The Lord of Rabinal," is the only textually preserved indigenous pre-Hispanic theatrical work. The words and music were preserved by the Abbé Brasseur de Bourbourg while in charge of the parish of Rabinal c. 1856.

radiocarbon (C¹⁴) dating Measurement in organic matter of the radioactive isotope carbon 14. It is uniformly present in all living things, but after their death, decays over thousands of years. Determining the proportion of C^{14} remaining establishes the time lapse since death of materials such as wood, charcoal, bone, and shell. The method was developed in the 1940s by Willard Libby, earned him the Nobel Prize, and revolutionized prehistoric archaeology.

A radiocarbon age expressed as the number of years B.P. (before present) is by custom converted to a calendar date by subtracting from A.D. 1950. An age or date is often followed by a notation, such as ±60, of its statistically probable error. Most published dates, including those in this volume, are "uncorrected," based on the 5,568 years first established as the half-life of C^{14}, that is, time in which one-half the C^{14} originally present will have decayed. Subsequent research has demonstrated that conventional C^{14} ages, although mainly correct relative to each other, do not correspond precisely to real age in solar years.

Dendrochronology, which gives absolute age by means of annual tree-ring growth, has revealed an increasing inaccuracy in C^{14} dates within its range of over 8,000 years. Analyses of wood from the bristlecone pine established correction tables and led to the identification of the Seuss effect, named for its discoverer. This inaccuracy results from a decreased proportion of radioactive to stable carbon in the atmosphere since the industrial revolution because of the burning of radioactive-free fossil fuels, causing C^{14} dates to appear too old and affecting the calculated C^{14} half-life.

Today three types of radiocarbon-related dates are used: 1. C^{14} age based on the conventionally accepted 5,568-year half-life of the radioactive isotope; 2. C^{14} age based on the revised 5,730-year half-life, producing somewhat older dates; and 3. C^{14} age corrected according to dendrochronological data, sometimes called "bristlecone age," which is considerably older for B.C. dates. See also **bristlecone.**

ramón Breadnut tree (*Brosimum utile*) found clustering about archaeological sites in the Petén of Guatemala; a supplementary food source of the Maya.

raxón Also called *ranchón* (*Cotinga amabilis*), a bird abundant in the Alta Verapaz Mountains of Guatemala, whose turquoise and purple feathers shared with *quetzal* feathers the honor of adorning headdresses of kings and gods among the Maya. See *xiuhtototl.*

137

"re" glyph "Rep-
tile's eye," inter-
preted as a symbol
of the earth, fer-
tility, and abun-
dance, is of Teoti-
huacán origin. It
is generally pic-

"re" glyph

tured in a cartouche, with a curl as its
most prominent component; found on ceramics, rarely in murals.

rebus writing A mode of expressing words
and phrases by pictures of objects whose
names resemble those words, or the sylla-
bles of which they are composed.

Relación de las Cosas de Yucatán An encyclopedia of Maya religion, rituals, history,
and ethnology, written in 1566 by the
Franciscan Diego de Landa, the third
bishop of Yucatán. It is the most important
source on the pre-Hispanic Maya and includes Landa's Maya alphabet, the first attempt to decipher Maya hieroglyphic writing. The original manuscript has been lost;
existing versions are based on an early
17th-century copy in the Royal Academy
of History, Madrid. First printed in 1864,
it is presented in 52 chapters.

Relación de Michoacán Chronicle taken
down by an anonymous Franciscan mis-
sionary, verbatim from native Tarascan
sources, c. 1539–41, at Tzintzuntzan,
Michoacán, Mexico. Relates pre-Conquest
and very early colonial Tarascan history.
Biblioteca del Monasterio de El Escorial,
Madrid.

religious ceremonies, Aztec Major ritual
ceremonies were the 18 annual *veintenas*
(20-day feasts) geared to the 365-day
Vague Year. They were supplemented
every 8 years by the Atamalcualiztli ceremony, and every 52 years by the Toxiuhmolpilia, the New Fire Ceremony. Another
group of important rituals, related to the
260-day *tonalpohualli*, were the "movable
ceremonies," so called because they did not
repeat according to the seasons. The most
prominent of these seems to have been the
4 Ollin ceremony, dedicated to the sun
and involving community fasting, blood-

letting, and the sacrifice of a messenger to
the sun at midday. See **months, Aztec.**

Remojadas Large, important early site of
central Veracruz, with occupation from c.
500 B.C. Active until the fall of Teotihuacán in the seventh century, when the creative center shifted to El Tajín. Best known
for the "smiling figure" hollow mold-made
figurines that appeared c. 100 B.C., reaching their zenith in the Late Classic period.

repoussé The process of "pushing out" a design in thin sheets of metal from the rear.
A common technique of Central American
and Oaxacan goldsmiths, probably worked
with tools of bone or deer antlers. Coclé
breastplates are outstanding examples of
the method, perhaps formed over a yielding surface of leather or pitch.

resist painting A technique of ceramic decoration in which a design is created by covering and protecting parts of the ceramic
surface with a resistant substance, such as
wax or clay, before applying ceramic pigments or carbon-yielding compounds. It is
essentially a positive-negative procedure
from which the inadequate reference to it
as "negative painting" is derived. With the
removal of the covering substance, the pattern is revealed in the base color. Sometimes this process is called batik after a
similar Southeast Asian technique of dye-
ing textiles.

Retes Site on the slope of the Irazú volcano,
central Costa Rica. Source of an important cache of stone sculptures and rare
wooden ceremonial artifacts preserved under the volcanic ash, 10th century A.D.

Retoño Terminal phase of the Suchil branch
of the Chalchihuites culture of Zacatecas,
along the Río Colorado, c. A.D. 650–750.

Reventazón River valley of the Atlantic watershed of eastern Costa Rica. The early
Middle Period, c. A.D. 400–850, is based
on excavations there, marking the first appearance of anthropomorphic ceramic decoration. Gold and *tumbaga* were worked,
the eagle motif being most popular. See
also **El Guayabo.**

Riego See **Tehuacán.**

Río Bec Late Classic period Maya site in the

forest of southeastern Campeche that lends its name to a distinctive regional style of temple architecture characterized by a lavishly decorated central building flanked by soaring solid towers of masonry. Stairways, inclining only 20 degrees from the vertical, were hardly designed for use and led to surmounting temples with false doors and no interior rooms. This ostentatious derivative of the Petén style is known at Río Bec, Becan, and Xpuhil.

Río Blanco Early Postclassic phase of the Ulúa-Yojoa area of western Honduras, A.D. 1000–1200.

Río Chiquito See **San Lorenzo Tenochtitlán.**

Río Cuautla Term for ceramic style identified with the sites of La Juana and San Pablo along the Cuautla River, Morelos. They furnished bottles with stirrup spouts, composite bottles, bottles with long tubular necks, resist painting, hollow figurines of types D and K, and small, solid type K figurines. The Río Cuautla style is represented alongside Olmec ceramics at Tlatilco; its inspiration may have come from South America by way of western Mexico. La Juana phase was earliest, 1350–1250 B.C., followed by San Pablo A and B to 900 B.C.

Ríos, Codex See **codex, early post-Conquest Mexican; Ríos, Codex.**

Río Tunal Middle phase of the Postclassic horizon of the Chalchihuites culture of north-central Mexico, A.D. 950–1150.

ritual calendar See **tonalpohualli, tzolkin.**

Ritual of the Bacabs Yucatecan Maya book of medicinal incantations. Its symbolism and allusions to a now lost mythology involving plants, birds, and insects make the incantations almost incomprehensible today.

Robles See **Plumbate.**

rocker stamping Preclassic decorative technique in which a curved sharp edge, probably a shell, is "walked" back and forth on a pottery vessel before firing, creating a curved zigzag incised line.

rocker stamping

roll See **codex.**

roof comb A tall stone superstructure built on the roof of lowland Maya temples, adding height and grandeur; often elaborately stuccoed, carved, and painted. Also called a roof crest. Roof combs were placed over the rear or medial wall of supporting buildings; those over the front wall were "flying facades." Roof combs were solid in section, or hollow, approximating an inverted V, frequently perforated with openings to relieve the massive weight. Hollow roof combs were generally limited to the central, Usumacinta, and western areas; "flying facades" appear restricted to the Chenes, Puuc, and northern plains areas.

Ruiz Early Postclassic phase of Chiapa de Corzo, Chiapas, c. A.D. 900–1250.

S

sacbé (*sacbeob*, pl.) Causeway or road of the lowland Maya, constructed of huge blocks of stone, leveled with gravel, and paved with plaster. Causeways connected parts of ceremonial centers, as well as cities, and in the absence of vehicular traffic must have served ceremonial parades and pedestrian use. Longest known *sacbé* extends 62 mi. (100 km) from Cobá to Yaxuna in the Yucatán peninsula.

sacred calendar See **tonalpohualli, tzolkin.**

Sacred Round See **Calendar Round.**

sacred well See **cenote.**

sacrifice Some sort of death sacrifice formed a part of most Mesoamerican cultures. Although its origin is found in the Preclassic period, the widest application of human sacrifice was in the Postclassic, becoming a diagnostic trait of that civilization.

Among the Aztecs, most ceremonies involved sacrifice, including the dispatching of animals, notably quail (identified with the sun-god). Human sacrifice (*tlamictiliztli*) was practiced widely. The Aztec sacrifice of human hearts was the "food" required to sustain the sun in its daily orbit across the sky. Victims were generally captives resulting from the "Flowery Wars" waged by Aztecs for that purpose. The record sacrifice must be the reputed 80,000 victims slain at the dedication of the Great Temple of Tenochtitlán in the reign of Ahuítzotl, A.D. 1487.

Some of the special sacrificial ceremonies included the flaying of victims to honor Xipe Totec (*Tlacaxipehualiztli*), the Arrow Sacrifice (*Tlacacaliliztli*), and the gladia-torial sacrifice (*tlahuahuanaliztli*). In auto-sacrifice, blood was drawn by the Aztecs from various parts of the body with the spine of the maguey or a sharp bone awl; and the sting of a stingray was used among the Maya. Aztecs allowed blood to fall on sheets of bark paper, or gathered it in a vessel to be offered to the gods.

Sahagún, Bernardino de (c. 1499–1590) Born in Sahagún de Campos, León, Spain; studied at the University of Salamanca; subsequently joined the Franciscan order; sailed for New Spain in 1529; and died in Mexico City. He became the foremost ethnographer of the 16th century in Mexico, largely based on his monumental work, *Historia General de las Cosas de la Nueva España*, an encyclopedia of the religion, customs, and natural history of the Aztecs.

The *Historia* was the final compilation based on numerous separate works, many now lost, written by native scribes based on information derived from ancient codices and answers to Sahagún's systematic questioning of elders familiar with the pre-Conquest traditions. The *Historia* was written in both Nahuatl and Spanish, with illustrations, principally in Tlatelolco and Mexico City. Two of the contributory works that make up the *Historia* are the Codices Matritenses in Madrid. The Florentine Codex is believed to be a copy of the *Historia* sent to Europe by Sahagún in 1580.

The *Historia* is divided into 12 books, each dealing with distinct aspects of the Aztec civilization: I. gods and related religious ceremonies; II. fixed and movable ceremonies; III. origin of the gods, religious mythology, customs; IV. divination, the sacred almanac; V. omens and prophecies; VI. rhetoric, moral philosophy, theology; VII. sun, moon, stars, and Tying of Years; VIII. kings and lords; IX. merchants and craftsmen; X. people: virtues, vices, sickness; Mexican nations; XI. natural history: animals, birds, trees, herbs; XII. conquest of Mexico.

Saint Andrew's cross See "crossed-bands" motif.

Sak Late Preclassic phase of Central Plateau of Chiapas, sparsely populated, with modest settlements.

Salinas de los Nueve Cerros Important salt deposits on a tributary of the middle Chixoy River, Guatemala; possibly once under Putún control.

Samac Early Postclassic-Protohistoric phase of the Chixoy River drainage, A.D. 1000–1530.

San Antonio Last phase of the Sierra Madre of southwest Tamaulipas, coeval with Los Angeles of the Sierra de Tamaulipas, c. A.D. 1300–Conquest.

San Augustín Acasaguastlán Late Classic site in the Motagua River valley of Guatemala. San Juan Plumbate appeared during its Magdalena phase, related to Amatle of the highlands, c. A.D. 600–750.

San Blas 1. Ceramic complex of the Pacific coast of Nayarit, with the earliest monochrome ware c. 500 B.C. 2. Province of northeastern Panama, including the San Blas Islands in the Caribbean Sea, today famed for their *molas*, textiles of reverse appliqué made by native Cuna Indians. Archaeologically little explored.

Sanchez-Solis, Codex See **codex, early post-Conquest Mexican; Sanchez-Solis, Codex.**

San Cristóbal 1. Preclassic phase of Zacualpa, western Guatemalan highlands, c. 300 B.C. 2. Part of the Great Lake of the Valley of Mexico in pre-Hispanic times.

San Gerónimo Archaeological site on the Costa Grande of Guerrero, northwest of Acapulco.

San Isidro Piedra Parada Preclassic site near Colomba on the Pacific slope of Guatemala where an Olmecoid petroglyph has been found.

San José 1. Maya center in north-central Belize with an occupation spanning 800 B.C.–A.D. 1000. 2. Capital of Costa Rica.

San José Mogote Earliest ceramic horizon of the Oaxaca region, c. 1500–900 B.C. White-rimmed blackware, excised designs, Olmec motifs, rocker stamping, and figurines of types C and D attest to Gulf Coast contact. Named after a site in the Etla valley, northwest of Oaxaca City.

San Juan 1. See **Plumbate.** 2. River draining from Lake Nicaragua into the Caribbean Sea, an early passage and trade route to the Pacific Ocean; forms part of the modern international boundary between Nicaragua and Costa Rica.

San Lorenzo 1. Period of highest achievement at the Olmec site of San Lorenzo Tenochtitlán, 1150–900 B.C. 2. Classic ceramic phase of the Choluteca area of southern Honduras, A.D. 600–800. 3. Ceramic phase of the Gulf of Chiriquí area of Panama, c. A.D. 800–1200. 4. Early Postclassic phase of the Sierra Madre of southwest Tamaulipas, c. A.D. 900–1300.

San Lorenzo Tenochtitlán Collective name for three related Olmec sites in the Coatzacoalcos River basin of southern Veracruz: San Lorenzo, Tenochtitlán (also called Río Chiquito to avoid confusion with the Aztec capital), and Potrero Nuevo. It has the longest history of any Olmec settlement studied, extending from c. 1500 B.C. until its abandonment c. 400 B.C. Reoccupied in Postclassic times, it never regained prominence. Earliest phase was Ojochí, c. 1500–1350 B.C., with ceramics related to the Barra and Ocós phases of the Chiapas coast. During the Bajío phase, 1350–1250 B.C., ceramics still lacked Olmec traits but work was underway to build the high plateau above the surrounding savannas on which San Lorenzo was situated. The Chicharras phase, 1250–1150 B.C., marks the emergence of Olmec figurines, white-black differential firing of pottery, and fine kaolin ware. San Lorenzo A and B, 1150–900 B.C., produced most of the monuments and brought the site to its final form. During the following Nacaste phase, 900–700 B.C., the Olmec period terminated, replaced by outside stylistic influences. For unknown reasons, monuments were defaced and some methodically concealed. The final phase, Palangana, ended c. 400 B.C.; remnants indicate contact with **La Venta**, Tres Zapotes, and Mamom peoples.

The site of San Lorenzo has produced six colossal heads, 48 major monuments, and the first conduit drainage system known in the Americas. The appearance of a south-north-oriented ceremonial center set a precedent followed throughout Mesoamerica to the Conquest. Fine Olmec pottery and figurines abound, but the variety of artifacts and new imported materials are proof of extensive trade. Jade, intimately associated with the Olmec, is strangely missing. After 900 B.C., La Venta replaced San Lorenzo as the center of the Olmec civilization.

San Luis Potosí Modern Mexican state, with capital of same name, bounded by the states of Nuevo León, Tamaulipas, Veracruz, Hidalgo, Querétaro, Guanajuato, Jalisco, and Zacatecas. Its principal site is Tamuín, a Postclassic site of the Huasteca.

San Martín Pajapán Volcano in the Tuxtla Mountains of Veracruz; a famous stone monument, the "Jaguar God of San Martín," was discovered near its peak.

San Miguel Amantla Center of the Teotihuacán cultural tradition in Atzcapotzalco, after the fall of Teotihuacán. Period is called Teotihuacán IV or Metepec.

San Miguel Amuco Site near Coyuca in the Balsas River Basin where discovery of an Olmec stela supports the theory of Olmec presence in Guerrero.

San Pablo See **Río Cuautla.**

San Salvador Capital of the Republic of El Salvador.

San Sebastián Red A pottery type named after a site in the Magdalena Lake basin of Jalisco. Characterized by deep red paste, its color clouded with a black burial patina (black manganese deposits), positive and negative painting, primarily in black and

cream slip, elaborately incised indications of hair, and punched wide slits for eyes and mouth. Modeling is highly expressive. Typical examples are the "mourners," "los desnudos," and figurines with elephantine legs. Radiocarbon dates extend from the time of Christ to A.D. 500. See also **Etzatlán.**

Santa Ana Site on the Ulúa River, Honduras, that gave its name to a class of Late Classic Ulúa Polychrome pottery distinguished by thickness of vessel walls, heavier than those of the Mayoid class. Cylindrical vases are supported by low, round or slab-footed feet. The main design is usually of human figures, mostly in processional sequence.

Santa Cecilia Restored small Aztec pyramid and temple outside Tenayuca.

Santa Clara Protoclassic ceramic phase of Guatemalan highlands, c. A.D. 100–300. The mammiform vessel supports are diagnostic. See **Kaminaljuyú.**

Santa Cruz 1. Site on the upper Grijalva River, Chiapas; ceramics are of Chiapa I and II periods. 2. Site on the Cuautla River, Morelos, contemporary with Tlatilco in the Valley of Mexico, c. 1000–500 B.C. The pottery is of great sophistication and technical accomplishment.

Santa Isabel Ixtápan Remains of imperial mammoths found here in conjunction with projectile points prove the presence of man in the Valley of Mexico c. 7000 B.C.

Santa Lucía Cotzumalhuapa See **Cotzumalhuapa.**

Santa María 1. Preclassic phase of Tehuacán Valley sequence, Puebla. Early Santa María, 850–650 B.C., is related to the Dili and Escalera phases of Chiapas, has same white pottery as lowland Maya Xe. Late Santa María is related to the Valley of Mexico, extending to 150 B.C. 2. Ceramic phase of Parita Bay, Panama, preceding Early Coclé, A.D. 300–500.

Santa Marta Cave near Ocozocoautla, Chiapas, that revealed preceramic human habitation from 6770–5360 B.C., related to early hunting-gathering levels at Tamaulipas.

Santa Rita 1. Maya site on northern tip of Belize, of post-Plumbate horizon, contemporary with Mayapán of Yucatán. Pottery figurines are decadent; frescoes of Mixtec style, now destroyed, were found there containing a unique text of the Mayapán period. 2. Archaeological site of western Honduras on the Comayagua River near its confluence with the Ulúa. Preclassic ceramic assemblage, called Ulúa Bichrome, was isolated at this site. During the Late Classic period Santa Rita was known for a Mayoid type of Ulúa Polychrome pottery, typically represented by cylindrical flat-bottomed vessels with a central band of figures.

Santa Rosa 1. El Salvador site where Classic period pottery sherds were found. 2. Archaeological site in the Central Depression of Chiapas whose ceramic history spans Chiapa II–VII, c. 1000 B.C.–A.D. 200.

Santa Rosa Xtampak Maya site in the Chenes area of northern Campeche with a continuous ceramic history from the Middle Preclassic to the Postclassic transitional period. Two stelae dated c. A.D. 511–771 may have been erected before the buildings in Chenes style, such as the multichambered palace.

Santiago 1. Mexican river. See **Lerma.** 2. Ceramic phase of central Nayarit, A.D. 1400–1500. See also **Amapa.**

sapodilla (*Achras zapota*) A large tree of the lowland rain forests and source of chicle used for chewing gum. Its wood is hard and resistant; employed by the Classic Maya for inner vault supports and temple-door lintels, often intricately carved. *Zapote* is another name for this tree.

Sarigua Ceramic complex at Monagrillo, Parita Bay, Panama, possibly dating to the beginning of the first millennium B.C.

Sarstún (*Sarstoon*) River that drains the depression between the Cockscomb (Maya) Mountains and the Sierra de Santa Cruz, marking the boundary between Guatemala and Belize as it flows into the Bay of Amatique on the Caribbean Sea.

sascab Weathered, disintegrated limestone employed by the lowland Maya as a building material in place of mortar.

Saxche A Uaxactún polychrome ceramic appearing in the Tepeu I phase and continuing into Tepeu II, with orange, cream, or red slips, and decorated with glyph bands, geometric motifs, sky-band signs and figures. Influenced Ulúa Polychrome and Copador styles of Honduras and El Salvador.

Sayil Late Classic Maya site in the Puuc region of southwestern Yucatán. Its three-storied palace is considered one of the most satisfactory architectural compositions ever created by the Maya.

scapulary tablet A Zapotec variation of the *talud-tablero* architectural feature of Teotihuacán. The Zapotecs heightened the chiaroscuro effect by two modifications of the *tablero* (panel). The bottom of the *tablero* frame was removed and the remaining three sides of the rectangular frame were repeated, recessed, to accent the shadow effect. Another variant was the superimposition of the *tablero* over a larger sloping *talud* (wall surface) to maximize the play of light and shadow in the strong Oaxacan sun. Scapulary tablets are diagnostic of Zapotec architecture and prominent on the stepped temple platforms, facades, and balustrades of the type site, Monte Albán.

scarification Cosmetic puncturing of the skin to produce small welts. The Maya seem to have practiced it to some degree, but the ceramic evidence is most pronounced in western Mexico. Jalisco, Nayarit, and Colima figurines show widespread scarification on the shoulders.

scarified ware A type of pottery decoration consisting of alternate groups of incised lines and patches, usually red in color. It is characteristic of La Concepción phase of Greater Chiriquí. Peculiar to this complex is a chimney-shaped vessel with three solid legs. Its style is close to the Zoned Bichrome of Costa Rica and Nicaragua. Scarified ware is found from southern Costa Rica to Coclé in Panama, including Veraguas. Contemporary with the Guacamayo type, c. 300 B.C.–A.D. 300. See **Central Panama.**

Schroeder site Ceremonial and residential site of the Guardiana branch of the Chalchihuites culture in Durango. It participated in all four phases: Ayala, A.D. 550–700, Las Joyas, 700–950, Río Tunal, 950–1150, and Calera, 1150–1350. Its greatest activity was stimulated by the Toltecs after A.D. 900.

screen-fold See **codex.**

secondary burial Burial of a dismembered corpse. In Middle America it refers to partially decomposed human remains whose bones were cleaned and buried, frequently in ceramic containers.

Secondary Series See **Distance Numbers.**

Segovia River between Nicaragua and Honduras. See **Coco.**

Seibal Maya site whose occupation dates back to the Preclassic period, but its importance is from the decline of Altar de Sacrificios c. A.D. 751. Both centers are

Seibal emblem glyph

on the Pasión River in the Petén. The Putún Maya controlled Seibal c. A.D. 850. Subsequently, stela erections continued, but showed Putún facial types introduced into the Classic Maya decoration.

Selden Codex See **codex, early post-Conquest Mexican; Selden Codex.**

Selin Ceramic phase of northeastern Honduras and the Bay Islands, blending Caribbean and Ulúa-Yojoa pottery types, c. A.D. 500–1000.

sello Spanish for an object, usually of clay, incised with a design for the purpose of imprinting that design on another surface; also called a stamp. Its form is either cylindrical or flat, in the latter case with a handle on the side opposite to the design. Appeared as early as the Olmec, before 1300 B.C., and used widely in Preclassic Mesoamerica. Its use diminished in the Classic period. It became a rarity in the

great Classic Maya sites, but reappeared in the centuries before the Conquest, especially in the Valley of Mexico. Pigments were applied to the *sello* surface for printing; it may also have been used for body decoration and/or printing bark paper.

serpent column A unique Toltec-inspired architectural support in the form of a feathered serpent (*quetzalcóatl*), whose open-fanged head serves as a base and whose tail-rattles are the roof support, as seen at Tula and Chichén Itzá.

serpent X A basic motif of Maya art, possibly with its origin in Olmec masks and early dragons. Further developed in the Izapan style, the baroque serpent head was baptized "serpent X" by archaeologists. Highly stylized, ten elements appear: the supraorbital plate, eye, nose or snout, fang, tongue, teeth, molar, beard, nose scroll and nose plug. Although Maya serpents occasionally show only an upper lip, they quite often have a lower one as well.

Seuss effect See **radiocarbon (C¹⁴) dating.**

shaft tomb Boot-shaped in its simplest form, examples consist of a vertical shaft, usually 13 to 20 ft. (4 to 6 m) deep, that leads to one or more horizontal chambers. The shaft-tomb complex in Mesoamerica is found only in the Jalisco, Nayarit, and Colima areas of western Mexico. Dating to c. 200 B.C.–A.D. 330, they suggest an influence from South America where shaft tombs appear from Peru to Colombia. See **Etzatlán.**

shaman Native religious practitioner, or medicine man, the link between the living and the unseen world of gods, spirits of ancestors, and manifestations of natural forces, frequently with the aid of hallucinogens.

Shield Jaguar The eighth-century ruler of Maya Classic center of Yaxchilán, Chiapas.

Short Count Abbreviated Maya date-recording system that replaced the

Shield Jaguar glyph

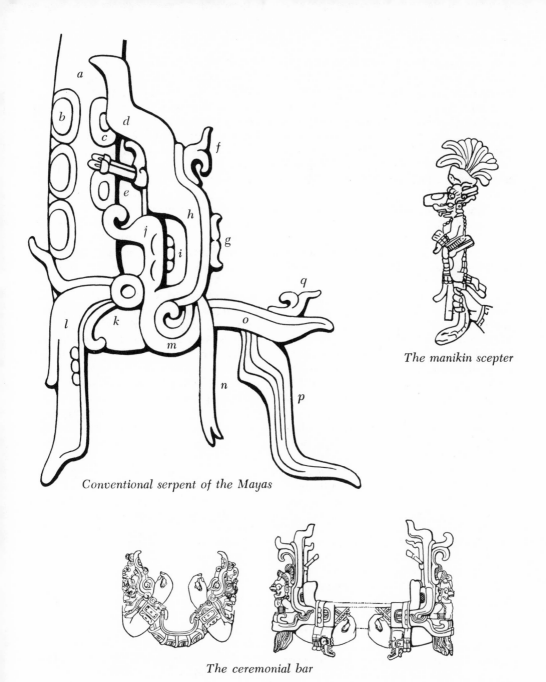

Conventional serpent of the Mayas

The manikin scepter

The ceremonial bar

Plate 16. Maya serpent motif. *Conventional serpent of the Mayas used for decorative purposes:* (*a*) body, (*b*) ventral scale, (*c*) dorsal scale, (*d*) nose, (*e*) noseplug, (*f*) incisor tooth, (*g*) molar tooth, (*h*) jaw, (*i*) eye, (*j*) supraorbital plate, (*k*) earplug, (*l*) ear pendant, (*m*) curled fang, (*n*) tongue, (*o*) lower jaw, (*p*) beard, (*q*) incisor tooth.

The manikin scepter: a grotesque figure with one leg modified into a serpent.

The ceremonial bar: a two-headed serpent held in the arms of human beings on stelae: (*left*) Stela P, Copán; (*right*) Stela N, Copán.

From H. J. Spinden, *Ancient Civilizations of Mexico and Central America,* pages 91, 98, 99.

Long Count of the Classic period lowland Maya in Postclassic Yucatán. It had the merit of requiring only one glyph (rather than ten) to express it, with the understanding that this day ended some *katun* in the Long Count. Its accuracy was limited to 13 *katuns* (13 x 7,200 days, or 256½ years), with each *katun* bearing the name of the day on which it ended, always Ahau. Thus, *katun* 13 Ahau was followed by *katun* 11 Ahau, and *katuns* 9, 7, 5, 3, 1, 12, 10, 8, 6, 4, 2, and again 13, after 256½ years. Although adequate for contemporary use, the Short Count date has the same inadequacy for historians as our saying it happened on July 4, '76, which does not clarify whether 1776, 1876, or 1976 is meant, lacking other references. The Short Count was called *U Kahlay Katunob* by the Maya, meaning "the record of the *katuns*."

Sierra Madre del Sur Mountain range south of the Balsas River, bordering the Pacific Ocean, and extending from southern Michoacán across Guerrero into southern Oaxaca.

Sierra Madre Occidental Broad mountain chain of western Mexico, an extension of the Rocky Mountains.

Sierra Madre Oriental Mountain range of eastern Mexico, mainly on a north-south axis, its principal sector forming the eastern edge of the Central Plateau.

Silho See **Orange, Fine.**

silhouetted relief In sculpture, a form cut out by perforations through a block of stone; the technique appeared in the Protoclassic period, A.D. 100–300, in highland Guatemala. Although similar, its reappearance at Telantunich, Yucatán, in the 16th century does not present a stylistic relationship.

Sinaloa Mexican state on the Pacific coast whose capital is Culiacán, bordered by the states of Nayarit, Durango, Chihuahua, and Sonora. Sinaloa represents the northwestern corner of Mesoamerica, but atypically for that civilization, it was at its peak development after A.D. 1000–Conquest. No definite Preclassic evidence of Mesoamerican tradition has yet materialized. The site of Chametla, near the Nayarit border, gave its name to the Sinaloa Classic horizon. Postclassic horizon, Aztatlán, spanned 500 years and was evident in all sites, including Chametla, Culiacán, and Guasave in the north. A late horizon, called Culiacán, overlapped Aztatlán and continued to the Conquest.

Sitio Conte Ceremonial site in Coclé province, central Panama, noted for its goldwork, which was cast, hammered, and embossed with characteristic Coclé designs. Included were circlets, helmets, many beads, nose and ear ornaments, and armbands. Most distinctive are the large hammered breastplates made to be worn on clothing as insignia of rank. Perishable objects were covered with sheet gold. Gold settings were fashioned for emeralds and carved whalebone ivory. Serpentine and agate were carved into beads and pendants. Polychrome ceramics included an unusual purplish color and date c. A.D. 500–800; highly stylized animal forms are arranged in curvilinear patterns. Principal shapes are round dishes, carafes, and long-necked jars.

skeuomorph In archaeology, a representation of an object ordinarily made of a different material or by a different technique, such as a pottery rendition of a woven basket.

slash-and-burn See **milpa.**

slip A thin coating of liquid clay applied to ceramic objects before firing, usually different in color from the vessel's paste.

"smiling figures" Famous Classic period central Veracruz ceramic figurine sculptures, possibly expressing a cult of sensuality related or antecedent to the Postclassic Xochipilli-Macuilxóchitl cult. See **Remojadas, Nopiloa.**

Soconusco Geographic region formed by the narrow Pacific coastal plain, backed by a hilly piedmont area, extending eastward along the Isthmus of Tehuantepec and southward into Guatemala. Excavations here suggest early contact with South

America. Soconusco was a rich cacao-producing region in the Postclassic period, appearing prominently in Aztec lists of trade and tribute. See **Altamira, Ocós, La Victoria, Izapa, Barra.**

solar year, Maya See **calendar, Mesoamerican.**

Solomec Maya linguistic group of the Department of Huehuetenango, Guatemala.

Soncautla Postclassic phase of Tres Zapotes, Veracruz, c. A.D. 1200, sometimes called Tres Zapotes V.

sótano Spanish word for cellar, applied in Oaxaca to the characteristic, small Mixtec tomb, not built but dug directly into the *tepetate,* the hard natural subsoil.

Sotuta Postclassic ceramic phase of Yucatán, c. A.D. 1000–1200, that takes its name from the capital city of the Cocom family at the time of the Conquest.

Southern Lowlands See **Maya areas.**

Spanish Lookout Cultural phase of Barton Ramie, Belize, c. A.D. 700–1000.

stamp See **sello.**

stela (*stelae,* pl.) Columnar stone monument erected to record historic and religious events, it was sometimes plain, more usually sculpted with figures and glyphs. First appeared in the New World among the Preclassic Olmec on the Gulf Coast of Veracruz and Tabasco. Stela 2, at Chiapa de Corzo, dated 36 B.C., followed by Tres Zapotes Stela C, 31 B.C., are the earliest recorded. Stelae were erected in Monte Albán I in Oaxaca, and at Protoclassic Izapa in the Soconusco region of Chiapas. Highland Guatemala stelae rarely had glyphic inscriptions; disappeared there abruptly in Classic times.

The southern lowland Maya brought stelae to the highest and broadest development. Inscribed with Initial Series dates, starting with Tikal Stela 29 in A.D. 292, they became a Classic lowland Maya horizon marker. Their use proliferated, with exception of a 50-year hiatus in the last half of the sixth century, until the end of the Classic period, c. A.D. 900.

stepped fret Abstract decorative motif, possibly inspired by serpents or waves, com-

stepped fret motif

prised of diagonally rising steps, and ending in an angular or curved hook. Called *xicalcoliuhqui* in Nahuatl, and *greca* in Spanish because of its similarity to Greek meanders. First seen on Monte Albán II vessels c. 350–100 B.C., it achieved broad popularity in Mesoamerica by the Postclassic. Prominent in stone mosaic at Mitla, in Mixtec codices, and the architecture of El Tajín and Tula.

stingray The ray whose spines served as spear and arrow points for natives of Costa Rica and Panama. Among the Maya to the north they were used to draw blood in rituals of autosacrifice. They are found in Maya burials, sometimes with glyphic inscriptions.

stirrup spout A distinctive ceramic form with two hollow tubes rising from the body of the vessel and joined in a single spout. Distribution in Mexico was spotty. It appeared in Colima c. 1500 B.C.,

stirrup spout, Tlatilco

then in Tlatilco, Chupícuaro, and Morelos, suggesting Pacific contact with South America where this form was common.

string-sawing The technique of pulling a cord back and forth, using an abrasive like sand, to cut stone such as jade or softer materials. Worked from an edge or from a drilled perforation to enlarge an opening or produce openwork.

Suchiate River providing the boundary between Chiapas, Mexico, and the Guatemalan coastal plains. It flows into the Pacific Ocean.

suffix See **affix.**

sukia 1. Costa Rican stone human figure shown on its haunches, elbows resting on raised knees, with a tubular object, possibly a cigar, held to its mouth. 2. Name ap-

Back view   Side view   Front view

Plate 17. Stela A, Copán. Catherwood engraving in J. L. Stephens, *Incidents of Travel in Central America, Chiapas and Yucatán*, vol. I, following page 158.

plied to medicine men by the Misquitos of Honduras and Nicaragua.

Sula Plain Region of northwest Honduras drained by the Ulúa River; includes the sites of Playa de los Muertos, Santa Rita, Las Flores, and Travesia.

Sultepec Site in the state of Mexico that lends its name to the northernmost variant of the Guerrero Chontal style of small stone sculpture, Late Preclassic, c. 300–100 B.C.

sun-god See **Tonatiuh, Kin, Kinich Ahau, Curicaueri.**

suns, Aztec See **Creation myth, Aztec.**

Sun Stone See **Calendar Stone, Aztec.**

superfix See **affix.**

Supplementary Series A series, usually of six glyphs, found on Classic period Maya stelae, inserted between the main body of the Initial Series and its final glyph stating the month of the date. This Supplementary Series of glyphs treated the age of the moon on the recorded date, length of this particular lunar month, and other not always identifiable lunar data. Also called Lunar Series and Moon Count.

sweat bath Separate building, called *temescalli* in Nahuatl, housed facilities for the steam bath (*temescal*), possibly connected ritually with the ball game. The buildings usually had a fire area for heating the stones over which water was poured to produce steam.

t

Tabasco State of Mexico situated on the Gulf Coast, bordered by Veracruz, Chiapas, Campeche, and Guatemala. Its capital of Villa Hermosa today has a regional museum and an outdoor installation, Parque Museo de La Venta, where many of the monuments from the Olmec site of La Venta are on view. Tabasco is the pre-Conquest name of the Grijalva River. See also **Comalcalco, Jonuta, La Venta, Potonchán.**

tablero A horizontal rectangular panel cantilevered from the outer wall of a structure by means of stone slabs. Its frame enclosed a recessed surface that was often decorated by painted or sculptured motifs, as on the Temple of Quetzalcóatl, in the Ciudadela of Teotihuacán. It formed the upper portion of the *talud-tablero,* a diagnostic feature of Teotihuacán architecture.

Taino High ceremonial culture of the Island Arawaks in the Greater Antilles during Period IV. Starting from eastern Hispaniola c. A.D. 700, it had spread through most of the Greater Antilles by A.D. 1000. Classic Taino pottery has its own unusual shapes, with distinctive incised-and-pitted patterns, but bears a resemblance to other circum-Caribbean styles that date after A.D. 800. Pottery stamps and rollers hint at the beauty of ancient textiles. Carving skills are expressed in their *duhos* and platform-topped human figures in wood and stone. Collar stones, *zemis,* and ball courts outlined with vertical slabs, incised with symbolic figures, are identified with this culture.

Tajín Rain-god of the Totonac peoples, corresponding to the Aztec god Tlaloc and the Maya god Chac. See also **El Tajín.**

Tajumulco Name of a volcano and an early Postclassic site in the western Guatemala highlands near the Chiapas border. May be where Tohil Plumbate pottery originated.

Talamanca 1. Mountain range in southeastern Costa Rica. 2. Cultural area represented by the plain of Limón, Costa Rica.

talpetate See **tepetate.**

talud Facade of the outer wall of a structure, sloping inward as the wall ascends. First noticed in Mesoamerica at the Olmec site of La Venta, Tabasco, c. 800 B.C.

talud-tablero Classic Teotihuacán architectural feature composed of a rectangular panel (*tablero*) cantilevered over a sloping wall (*talud*). Repeated on stepped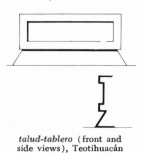

talud-tablero (front and side views), Teotihuacán

temple pyramids, it accented the terracing of the receding structure. It was widely copied, with regional variations, throughout Mesoamerica after A.D. 300. At Teotihuacán the *tablero* was always larger than the *talud.* See **scapulary tablet.**

Tamarindito Classic Maya site on the Pasión River of Petén, Guatemala.

Tamaulipas Mexican state on the Gulf Coast, with capital of Cuidad Victoria, bounded by the Río Grande on the north and by the Mexican states of San Luis Potosí and Nuevo León. In southern Tamaulipas, which is the northeastern limit of Meso-america, a regional sequence was born of two local sequences, the Sierra de Tamaulipas (T) and the Sierra Madre of southwest Tamaulipas (M). Its main archaeological importance derives from the study of earliest man to the beginnings of agriculture and maize cultivation. Arid desert conditions were not conducive to full participation in the rise of Mesoamerican civilization. Applicable cultural phases are:

alcóatl bringing bones from the underworld to Tamoanchán, where they are ground and mixed with the autosacrificial blood of the assembled gods to create man. See also **Xochicalco.**

Tamuín The most explored Huastec site with an 11th-century temple whose frescoes depict a procession of gods or priests in a style related to Mixtec codices. The site is the source of the famous stone sculpture, *The Adolescent.*

Tancah Maya center north of Tulum in Quintana Roo with an almost continuous ceramic record from the Late Preclassic

Diablo (T)	to 12,000 B.C.	nomadic hunters
Lerma (T)	12,000–7000 B.C.	hunting, some gathering
Infiernillo (M)	7000–5000 B.C.	incipient agriculture
Nogales (T)	5000–3000 B.C.	seasonal macrobands
Ocampo (M)	4000–3000 B.C.	domesticated plants to 5% of food
La Perra (T)	3000–2200 B.C.	domesticated plants 10% of subsistence; traces of nal-tel corn
Flacco (M)	2200–1800 B.C.	Bat Cave–type corn, semisedentary macrobands
Almagre (T)	2200–1800 B.C.	
Guerra (M)	1800–1400 B.C.	semipermanent villages
Mesa de Guaje (M)	1400–500 B.C.	hybridized corn, pottery
La Florida (M)	500 B.C.–A.D. 1	temple-oriented villages
Laguna (T)	500 B.C.–A.D. 1	variety of ceramics
Eslabones (T)	A.D. 1–500	centers about plazas
Palmillas (M)	A.D. 1–500	figurines, ceramic vessels
La Salta (T)	A.D. 500–900	small sites without temples
San Lorenzo (M)	A.D. 900–1300	agriculture 40% of diet
Los Angeles (T)	A.D. 1300–	cultural decline,
San Antonio (M)	A.D. 1300–	some return to cave habitation

Tamoanchán Referred to in post-Conquest native accounts as the terrestrial paradise, mythical land of man's origin. A Toltec-Mexica concept, probably of Huastec origin, the word is a Mayan toponym: *ta* is a locative prefix meaning "of"; *Moan* is a mythical bird, lord of the 13th heaven; *chan* is an archaic form of *can*, denoting snake or sky. Thus translated, Tamoanchán is "land of the bird-snake (feathered serpent)." It is sometimes confused with Tlalocán, the paradise of the Aztec rain-god Tlaloc.

One Mexican saga of creation has Quetz-

period through the Late Postclassic. Rooms in a Postclassic palace are decorated with murals in the style of Codex Tro-Cortesianus.

Tangancicuaro Postclassic Tarascan site in Michoacán.

tapadera A usually hemispheric clay object with three or four supports placed over burning incense. Capiral *tapaderas* are incense burner covers found in the Tepetate phase of Michoacán c. A.D. 800.

tapextle Crude bed, consisting of a framework of wood, reinforced with cane and supported on four forked sticks.

tapia Puddled adobe used in construction.

Tarascan Most important nation of western Mexico from the 10th century to Conquest. It extended its empire from its capital of Tzintzuntzan on Lake Pátzcuaro to northwest Michoacán, part of Jalisco, the lowlands of Michoacán, and northwest Guerrero. The last lord, Caltzontzin, fell to the Spanish in 1528. Tarascans were famed for feather mosaics, copperwork, fine textiles, and painted pottery. The term *Tarascan* was earlier and erroneously applied to the combined cultures of Colima, Jalisco, and Nayarit, which had long disappeared when the Tarascans reigned.

Tariácuri Tarascan lord who consolidated the kingdom, with his seat at the first capital of Pátzcuaro. His successors made Tzintzuntzan the capital; made him a hero, finally a wind-god, a sort of Quetzalcóatl.

Tases Yucatecan cultural phase, A.D. 1300–1450.

Tayasal Island in Lake Petén-Itzá, Guatemala; the last stronghold of the Itzá Maya, conquered by the Spanish in 1697. See also **Flores, Canek.**

Tazumal Large mound group in the Chalchuapa archaeological zone of El Salvador, near Guatemalan border, primarily active A.D. 400–1200. Although its architecture is influenced by Kaminaljuyú, its pottery reflects a Classic period connection with Copán and the Ulúa region to the north.

tecali Referred to as Mexican "onyx," or "alabaster," the mineral aragonite.

Tecciztécatl Aztec god of the moon, represented in masculine (Codex Vatican B) or feminine (Codex Borgia) form. Sometimes a nocturnal aspect of Tezcatlipoca. God of fertility, related to the marine snail. Patron deity of the Aztec day Miquiztli.

In one version of the Aztec Creation myth, he sacrifices himself in the fire, becoming the moon after Nanahuatzin had preceded him to become the fifth sun. Synonymous with *meztli*.

tecciztli See **atecocolli.**

téchcatl Sacrificial stone shaped so that a victim's chest was arched upward as he was held on his back by four priests. A fifth priest plunged the flint knife into his breast, extracting the heart as a gift to the gods.

tecolotl Nahuatl for owl, associated with death and the underworld. A bird of ill omen whose nocturnal song is even today considered to be fatal to anyone who hears it.

Tecolpan Maya site northeast of Palenque at the Tabasco border. Its principal period is Late Classic to Early Postclassic, yielding fine Balancán Z Fine Orange pottery.

tecomapiloa Resonant gourd, played by women at feasts of the Aztec young corn- (Xilonen) and mature corn- (Toci) goddesses.

tecomatl Nahuatl for a common spherical pottery vessel, today also called *tecomate*, in imitation of natural gourds, with a restricted opening and no collar.

tecpan Aztec community house, or "city hall," of the *calpulli.*

tecpantli Nahuatl for the number 20, expressed pictographically by a small flag.

Técpatl Eighteenth of the 20 Nahuatl day signs, pictured in the Mexican codices as a flint knife; corresponds to the Maya day Etz'nab. Técpatl, as a Year Bearer, along with the days Ácatl, Calli, and Tochtli, served to begin the years, there being 13 Técpatl years in the 52-year cycle. Its orientation was North. Calendrical names of Técpatl are: 1 Técpatl: Huitzilopochtli-Camaxtli; 4 Técpatl: Tecciztécatl; 7 Técpatl: Chicomecóatl; 8 Técpatl: name for maguey; 12 Técpatl: earth- or death-god.

Chalchiuhtotolin, a manifestation of Tezcatlipoca, was patron of the day; its augury was favorable.

tecuhtli Meaning lord in Nahuatl, it also designated the privileged class of Aztec society, which included holders of titles and offices appointed for life by the *tlatoani.* Commoners could achieve this rank through war service. Also called *teuctli (teteuctin,* pl.).

Tecuilhuitontli Eighth of the 18 20-day months of the Aztec year of 365 days, as celebrated at Tenochtitlán. Principal celebration honored Huixtocíhuatl, goddess of salt. See also **months, Aztec.**

Tegucigalpa Capital of the Republic of Honduras.

Tehuacán An arid valley of southern Puebla, Mexico, whose dry caves preserved the longest record, 8,000 years, of human habitation in the Western Hemisphere. Three phases, Riego, 6800–5000 B.C., Coxcatlán, 5000–3400 B.C., and Abejas, 3400–2300 B.C., span the period from nomadic hunters to incipient agriculturists and a gradual transition to sedentary life. Primitive, tiny ears of corn, carbon-dated 5200–3400 B.C., are the earliest in any part of the world.

The Purrón phase, 2300–1500 B.C., reveals hybrid corn supporting settled village life and the earliest appearance of pottery in Mesoamerica. The Tehuacán sequence continued through these phases: Early Ajalpan, 1500–1200 B.C., Late Ajalpan, 1200–850 B.C., Early Santa María, 850–650 B.C., Late Santa María, 650–150 B.C., Early Palo Blanco, 150 B.C.–A.D. 250, Late Palo Blanco, A.D. 250–700, Early Venta Salada, A.D. 700–1150, Late Venta Salada, A.D. 1150–1520.

Although cultures of more fertile Mexican valleys overshadowed Tehuacán from the Middle Preclassic to the Conquest, the Tehuacán sequence, especially when related to contemporary ceramic phases in other areas, provides a helpful reference to the study of emerging Mesoamerican civilization. See separate references to phases.

tejar ware Bowls and jars decorated with small circular appliqué buttons, found in the Amatle and Pamplona phases of the Guatemalan highlands.

Telantunich Postclassic Maya site noted for "silhouetted" reliefs with strong phallic motifs; west of Lake Chichancanab, Yucatán.

Tella Tenth of the 20 Zapotec days of the month. Equivalent to the Aztec day Itzcuintli and the Maya day Oc.

Telleriano-Remensis, Codex See **codex, early post-Conquest Mexican; Telleriano-Remensis, Codex.**

telpochcalli Aztec school for *macehuals,* the standard school for training commoner youth, especially for warfare. Tezcatlipoca was its patron. See also **calmécac.**

temalacatl Circular stone platform from which the victim attempted to defend himself in the ritual of a "gladiatorial sacrifice."

temescal Sweat bath, often used for ritual purification; Nahuatl for sweathouse is *temescalli.* See **sweat bath.**

Temiminaloyán See **universe, Aztec.**

Tempisque Valley of the Guanacaste region of Costa Rica terminating at the tip of the Gulf of Nicoya.

temple Building used for ritual ceremonies, placed on a raised platform (pyramid). Used only by the hierarchy; public view was restricted to ceremonies conducted on the pyramid platform in

Great Temple, Tenochtitlán

front of the temple, which could be seen from the plaza below. Earlier temples were of perishable materials and similar to native huts. By Classic times the Maya built them of stone and mortar, with an outer chamber leading to an inner sanctuary, as in the Temple of the Cross, Palenque. They were frequently surmounted by an impressive roof comb. The Aztecs at Tenochtitlán erected twin temples honoring Tlaloc and Huitzilopochtli on a common platform.

Tenahuatiliztli Alternate designation for Ochpanitztli, 12th of the 18 months of the Nahuatl calendar of 365 days.

Tenam Late Classic site in the Comitán Plain, Chiapas, with sculptured monuments and stelae with cycle and *katun* counts, same as the lowland Maya.

Tenampúa Fortified site on a mesa above the Comayagua plain in central Honduras, strongly influenced stylistically by the Late Classic period Maya, A.D. 550–950. Gave its name to a distinctive type of the Ulúa Polychrome ceramic group.

Front Elevation

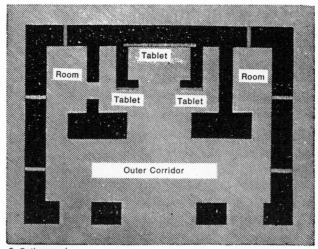

F. Catherwood

Ground Plan

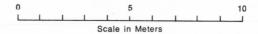

Scale in Meters

Plate 18. Temple of the Cross, Palenque. Catherwood engraving in J. L. Stephens, *Incidents of Travel in Central America, Chiapas and Yucatán*, vol. II, facing page 350.

Tenayuca Old settlement of the Chichimec chief Xólotl, near modern Tampantla, Valley of Mexico. Its pyramid represents eight successive superimpositions, probably built every 52 years; the first dates A.D. 1064–1116, including the row of serpents (*coatepantli*) at its base. The last pyramid, dating A.D. 1450–1500, and surmounted by twin temples, may have been the model for the Great Temple at Tenochtitlán.

Tenexpan Preclassic site of southern Veracruz. See **baby face.**

Tenocelome An appellation proposed for the Preclassic period Olmec of the Mexican Gulf Coast to avoid confusion with the unrelated Historic Olmec of the Late Postclassic. It has not been generally adopted.

Tenoch Semilegendary priest-leader associated with founding of Tenochtitlán.

Tenochca An inhabitant of Tenochtitlán.

Tenochtitlán Island capital of the Aztecs in Lake Texcoco, traditionally founded A.D. 1325, at the Conquest a city of perhaps 100,000 inhabitants. It was laid out in a grid of streets and canals connected to the mainland by three great causeways. It was completely leveled by the Spanish to whom it capitulated on August 13, 1521. Its ruins underlie modern Mexico City. Its ceremonial precinct, surrounded by a serpent wall and containing the twin-templed pyramid dedicated to Huitzilopochtli and Tlaloc, covered the area now occupied by the modern Zócalo, the cathedral, and the Presidential Palace. See also **Mexica.**

Teocalco Last Postclassic phase of the Valley of Mexico, also called Aztec IV.

teocuítlatl Nahuatl word for gold, meaning "excrement of the gods."

teoicpalli Chair of the gods in temples as shown in Mexican codices; carved wooden throne of rulers. See **icpalli.**

teomama (*teomamaque,* pl.) Title of those who carried idols of the tribal gods on their shoulders during the early migrations, and later in Aztec festivals.

teonanacatl Nahuatl for "divine mushroom," which was restricted to ritual use by the natives. Ceremonial use of hallucinogenic mushrooms dates back to 1500 B.C. in Middle America; still used in Oaxaca and other parts of Mesoamerica.

Teopanzolco Aztec ceremonial site, with pyramid, in Cuernavaca, Morelos.

teopixque Aztec priests who instructed in the schools for commoners, the *telpochcalli.*

teosinte (*Euchlaena mexicana*) A grass formerly considered to be the ancestor to domesticated maize, now proven a hybrid of maize and its truly wild relative, *Tripsacum;* today grows as an unwanted weed in Indian *milpas.*

Teotenango Fortified hilltop site overlooking the southern Toluca valley in the state of Mexico. Erected by the Matlatzincas by A.D. 700, it shows strong Teotihuacán architectural influence; occupied by the Aztecs in the reign of Axayácatl.

Teotihuacán The earliest true urban complex of Middle America, 30 mi. (50 km) north of Mexico City. Its development spans the period from c. 100 B.C. to its destruction in the seventh century A.D.

The grandeur of the site lies in the central plan about a north-south axis described as the "Avenue of the Dead," which originally extended another $1\frac{1}{4}$ mi. (2 km) to the south. The Pyramid of the Moon overlooks a plaza at the north end, and the Pyramid of the Sun rises on its eastern side. The latter is one of the largest structures in Mesoamerica, c. 700 sq. ft. (225 m^2) at its base, built in five terraces to a temple platform 215 ft. (65 m) above the valley floor. The Ciudadela, a square compound approx. 1,300 ft. (400 m) on a side and east of the "Avenue of the Dead," originally constituted the center of the city, probably the seat of the hierarchy, and contains the pyramid of Quetzalcóatl. Various platforms and clusters of chambered buildings are aligned along the avenue. This civic-religious center alone covered some 2 sq. mi. (5 km^2), 12 times the size of the later sacred precinct of Aztec Tenochtitlán. The overall extent of Teotihuacán is estimated at $22\frac{1}{2}$ sq. mi. (58 km^2), supporting a population of perhaps 85,000. On the periphery of the site as seen today

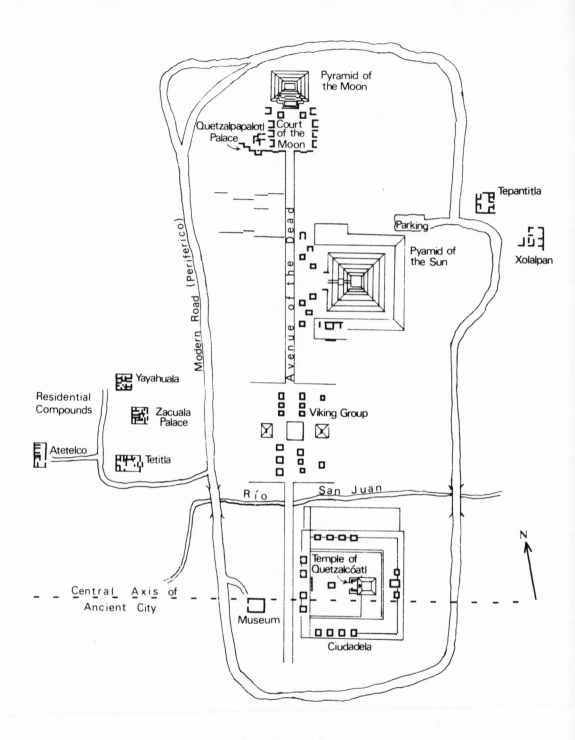

Plate 19. Teotihuacán.

are large residential compounds that housed the urban population, resident artisans of all types, reflecting the far-flung trade of the metropolis. These include Tlamimilolpa, Tepantitla, Tetitla, Zacuala, Yayahuala, Atetelco, and Xolalpan.

In architecture Teotihuacán contributed the *talud-tablero*, the widely copied facing of ceremonial structures. Its site planning, borrowed from the Olmec, was likewise imitated. In ceramics the distinctive tripod cylindrical vase, decorated in polychromed gesso or incised, was widely traded along with Thin Orange ware. Complex pottery *incensarios* were decorated with molded appliqué. In sculpture large examples were rare and architectonic in style. The most notable carvings were the serene, stone face masks created for funerary use. Polychrome murals of religious inspiration decorated the inside walls of many buildings and showed stylistic influences of both the Gulf Coast and the Maya. Best preserved are those at Tetitla and Atetelco; most publicized are those from Tepantitla, among which is the *Paradise of Tlaloc*. Cultural phases of Teotihuacán, described under separate listings, are: Tzacualli (Teotihuacán I): A.D. 1–150; Miccaotli (Teotihuacán II): A.D. 150–250; Tlamimilolpa (Teotihuacán III): A.D. 250–500; Xolalpan (Teotihuacán IIIa): A.D. 500–650; Metepec (Teotihuacán IV): A.D. 650–750.

Teotihuacán's influence dominated Classic Mesoamerica as far as western Mexico, the Gulf Coast, and the Maya areas of Guatemala, western El Salvador, and the Yucatán peninsula. See also **Middle Classic horizon.**

Teotl See **universe, Aztec.**

Teotlalpan Aztec designation for the desert region north of Teotihuacán, place of origin of the Otomí and Chichimec; in mythology it is identified with Mictlampa.

Teotleco See **Pachtontli; months, Aztec.**

teoxíhuitl Nahuatl for "turquoise of the gods"; turquoise was extensively used in mosaic work during the Toltec and Aztec periods; its only known Mesoamerican source is in Zacatecas.

Teoyaomiqui Aztec god of those who died in the Flowery Wars, he was sometimes identified as 6th of the 13 Lords of the Day, replacing Mictlantecuhtli. Also called Huahuantli.

Teozacoalco Mixtec city of central Oaxaca, mentioned in and possibly provenance of Codex Nuttall.

Tepaneca Traditionally one of the seven Aztec tribal groups believed to have left the legendary Chicomoztoc ("seven caves") in A.D. 1168, starting the migration to the Valley of Mexico. Meaning "those on the rocks" in Nahuatl, their name may relate to their first settlement in the Pedregal, an area of volcanic outcroppings at modern San Ángel, Mexico City. Under Tezozómoc they founded the Tepanec empire, ruling the Valley of Mexico from their capital, Atzcapotzalco, until subdued by the Mexica under Itzcóatl, A.D. 1428.

Tepantitla Residential compound east of the Pyramid of the Sun at Teotihuacán noted for its wall paintings, especially of Tlalocán, the paradise of the rain-god Tlaloc.

Tepeílhuitl See **Hueypachtli; months, Aztec.**

tepescuintli Nahuatl for "stone dog," it describes a species of hairless Mexican dog rare today but anciently raised and fattened to be eaten; a popular subject of Colima potters.

tepetate 1. Fine-grained earth of volcanic origin that forms a hard natural subsoil. The shaft tombs of western Mexico were cut into this layer to avoid cave-ins. Called *caliche* in central Mexico. 2. Earliest Postclassic phase of Apatzingán, Michoacán, c. A.D. 800.

Tepetl Imonamiquiyán See **universe, Aztec.**

Tepeu 1. Terminal lowland Maya Classic period, c. A.D. 600–900, in which the Maya civilization achieved its highest development. Teotihuacán influence from the Valley of Mexico, intruding late in the preceding Tzakol phase, marked the early Tepeu evolution. 2. Meaning "conqueror" in Nahuatl, Tepeu was a creator-god of the Quiché Maya, mentioned in the Popol Vuh. 3. One of the tribes of Toltec origin that emigrated from the Gulf Coast to the Guatemalan highlands with the ancestors of the Quiché, the Yaqui-Tepeu.

Tepexpan Place where "Tepexpan Man" (a 30-year-old woman) was found in lacustrine deposits on the northeast edge of Lake Texcoco, Valley of Mexico. The oldest known remains of man in Mesoamerica, they date to c. 8000 B.C.

Tepeyolohtli Nahuatl for "heart of the mountain," he is the jaguar-god of the interior of the earth, possibly originating in the Olmec jaguar cult. An aspect of Tezcatlipoca, eighth of the nine Lords of the Night; 8 Océlotl (jaguar) is his calendrical name; patron of day Calli.

Tepic Capital of the Mexican state of Nayarit.

Tepictoton Mountain-rain deities, little Tlalocs, conceived by the Nahuatl as dwarfs.

teponaztli Nahuatl name for a Mesoamerican musical instrument consisting of a wooden cylinder (a hollowed-out log) played in a horizontal position. The upper surface had two tongues cut out that were struck by a rubber-tipped mallet (*olmaitl*) to produce two pitches. Called *tunkul* by the Maya, *cuiringa* by the Tarascans, *nicache* by the Zapotecs, *nobiuy* by the Otomí.

Tepopochtli Alternate Nahuatl name for Tóxcatl, 6th of the 18 20-day months, as celebrated at Tenochtitlán. See **months, Aztec.**

Tepoztécatl God of Tepoztlán, Morelos; a pulque god whose calendrical name was Ometochtli (2 rabbit).

Tepoztlán Village northwest of Cuernavaca, Morelos, with its earliest occupation contemporary with Zacatenco, Valley of Mexico. It was inhabited until Aztec IV. On a nearby mountain is a two-storied temple dedicated c. A.D. 1500 to Tepoztécatl.

Tequilita See **Las Cebollas.**

Tequixquiac Place north of Mexico City where a fossil camel sacrum with manmade alterations simulating the head of a dog or coyote was found. Earliest example of a Paleo-Indian *art mobilier*, it dates back 12,000 to 15,000 years. Now on display at Museo Nacional de Antropología, Mexico City.

tetehuitl See **amatetehuitl.**

Tetelpan Middle Preclassic period site contemporary with Tlatilco, Valley of Mexico.

Teteoinnan Nahuatl for "mother of the gods," it represents the earth-mother complex of the Late Postclassic period in the Valley of Mexico. Related to fertility it is also represented by Toci, Coatlícue, Tlazoltéotl, Cihuacóatl. The earth-mother concept was highly developed on the Gulf Coast and Chinampa areas of the Valley of Mexico. Teteoinnan was honored by the Ochpanitztli, 12th monthly feast of the Aztec year.

Tetitla Residential compound of patios connected by alleys, west of today's Teotihuacán archaeological zone; well-preserved polychrome murals decorate the buildings' *taluds* and walls. Symbolic subjects concentrate on the rain-god, a person disguised as a jaguar in a net suit, and a panel of hands. Largest patio has an altar with carved decoration.

Tetlamixteca Term coined to designate a group of peoples in Postclassic times that included the Mixtec proper and their neighboring linguistic and cultural relatives, but excluding the Zapotecs. As cultural innovators they are credited with the Mixteca-Puebla style that centered about Cholula.

teuctli See **tecuhtli.**

Texcoco City-state across the lake from Tenochtitlán. Originally settled by the Otomí who called it Katenikko. The Chichimec under Xólotl arrived c. A.D. 1200 from Tenayuca. It became the capital of the Acolhuacán state and a member of the Triple Alliance with Tenochtitlán. Flowered with the accession of Nezahualcóyotl, A.D. 1430. He and his son Nezahualpilli made it the intellectual center of the Valley of Mexico. Cortés built his ships there for his attack by lake on Tenochtitlán.

Texcoco, Lake Great Lake of the Valley of

Plate 20. Lake Texcoco and pre-Conquest sites in the Valley of Mexico.

Mexico, it incorporated separate parts, from north to south: Zumpango, Xaltocán, Texcoco, Xochimilco, and Chalco. Esoterically, the lake was also called Meztliapán, Nahuatl for "moon lake." Because there was no outlet, all parts were saline except the two most southern. Nezahualcóyotl cooperated with Tenochtitlán to construct a dike across the lake, thereby protecting the fertile *chinampas* to the south. By means of artificial drainage, completed in 1900, Lake Texcoco is today a source of the Pánuco River; only a small portion of the original lake remains.

Texcotzingo Remains of a 15th-century summer palace of the poet-king Nezahualcóyotl, east of Texcoco; set in the mountains, it includes his bath, cut out of the natural rock.

Teyollocualoyán See **universe, Aztec.**

Tezcatlipoca Creator-god with many diverse forms, he is usually recognizable by the "smoking mirror," his name in Nahuatl, replacing his left foot, which was wrenched off by the earth monster. He is the god of night, closely associated with deities of death, evil, and destruction and the patron of sorcerers and robbers. Very important because of his direct intervention in human affairs. Prominent in Toltec mythology as the adversary of his brother Quetzalcóatl. Later revered in Aztec Tenochtitlán as the 10th of the 13 Lords of the Day, he was also the tutelary god of Texcoco, known in many parts of Mexico and appearing on sculpted columns at Chichén Itzá.

Tezcatlipoca is represented in directional colors as:

Red Tezcatlipoca: The "flayed one," Xipe Totec; and Camaxtli, god of Tlaxcala; synonym of Mixcóatl. Patron of the Aztec day Cuauhtli; associated with the East.

Black Tezcatlipoca: "Smoking Mirror," principal god of Texcoco; patron of the Aztec day Ácatl; warrior of the North.

White Tezcatlipoca: "Plumed Serpent," Quetzalcóatl; god of education and priesthood. Principál god of Cholula; associated with the West.

Blue Tezcatlipoca: "Hummingbird Sorcerer," Huitzilopochtli, god of sun and war and principal deity of Tenochtitlán; associated with the South.

Chalchiuhtotolin is another form of Tezcatlipoca, patron of day Técpatl. The jaguar is the *nahual* of Tezcatlipoca. He was ruler of the first "sun," or world, in the Aztec Creation myth. Another myth credits him with the abduction of Tlaloc's first wife, Xochiquetzal.

Tezcatzontécatl A pulque god, perhaps identified with stone Chacmool sculptures.

tezontle Porous, lightweight, and weather-resistant volcanic stone, usually red, gray, or black; used for construction in the Valley of Mexico.

Tezoyuca See **Ticomán.**

Tezozómoc (1343–1426) Long-lived ruler of Atzcapotzalco, an able and ruthless administrator whose Tepanec realm covered the Valley of Mexico. His methods provided a pattern for the Aztec expansion to follow. He ordered the assassination of Chimalpopoca, the Aztec ruler and his grandson, when he opposed Tepanec dominance. In the course of his conquests he also slew Ixtlilxóchitl, king of Texcoco and father of Nezahualcóyotl, who in turn helped to destroy the Tepanec empire.

thermoluminescence A modern scientific method based on radioactivity used to establish the age of pottery by determining the date of firing. Still experimental, it provides an important check on radiocarbon (C^{14}) dating where both ceramics and organic materials are found together.

Thin Orange See **Orange, Thin.**

Ticomán Site on a terraced peninsula jutting into Lake Texcoco near Zacatenco. Gave its name to the late Preclassic phase of the Valley of Mexico during which Cuicuilco was an important center. Sometimes referred to as Cuanalan-Ticomán, referring to the other site sharing its ceramics: Early Cuanalan-Ticomán I: 550–400 B.C.; Middle Cuanalan-Ticomán II: 400–300 B.C.; Late Cuanalan-Ticomán III: 300–200 B.C.; Tezoyuca-Ticomán IV: 200–100 B.C.; leading into proto-Teotihuacán Patlachique.

Tierra del Padre See **Chametla.**

Tiger Run Cultural phase of Barton Ramie, Belize, A.D. 600–700.

Tihoo Pre-Hispanic name of Mérida, Yucatán.

Tihosuco Cultural phase of Yucatán, 800 B.C.–A.D. 1.

Tikal The largest lowland Maya ceremonial center, in the dense forest of the Petén, Guatemala, occupied uninterruptedly for over 1,000 years. Six sq. mi. (c. 16 km²) of central Tikal  have been mapped, revealing over 3,000 structures: temples, palaces, shrines, ceremonial platforms, residences, ball courts, terraces, causeways, plazas both small and huge, as well as over 200 carved stelae and altars, hundreds of burials, and ritually cached offerings.

Tikal emblem glyph

The main structures, including Temples I and II, the North and Central Acropolis, rise about the Great Plaza. Highest of the five temple pyramids, Temple IV, is 212 ft. (65 m) to the top of its roof crest, the highest aboriginal structure in the New World. Four wide causeways radiate out from the site's center. The evolution of Tikal is charted by a sequence of local phases:

Eb: c. 600–500 B.C., revealed rare burials containing simple pottery of technical sophistication; presence of obsidian indicates trade with the Guatemalan highlands.

Tzec: 500–200 B.C., marked continued pottery development; no architectural construction remains except the presence of floors.

Chuen: 200–50 B.C., saw the appearance of ceremonial architecture, earliest vestiges of the North Acropolis. Tikal became a major city; its center was the Great Plaza as seen today.

Cauac: 50 B.C.–A.D. 150, witnessed the rebuilding of the North Acropolis, erection of large temples with polychromed stuccowork and masks.

Cimi: A.D. 150–250, concluded with the emergence of polychrome ceramics, corbeled arches in buildings, and hieroglyphic writing, heralding the opening of the Classic period of lowland Maya civilization.

Tzakol: A.D. 250–550, Tikal participates in the Early Classic period. Stela 29 provides the earliest known Long Count date of the Maya lowland region, A.D. 292. Extensive trade with Teotihuacán of the Valley of Mexico is reflected in pottery styles and architecture.

Tepeu: A.D. 550–900, Tikal partakes of the final evolution of Maya Classic civilization. Most extant structures date from this time, including elaborately carved stelae and altars. Tikal, for unverified causes, joined the collapse of lowland Maya Classic civilization at the end of the ninth century.

Burials at Tikal contained rich stores of carved jade, flint, obsidian, shell, bone, murals with glyphs, and a wide variety of ceramics. Tikal retained a limited ceremonial function in the Postclassic period, but new construction had ceased.

Tilantongo Leading town of the Mixteca beginning c. A.D. 875. Its second dynasty, recorded in the codices, featured the ruler Eight Deer Tiger Claw.

tilmantli Aztec mantle, a rectangular piece of woven fabric, originally of maguey fibers, later of cotton.

Tinaja Spanish word for a large earthen jar; it was applied to the Tepeu III ceramic complex of the southern lowlands Maya, A.D. 800–1000.

Tipo de los Cerros Name applied to the oldest group of sherds found in the Valley of Mexico, discovered in the hilly terrain about Zacatenco and Ticomán.

Tiquisate Site in the Pacific coastal range of Guatemala, source of a style of ceramic ware with a wide range of shapes and decorative techniques, c. A.D. 400–800. Recent research reveals strong influence from Teotihuacán, Mexico, in the form and decorative symbolism of its pottery,

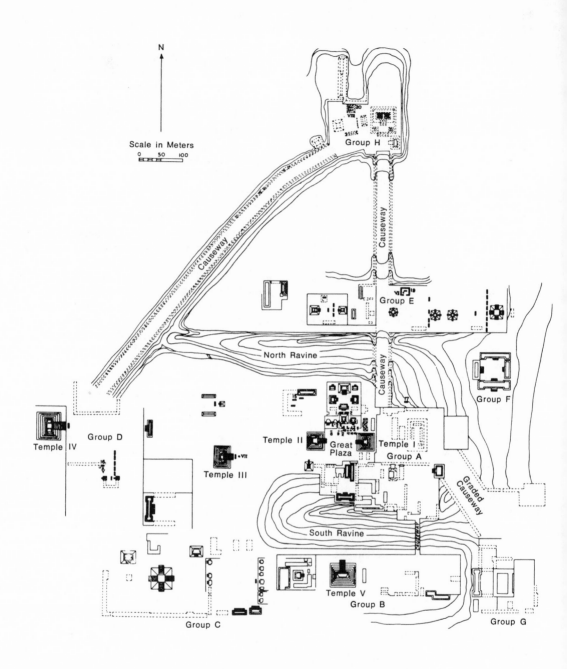

N

Scale in Meters
0   50   100

Group H

Causeway

Causeway

Group E

North Ravine

Causeway

Group F

Temple IV

Group D

Temple II

Temple III

Great
Plaza

Temple I

Group A

Graded
Causeway

South Ravine

Temple V

Group B

Group G

Group C

Plate 21. Map of the central section of Tikal. From S. G. Morley, *The Ancient Maya*, page 273.

especially in the elaborate incense-burner lids on hourglass bases and cylindrical tripod vessels. While borrowing from Mexico, the Tiquisate art style developed on its own, portraying new renditions of deities, and may prove to be antecedent to the important Cotzumalhuapa style at nearby Bilbao in the Late Classic period. In the Esperanza phase it mixed basal-flanged Tzakol vessels of lowland Maya inspiration with the cylindrical tripods borrowed from Teotihuacán. Cream to beige in color, Tiquisate ware was predominantly monochrome. Decoration was achieved by incising, grooving, planorelief, modeling, molding, and appliqué. The form of architecture at Tiquisate was determined by Kaminaljuyú, Guatemalan highlands, in turn a satellite of Teotihuacán.

tira See **codex.**

Tira de la Peregrinación See **codex, early post-Conquest Mexican; Boturini, Codex.**

Tiradero Maya site in eastern Tabasco, closely linked culturally to the Petén, that produced pottery from the Middle Preclassic through the Late Classic period.

Títitl Eighteenth of the 18 months of the Aztecs, as celebrated at Tenochtitlán. Its feast was observed during the winter solstice, principally honoring the goddess Ilamatecuhtli. See **months, Aztec.**

Tizapán Town at the southern limits of modern Mexico City where the Aztecs had settled prior to founding Tenochtitlán.

Tizatlán Archaeological remains in Tlaxcala of baked clay (brick) construction, known elsewhere in Mesoamerica only at Tula and Comalcalco in Tabasco. Polychrome alfresco murals found on two rectangular altars are in the Cholula-Puebla style of Codex Borgia. Ceramics are similar to those of Cholula, including *laca* polychrome. Also found are representations of Coyotlatelco, Mazapán, Aztec I–III.

Tizimín Town of northeastern Yucatán. See also *Chilam Balam.*

Tizoc Seventh Aztec sovereign, 1481–86, brother of his predecessor Axayácatl and his successor, Ahuítzotl. The Stone of

Tizoc in the Museo Nacional de Antropología, Mexico City, is a carved monolithic cylinder recounting his victories and presumably a sacrificial block; it is the finest and latest example of Aztec historically oriented sculpture.

Tlacacaliliztli See **Arrow Sacrifice.**

Tlacaélel (d. 1480) Historic figure who served as councilor (*cihuacóatl*) under three Aztec rulers, beginning with Itzcóatl in 1435, and including Moctezuma I. His ideas underlay Aztec economic, cultural, and political expansion. During the period of his influence the Triple Alliance of Tenochtitlán, Texcoco, and Tlacopan was created and the Flowery Wars for securing sacrificial victims were initiated. He caused the books of conquered peoples to be burned and rewrote Aztec history to make the Mexica the "chosen people," true heirs of the Toltec tradition, who would fight wars and sacrifice victims to the gods to keep the sun moving across the sky. He can be credited with the master plan for the Aztec civilization that so impressed Cortés on his arrival.

Tlacatecuhtli Title of Aztec ruler in his role as high priest.

Tlacaxipehualiztli Third of the 18 20-day months of the Aztec year of 365 days, as observed at Tenochtitlán. Feast honored Xipe Totec, god of spring, at seedtime. Sacrificed victims were flayed, their skins were then worn by priests. Evoking ancient fertility rites, this seasonal ceremony was probably of Huastec origin. The bravest of the victims were subjected to the "gladiatorial sacrifice," called *tlahuahuanaliztli.* Coaílhuitl is another name for this monthly ceremony. See **months, Aztec.**

tlachtli Nahuatl word for the ritual ball court, usually in the form of a Roman I. Also applied to the game itself, which was called *pok-ta-pok* by the Maya. See **ball game, Mesoamerican.**

tlacolol A highland variant of the slash-and-burn system of agriculture in which some sections are cultivated while others are left fallow for three to four years. See also **milpa.**

Tlacopan Smallest member of the Triple Alliance with Tenochtitlán and Texcoco in the 15th century; today the part of Mexico City called Tacuba.

Tlacoquecholli See **Quecholli; months, Aztec.**

tlacotin (*tlacotli,* sing.) Slaves in Aztec society.

tlahuahuanaliztli See **gladiatorial sacrifice.**

Tlahuica See **Tlalhuica.**

Tlahuizcalpantecuhtli Aztec deity of the planet Venus in its aspect of both morning and evening stars, attesting to the importance of Venus in the religion and calendrics of Mesoamerica. Represented in the morning by Quetzalcóatl, in the evening by his twin Xólotl. Was 12th of the 13 Lords of the Day, therefore the codices represent him in two forms: that of a living man and that of a skull. Worshiped in Postclassic central Mexico.

tlailotlaque Mixtec wise men from Oaxaca who settled in Texcoco, bringing knowledge of writing and painting of codices.

Tlalchitonatiuh Mexican deity introduced to the Guatemalan highlands in the Early Classic period from Teotihuacán, referred to as the Jaguar Sun, or Falling Sun (sunset). As the god of the warrior cult he appears in the Postclassic on a frieze of the Temple of the Warriors at Chichén Itzá, dated c. A.D. 1200, receiving human hearts from the warrior fraternities of Jaguar and Eagle Knights.

Tlalhuica 1. Traditionally one of seven Aztec tribal groups believed to have left the legendary Chicomoztoc ("seven caves") in A.D. 1168, on the migration to the Valley of Mexico. They were settlers of what is now the Mexican state of Morelos. 2. Pottery type, also called Tlahuica, found at Teopanzolco, Morelos, believed contemporary with Gualupita III phase of Morelos and Aztec II, or Tenayuca Black-on-Orange, of the Valley of Mexico. Lacquered decorated ware is typical.

Tlaloc Mexican rain-god, associated with serpent, mountains, flood, drought, hail, ice, and lightning. One of most ancient Mesoamerican deities, probably originating in Olmec god IV. Depicted with rings about his eyes, fangs, and frequently a volute over his mouth. His counterparts are Chac of the Maya, Tajín of the Totonacs, Tzahui of the Mixtecs, and Cocijo of the Zapotecs. Rain-god representations are seen at Classic Copán, Maya sites of the Petén and Puuc regions, and in Postclassic Chichén Itzá. His wives were, successively, Xochiquetzal and Matlalcueitl; his sister was the rain-goddess Chalchiúhtlicue. He was thought of as fourfold, a Tlaloc of a different color for each of the cardinal points. He was the patron deity of the seventh Nahuatl day, Mázatl; 8th of the 13 Lords of the Day, 9th of the 9 Lords of the Night. His calendrical name was 9 Océlotl.

Tlalocán Those who died by drowning, by lightning, from leprosy, or any of the illnesses considered related to the rain-god, went to the "place of Tlaloc," conceived as a paradise of abundance and pleasure. Identified with the South. See also **afterlife.**

Tlalpan Cultural phase designation tentatively assigned to pre-Olmec settlers in the Cuicuilco area of the Valley of Mexico, c. 2100–1800 B.C.

Tlaltecuhtli The earth monster pictured as a fantastic toad whose mouth had great tusks, and arms and feet armed with claws. It swallowed the sun in the evening, disgorging it at dawn; also devoured the hearts and blood of sacrificial victims. It is often depicted on the undersides of Aztec carved stone containers, especially *cuauhxicalli,* the receptacle for the heart and blood of sacrificed victims. With both male and female aspects; as an earth god is second Lord of the Day.

Tlaltícpac Meaning "earth" in Nahuatl, in Aztec thought it represented the visible, the here and now; as opposed to Topán and Mictlán, "what is above us and below us—the regions of the dead," the earth's surface. See also **universe, Aztec.**

tlamacazqui Young priests of the Mexican hierarchy.

tlamacazton Young Aztec boys who served

as "little priests" while enrolled in the *calmécac,* in preparation to becoming *tlamacazqui.*

tlamani Aztec warrior who has captured a prisoner, thereby demonstrating his valor and value in supplying sacrificial victims.

Tlamatinime Earliest reference is to leaders who, after fall of Tula, led their tribe out of the mythical Tamoanchán to the east, to Guatemala. Transcriptions in Nahuatl use this title for a group of enlightened philosophers in the Valley of Mexico who questioned the mysticomartial Aztec concepts and the meaning of man's existence. The advanced thoughts expressed by Nezahualcóyotl of Texcoco may represent their thrust. They were the guardians and interpreters of the codices, the "black and red ink."

tlamictiliztli Nahuatl word for human sacrifice.

Tlamimilolpa 1. Largest residential complex of Teotihuacán, with 176 rooms, 21 patios, and 5 large courts with interconnecting alleys. 2. Early Classic phase of Teotihuacán, c. A.D. 250–500. Contact with the Gulf Coast was close, and Maya influence is evident at its end. These contacts are reflected in the form and style of ceramics and in mural painting. Tajín-style scrolls, appliqué ornamentation, and the first planorelief decoration appear on vases. Thin Orange ware was also distinctive. Stone face masks may date from this period. The Ciudadela was completed; the original Temple of Quetzalcóatl was buried under a new pyramid, which today has been partially removed to reveal the richly decorated *talud-tablero* facade of the underlying structure.

Tlamiquecholli See **Quecholli; months, Aztec.**

Tlapacoya Preclassic site in the Valley of Mexico, with Colonial Olmec occupation carbon-dated 1070–940 B.C. See **Olmec, Colonial.** Along with Tlatilco, shares the earliest identified use of pottery in the Valley. Its pyramid, erected c. 100 B.C., is the most elaborate architecture of the Ticomán period.

Tlapallán According to the Popol Vuh, the area to which Nacxit (Quetzalcóatl) emigrated from Tula; the "land of sunrise," it is identified with the modern Mexican states of Tabasco, Campeche, and western Yucatán.

Tlapanec Linguistic group whose principal town was Tlapa, Guerrero, near the Oaxacan border.

Tlapaneca-Yope See **Maribio.**

Tlapcopa Among the Aztecs, the East; also the designation of the first quarter of the *Tonalamatl.* Identified with the color yellow, mesquite tree, *quetzal* bird, and Tlahuizcalpantecuhtli, the Venus god. Related day signs were Cipactli, Ácatl, Cóatl, Ollin, and Atl, Ácatl also served as its year sign; augury was favorable. See also **cardinal points.**

tlapitzalli Aztec clay flute of the type that the youth who impersonated Tezcatlipoca in the ceremony of Tóxcatl broke one by one as he ascended the temple steps to be sacrificed.

tlaquimilolli Container of sacred objects related to the cult of a deity; it was often the symbol of a community when the god was its patron.

Tlatelolco Twin city with Tenochtitlán on an island in Lake Texcoco, a great market and commercial center. Founded A.D. 1370, it was conquered by Tenochcas in 1473. Colegio de la Santa Cruz, established by the Order of Saint Francis for the Indians, is identified with Bernardino de Sahagún whose native scribes painted the illustrations for the Florentine Codex there. Today Tlatelolco is represented by its Plaza of the Three Cultures within Mexico City.

Tlatilco Important Preclassic period cemetery site of over 300 burials, discovered in a brickyard within modern Mexico City. Its occupation coincides with the Zacatenco phase of the Valley of Mexico, 1050–550 B.C., but earliest deposits date from c. 1200 B.C., the newly designated Ixtapaluca phase, which provides the earliest known pottery in the Valley of Mexico, coeval with the Ayotla phase of Tlapacoya. Appears to have been an Olmec "colony" from the earliest times. Noted for its great variety of figurines, including fine white-slipped hollow figurines with Olmec facial traits. Vessels included Black Channeled Ware and zoomorphic pottery.

tlatoani (*tlatoyue,* pl.) The hereditary ruler of the Aztec state, sharing some of his powers with the *cihuacóatl.* His lineage enjoyed superior prestige, collectively called the *pilli.* See also **altepetl.**

Tlaxcala 1. Smallest Mexican state, with capital of same name, bounded by the states of Mexico, Hidalgo, and Puebla. 2. City-state reputedly founded A.D. 1328; a white heron was its symbol. Became an ally of Cortés in 1519 against Tenochtitlán, with whom they waged Flowery Wars but by whom they were never subdued.

tlaxcalli Nahuatl word for corn bread. See **tortilla.**

Tlaxcalteca Traditionally one of seven Aztec tribes believed to have emigrated from legendary Chicomoztoc ("seven caves") in A.D. 1168, eventually reaching the Valley of Mexico. Also known as Teochichimec, they settled in southern Acolhuacán before being ousted by the Tepanec, Colhua, and Mexica. Some then migrated to Chalco, others to Tlaxcallán, the area of modern Tlaxcala. Mixcóatl-Camaxtli was the patron deity.

Tlaxochimaco See **Miccailhuitontli; months, Aztec.**

Tlazoltéotl A manifestation of the earth-goddess, others being Coatlícue and Cihuacóatl. Of Huastec origin, appeared in the Mexican pantheon after the Aztecs subjugated the Gulf Coast. Goddess of fertility and carnal love and, like Xipe Totec, often portrayed wearing the skin of a sacrificial victim. Nahuatl name translates as "goddess of filth." Codices identify her by a band of raw cotton decorated with two spindles or bobbins on her headdress. She was honored during the feast of Ochpanitztli. She was patron of the 14th day of the 20-day Aztec month Océlotl; also 5th of the 13 Lords of the Day and 7th of the 9 Lords of the Night.

tlemáhuitl Incense burner in the form of a ladle. See **incensario.**

tlenamac Intermediate grade of Aztec priest, the "firegiver."

Tlillan Tlapallán Legendary destination of Quetzalcóatl after leaving Tula and from which he prophesied his return in a year Ce Ácatl. Nahuatl for "land of black and red," it is a mythical explanation of the death of the planet Venus, its descent into the West where black and red, night and day, merge, and its reappearance in advance of the sun in the East as the morning star. See **Tlapallán, Quetzalcóatl.**

Tloque Nahuaque Abstract, invisible god, "lord of the everywhere," conceived under Nezahualcóyotl in Texcoco. Not represented materially, he was worshiped in temples without idols. It was the idea closest to monotheism in Mesoamerica, but did not achieve general veneration because its concept was in opposition to the tenor of the times.

Tlotzin Chichimec chieftain, grandson of Xólotl.

tocado Spanish word in general modern use to describe the ceremonial headdress depicted in Mesoamerican sculpture, ceramics, murals, and codices.

Tochtli Eighth of the 20 Nahuatl day signs pictured in Mexican codices by a rabbit, its meaning in Nahuatl. The Maya equivalent day was Lamat and the Zapotec day was Lapa. Tochtli, as a Year Bearer, along with the days Ácatl, Calli, and Técpatl, served to begin the years, there being 13 Tochtli years in the 52-year cycle; oriented to the South. Calendrical names related to Tochtli are: 1 Tochtli: Mayáhuel, pulque-goddess; 2 Tochtli: Ometochtli, pulque-god; 7 Tochtli: Coatlícue, earth-goddess; 400 Tochtli: Centzóntotochtin, collective name of the pulque-gods.

Mayáhuel was the patron deity of the day, related to fertility and the moon, with a favorable augury.

Toci A designation of the earth-goddess, "our grandmother." Of Huastec origin, she was also Tlazoltéotl, and was worshiped there in the first rank. Honored during the Aztec Ochpanitztli ceremony.

Tohcock Postclassic site of northern Campeche. Paintings on doorjambs were found there.

Tohil 1. Major Quiché Maya deity mentioned in the Popol Vuh, associated with rain and fire and sometimes with Quetzalcóatl. 2. See **Plumbate**. 3. Postclassic phase of Zacualpa, Guatemalan highlands, A.D. 1000–1200.

Tojolabal Maya group of the Chiapas Plateau, Mexico, affiliated with the Tzeltal and Tzotzil.

Tolimán See **Tuxcacuesco**.

Tollán See **Tula**.

Toltec Postclassic culture of Mexico, conceived between the 9th and 11th centuries A.D. at the legendary capital of Tollán (Tula). The Toltecs represented a mingling of backgrounds, primarily composed of Nahua-Chichimecs who had migrated from the northwest frontier and intermingled with the Nonoalca from southern Veracruz. The resulting culture combined those of remote Teotihuacán, Xochicalco, and the Gulf Coast.

In ceramics, the Coyotlatelco phase, popular after the fall of Teotihuacán, developed into the Mazapán phase. Diagnostic of the Toltec horizon in Mesoamerica were Fine Orange and Plumbate pottery, although neither was their creation. Metallurgy appeared c. A.D. 900.

Their religion was centered upon human sacrifice expressed in an aggressive expansionist relationship to neighboring tribes. The later Aztecs so admired them they took measures, through marriage and the burning of history books, to establish their descent from them. After the fall of Tula, Toltec migrations encompassed Cholula, the Tabasco-Campeche Gulf Coast, Yucatán, and parts of Central America, c. A.D. 1000–1200. See **Tula, Quetzalcóatl, Nonoalca, Chichén Itzá, Quiché**.

Toltec architecture Founded on Teotihuacán and its pyramids, it added colonnaded edifices several ranks deep, Atlantean and carved, square-pillar building supports that are visible today at Tula and Chichén Itzá. Sculptured architectural innovations included monumental serpent columns and balustrádes, serpent walls, and narrative relief panels set in plain wall surfaces. Austerity and geometric stylization mark the style, setting the stage for the Aztec and Postclassic styles throughout Mesoamerica.

Tomb 7 Richest Mixtec tomb discovered at Monte Albán, containing a treasury of artifacts of gold, precious stones, and ceramics. Its contents are the prize archaeological exhibit at the Oaxaca Regional Museum. A replica of Tomb 7 is on view at the Museo Nacional de Antropología, Mexico City.

Tonacacíhuatl See **Omecíhuatl**.

Tonacatecuhtli See **Ometecuhtli**.

Tonacatépetl "Sustenance Mountain" in Nahuatl, it is where, according to the Codex Chimalpopoca, Quetzalcóatl was led by a red ant, Azcatl, and transformed into a black ant to obtain grains of maize hidden there to sustain mankind. Some identify the mythical mountain with Iztaccíhuatl.

Tonacatlalpan Aztec name for the Huasteca, "place of our sustenance." It was also broadly applied to moist lands of the Gulf region.

Tonalá 1. River partly constituting the border between Veracruz and Tabasco, on which the Olmec site of La Venta is located. 2. Elevated religious center near the Pacific coast of western Chiapas, occupied in the Preclassic period; its massive stone-faced platforms date from the Postclassic. 3. Town in Jalisco famed for its glazed pottery.

Tonalamatl Mexican Book of the Days, usually recording a *tonalpohualli* ritual calendar of 260 days. Auguries based on its interpretation were provided by priests, the *tonalpouque*. It was generally written on deerskin or bark paper, with its pages presented in the form of a screen-fold, today referred to as a codex.

tonalpohualli Nahuatl term, "count of the

days," for the ritual or sacred calendar, corresponding to the Maya *tzolkin,* and the Zapotec *piye.* Earliest known reference to it is from Oaxaca, during the Monte Albán I phase, sixth century B.C. The *tonalpohualli* represents a 260-day cycle, rotating the 20 named days against the numbers 1 to 13. Thus, it begins with 1 Cipactli, followed by 2 Ehecatl, 3 Calli, etc., to 13 Ácatl. Then followed 1 Océlotl, 2 Cuauhtli, and so on. When the day Xóchitl is reached, it is necessary to use Cipactli again, with its corresponding number. Time repeats itself endlessly, with the same conjunctions, furnishing the basis for its consultation by priests for auguries related to personal and agricultural predictions. In its elaborate forms, it also has associations with 13 birds, 9 Lords of the Night, and 13 Lords of the Day. See also **calendar, Mesoamerican.**

tonalpouque Aztec priests who interpreted the *Tonalamatl* to foretell the future, cast horoscopes, and determine favorable and unfavorable days.

Tonalteuctin See **Lords of the Day.**

Tonantzin Nahuatl name, meaning "little mother," for the earth-goddess in her benevolent role as mother of mankind. The site of the temple dedicated to Tonantzin is today occupied by the Basilica of Tepeyac, the shrine of the Virgin of Guadalupe, Mexico's patron saint, in Mexico City. Nahuatl-speaking natives still occasionally refer to the Virgin as Tonantzin.

Tonatiuh Mexican sun-god, associated with the young warrior deity Huitzilopochtli; the sun itself. The rising sun was named Cuauhtlehuánitl, the setting sun Cuauhtémoc, respectively conceived as the ascending and descending eagle. He is the 4th of the 13 Lords of the Day and also the patron of the 19th Nahuatl day, Quiáhuitl. On the Aztec Calendar Stone, now exhibited in the Museo Nacional de Antropología, Mexico City, the central figure is popularly identified as Tonatiuh. Recent studies favor its interpretation as Yohualtonatiuh, his nocturnal manifestation,

clutching in his eagle claws his sustenance, the hearts of human beings.

Tonatiuh Ichan Nahuatl for "house of the sun," the eastern paradise of warriors who fell in combat or died as victims on the sacrificial stone. It was an existence of pure delight; after four years they returned to earth as hummingbirds and fed on the nectar of flowers.

Toniná Late Classic Maya ceremonial center near modern Ocosingo, Chiapas, briefly reoccupied in the Postclassic period. Especially noted for rare figure (now mostly headless) sculpture in the round.

Tonosí See **Central Panama.**

Topán See **Tlaltícpac.**

Topoxte Postclassic Maya island site in Lake Yaxhá, Petén, Guatemala.

tortilla Spanish word for the Mesoamerican corn cake, *tlaxcalli* in Nahuatl. Lime-treated corn was ground on a stone *metate* with a *mano,* a handstone. The resulting paste was fashioned into thin pancakes, *tortillas,* and roasted on a *comal,* a flat pottery griddle. It is the staff of life, the bread of Mesoamerica.

Tortuguero Small Maya site in Tabasco, closely related to Palenque.

Totoate Northern Jalisco site with Mesoamerican traits, occupied c. A.D. 200–900. See **Bolaños-Juchipila.**

Totonac A people linguistically of the Macro-Mayan group who settled in the mountains of northern Puebla and northern Veracruz. Modern Totonac Indians inhabit the El Tajín area, but it has not been proven that they were the founders of that site. They did inhabit central Veracruz by the 16th century, with their capital at Cempoala. They were the first ally of Cortés in 1519 as he began his expedition against the Aztecs.

Totonacapán Anciently the land of the Totonacs, comprising the central Gulf Coast and extending inland to the mountains of Puebla.

Tóxcatl Sixth of the 18 months of the Aztec calendar, as celebrated at Tenochtitlán. The feast of Tóxcatl honored the god Tezcatlipoca. He was impersonated for a year by a young warrior whose final sacrifice crowned the activities. It was one of the great festivals of Tenochtitlán, attended by nobles in their gold-bedecked finery. The greed of Cortés's lieutenant, Pedro de Alvarez, in his absence precipitated the "massacre of Tóxcatl" in which the Spaniards reputedly slew 8,600 unarmed Aztecs. Tepopochtli is an alternate name for Tóxcatl. See **months, Aztec.**

Toxiuhmolpilia "Tying of Years" in Nahuatl, the New Fire Ceremony marked the completion of one and the renewal of another 52-year cycle; celebrated the avoidance of the end of the world. See also **Calendar Round, Tying of Years.**

Tozoztontli Fourth of the 18 months of the Aztec calendar of 365 days, as observed at Tenochtitlán. Major feasts were dedicated to the rain-god Tlaloc, with offerings of flowers. Other fertility deities propitiated were Centéotl, Chalchiúhtlicue, Chicomecóatl, and Coatlícue. This month also completed Tlacaxipehualiztli rites: human skins worn by alms-begging priests were deposited in a "cave" in the temple of Xipe Totec. Another name for the month was Xochimanalo, "offering of flowers." See also **months, Aztec.**

tradition In archaeology, a temporal continuity manifested by the persistence of technologies, styles, or other cultural traits. Its long application in time contrasts with the broader geographic but generally shorter-lived cultural horizon. Tradition has a lasting quality, in depth; in cultural-historical relationships, tradition can be thought of as the "vertical" continuum as opposed to the recurring "horizontal" unifying effect over a larger area of the horizon. See also **co-tradition, horizon.**

Trapiche See **El Trapiche.**

Travesia Ceremonial site in the Sula Plain of western Honduras with Late Classic Ulúa Polychrome ceramics; Tlaloc faces on the facade of the Temple of the Carvings suggest Mexican contact.

trecena Modern appellation for a 13-day period of the *Tonalamatl*, 20 of them constituting the 260-day ritual calendar.

Tres Islas Classic Maya site on the Pasión River, Petén, Guatemala.

Tres Zapotes Ceremonial center nestled in the Tuxtla Mountains of southern Veracruz. Its beginnings overlapped with Olmec La Venta, which it succeeded as the most important Olmec center. The first of the Olmec "colossal heads" was found there. Active from perhaps 1000 B.C. into Classic times when the influence of Teotihucán was pronounced. Stela C is the second-oldest dated monument in the New World, 31 B.C., five years later than Stela 2 at Chiapa de Corzo.

triadic symbol See **quadripartite badge.**

Triple Alliance 1. In the Valley of Mexico under Moctezuma I, Tenochtitlán, Texcoco, and Tlacopan united against the neighboring Nahuatl-speaking states of Tlaxcala and Huexotzinco in the conduct of Flowery Wars to secure prisoners for sacrifice. The alliance continued until the Spanish Conquest in support of the political and military expansion of the Aztecs. 2. In Yucatán native accounts tell of the Triple Alliance of Chichén Itzá, Mayapán, and Uxmal as controlling the region A.D. 989–1185. Current research favors the inclusion of Izamal in place of Uxmal, making it totally an Itzá alliance.

Tripsacum A wild grass that will hybridize with maize. See **maize.**

Trique A small linguistic group in the Mixteca of western Oaxaca.

Tro-Cortesianus, Codex See **codex, pre-Conquest Maya; Madrid Codex.**

trophy-head cult Believed to be of South American origin, the cult is associated with ritual sacrifice and possibly war. Trophy heads are prominent in Costa Rican stone sculpture to the time of the Conquest, both with human figures and on *metates*. Evidence of the cult is sometimes difficult to separate from evidence of decapitation, which was practiced in Olmec times and later pictured at such widely separated locales as Chichén Itzá and Bilbao.

Tsah Late Classic phase of the Chiapas Central Plateau, a period of widespread occupation and defensive settlements, such as at Yerba Buena and Cerro Chavin, c. A.D. 500–800.

Tula Modern town and archaeological site in the state of Hidalgo, 50 mi. (80 km) north of Mexico City. It is believed to be the legendary Tollán, capital of the Toltecs whose culture dominated the Mesoamerican Postclassic period from the 10th to the 13th century. Traditionally founded by Ce Ácatl Topiltzin Quetzalcóatl in A.D. 968, it was destroyed c. 1160.

Prominent about Tula's two plazas are the ball court, serpent wall, the pyramid and temple of Quetzalcóatl with its 15-ft. (4.6 m)-high Atlantean roof supports representing him as Tlahuizcalpantecuhtli ("morning star"), a larger, badly destroyed pyramid (bldg. C), and the Burned Palace with two large colonnaded halls. Toltec innovations to be observed are a Chacmool, relief-paneled benches, and processional carved panels of heart-devouring eagles and jaguars. The last named anticipate the later Aztec adoption of them as symbols for their warrior fraternities. See **Toltec.**

Tulum Postclassic period Maya fortified site on a high cliff on the eastern coast of Quintana Roo, contemporary with Mayapán. The Castillo, the tallest structure, is crowned by a temple with Toltec serpent pillars, and was probably the first Maya structure seen by the seafaring Spaniards. Tulum is protected on the three land sides by a wall. The Temple of the Descending God and the Temple of the Frescoes, c. A.D. 1500, both have polychrome murals in the Mixtec style.

tumbaga A gold-copper alloy, ideally 82 percent gold, resulting in a lower melting point than either contributory metal, makes it especially practical for casting purposes. Can be hammered to a bronzelike hardness. Widely employed in Central America, it was introduced to Mexico in the Early Postclassic period. *Tumbaga* artifacts were given a surface appearance indistinguish-able from gold by the *mise-en-couleur* process.

tumpline A carrying strap passed over either chest or forehead, facilitating the transport of a burden carried on a human back.

tun 1. Maya word for stone in general, but particularly for jade, in turn a symbol for "precious." In a play on words, the term is also used for maize. 2. In the Maya calendar, the year of 360 days, or 18 *uinals,* its Mexican equivalent was *xíhuitl.* Sometimes called *haab.* See also **Long Count.**

tun (2)

tunkul See **teponaztli.**

Tuxcacuesco Archaeological site of southern Jalisco. Cultural phases include Early Tuxcacuesco, c. A.D. 1, and Postclassic Coralillo, c. A.D. 1000, and Tolimán, c. A.D. 1350.

Tuxpan Ceramic phase of central Nayarit, c. A.D. 700. See also **Amapa.**

Tuxtla 1. Mountain range of coastal southern Veracruz. Source of stone for the Olmec site of La Venta. 2. The Tuxtla statuette, in late Olmec style, is a small, jade, duckbilled, winged figure with human features. The Long Count date is equivalent to A.D. 162 and the other hieroglyphs were inscribed long after the figure itself was carved. Smithsonian Institution, Washington, D.C. 3. Protohistoric phase of Chiapa de Corzo, A.D. 1250–1524.

Tuxtla statuette

Tuxtla Chico Site of eastern Chiapas near Izapa at the Guatemalan border.

two-headed dragon Classic lowland Maya sculptural motif found on altars at Copán and Quiriguá, on stelae at Piedras Negras, and on doorways at Palenque. Related to the ceremonial bar.

Tying of Years Esoteric reference to the Cal-

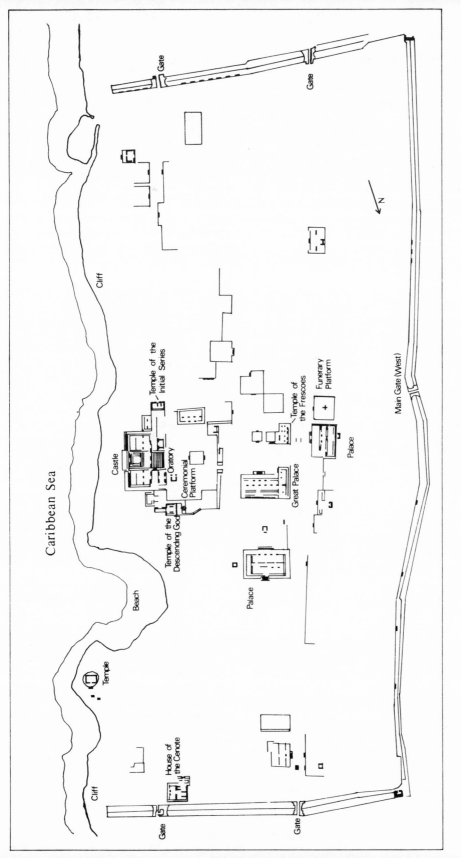

Caribbean Sea

Cliff

Cliff

Temple

Beach

House of
the Cenote

Temple of the
Descending God

Castle

Oratory

Ceremonial
Platform

Temple of the
Initial Series

Palace

Great Palace

Temple of
the Frescoes

Funerary
Platform

Palace

Gate

Gate

Gate

Main Gate (West)

Gate

N

Plate 22. Tulum.

endar Round, the Aztec "century" of 52 years, called Xiuhmolpilli in Nahuatl. Pictorially it was rendered as a tied bundle of reeds. When carved three-dimensionally in stone or wood, it also served as a ceremonial seat for dignitaries. The ceremony marking the initiation of a new 52-year cycle was called Toxiuhmolpilia, celebrated in the year 2 Ácatl ("reed").

Tzacualli Cultural phase of the Valley of Mexico, also called Teotihuacán I, c. A.D. 1–150. It marks the beginning of Teotihuacán as a regional religious center, and the inception of important architecture. The Temple of the Sun was built and probably completed at this time. Population reached about 30,000, but the influence of Teotihuacán did not yet extend to other parts of Mesoamerica, although there is evidence of trade with points as far removed as Monte Albán, Oaxaca. Ceramics show affinity with Ticomán.

Tzakol Early Classic ceramic phase of the Maya lowlands, c. A.D. 200–600. It saw the rapid spread of religious symbolism, technology in architecture, the stela cult, hieroglyphic writing, and astronomy. Distinguished from the later Tepeu phase by the still discernible Izapa influence on the Maya style. The commonest Tzakol vessel is the polychrome, basal-flanged bowl, but cylindrical tripods of Teotihuacán style penetrated from Mexico c. A.D. 500. Contemporary with the Esperanza phase of the Guatemalan highlands and Teotihuacán III; type sites are Uaxactún and Tikal. Its name is derived from Tzakol, mentioned as the creator-god of the Quiché in the Popol Vuh.

Tzec 1. Fifth month of the *tun*, the Maya year of 360 days. 2. Preclassic ceramic phase of Tikal, c. 500–200 B.C.

Tzeltal A linguistic group of the Chiapas Plateau, of lowland Maya origin, related to the Tzotzil, Tojolabal, and Chuj of western Guatemala.

Tzibanche Maya site in Quintana Roo where an incised jade bead provided the latest known inscription in the Initial Series, cor-responding to A.D. 909. Earliest is the Leyden Plate, A.D. 320.

Tzintzuntzan Tarascan capital on Lake Pátzcuaro, Michoacán. Remains show a distinctive architecture with five *yácatas*. Gave its name to the Late Postclassic period of Michoacán, A.D. 1200–1521.

Tzitzimime Nahuatl for "demons of darkness," the term refers to the stars visible during an eclipse of the sun. They were feared as demons who would descend to devour man at the end of the fifth "sun," the current world in Aztec mythology.

tzoalli Amaranth (*Amaranthus paniculatus*) seed dough used by the Aztecs to fashion cookies in the images of gods during festive ceremonies.

tzolkin Maya term for the sacred almanac, the ritual calendar of 260 days, arrived at by matching the 20 named days against the numbers 1 to 13. Corresponds to the Aztec *tonalpohualli* and the Zapotec *piye*. Running concurrently with the Vague Year of 365 days, it produced the Calendar Round of 52 years. See also **calendar, Mesoamerican.**

tzompantli Skull rack, usually placed near a temple, to which the severed heads of sacrificial victims were skewered by the Aztecs. The name is also applied to their carved representations in stone.

tzontémoc Word meaning "who falls head-first" in Nahuatl, it is similar to the "descending god" of the Postclassic Maya as observed at Tulum; symbol of the sun descending in the west, synonymous with *cuauhtémoc*, the descending eagle, or setting sun.

Tzotzil Maya linguistic group of lowland Maya origin, still populous today around Chamula in the Central Chiapas Plateau. Not to be confused with a branch of the Cakchiquel of Guatemala whose ruling family took the bat (*zotz*) as their symbol. See also **Tzeltal.**

tzotzocolli Aztec haircut in two different lengths, which distinguished their warriors and their patron deity, Tezcatlipoca.

Tzutuhil Maya linguistic group related to

the Quiché and Cakchiquel who settled on the shores of Lake Atitlán, Guatemala. Their capital was Tziquinaha, and its ruins remain in the place that is now called Chuitinamit. After conquering the Tzutuhil in 1524, the Spaniards moved them across a bay of Lake Atitlán to what is now Santiago Atitlán.

u

u Maya word for moon; can also be the possessive *of* in hieroglyphic writing.

U-symbol A sculptural motif of Olmec origin found on Preclassic Izapa stone carvings, then called the "Izapa signature." May be antecedent of the Maya glyph for the moon.

uac Number 6 in Maya.

uaxac Number 8 in Maya.

Uaxac Canal Early Postclassic Maya site near Chacula in the western Guatemala highlands.

Uaxactún Important Maya ceremonial site north of Tikal in the Petén forests of Guatemala, where extensive excavations show occupation c. 600 B.C.–A.D. 900. Large jaguar masks on the terraces of Pyramid E-VII Sub, of the Chicanel period, resemble the mask on Stela C at Tres Zapotes, a late Olmec settlement in Veracruz. Uaxactún was the type site for the establishment of the lowland Maya ceramic sequence: Mamom: 1000–300 B.C.; Chicanel: 300 B.C.–A.D. 100; Matzanel: A.D. 100–200; Tzakol: A.D. 200–600; Tepeu: A.D. 600–900.

Uayeb The last 5 days of the Maya Vague Year, following the 360 days of the *tun*. Also called *Xma Kaba Kin,* "days without name." Corresponds to the Aztec *Nemontemi.*

uinal Maya month of 20 days. See also **Long Count.**

U Kahlay Katunob See **Short Count.**

Ulúa 1. Culturally, the most important river of

uinal glyph

western Honduras, it flows north to the Caribbean Sea, past the sites of Santa Rita, Playa de los Muertos, Santa Ana, Travesia, and Las Flores. 2. Ulúa Bichrome is a Middle Preclassic ceramic phase identified with Santa Rita. 3. Ulúa Polychrome is the Late Classic ceramic period of Honduras and El Salvador, sometimes called Ulúa-Yojoa Polychrome, c. A.D. 500–800. 4. Ulúa Mayoid and Copador phases resulted from Late Classic Maya polychrome pottery exerting its influence in Honduras after A.D. 600. 5. Related Ulúa ware found in the Nicoya region of Costa Rica is noted for its brilliant finish, achieved with a mixture of beeswax and vegetable resins.

Ulva A linguistic group of southern Honduras and central Nicaragua. See also **Macro-Chibcha.**

universe, Aztec The Mexicans did not share the Christian concept of a heaven and hell. The universe was conceived as a vertical stratification comprising 13 celestial layers over 9 layers of the underworld. The earth itself, conceived as an enormous saurian lying in water, was the first layer counting in both directions. See the table on page 175 for a presentation of this scheme, from top to bottom, according to the Codex Vaticanus. See also **afterlife.**

universe, Maya The Maya had two conflicting concepts of the structure of the universe: 1. Like the Mexicans, they conceived of the earth as resting on the back of a crocodile or cayman. They also visualized 13 celestial and 9 underworld stations. The celestial layers were represented

13. Omeyocán	place of duality
12. Teotl Tlatlauhcán	red god place
11. Teotl Cozauhcán	yellow god place
10. Teotl Iztacán	white god place
9. Itztapal Nanatzcayán	where the stone slabs crash together (thunder?)
8. Ilhuicatl Xoxouhcán	blue heaven
7. Ilhuicatl Yayauhcán	blackish heaven
6. Ilhuicatl Mamalhuazocán	heaven of the fire drill
5. Ilhuicatl Huixtotlan	heaven of salt-fertility goddess (Huixtocíhuatl)
4. Ilhuicatl Tonatiuh	heaven of the sun
3. Ilhuicatl Citlalicue	heaven of the star-skirted goddess
2. Ilhuicatl Tlalocán Ipan Meztli	heaven of paradise of the rain-god and the moon
1. Tlaltícpac	on the earth (surface?)
2. Apanohuayán	water passage
3. Tepetl Imonamiquiyán	where the hills clash together
4. Itztepetl	obsidian knife hill
5. Itzehecayán	place of obsidian-bladed wind
6. Pancuecuetlayán	where banners are flourished
7. Temiminaloyán	where someone is shot with arrows
8. Teyollocualoyán	where someone's heart is eaten
9. Iz Mictlán Opochcalocan	place of the dead, where the streets are on the left

by 6 steps ascending from the eastern horizon to the top, or 7th layer, from which 6 steps descended to the western horizon. Similarly, the underworld layers descended 4 steps down from the west to the 5th layer, the nadir of the nether regions, rising again by 4 steps to the eastern horizon. Thus, the Maya concept in reality had only 7 celestial and 5 underworld layers, for which there are no known names. 2. Another Maya concept is expressed by "iguana house," or Itzamná. This is a reptilian configuration in which the world is pictured as within a house (*na*). Giant iguanas (*itzam*) form the roof (heaven) and walls, continuing their course to form the floor, too, generally interpreted as the earth's surface.

Uo 1. Second month of the *tun*, the Maya year of 360 days. 2. A little black frog whose croaking announces rain; *uos* were likewise considered attendants and musicians of the Chacs.

Uolantun Early Classic Maya site of the central Petén where the Stela I figure recalls style of Santa Lucía Cotzumalhuapa of the Guatemalan Pacific slope.

Urbina Late Postclassic stage, preceding the Conquest, of the Central Depression of Chiapas.

urns of Oaxaca Early Classic Monte Albán IIIa tombs disgorged enormous quantities and a great variety of grayware pottery urns (*incensarios*) depicting their gods. They are generally seated tailor-fashion, and are richly adorned with elaborate face masks and headdresses containing identifying symbols; a hollow cylindrical urn rises in the back. Ornamentation was intricate and hand-modeled. Oaxacan ceramic sculptures have been categorized, identified by numbers and description: 1. Cocijo, the rain-god; 2. goddess "F," also called the goddess Quetzal; 3. with mask of Cocijo as headdress medallion; 4. goddess "1 Z," characterized by simulated "pouring lip" at the orifice of the urn; 5. god with a headdress

urn of Oaxaca 1, the rain-god Cocijo

composed of the upper jaw of a serpent; 6. goddess with regional coiffure of Yalalteca; 7. butterfly god, mask element influenced by the style of Teotihuacán; 8. goddess "8 Z," with serpent's nasal mask; counterpart of "god with buccal serpent mask" (17); 9. old-man god "2 tiger"; 10. god Xipe Totec, with two prominent lines on cheeks; 11. god with earth monster in headdress; 12. god "11 death"; 13. god "5 turquoise"; 14. goddess with headdress incorporating large plume worn horizontally; 15. god of glyph "L" (Zapotec day sign for Xoo); 16. little heads with headdresses of plumes, with glyph "F" as a medallion; 17. god with buccal serpent mask; 18. goddess with the beaded turban; 19. old-man god "5 F," oldest of deities, jaguar; 20. opossum-god; 21. *acompañante* (see); 22. jaguar-god; 23. god "1 tiger"; 24. bat-god; 25. god "5 flower"; 26. goddess "2 J" (glyph J is the day sign for Quij); 27. god with ear of maize as headdress medallion; 28. goddess "13 serpent"; 29. braziers of the fire-god; 30. god with headdress composed of the mask of a bird, and young god with helmet of a broad-beaked bird; 31. jaguar-god displaying nasal mask of the god with headdress of a broad-beaked bird; 32. figurines of a god displaying an idol in headdress; 33. god with a bowknot in his headdress; 34. urns and ceremonial whistles belonging to the category of young god with asymmetrical headdress; 35. god with headdress with double points, built-up layers; 36. deity with flat-topped headdress; 37. ceremonial whistles with body of a bird, head of an old-man god with headdress of plumes; 38. goddess with the woven headdress; 39. ceremonial whistles showing old-man god wearing headdress of plumes and a cape; 40. deity with headdress composed of a horizontal band; 41. deities having two vases on back or lap; 42. anthropomorphic and zoomorphic Oaxacan vessels; 43. unclassified personages: musicians, jugglers, ballplayers, etc.; 44. Oaxacan vessels in animal form.

Uspantán Maya site in the Altos Cuchumatanes Mountains of central Guatemala. Uspantec, which is related to Quiché, is the regional language.

Usulután Town in southern El Salvador that gave its name to a distinctive Late Preclassic ceramic ware. The parallel-line decoration was accomplished with multiple brushstrokes in the negative or resist technique, leaving light lines on a dark orange or brownish ground. Found from southern Mexico to northern Nicaragua, most popular in western El Salvador and at Copán, Honduras. The technique persisted into Classic times.

Usumacinta Major river formed by three tributaries in Guatemala: the Pasión, Chixoy (Salinas), and the Lacantún. It forms the western boundary of the Petén and empties into the Gulf of Mexico through several channels in Tabasco. The Usumacinta-Pasión drainage supported the Maya sites of Piedras Negras, Yaxchilán, Palenque, Bonampak, Altar de Sacrificios, Seibal, and Cancuén.

Utatlán 1. Nahuatl name for Gumarcaah, last capital of the Quiché Maya. Conquered by the Spanish in 1524, it was renamed Santa Cruz del Quiché. 2. Name applied to Zoned Bichrome pottery of Preclassic Kaminaljuyú and the Quetzaltenango valley of Guatemala.

Uto-Aztecan Largest, most important language group of Mesoamerica, comprising dozens of languages distributed from the northwestern United States to as far south as Panama. Far western Mexico may be the heartland of the Uto-Aztecan people. Nahua is the major linguistic division, with two main dialects, Nahuatl and Nahuat.

Nahuatl became the lingua franca of the Aztec empire, and was spoken by colonies of Mexican traders settled about Honduras, El Salvador, and Nicaragua. Nahuat was spoken along the Gulf Coast and by Pipil groups that migrated to Central America, principally in western El Salvador and among the Nicarao of Pacific Nicaragua.

Utuado Town of central Puerto Rico near which Capa, the Arawak ceremonial center with several ball courts, has been preserved. See also **Taino; ball game, Arawak.**

uuc Number 7 in Maya.

Uxmal Late Classic Maya center in the Puuc hills of western Yucatán; traditionally linked with the ruling Xiu family who abandoned it in the 10th century for a new seat at Maní. Its original name may have been Oxmal, "built three times."

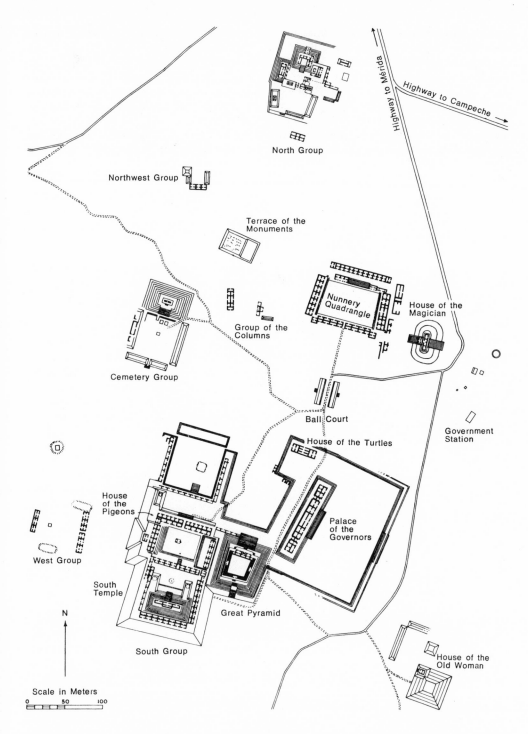

Plate 23. Map of the central section of Uxmal. From S. G. Morley, *The Ancient Maya*, page 298.

Noted for outstanding Puuc architecture, with some Chenes-style intrusion. The imposing 325-ft. (98 m)-long Palace of the Governors exhibits the Puuc style in its most refined and highly developed plane. The Nunnery Quadrangle, a group of four freestanding palaces about a court, with walls of negative batter, is decorated with a horizontal frieze in a mosaic technique that recalls Mitla in Oaxaca. Its roofs are edged by "flying facades." Other prominent structures are the dominating Pyramid of the Magician, the Great Pyramid, Turtle House, and House of the Pigeons with its immense open-work roof crest. See also **Puuc.**

Uxul Classic Maya site of Campeche, near the Petén, Guatemala, border.

V

Vague Year Modern term for the year of 365 days. Among the Maya it was composed of the *tun* or *haab* of 18 months of 20 days each, followed by the *Uayeb* of 5 unlucky days. Among the Aztecs, the *xíhuitl* of 360 days was similarly followed by the 5 days of the *Nemontemi*. The term is based on the fact that the true year is about 365¼ days, the reason for our leap year correction.

Valdivia 1. A Spanish expedition, in charge of a Captain Valdivia, proceeding from Darién to Santo Domingo was shipwrecked off the coast of Yucatán in 1511, the first European contact with the Maya. Only 2 of 20 survivors outlived sacrifice by the natives. Gerónimo de Aguilar was rescued by Cortés to become his interpreter. Gonzalo de Guerrero remained, having married a Maya chief's daughter, and finally died in battle against the Spanish. 2. Coastal site of Guayas Province, Ecuador, and Formative ceramic phase, 2600–1500 B.C., which may have influenced the pottery style of the Barra phase of the Soconusco region of Chiapas, Mexico.

Valladolid 1. Modern city of Yucatán, east of Chichén Itzá, called Saki by the Maya. 2. Valladolid incised-dichrome ceramic, a glossware type, is a marker for the Early Classic period of the northern Maya lowlands, c. A.D. 200–400.

Varajonal Late Classic Maya site in the Central Depression of Chiapas, c. A.D. 550–950, with the only corbeled vault in the region and a huge I-shaped ball court.

Valley of Mexico The heartland of Mesoamerica, it measures 5,000 sq. mi. (c. 13,000 km²) at an elevation of c. 7,000 ft. (2,240 m). It was contained on the east, before the Pliocene epoch, by a transverse chain of volcanos that locked five connected lakes within the basin. Rich in lake shores and mountain slopes, it supported Preclassic populations, its adaptability to agriculture giving rise to Teotihuacán and ultimately to Postclassic Tenochtitlán.

Vaticanus A, Codex See **codex, early post-Conquest Mexican; Ríos, Codex.**

Vaticanus B, Codex See **codex, pre-Conquest Mexican; Vaticanus B, Codex.**

veintena A Spanish post-Conquest term applied to the 18 20-day Aztec months and the religious festivals associated with them. Most were linked to the annual agricultural cycle and concerned with fertility promotion. Primary or other names for the *veintenas* are the same as the month names used in particular localities. See also **months, Aztec.**

Venado Beach Site west of the Pacific entrance to the Panama Canal. The distinctive type of goldwork here was a cast-filigree effigy pendant reminiscent of the Sinu culture of Colombia. Earliest gold found there radiocarbon-dates to c. A.D. 250. See also **Panama.**

Venta Salada Last phase of the Tehuacán Valley sequence, Puebla. Early Venta Salada is dated A.D. 700–1150, with Tohil Plumbate in late levels. Late Venta Salada, A.D. 1150–1520, adds X Fine Orange, outlasting Plumbate, coeval with Cempoala

II–III, with Isla de Sacrificios polychrome evident.

Venus cycle The synodical revolution of the planet Venus, totaling 584 days, was in Mesoamerica divided into four periods of 236, 90,

Venus glyph

250, and 8 days. The Maya saw Venus as the morning star for 236 days; it became invisible during superior conjunction for 90 days; it reappeared as the evening star for 250 days; and again became invisible during inferior conjunction for 8 days. The planet was considered sinister and a threat to man's affairs. The Maya Dresden Codex is mainly concerned with study of this time cycle; the Grolier Codex also contains Venus tables.

Central Mexicans as well as the Maya recognized that 8 solar years are equal to 5 Venus cycles. At the completion of 104 years several time cycles spectacularly coincided: the 584-day Venus cycle, the 365-day solar year, the 52-year Calendar Round, and the *tonalpohualli* or *tzolkin* of 260 days.

Veracruz State of the Republic of Mexico, with capital of same name, extending along the Gulf of Mexico and enclosed by the states of Tamaulipas, San Luis Potosí, Hidalgo, Puebla, Oaxaca, Chiapas, and Tabasco. Principal sites are El Tajín, Cempoala, Remojadas, Isla de Sacrificios, Cerro de las Mesas, Tres Zapotes, and San Lorenzo.

Veraguas Province of Panama, bounded by Chiriquí, Bocas del Toro, the Caribbean Sea, Colón, Coclé, Herrera, Los Santos, and the Pacific Ocean. Archaeologically, the area produced grinding stones with stylized birds or animals in high relief under the grinding surface. It is best known for the expert casting of open-backed *tumbaga* figures of birds, animals, frogs, crocodiles, and anthropomorphic figures that were gilded by the *mise-en-couleur* technique. Protruding eyes are characteristic, as is the use of bells incorporated in large pendants. Traditional ceramic phases include Scarified/Guacamayo, 300 B.C.–A.D. 300, followed by "Classic Veraguas." See also **Central Panama**.

Vesuvio Phase of the Río Suchil branch of the Chalchihuites culture in Zacatecas, Mexico, c. A.D. 500–950.

Vienna, Codex See **codex, pre-Conquest Mexican; Vienna Codex**.

vigesimal system Mesoamerican system of counting that uses the base 20, comparable to our decimal system using the base 10. Its origin may come from the total number of digits on hands and feet.

Volador Ritual ceremony of Gulf Coast origin, enacted as far away as Nayarit and Nicaragua. Four men, dressed as gods or eagles, jumped simultaneously from a revolving square platform atop a high pole. On their descent they whirled 13 times about the pole, symbolizing the movement of the sun. The 4 x 13 revolutions by the participants represented the 52-year cycle, or Calendar Round.

volátiles Each of the 13 Lords of the Day was assigned a bird in the Book of Days, the *Tonalamatl*. They are referred to collectively by the Spanish word *volátiles*, literally, "flying." See also **Lords of the Day**.

votive axe A ceremonial Olmec form, essentially a celt with its thicker end carved to suggest an anthropomorphic figure. Generally of basalt, rarely jade, some are very large. The Kunz Axe at The American Museum of Natural History, New York, is

votive axe representing Olmec god I

shaped from a boulder of blue-green jade and is 11 in. (28 cm) high. Another, in The British Museum, London, is slightly larger. Only about 20 votive axes are known. They generally have cleft heads, flame eyebrows, flattened noses, toothless mouths, their hands meeting across the chest. The oldest Olmec celt with figure carving was excavated from Tomb E, La Venta, dated c. 700–600 B.C. Characteristic Olmec features refer to gods I, III, IV, or V.

Vucub-Camé Lord of Xibalba, as related in the Popol Vuh, the sacred book of the Quiché Maya.

Vucub-Caquiz Mythical character in Popol Vuh of the Quiché Maya who proclaimed himself both sun and moon during the Creation. He was destroyed, along with his sons Zipacná and Cabracán, by the hero twins Hunahpú and Xbalanqué.

Waecker-Götter, Codex See **codex, early post-Conquest Mexican; Sanchez-Solis, Codex.**

weapons Pre-Hispanic weapons, in the absence of iron, included the dreaded *macuauhuitl*, spears, bows and arrows, *atlatl*, slings, and blowguns. Defensively, shields of wood and basketry were used; the warriors themselves were protected by tufted cotton armor, later adopted by the Spaniards as more practical than their heavy metal armor.

werejaguar See **baby face.**

Western Mexico Term used to describe a subarea of Mesoamerica comprising the states of Sinaloa, Nayarit, Jalisco, Colima, Michoacán, part of Guanajuato, and Guerrero. Zacatecas and Durango are sometimes considered separately, not properly a part of Mesoamerica.

West Indies See **Antilles.**

whistling jar A ceramic vessel composed of two connected pots, one open at the top, the other provided with a small hole. As water is poured, the air passing through the small aperture produces a whistling sound. First appearance in Mesoamerica may have been during the Monte Albán I phase of Oaxaca.

white-rimmed blackware Preclassic pottery with a contrast in surface color produced by differential firing.

world creation See **Creation myth; Aztec, Maya.**

world directions and associations, Aztec From the center of the earth (navel) four quadrants extended out to the four cardinal points, each with a sacred tree upon which was perched a sacred bird. Each direction had its own associations, with considerable variation in colors, trees, and birds. Primary references below reflect late pre-Hispanic sources:

East: called Tlapcopa, associated with red (or yellow, blue-green), with mesquite (or *ceiba*) tree, and the *quetzal* (or eagle) bird. Tlahuizcalpantecuhtli, the Venus god, was the sky bearer. Related days were Cipactli, Ácatl, Cóatl, Ollin, and Atl; Ácatl was also the year sign. Augury was favorable.

North: called Mictlampa, associated with black (or red, white), the *ceiba* (or mesquite) tree, and the eagle (or jaguar). A fire-god (?) was the sky bearer. Related days were Océlotl, Miquiztli, Técpatl, Itzcuintli, and Éhecatl; Técpatl was also the year sign. Augury was unfavorable.

West: called Cihuatlampa, associated with white (or blue-green, yellow), the cypress (or maguey) tree, and the hummingbird (or serpent). Éhecatl-Quetzalcóatl was the sky bearer. Related days were Mázatl, Quiáhuitl, Ozomatli, Calli, and Cuauhtli; Calli was also the year sign. Augury was "too humid."

South: called Huitzlampa, associated with blue (or red, white), the willow (or palm) tree, and the parrot (or rabbit). Mictlantecuhtli was the sky bearer. Related days were Xóchitl, Malinalli, Cuetzpalin, Cozcacuauhtli, and Tochtli. Tochtli was also the year sign. Augury was indifferent.

A fifth, or central direction, up and down, represented heaven and earth, ruled by the divine pair, Ometecuhtli and Omecíhuatl. The numbers 4 and 5 were therefore important to the Aztecs, representing the 4 cardinal points and their combination with the vertical direction. Their role in Mexican thought can be compared to 3 (the Trinity) in Occidental magic.

world directions and colors, Maya Unlike the Aztec, Maya associations were uniform, as follows:

East: called Likin, associated with the color red (*chac*); the Year Bearer was Kan.

North: called Xaman, associated with the color white (*zac*); the Year Bearer was Muluc.

West: called Chikin, associated with the color black (*ek*); the Year Bearer was Ix.

South: called Nohol, associated with the color yellow (*kan*); the Year Bearer was Cauac.

The fifth direction, up and down, in the center of the earth, was depicted by the sacred *ceiba* tree. Its roots penetrated the underworld; its trunk and branches reached into the various layers of the skies.

writing, pre-Hispanic See **hieroglyphic writing, ideogram, pictogram.**

X

X Fine Orange Horizon marker of Early Postclassic Mesoamerica. See **Orange, Fine.**

Xaltocán Aztec island town in the northern part of the Great Lake of the Valley of Mexico, sometimes called Lake Xaltocán.

Xamantún Maya site in southern Campeche. One of only three cities, along with Uaxactún and Xultún, to erect a monument to commemorate the last *katun* of the Classic period, 10.3.0.0.0 (A.D. 889).

Xamen Ek Fifth most common god in the Maya codices, the North Star god, depicted as snub-nosed, with peculiar black markings on his head. Associated with Ek Chuah, god of merchants; probably god C and patron of the day Chuen. A benevolent deity, in association with the rain-god Chac. Xamen is the Maya word for North.

xantile Modern Zapotec word for an anthropomorphic bottomless cylindrical pottery vessel. Was probably placed over burning incense, with smoke escaping from the orifices. Commonly found in the region of Teotitlán del Camino, Oaxaca. It can usually be identified with a Postclassic deity of the Mixteca-Puebla region, such as Xochipilli.

Xaratanga Tarascan moon-goddess, deity of sustenance, germination, and growth, born of the union between Curicaueri and Cuerauáperi.

Xbalanqué Mythical figure, one of the hero-twins of the Popol Vuh. See **Hunahpú.**

Xcalumkin See **Holactún.**

Xcaret Maya site on the east coast of Quintana Roo, representing the decadent Late Postclassic period. May be Polé, referred to as the point of entrance to the Yucatán peninsula for the Putún Maya from Cozumel Island. The Yaxuna-Cobá causeway is believed to have extended to Xcaret. Principal occupation was after A.D. 1300.

Xe Name, meaning "vomit" in Maya, applied to the earliest occupation of the southwestern Maya lowlands, at bottom of the Altar de Sacrificios cultural sequence. Dated c. 900 B.C., it antedates the Mamom phase of Uaxactún.

Xelha Small fortified Late Postclassic Maya town on the east coast of Quintana Roo, north of Tulum.

Xibalba Highland Maya designation for the underworld mentioned in the Popol Vuh of the Quiché; derived from the root *xib*, "fear, terror, trembling with fright." The Yucatec Maya equivalent was Mitnal.

Xicalango An important port and trading center in the Postclassic period at the west end of the Laguna de Términos, Tabasco; controlled by the seafaring Chontal Maya. Mentioned in the Popol Vuh as a temporary way station of the Guatemalan highland tribes during their migration from Mexico.

xicalcoliuhqui Nahuatl word for the popular design motif of Mesoamerica called the "stepped fret."

xicalli Nahuatl word for a bowl made of a gourd, also called *jícara*. Translated into stone, it became the *cuauhxicalli*.

Xico 1. Classic site in Veracruz, near Coatepec. 2. Place on the southern shore of Lake Texcoco, formerly Lake Chalco, where a human infant's jaw was discovered, probably coeval with "Tepexpan Man," c. 8000 B.C. The famous Late Classic period Xico Stela exhibits the style of Xochicalco.

xicolli Nahuatl word for a sleeveless jacket, previously appearing only in Teotihuacán II, that later became the typical garb of the Mixtec, also worn by Aztec priests. The Tarascans of Michoacán adopted it in a varied form—extending only to the navel, worn without breechcloth.

Xictli Small volcano in the Valley of Mexico. It erupted during the Protoclassic period, covering Cuicuilco and Copilco, creating a rocky lava area today known as the "Pedregal of San Ángel" on the outskirts of Mexico City.

xíhuitl 1. Mexican year of 360 days, composed of 18 months of 20 days each, equivalent to the *haab* or *tun* of the Maya. It was followed by 5 unlucky days, called *Nemontemi,* to complete the solar calendar of 365 days. See also **calendar, Mesoamerican.** 2. Nahuatl word for turquoise, frequently employed in compound words to denote "precious." In combining forms *xíhuitl* becomes *xiuh,* as in *xiuhpohualli,* a synonym for the word *xíhuitl* in its calendrical application.

Xilomanaliztli See **Atlcahualo; months, Aztec.**

Xilonen Adolescent corn-goddess, subject of a cult in her honor established by the virgins of Tenochtitlán. Closely related to the fertility deity Chicomecóatl. See also **Centéotl.**

Ximba Fine Orange ceramic phase at Altar de Sacrificios. The style was introduced into the Pasión River drainage, c. A.D. 909–948, by peoples from the lowlands of Tabasco. See **Orange, Fine.**

Xinabahul Protohistoric phase of the western Guatemala highlands.

Xinca Non-Maya linguistic group of uncertain affiliation, southeast Guatemala.

Xipe Totec Mexica god of springtime, seeding, and planting; the red Tezcatlipoca, associated with the East. Patron deity of the Aztec day Cuauhtli; second month of the Nahuatl year, Tlacaxipehualiztli, honored him by dressing priests in skins of flayed sacrificial victims, a ritual signifying the renewal of vegetation in the spring. Also called Yope. His cult probably originated in the Oaxaca-Guerrero border region and his ultimate origin may be found in Olmec god VI. Revered in central Mexico, especially in Tlaxcala. Patron of lapidaries and smiths. Introduced late into Maya region, as at Oxkintok, Chichén Itzá, and Mayapán.

Xiu An important family of northern Yucatán that defeated the Cocom dynasty of Mayapán A.D. 1441, thereby ending its dominance over the northern lowlands: beginning of the period of city-states as found by the Spaniards. Although Uxmal was in Xiu territory and has been traditionally linked with that family, archaeology suggests Uxmal's abandonment before the time of Tutul Xiu. After the fall of Mayapán, the Xiu established their capital at Maní.

xiuhamatl Codices, "book of the years" in Nahuatl, in which the Mexica recounted the events of the years; some comprised cycles of 52 years.

xiuhatlatl Nahuatl for "blue (turquoise) spear-thrower," it was the weapon and sign of office of the fire-god and such related deities as Huitzilopochtli.

xiuhcóatl Meaning "turquoise serpent" in Nahuatl, it was the alter ego and symbol of Xiuhtecuhtli, the fire-god; also an accouterment of Huitzilopochtli and Tezcatlipoca. In contrast to the benevolent Feathered Serpent (Quetzalcóatl), it represents fire, aridity, and drought. In Aztec mythology *xiuhcóatl* carries the sun through the sky from dawn to zenith; two of them encircle the famous Calendar Stone in the Museo Nacional de Antropología in Mexico City. Repeated in endless series, they constituted the *coatepantli* ("serpent wall") enclosing the sacred precinct of Tenochtitlán.

Xiuhmolpilli See **Tying of Years.**

xiuhpiltontli Nahuatl word for the sun, "turquoise child."

xiuhpohualli Aztec solar year. See **xíhuitl.**

Xiuhtecuhtli God of fire, first of the 9 Lords of the Night, and first of the 13 Lords of the Day, patron of the Aztec day Atl; he is one of most ancient Mexican deities, also called Huehuéteotl, the "old god," in Nahuatl. He is often depicted as a wrinkle-faced toothless old man bearing a brazier on his head. He is found in Preclassic cultures of the Valley of Mexico and may have his origin in god I of Olmecs. Associated with the number 3, symbolic of the three hearthstones.

xiuhtototl Nahuatl name for "turquoise bird" (*Cotinga amabilis*), called *raxón* or *ranchón* in Guatemala. Its feathers, worn on the front of his headband, formed a part of the accouterment of the Aztec fire-god Xiuhtecuhtli.

xiuhuitzolli Headband of turquoise mosaic worn as sign of royalty by Mexican rulers. Shown as symbol of the East to the left above the face of the central figure on the Aztec Calendar Stone. The device adorned nobles and warriors at their burials.

Xkichmook Late Classic Maya site, also called Xkichmul, of southwest Yucatán.

Xmucané In Quiché Maya mythology the "grandmother," the maker of man. Xpiyacoc and Xmucané were equivalents of the Mexican gods Cipactonal and Oxomoco, the active creator-couple. In the Popol Vuh, Xmucané is the mother of Hun-Hunahpú and Vucub-Hunahpú, grandmother of the hero-twins Hunahpú and Xbalanqué. See **Hunahpú.**

Xmulzencab Maya bee-gods who appear in the story of the Creation, each with a world color and directional associations, as reported in the *Chilam Balam* of Chumayel. The deity that appears at Tulum as the "descending god" may represent the Xmulzencab.

xoc Mythical fish whose glyphic representation was used as a rebus for *xoc* ("to count") in lowland Maya inscriptions dealing with the passage of time. See **glyph, introducing.**

In Yucatec Maya, *xoc* may be a rebus for "waist" or "lady," incorporated in some stelae to identify female figures.

Xochicalco Large defensible site on steep terraced hills in the state of Morelos. It appears to have been transitional between the terminal phase of Classic Teotihuacán and the Postclassic emergence of Tula, although its history antedates and also continues beyond this period in time. Maximum building activity was in the Late Classic.

Structures employ the *talud* and *tablero,* but unlike their Teotihuacán model, the *talud* here is tall, the *tablero,* short. The *talud* of the main pyramid of Quetzalcóatl is carved with a feathered serpent undulating about seated dignitaries, suggesting a meeting of Mesoamerican astronomers similar to the scene on Altar Q at the Classic Maya site of Copán. Old chronicles refer to the site as Tamoanchán, the legendary seat of the "bird serpent." The large ball court is in the style of Tula; the style of the pottery and the reliefs on monuments indicate a convergence of Toltec, Zapotec, Mixtec, and Maya influences.

Xochimanalo Alternate name for Tozoztontli, 4th of the 18 months of the Aztec calendar of 365 days.

Xochimilca One of seven Aztec tribal groups believed to have left the legendary Chicomoztoc ("seven caves") in the far northwest, starting the long migration to the Valley of Mexico; founded Xochimilco.

Xochimilco Town founded by the Xochimilca in the 12th century; its name in Nahuatl signifies "place of flower-growing." Became a tributary state of Tenochtitlán under the Mexican ruler Axayácatl. A vital source of agricultural products, grown on their *chinampas,* still famous today as the "floating gardens."

Xochipala Preclassic site in the Mezcala region of Guerrero, active c. 1800–800 B.C. Stylistically, its early figurines relate more to the naturalistic Olmec style than to the more expressionistic conventions of the

Mexican highland. Early Xochipala provides portraitlike works of great sophistication, with the sex indicated but with no suggestion of Mongoloid ancestry. Middle period, c. 1400–1200 B.C., produced solid C-9 figurines, white-slipped hollow "baby-face" types, and Morelos type D-2 figurines. Solid figures of the Late period show degeneration, with less emphasis on anatomical detail. The absence of controlled excavations precludes absolute dating and verification of the Xochipala ceramic complex as belonging to the Formative period of the Olmec tradition, predating its presence in the Mexican highlands and on the Gulf Coast.

Xochipilli Nahuatl name for the "flower prince," the youthful aspect of the solar god, patron of youth, gaiety, poetry, and masculine fecundity. Patron of the Aztec day Ozomatli. A deity so similar to him that it may only be his calendrical name is Macuilxóchitl (5 flower), god of the dance and the game *patolli*. Another manifestation of Xochipilli was Ahuíatl. Xochipilli and Xochiquetzal, his female counterpart, were principally worshiped by peoples of the *chinampas* in the Xochimilco area of the Valley of Mexico.

Xochiquetzal Nahuatl goddess, "flower of the rich plume," who was, according to one legend, the first wife of the rain-god Tlaloc before her abduction by Tezcatlipoca. As the female counterpart of Xochipilli, she was the personification of beauty and love, goddess of flowers, patroness of domestic work, and also of courtesans, the *auianime*. Patroness of Aztec day Xóchitl. Pictorially she is represented with two large panaches—erect *quetzal* feathers.

Xóchitl Name and symbol, "flower," of the 20th of the 20 Nahuatl days. Xochiquetzal was its patron. Equivalent to the Maya day Ahau and the Zapotec day Lao or Loo. Calendrical days of Xóchitl include: 1 Xóchitl: Centéotl, corn-god; 2 Xóchitl: feast day of merchants; 5 Xóchitl: Macuilxóchitl, god of pleasure; 7 Xóchitl: sun; 10

Xóchitl: god of war of Huaxtepec, Morelos.

Xochitlalpan "Land of flowers" in Nahuatl, name for the South, region of flowers, home of the gods of music, dance, games, and pleasure; abode of Macuilxóchitl.

Xochiyaóyotl Nahuatl word for Flowery War.

Xócotl See **Otontecuhtli.**

Xocotlhuetzi See **Hueymiccailhuitl; months, Aztec.**

Xolalpan Great Late Classic phase of Teotihuacán, c. A.D. 500–650, called Teotihuacán IIIa. Murals painted in Tepantitla and Tetitla show relationships with the Gulf Coast, Oaxaca, and the Maya region. In ceramics, Fine Orange and the lidded cylindrical tripod reached full development as a hallmark of Teotihuacán throughout Mesoamerica, decorated with painting, planorelief, fresco, incising, or simply burnished.

Xolchún Postclassic site in the Department of Quiché, Guatemala, c. A.D. 900–1500.

Xólotl 1. Aztec god of the planet Venus as the evening star, twin brother of Quetzalcóatl. Probably referring to him as a dog guide to the underworld, Postclassic renditions of him frequently show him with the head of a dog. Nanahuatzin, the syphilitic god, seems to have been an aspect of Xólotl. He is the patron of the Aztec day Ollin. 2. A legendary chief of the Chichimeca. 3. Texcocan codex, important source of the history of Anáhuac, written c. 1542–46, Bibliothèque Nationale, Paris.

Xometla Early Postclassic phase of the Valley of Mexico, also called Coyotlatelco, A.D. 900–1100.

Xoo Seventeenth of the 20 Zapotec days, equivalent to the Aztec day Ollin and the Maya day Caban.

Xpiyacoc The "grandfather" of the Quiché Maya, companion of Xmucané, mentioned in the Popol Vuh.

Xpuhil Classic Maya site of eastern Campeche, with a temple in the Río Bec style, c. A.D. 875.

Xtampak See **Santa Rosa Xtampak**

Xul Sixth month of the *tun*, the Maya year of 360 days.

Xultún Maya site of northeastern Petén, Guatemala; Stela 10 is one of the last dated monuments from the time of the lowland Maya civilization's collapse, 10.3.0.0.0 (A.D. 889).

Xunantunich Classic Maya site in the Cayo district of Belize.

y

yacameztli Nahuatl word for a nose pendant in the form of a half-moon, an insignia of Tlazoltéotl, a manifestation of the earth-goddess. It is also identified with various pulque deities and Xipe Totec.

yácata A Tarascan temple base combining terraced, rectangular and circular elements. The Tarascan capital, Tzintzuntzan, has an installation of five *yácatas*.

yácata

Yacatecuhtli Aztec god of the *pochteca*, the traveling merchant class, sharing some attributes with Quetzalcóatl. His symbols were a bamboo staff and a fan. Equivalent to the Maya god Ek Chuah, he was venerated in Postclassic central Mexico, especially at Cholula and Tenochtitlán-Tlatelolco. Central American versions of the merchant god were Yacapitzauac ("he with the pointed nose") and Yacacoliuhqui ("he with eagle-beaked nose").

Yagul Zapotec city-fortress on a hill near Mitla, Oaxaca, along the Pan American Highway. Main area is a complex consisting of a palace with six courts, a large ball court, and numerous tombs. A look-out fort is situated on high cliffs. Continuity of occupation is Monte Albán I-V, but the visible buildings are Monte Albán IV, showing some Mixtec influence with stone mosaic similar to Mitla.

yalba uinic Maya term for the commoners constituting the main body of the population, including farmers, small merchants, artisans, and poorer fishermen.

yáotl Nahuatl for enemy in general; a synonym for Tezcatlipoca as a nocturnal, destructive deity, and of Huitzilopochtli as his diurnal counterpart.

yaóyotl Nahuatl word for war. Its hieroglyph depicted a shield, a bundle of arrows, and a spear-thrower.

Yaqui 1. Term applied to the Mexican-Toltec followers of Quetzalcóatl in the Popol Vuh, the sacred book of the Quiché Maya. They migrated after the fall of Tula from the Gulf Coast to the Guatemalan highlands. Yaqui were "the chiefs and sacrificers," ancestors to the Quiché. 2. Protohistoric phase of Zacualpa, Guatemala, A.D. 1200–1524.

Yarumela Preclassic site near the center of a transcontinental pass on the Humuya (Comayagua) River of Honduras. Contemporary with the Arévalo phase of the Guatemalan highlands and Ocós of the Pacific coast, c. 1500–1000 B.C.

Yash Early and Middle Postclassic phase of the Central Plateau of Chiapas.

Yax Tenth month of the *tun*, the Maya year of 360 days.

yaxche Maya name for the ceiba (*Bombax pentandra*) tree, sacred to the Maya. Represented the fifth world direction (up and down), standing at the center of the earth, its trunk and branches piercing the various layers of the skies, its roots penetrating the underworld. Also called kapok.

Yaxchilán Meaning "place of the green stones," this Classic Maya center rises on a forested hill contained in a loop of the Usumacinta River at the

Yaxchilán emblem glyph

Guatemalan border of Chiapas. The upper facades and roof combs of the temple-pyramids are ornamented with figures in stucco and stone. Famed for its carved stelae and many stone lintels depicting scenes of conquest and ceremonial life. The eighth-century rulers Shield Jaguar and Bird Jaguar are identified by their glyphs. Stelae were erected until A.D. 870. Yaxchilán was originally called Menché, Maya for "green tree," then Lorillard in honor of American patron of the Désiré Charnay expedition in the 1880s. Current name was applied by Teobart Maler of the Harvard Expedition at the turn of the century.

Yaxhá Classic Maya ceremonial center, on lake of the same name, in the eastern Petén of Guatemala.

Yaxkin Seventh month of the *tun*, the Maya year of 360 days. Patron was the sun-god.

Yaxuna Maya site in central Yucatán connected to Cobá by the longest known causeway (*sacbé*), a distance of 62 mi. (100 km).

Yayahuala Residential compound of Teotihuacán, north of Tetitla and Zacuala.

Year Bearer In the meshing of the Aztec and Maya 365-day calendars with the 260 days of their ritual calendars, the same four days would repeatedly arise to mark the start of a new year. These days were called Year Bearers, determining the luck of the years as well as giving their names to designate them. Aztec Year Bearers were the days Ácatl, Calli, Técpatl, and Tochtli; at the time of the Conquest, Maya Year Bearers were Muluc, Ik, Cauac, and Kan.

Year Bundle See **Tying of Years, Calendar Round.**

year sign The year sign or "trapeze-and-ray," a motif of interlacing lines often pictured on Teotihuacán headdresses, appears throughout Mesoamerica. The Mixtec year sign is represented by inter-

Mixtec year sign

lacing a capital *A* with a horizontal *O*, a popular glyph in the codices and goldwork.

Yerba Buena A site in the Central Plateau of Chiapas.

Yerbalito See **Culiacán.**

yeyi Number 3 in Nahuatl.

Yestla-Naranjo Zone in the Sierra Madre del Sur of central Guerrero; late archaeological materials are related to the Mixteca-Puebla and Aztec cultures.

Yocahu Patron god of the Island Arawak, giver of manioc.

yohualli éhecatl An esoteric term applied to divinity in general, but particularly to Quetzalcóatl, expressing the invisible and intangible.

Yohualtecuhtli Nahuatl for "Lord of the Night," it represented both the sun and the planet Venus as they join in the underworld at the completion of the cosmic cycle. The counterpart of Tonatiuh, sun-god of the daytime sky, it was also known as Yohualtonatiuh, the night sun. Associated with midnight, darkness, earth, cyclic completion, and the central world direction. See also **Calendar Stone, Aztec.**

Yohualtecuhtli was the name given the star that appeared in the center of the sky at midnight on the final day of a 52-year cycle, denoting for Aztecs the successful completion of that cycle and the initiation of a new one. See **Calendar Round.**

Yohualteuctin Collective name for the nine Aztec Lords of the Night.

Yohualtonatiuh See **Tonatiuh, Yohualtecuhtli.**

Yojoa Only important lake in Honduras, possibly of volcanic origin, with no surface outlets. Sites of Los Naranjos and La Ceiba are at its northern end.

yoke Large U-shaped stone, often elaborately carved, presumed to be a ceremonial imitation of the protective belt worn by players in the Mesoamerican ritual ball game. A few closed-end

yoke

yokes are known. It may have been employed in play, but it may also have been a ceremonial reproduction in stone of perishable materials actually used, such as leather and wood. It forms part of the *yoke-hacha-palma* complex of Classic Veracruz sculpture. See also **ball game, Meso-american.**

Yope Linguistic group of Guerrero whose area is called Yopitzingo; thought to be place of origin for the cult of Xipe Totec.

yuca See **manioc.**

Yucatán 1. Peninsula extending north into the Caribbean Sea from the Central American mainland. 2. Its northern extremity is the Mexican state of Yucatán, contained by the Gulf of Mexico, and states of Campeche and Quintana Roo. Among its sites are Chichén Itzá, Uxmal, Kabah, Sayil, Labná, Acancéh, Dzibilchaltún, Mayapán, and Izamal, as well as the Cave of Loltún.

yugo Popularly used Spanish word for *yoke.*

yuguito Small stone carving, "little yoke," of unknown use. Its shape is an inverted U, domed with the concavity somewhat flattened at its apogee, the convex surface is frequently carved. Of Olmec origin, it is found at Tlatilco, Las Bocas; possibly an imitation of a thigh, elbow, or hand protector used in the ball game.

Yum Cimil Name of a Maya death-god, associated with Ah Puch.

Yum Kaax See **Ah Mun.**

yza The Zapotec year, corresponding to the Aztec *tonalpohualli.*

Z

Zaachila Capital of the Zapotecs after the fall of Monte Albán, c. A.D. 1000–Conquest. Plaster sculptures on the walls of tombs, as well as fine polychrome ceramics, show Mixtec influence. Located in the valley of Ocotlán, Oaxaca.

Zac Eleventh month of the *tun*, the Maya year of 360 days; the word means "white," and as such is related to the North.

Zacatecas 1. State of the Republic of Mexico, with capital of same name, bounded by Coahuila, San Luis Potosí, Jalisco, Aguascalientes, and Durango. See also **Chalchihuites, La Quemada.** 2. "Zacatecas" figures are of a style formerly classified as Nayarit, but they are found in northeast Jalisco, Zacatecas, and Mexico. The little-known style differs from Nayarit, especially in the headdresses of male figures, which extend on both sides like two horns.

Zacatenco Middle Preclassic site in the Valley of Mexico whose graves furnished early figurines, mostly female. Its name is applied to a basin-wide phase, c. 1050–550 B.C., between the earlier Ixtapaluca and Ticomán (Cuicuilco); subphases were El Arbolillo, La Pastora, and Cuautepec.

Zacuala Residential compound of Teotihuacán, between Tetitla and Yayahuala.

Zacualpa Postclassic Maya site in the Department of Quiché, western Guatemalan highlands. Extensively excavated, its phases are Tohil, A.D. 1000–1200, and Yaqui, A.D. 1200–Conquest. The presence of X Fine Orange ware suggests Mexican influence.

Zaculeu Major western Guatemalan highlands site in the Department of Huehuetenango. On a defensible plateau, it was occupied from the Early Classic period until its capitulation to the Spaniards under Pedro de Alvarado in 1525. Architecture is stylistically Toltec, its main temple of Early Postclassic date has been restored.

Zapatera Island in Lake Nicaragua, "shoemaker" in Spanish, so named because of burials containing shoe-shaped vessels (*patojos*) there.

Zapotal Classic funerary site of Veracruz, active from the sixth to the ninth centuries. An unbaked clay statue of Mictlantecuhtli was unearthed there.

zapote See **sapodilla.**

Zapotec Nahuatl word meaning "cloud people," applied to an important branch of the Oto-Zapotecan language group that entered the valley of Oaxaca sometime before A.D. 300, becoming major builders of Monte Albán. While accepting outside influence, the Zapotecs developed an unmistakable and individual regional style in their buildings, tombs, ceramics, and the *lápidas*, which replaced the earlier stelae. The Zapotecs are still the dominant group in Oaxaca today. See also **Monte Albán.**

Zayamuincob Strong dwarfs who built the ancient sites, according to Maya myths, and were turned to stone when the sun appeared during the world Creation. They may be represented by small Atlanteans found at Chichén Itzá.

Zee Fifth of the 20 Zapotec day names, sometimes called Zij. Corresponds to the Aztec day Cóatl and the Maya day Chicchan.

zemi Taino word for deity, also applied to the characteristic Arawak three-cornered idol form of the West Indies, originally of shell but superseded c. A.D. 600 by tricorn or three-pointed stones. After A.D. 1000 the Taino made larger, decorated types.

Zempoala See **Cempoala.**

zero The discovery and use of the concept of zero was exclusive to the Maya in the New World, antedating its introduction into Europe from the East. It permitted the Maya to develop their vigesimal system of position numerals for limitless calculations, especially in time. The use of the zero is also basic to their calendrical writings in which they expressed themselves only in terms of elapsed time, which is impossible to do without the concept of zero. Maya glyphs for zero are found in codices and inscriptions. The most common form in writing is lenticular, or like the side view of a clam, with unpredictable inside decorations. The "head variant" for zero in monumental inscriptions always has a hand clasping the lower part of the face, probably denoting "ending" or "closing." See also **numerical recording, Maya; months, Maya.**

Zip 1. Third month of the *tun,* the Maya year of 360 days. 2. In Yucatán, also the name of a god of hunting, of deer in particular.

Zoned Bichrome Ceramic period of Greater Nicoya, c. 300 B.C.–A.D. 300. The pottery is red on buff or black on red, with painted zones set off by incised lines. Two phases are defined in Pacific Nicaragua: Aviles followed by San Jorge. Northwest Costa Rica had three interrelated phases: Chombo near the Nicaraguan border, Monte Fresco at Tamarindo Bay, and Catalina in the Tempisque valley. From the same period there are other two-color wares without incising, and unpainted types with zoned decoration that contrast smooth surfaces with areas textured by punctation, rocker and dentate stamping. The zoned incised mode was common to many early styles throughout the Americas.

zoomorphic 1. A representation in the shape or having attributes of an animal. 2. The term *zoomorph* has been applied to the large, elaborately carved stone boulders found at the Classic Maya site of Quiriguá, Guatemala. It may be a variant on the theme of a beast with heads at both ends, such as Altar 41 at Copán, with which Quiriguá had close ties. Zoomorph P is outstanding testimony to the intricacy of Maya carving and commemorates an event in the life of a ruler. It measures 33 ft. (10 m) in girth, 7¼ ft. (2.2 m) in height, and weighs 20 tons. Zoomorphs seemed to have served the same function as stelae, similarly accompanied by altars.

Zoque A branch of the Macro-Maya language group of eastern Oaxaca and Chiapas.

Zotz 1. Fourth month of the *tun,* the Maya year of 360 days. Zotz means "bat" in Maya; its glyph is the head of the leaf-nosed vampire bat, which also dominates the emblem glyph of Copán. 2. Name of the royal house of the Cakchiquel Maya of the Guatemalan highlands, whose king was Ahpozotzil, Lord Bat. 3. Zotzihá is the terrible House of Bats in Xibalba, the Quiché Maya underworld described in the Popol Vuh, where Cama Zotz, the killer bat, was the formidable enemy of Hunahpú and Xbalanqué.

Zouche, Codex See **codex, pre-Conquest Mexican; Nuttall Codex.**

Zumpango Most northerly portion of the Great Lake of the Valley of Mexico in pre-Hispanic times, now completely drained.

Zutuhil See **Tzutuhil.**

CHRONOLOGY TABLES

NORTHERN MESOAMERICA (Central Mexico)

	Valley of Mexico	Puebla	Oaxaca	North and Central Veracruz	Southern Veracruz and Tabasco
Postclassic — Late (1500–1200)	Aztec II–IV / Aztec I (Chichimec)	Late Venta Salada — Mixteca-Puebla	Monte Albán V (Mixtec)	Teayo / Cempoala / Isla de Sacrificios II–III	Soncautla
Postclassic — Early (1200–900)	Tula-Mazapán / Xometla (Coyotlatelco) — *Toltec*	Early Venta Salada — Olmec-Xicalanca	Monte Albán IV	Isla de Sacrificios I	Upper Cerro de las Mesas
Classic — Late (900–500)	Oxtotícpac / IV Metepec / IIIa Xolalpan — *Teotihuacán*	Late Palo Blanco	Monte Albán IIIb	Nopiloa / Tajín III / Upper Remojadas II	Upper Tres Zapotes
			Monte Albán IIIa	Tajín II / Upper Remojadas I	Lower Cerro de las Mesas II
Classic — Early (500–200)	III Tlamimilolpa / II Miccaotli	Early P[...]	Transitional	Tajín I	Middle Tres Zapotes
Protoclassic (200–100)					

Sequence

Time scale (years): 1500, 1400, 1300, 1200, 1100, 1000, 900, 800, 700, 600, 500, 400, 300, 200, 100

Chronological chart (rotated in original). Time scale in B.C. runs vertically; Preclassic period divided into Late, Middle, and Early.

B.C.	Preclassic	Valley of Mexico	Tehuacán	Oaxaca (Monte Albán)	Central Veracruz	San Lorenzo (Olmec) La Venta
100	Late	Patlachique (Ticomán)	Late Santa María	Monte Albán II	Lower Remojadas	Lower Cerro de las Mesas I
200	Late	IV Tezoyuca (Ticomán)	Late Santa María	Monte Albán II	Lower Remojadas	La Venta Palangana
300	Late	III (Ticomán)	Late Santa María	Monte Albán I	Lower Remojadas	La Venta Palangana
400	Late	II (Ticomán)	Late Santa María	Monte Albán I	El Trapiche	La Venta Palangana
500	Late	I (Ticomán)	Late Santa María	Monte Albán I	El Trapiche	La Venta Palangana
600	Middle	Cuautepec (Zacatenco)	Early Santa María	Guadalupe	El Trapiche	Lower Tres Zapotes Nacaste
700	Middle	La Pastora (Zacatenco)	Early Santa María	Guadalupe	El Trapiche	Lower Tres Zapotes Nacaste
800	Middle	El Arbolillo (Zacatenco)	Late Ajalpa	San José Mogote	El Trapiche	Lower Tres Zapotes Nacaste
900	Middle	El Arbolillo (Zacatenco)	Late Ajalpa	San José Mogote		San Lorenzo
1000	Middle	Bomba (Ixtapaluca)	Early Ajalpa	San José Mogote		San Lorenzo
1100	Early	Bomba (Ixtapaluca)	Early Ajalpa	San José Mogote		Chicharras
1200	Early	Ayotla (Ixtapaluca)	Early Ajalpa	San José Mogote		Chicharras
1300	Early	Ayotla (Ixtapaluca)	Early Ajalpa	San José Mogote		Bajío
1400	Early	Coapexco (Ixtapaluca)	(Purrón 2300–1500 B.C.)			Ojochí
1500	Early	Coapexco (Ixtapaluca)	(Purrón 2300–1500 B.C.)			Ojochí

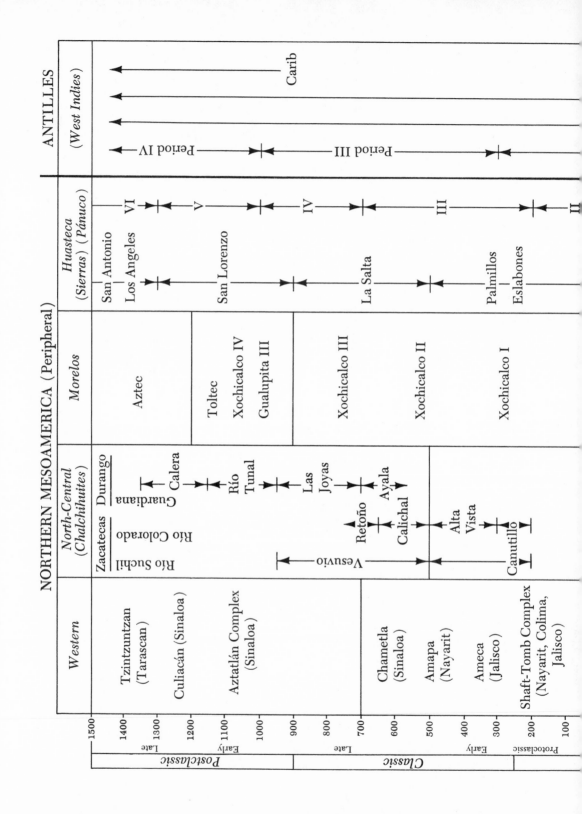

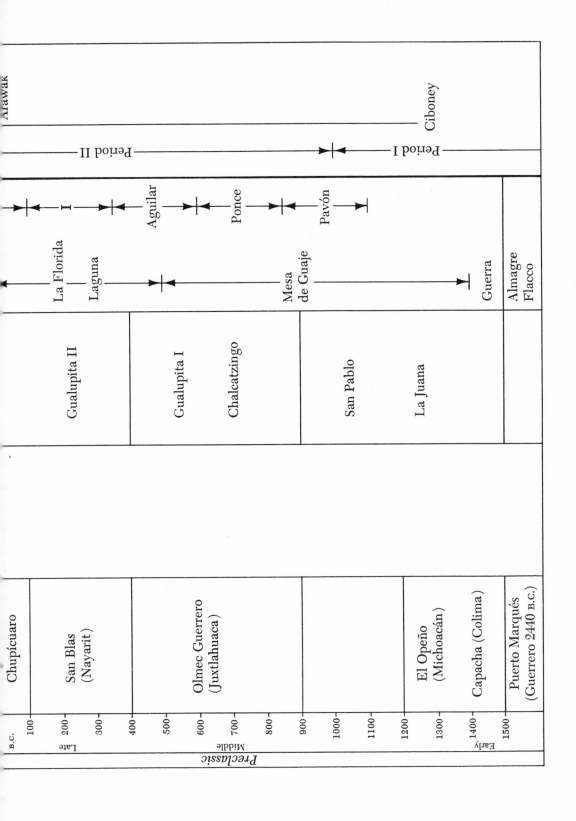

SOUTHERN MESOAMERICA (Area of Maya Influence)

	Central Chiapas	Soconusco	Guatemalan Pacific Coast	Guatemalan Highlands	Southern Lowlands	Northern Lowlands
Postclassic – Late (1500–1300)	XII Tuxtla		Peor es Nada	Chinautla		Independent States
						Mayapán
Postclassic – Early (1300–1000)	XI Ruiz			(Tohil) / Ayampuc		Toltec Maya (Chichén Itzá)
Classic – Late (1000–600)	X Maravillas		Santa Lucía Cotzumalhuapa	Pamplona	Tepeu	Puuc / Chenes-Río Bec
			Laguneta (Tiquisate)	Amatle		
Classic – Early (600–300)	IX Laguna		Mejor es Algo	Esperanza	Tzakol	
	VIII Jiquipilas			Aurora		
Protoclassic (300–100)	VII Istmo	Izapa		Santa Clara	Matzanel	

Time scale (years): 1500, 1400, 1300, 1200, 1100, 1000, 900, 800, 700, 600, 500, 400, 300, 200, 100

Chronological chart (Preclassic period correlations). Rotated table; read as columns of regional phase sequences aligned against a date/period scale.

Date	Period	Chiapa de Corzo Sequence				
100	Late	V Guanacaste	Crucero	Ilusiones	Miraflores-Arenal	Chicanel
200	Late					
300	Late					
400	Middle	IV Francesa	Conchas II	Algo es Algo	Providencia (Majadas)	Mamom
500	Middle					
600	Middle	III Escalera	Conchas I		Las Charcas	Xe
700	Middle					
800	Middle	II Dili	Jocotal		Arévalo	
900	Middle					
1000	Middle	I Cotorra	Cuadros			
1100	Middle					
1200	Middle					
1300	Middle		Ocós			
1400	Early	Barra				
1500	Early		Barra			

CENTRAL AMERICA I (Zone of Mesoamerican Influence)

Date	El Salvador	Western Honduras	Southern Honduras	Greater Nicoya
1500				
1400		Naco	Malalaca	Late Polychrome
1300				
1200				
1100	Plumbate (Cihuatan)	Río Blanco, Las Vegas	Amapala	Middle Polychrome
1000				
900	Ulúa Polychrome Copador Tazumal, Los Llanitos	Ulúa Polychrome Copador (at Copán)	Fonseca	
800				
700		Yojoa	San Lorenzo	Early Polychrome
600				
500	Tazumal, Quelepa	Eden	Chismuyo	
400				Linear Decorated
300				
200				Zoned Bichrome
100				

B.C.

100
200
300
400
500
600
700
800
900
1000
1100
1200
1300
1400
1500

Cerro Zapote

Jaral

Yarumela

CENTRAL AMERICA II (Zone of South American Influence)

Date (A.D.)	Northeast Honduras	Costa Rica — Highlands	Costa Rica — Atlantic	Greater Chiriquí	Panama — Veraguas	Panama — Parita-Coclé
1500						
1400	Cocal	Orosí		"Classic" Chiriquí		Herrera
1300	Cocal	Orosí		"Classic" Chiriquí		Herrera
1200	Cocal	Chircot (El Guayabo)	Las Mercedes	"Classic" Chiriquí		Late Coclé
1100	Cocal	Chircot (El Guayabo)	Las Mercedes	San Lorenzo (Gulf)	Classic Veraguas	Late Coclé
1000	Cocal	Chircot (El Guayabo)	Las Mercedes	San Lorenzo (Gulf)	Classic Veraguas	Late Coclé
900	Selin	Chircot (El Guayabo)	Las Mercedes	San Lorenzo (Gulf)	Classic Veraguas	Late Coclé
800	Selin	Curridabat	Las Mercedes	Burica (Gulf)	Classic Veraguas	Early Coclé
700	Selin	Curridabat	Las Mercedes	Burica (Gulf) / Aguas Buenas	Classic Veraguas	Early Coclé
600	Selin	Curridabat		Aguas Buenas	Classic Veraguas	Early Coclé
500	Selin	Curridabat	El Bosque	Aguas Buenas	Classic Veraguas	Early Coclé
400			El Bosque	La Concepción (Scarified)		Santa María
300		Pavas	El Bosque	La Concepción (Scarified)		Santa María
200		Pavas	El Bosque	La Concepción (Scarified)	Scarified/ Guacamayo	Scarified
100		Pavas	El Bosque	La Concepción (Scarified)	Scarified/ Guacamayo	Scarified

[Note: See Central Panama]

Formative

Sarigua
(c. 1000 B.C.)

Monagrillo
(c. 2130 B.C.)

Cerro Mangote
(c. 4850 B.C.)

100 200 300 400 500 600 700 800 900 1000 1100 1200 1300 1400 1500

SELECTED BIBLIOGRAPHY

compiled by Allan Chapman

This annotated guide for further reading offers titles in English selected from a vast literature. They are generally available in bookstores and libraries. Major bibliographies with more complete coverage are listed first. Current popular material appears in such magazines as *Archaeology, Expedition, Natural History,* and *Scientific American.* More scholarly materials are found in *American Antiquity, Science,* and the publications of The American Museum of Natural History; The Carnegie Institution of Washington; The Museum of the American Indian (Heye Foundation); and The Peabody Museum of Harvard University.

BIBLIOGRAPHIES

Bernal, Ignacio. *Bibliografía de Arqueología y Etnografía: Mesoamerica y Norte de México, 1541–1960.* México, 1962. 634p. (Instituto Nacional de Antropología e Historia, México. Memorias, 7).

The definitive bibliography listing virtually all of the literature, in all languages, up to 1960.

Chevrette, Valerie. *Annotated Bibliography of the Precolumbian Art and Archaeology of the West Indies.* New York: Library, The Museum of Primitive Art, 1971. 18p. (Primitive Art Bibliographies, 9).

Lists 275 publications with brief descriptions. The introduction offers a survey of the subject, and a short history of the study.

Kendall, Aubyn. *The Art of Pre-Columbian Mexico; an Annotated Bibliography of Works in English.* Austin: University of Texas at Austin, 1973. 115p. illus. (Guides and Bibliographies Series, 5).

Good guide to English-language materials with brief descriptions. Includes archaeology as well as art.

See also bibliographies in: Adams, Baudez, Coe (Michael), Covarrubias, Kubler, Paddock, Stone, Wauchope, Weaver, Willey.

BOOKS

Adams, Richard E. *Prehistoric Mesoamerica.* Boston: Little, Brown and Co., 1977. 307p. illus.

Basic standard archaeology text, well illustrated, with good bibliography. Covers the most recent work in the field.

Andrews, George F. *Maya Cities: Placemaking and Urbanization.* Norman, Okla.: University of Oklahoma Press, 1975. 468p. illus. (The Civilization of the American Indian Series, 131).

Scholarly discussion of Mayan architecture and city planning with good photographs and plan drawings of all major sites.

Baudez, Claude F. *Central America.* London: Barrie & Jenkins, 1970. 255p. illus. (Ancient civilizations).

General introduction to the art and archaeology of Honduras, El Salvador,

Nicaragua, Costa Rica, and Panama with good illustrations and bibliography. Includes discussion of the relationships of the area to Mesoamerica and to South America.

Benson, Elizabeth P. *The Maya World.* New York: Crowell, 1967. 172p. illus.

Basic introduction to all aspects of Maya civilization by topic. Includes information for the traveler.

Bernal, Ignacio. *The Olmec World.* Berkeley: University of California Press, 1969. 273p. illus.

Scholarly summary work by a leading Mexican archaeologist with illustrations of major materials and discussion of work in the area.

——, et al. *3000 Years of Art and Life in Mexico, as Seen in the National Museum of Anthropology, Mexico City.* New York: Harry N. Abrams, 1968. 216p. illus.

Guide to the museum with fine photographs of objects by Irmgard Groth. Discussion of objects and cultures by the director.

Boos, Frank H. *The Ceramic Sculptures of Ancient Oaxaca.* South Brunswick, N.J.: A. S. Barnes, 1966. 488p. illus.

A presentation in text and photographs of the urns from Monte Albán, with a classification by type of gods represented. Includes a discussion of the religion.

Caso, Alfonso. *The Aztecs: People of the Sun.* Norman, Okla.: University of Oklahoma Press, 1970. 125p. illus. (The Civilization of the American Indian Series, 50).

Major work on religion and the gods by the leading authority. Illustrations by Miguel Covarrubias.

Coe, Michael D. *America's First Civilization.* New York: American Heritage, 1968. 159p. illus. (The Smithsonian Library).

Authoritative, well-illustrated, popular account of the Olmecs by a leading scholar who worked at San Lorenzo Tenochtitlán.

——. *The Jaguar's Children: Pre-Classic Central Mexico.* New York: The Museum of Primitive Art, 1965. 126p. illus.

Documents an exhibition of the same title at The Museum of Primitive Art, New York. Text, by a leading Olmec scholar, covers the early cultures of the Valley of Mexico with emphasis on the Olmec presence there. Heavily illustrated.

——. *The Maya.* New York: Praeger, 1966. 252p. illus. (Ancient Peoples and Places, 52).

Basic introductory text with good illustrations and documentation.

——. *Mexico.* New York: Praeger, 1962. 244p. illus. (Ancient Peoples and Places, 29).

Basic introductory text with good illustrations and documentation.

Coe, William R. *Tikal, a Handbook of Ancient Maya Ruins, with a Guide Map.* Philadelphia: University Museum, University of Pennsylvania, 1967. 123p. illus.

Guide to the site by the director of the archaeological work there. Includes good general introduction to the Maya and perhaps the best concise introduction to the writing and counting system.

Covarrubias, Miguel. *Indian Art of Mexico and Central America.* New York: Knopf, 1957. 360p. illus.

All aspects of the field are covered by a well-known authority, heavily supported with illustrations and bibliography. Still the major introductory work in the field despite the early date.

Davies, Nigel. *The Aztecs: a History.* New York: Putnam, 1974. 363p. illus.

Very readable history based on native and colonial sources, with good illustrations and documentation.

Díaz del Castillo, Bernal. *The Discovery and Conquest of Mexico, 1517–1521.* Edited from the only exact copy of the original MS by Genaro García. Translated with an introduction and notes by A. P. Maudslay. New York: Grove Press, 1956. 478p. illus. (Evergreen Books, E-86).

Classic account of the Conquest by a soldier with Cortés; many editions available. An exciting adventure with much firsthand material on the Aztecs.

Durán, Diego. *The Aztecs; the History of the Indies of New Spain.* Translated with notes by Doris Heyden and Fernando Horcasitas. New York: Orion Press, 1964. 381p. illus.

A history of the Mexica. Translation, with scholarly notes, of a major sixteenth-century source on all aspects of Aztec life and culture. Includes the original illustrations.

——. *Book of the Gods and Rites and the Ancient Calendar*. Translated and edited by Fernando Horcasitas and Doris Heyden. Norman, Okla.: University of Oklahoma Press, 1971. 502p. illus. (The Civilization of the American Indian Series, 102).

Early description of the religion, ceremonies, and calendar of the Aztecs. Together with *The Aztecs* completes the translation of the *Historia de las Indias*, 1581. Includes the original illustrations, and scholarly notes.

Easby, Elizabeth K. *Pre-Columbian Jade from Costa Rica*. New York: André Emmerich, 1968. 103p. illus.

Thorough study based on archaeological investigation with fine photographs, many in color, by Lee Boltin. Includes discussion of Olmec relationships.

——, and Scott, John F. *Before Cortés: Sculpture of Middle America*. New York: The Metropolitan Museum of Art, 1970. 322p. illus.

Catalogue of a major exhibition at The Metropolitan Museum of Art, New York. Documents and illustrates a wide range of major pieces from public and private collections.

Emmerich, André. *Art Before Columbus; the Art of Ancient Mexico, From the Archaic Villages of the Second Millennium* B.C. *to the Splendor of the Aztecs*. New York: Simon and Schuster, 1963. 256p. illus.

Basic survey with good illustrations and discussion of the material.

——. *Sweat of the Sun and Tears of the Moon; Gold and Silver in Pre-Columbian Art*. Seattle: University of Washington Press, 1965. 216p. illus.

Definitive general text. Discusses material and technique and offers many illustrations of the finest metalwork.

Fernández Méndez, Eugenio. *Art and Mythology of the Taino Indians of the Greater West Indies*. San Juan, P.R.: Ediciones "El Cemi," 1972. 95p. illus.

Well-illustrated introduction to the major art styles, with discussion of the mythology and possible Mesoamerican connections.

Greene, Merle, *et al. Maya Sculpture*. Berkeley, Calif.: Lederer, Street & Zeux, 1972. 432p. illus.

Illustrates relief sculpture by a series of photographs of Greene's rubbings of monuments from the southern lowlands, the highlands, and piedmont of Guatemala, Mexico, and Honduras. Descriptive text by Greene, Robert L. Rands, and John A. Graham.

Helfritz, Hans. *Mexican Cities of the Gods; an Archaeological Guide*. New York: Praeger, 1970. 180p. illus.

General guide with good maps and illustrations. Includes advice for the traveler.

Instituto Nacional de Antropología y Historia, Mexico. *Official Guides*. Mexico, various dates.

A series of English-language guides to major Mexican sites and museums. Usually 25–35 pages, with illustrations, plans, and discussion. Available for: Calixtlahuaca, Chichén Itzá, Copilco-Cuicuilco, El Tajín, Malinalco, Maya Cities, Monte Albán-Mitla, Morelos, Museum of Huastecan Culture, Palenque, Tabasco Museums, Tenayuca, Teotihuacán, Tula, Tulum, Uxmal.

Joralemon, Peter D. *A Study of Olmec Iconography*. Washington, D.C.: Dumbarton Oaks, Trustees for Harvard University, 1971. 95p. illus. (Studies in Pre-Columbian Art and Archaeology, 7).

A specialized study illustrated with drawings and offering a classification of gods. Includes "A Dictionary of Olmec Motifs and Symbols."

Kubler, George. *The Art and Architecture of Ancient America*. 2d ed. Baltimore: Penguin Books, 1975. 402p. illus. (The Pelican History of Art).

Recently revised major study by a well-known art historian. Good illustrations, with extensive bibliography. Includes Middle and South America.

Landa, Diego de. *Landa's Relación de las Cosas de Yucatán*. Translated and edited with notes by Alfred Tozzer. Cambridge, Mass., 1941. 394p. (Papers of the Peabody Museum of American Archaeology and Ethnology, Harvard University, 18).

Definitive translation, by a major scholar, with complete notes. The chief sixteenth-century source for all aspects of the Maya.

León-Portilla, Miguel. *Aztec Thought and Culture; a Study of the Ancient Nahuatl Mind*. Norman, Okla.: University of Oklahoma Press, 1971. 241p. illus. (The Civilization of the American Indian Series, 67).

A major study of Nahuatl philosophy based on native sources, colonial documents, and a study of the language.

——. *The Broken Spears: the Aztec Account of the Conquest of Mexico*. Boston: Beacon Press, 1962. 168p. illus.

The story of the Conquest as told in native sources. Illustrations in the Aztec style by Alberto Beltran. Offers an insight into Aztec life and thought as well as another view of the Conquest.

——. *Pre-Columbian Literatures of Mexico*. Norman, Okla.: University of Oklahoma Press, 1969. 191p. illus. (The Civilization of the American Indian Series, 92).

Complete introduction to the native literature by type, offering many examples in translation. Bibliography constitutes a list of nearly all the major manuscripts and codices.

Martí, Samuel, and Kurath, Gertrude P. *Dances of Anáhuac; the Choreography and Music of Precortesian Dances*. Chicago: Aldine Publishing Co., 1964. 251p. illus. (Viking Fund Publications in Anthropology, 38).

Scholarly work based on early sources and archaeology, with reference to contemporary Mexico. Illustrates musical instruments and gives dance notation.

Morley, Sylvanus G. *The Ancient Maya*. 3rd ed. Stanford, Calif.: Stanford University Press, 1956. 494p. illus.

The classic general work since 1946; revised by George W. Brainerd. A complete introduction by a major Maya scholar.

Paddock, John, ed. *Ancient Oaxaca: Discoveries in Mexican Archeology and History*. Stanford, Calif.: Stanford University Press, 1966. 416p. illus.

Includes "Mesoamerica Before the Toltecs" by Wingberto Jimenez Moreno and "Oaxaca in Ancient Mesoamerica" by Paddock, together with a series of other specialized papers.

Popol Vuh; the Sacred Book of the Ancient Quiché Maya. English version by Delia Goetz and Sylvanus G. Morley from the Spanish translation of Adrián Recinos. Norman, Okla.: University of Oklahoma Press, 1950. 267p. (The Civilization of the American Indian Series, 29).

Complete text, with notes, of the Mayan epic, first reduced to writing in the sixteenth century. A classic of world literature covering cosmology, mythology, traditions, and history.

Proskouriakoff, Tatiana A. *An Album of Maya Architecture*. Norman, Okla.: University of Oklahoma Press, 1970. 142p. illus.

A series of drawings depicting the buildings at the time of their use, together with discussion and illustration of the buildings today.

Rouse, Irving. "Prehistory of the West Indies." *Science*, 144, no. 3,618 (May 1964): 499–513. illus.

Complete concise coverage of the subject with discussion of the cultures and chronology charts.

Sahagún, Bernardino de. *Florentine Codex; General History of the Things of New Spain*. Translated from the Aztec into English with notes and illustrations by

Arthur J. O. Anderson and Charles E. Dibble. Santa Fe, N.M., 1950–1969. 12 vols. illus. (Monographs of The School of American Research, 14).

Definitive translation, with complete notes, of one of the chief sixteenth-century sources for the Aztec, covering all aspects of their life and history. Illustrated with drawings by artists of the time.

Sanders, William T., and Price, Barbara J. *Mesoamerica: the Evolution of a Civilization.* New York: Random House, 1968. 264p. illus. (Studies in Anthropology).

Scholarly study of history from an ecological and evolutionary point of view.

Stephens, John L. *Incidents of Travel in Central America, Chiapas and Yucatán,* 2 vols. illus. Reprint. New York: Dover Publications, 1969.

Classic travel book first published in 1841; describes visits to the major sites and includes the fine Catherwood engravings.

——. *Incidents of Travel in Yucatán, with Engravings by Frederick Catherwood,* 2 vols. illus. Reprint. New York: Dover Publications, 1963.

A classic travel book first published in 1843; describes visits to the major sites and includes the Catherwood engravings.

Stevenson, Robert M. *Music in Aztec & Inca Territory.* Berkeley: University of California Press, 1968. 378p.

Scholarly coverage from pre-Columbian times to about 1800, based on original sources. Includes music.

Stierlin, Henri. *Living Architecture: Ancient Mexican.* New York: Grosset & Dunlap, 1968. 192p. illus.

Survey of architecture north of the Mayan area. Includes site plans, elevation drawings, and especially fine photographs.

Stone, Doris. *Pre-Columbian Man Finds Central America: the Archaeological Bridge.* Cambridge, Mass.: Peabody Museum Press, 1972. 231p. illus.

Popular presentation of the archaeology of the area from Guatemala through Panama with discussion of Mesoamerican

and South American influences. Good illustrations and bibliography.

Thompson, J. Eric S. *A Catalog of Maya Hieroglyphs.* Norman, Okla.: University of Oklahoma Press, 1962. 458p. illus. (The Civilization of the American Indian Series, 62).

Compilation of glyphs with illustrations and discussion. The catalogue numbers assigned are now the standard reference for those working with the material.

——. *Maya Hieroglyphic Writing; an Introduction.* 2d ed. Norman, Okla.: University of Oklahoma Press, 1960. 347p. illus.

Technical study of all aspects of the subject by the dean of scholars in the field.

Vaillant, George C. *Aztecs of Mexico: Origin, Rise, and Fall of the Aztec Nation.* Revised by Suzanna B. Vaillant. Garden City, N.Y.: Doubleday, 1962. 312p. illus.

Classic work since 1941; revised by Suzanna B. Vaillant. Despite the title, covers the cultures of the Valley of Mexico from the Preclassic, with emphasis on the Aztecs.

Wauchope, Robert, ed. *Handbook of Middle American Indians.* Austin: University of Texas Press, 1964–73. 16 vols. illus.

A series of survey articles by specialists on all aspects of the subject—the most important single reference. The individual bibliographies and the compilation in volume XVI constitute an extensive bibliography. Contents: I. Natural Environment and Early Cultures; II, III. Archaeology of Southern Mesoamerica; IV. Archaeological Frontiers and External Connections; V. Linguistics; VI. Social Anthropology; VII, VIII. Ethnology; IX. Physical Anthropology; X, XI. Archaeology of Northern Mesoamerica; XII–XV. Guide to Ethnohistorical Sources; XVI. Sources Cited and Artifacts Illustrated.

Weaver, Muriel P. *The Aztecs, Maya and Their Predecessors: Archaeology of Mesoamerica.* New York: Seminar Press, 1972. 347p. illus. Basic introductory survey with good illustrations and bibliography.

Willey, Gordon R. *An Introduction to Amer-ican Archaeology*. Vol. 1, *North and Middle America*. Englewood Cliffs, N.J.: Prentice-Hall, 1966. 530p. illus.

Major text by a well-known American archaeologist. Good illustrations and bibliography.